"Cardinal George represented the best of Chicago; super smart, tough, direct, compassionate. It is important that his story has been well told by Michael Heinlein, for us and for future generations."
— **Cardinal George Pell**, Prefect Emeritus of the Secretariat for the Economy, Holy See

"The Archdiocese of Chicago was the crucible, where this 'head man' became a 'heart man,' suffering and living through the pains and doubts of a Shepherd and emerging with deeper faith in God. The beauty of his life for God and Church emerges in this book of love. A must-read for everyone."
— **Cardinal Orlando B. Quevedo, O.M.I.**, Archbishop Emeritus of Cotabato, Philippines

"Cardinal George was a man, as Tacitus states, *sine ira et studio*, a man without bitterness or partiality. In Cardinal George, we see a churchman of deep intellectual objectivity and compassionate missionary zeal. Michael Heinlein's work presents to us once again the steady wisdom and fortitude which so marked the life of Cardinal George."
— **Cardinal Daniel N. DiNardo**, Archbishop of Galveston-Houston

"For over two decades I've heard the chant from so many, 'We need a biography of Cardinal Francis George!' Thanks to Michael Heinlein, we've got one! Cardinal George was a man of intense intellectual depth, with a heart that was soft and big. We benefit from his wisdom and focus more than ever!"
— **Cardinal Timothy M. Dolan**, Archbishop of New York

"I am deeply grateful that this volume has been prepared. It presents great insight into this churchman, who was one of our most gifted ecclesiastical leaders. Cardinal George was a friend to all in need, especially the poor. And he was a holy man."
— **Most Reverend Roger L. Schwietz, O.M.I.**, Archbishop Emeritus of Anchorage

"As bishop, archbishop, and cardinal, Francis George emulated the example of our Founder St. Eugene de Mazenod, who had great devotion to the Cross of Jesus Christ and saw the world through the eyes of the Crucified Savior, uniting himself compassionately to those who suffered from poverty, violence, racism or abuse. We thank God for his life and are happy that others can now read this testimony of his well-lived life."
— **Very Reverend Luis Ignacio Rois Alonso, O.M.I.**,
Superior General, Missionary Oblates of Mary Immaculate

"Francis George was a personal friend; a mentor and adviser; a man of gifted intellect and wisdom; and one of the truly great American bishops of the last century. He is very sorely missed. But in capturing the fullness of Cardinal George's life, ministry, and the meaning of his legacy in this superb biography, Michael Heinlein has done a service for the entire American Catholic community. I will treasure and share this book."
— **Most Reverend Charles J. Chaput, O.F.M. Cap.**, Archbishop Emeritus of Philadelphia

"As a successor of Francis George, who is still beloved in the Archdiocese of Portland despite his short tenure as our ninth archbishop, I am pleased and gratified to see this fine account of Cardinal George's life. Heinlein offers a comprehensive, informative and insightful narrative, giving the reader a unique perspective into the witness and ministry of this holy man."

— **Most Reverend Alexander K. Sample**, Archbishop of Portland-in-Oregon

"I learned an abundance of important lessons that have shaped my life and ministry as a bishop by observing and working closely with this brilliant and holy churchman over the span of almost two decades. Now, thanks to this outstanding biography by Michael Heinlein, people who never had the opportunity to meet Cardinal George will get to know this saintly and towering figure who dedicated his life to giving glory to Christ in the Church and in the world."

— **Most Reverend Thomas J. Paprocki**, Bishop of Springfield in Illinois

"From the day he was introduced as Archbishop of Chicago until the day the Lord called him to eternal life, I lived, conversed, laughed, and prayed with Cardinal George. Michael Heinlein has done a fine job on this biography, employing his skills as a researcher and a writer to accurately present the authenticity and holiness of a man with whom I was pleased to serve as a brother bishop and knew as a friend."

— **Most Reverend Raymond E. Goedert**, Auxiliary Bishop Emeritus of Chicago

"In a religious life and ministry that spanned six pontificates, Cardinal Francis George was a pivotal figure in American Catholic life. As a religious, an intellectual, and a shepherd, he navigated through turbulent times in a way that was deeply faithful to the Gospel and, precisely because of that fidelity, was innately pastoral. We can be grateful to Michael Heinlein for making the life and ministry of Francis George available to us in this engaging biography."

— **Most Reverend Kevin C. Rhoades**, Bishop of Fort Wayne-South Bend

"In the extraordinary life of Francis Cardinal George, we see the grace of Christ powerfully at work. Michael Heinlein has masterfully sketched both the grace-filled sweep and the moving details of Cardinal George's life of service to the Church and his heroic death, a narrative which leaves the reader with both joy and gratitude for the mysterious workings of divine providence."

— **Most Reverend Donald J. Hying**, Bishop of Madison

"In the midst of the drama and struggle of human life, by his wise leadership and personal example, Cardinal George exhibited what it takes to be a disciple of Jesus Christ. Michael Heinlein has done us an inestimable service by penning an insightful biography of Cardinal George. In this moment of crisis for the Church and the human family, I invite you to learn from the Cardinal's life and ministry and give Christ glory in all things."

— **Most Reverend Robert P. Reed**, Auxiliary Bishop of Boston

"Jesus Christ glorifies those who glorify Him. Michael Heinlein shows this to be true with Cardinal George in this luminous book."

— **Gloria Purvis**, Host and Executive Producer, *The Gloria Purvis* Podcast.

"Modeling the courage, persistence, and holiness of Cardinal George himself, Heinlein has given us a wonderful gift in writing this book. I recommend it unreservedly, but perhaps with this one warning: if you wish to keep the former Archbishop of Chicago in a comfortable or dismissible ideological box, then get ready for a challenging read."

— **Charles C. Camosy**, Author and Professor of Medical Humanities, Creighton University School of Medicine

"During an era when the Church had yet to begin to care for survivors of clergy abuse, Cardinal George is counted among the few who ventured to listen to survivors. Michael Heinlein has created an exhaustively researched account of the late Cardinal's prophetic and often unsung contributions to the ongoing reform and renewal of the Church, particularly his efforts to ensure systemic abuse never happens again."

— **Teresa Pitt Green**, Cofounder, Spirit Fire

"Amid the tumultuous changes enveloping the Church in the United States, Cardinal George's life attests to the one necessary thing: to become saints. This masterful biography holds up for us one man who exemplifies passionate love for God, for people, and for truth."

— **Sister Nancy Usselmann, F.S.P.**, Director, Pauline Center for Media Studies

"Reading this biography of Cardinal George's entire life made me realize how much I miss him and how much of him I had missed when I knew and worked with him. What a blessing Cardinal George was and still is for the Church!"

— **Abbot Jeremy Driscoll, O.S.B.**, Abbot of Mount Angel Abbey

"This book is for the many who need reassurance today about 'whether it's possible to live this way.' To live intelligently, unafraid of a changing world, capable of handling a lifetime of suffering, and throughout, to be person of unwavering faith, a Christian. Cardinal Francis George did it all by answering God's call a day at a time, a task at a time, in the midst of frequent opposition and suffering. He can inspire us to do the same."

— **Helen M. Alvaré**, The Robert A. Levy Chair in Law & Liberty, Antonin Scalia Law School, George Mason University

"The good cardinal was a man of deep faith, warm humanity, and profound intellect, but was unfairly maligned and misrepresented in both the Catholic and secular media as a right-wing 'hardliner' who was out of touch with the needs of modern Catholics. Heinlein's detailed and exhaustive biography explodes these caricatures and shows us a complex and richly textured man who was a genuine prophet for our times."

— **Dr. Larry Chapp**, retired professor of theology, DeSales University

Glorifying Christ

Glorifying Christ

THE LIFE OF
Cardinal Francis E. George, O.M.I.

Michael R. Heinlein

Huntington, Indiana
Our Sunday Visitor

Contents

Foreword

By Archbishop José H. Gomez

In late February 2015, two months before he would die from cancer, Cardinal Francis George finished the preface to his final book, a selection of essays titled, *A Godly Humanism.* He wrote:

> As the years here grow shorter, it fills in with the realization that, just as we pray to see God face to face, so God wants to see us face to face. We give him our time, which is all that we have, he takes the gift and calls us when he is ready to do so. In the end, that is all there is, and everything is summed up and integrated in that vision and desire.

This is the Cardinal George whom I was privileged to call my friend and mentor. He was a man of depths, spiritual and intellectual, with a priestly heart, who loved his people to the end.

We first met after he had been appointed bishop of Yakima, Washington. At the time, I was a priest serving in Houston, Texas. His new diocese was majority Hispanic, and many of his people were migrant farmworkers. Cardinal George immersed himself to learn the language and became a fluent, often eloquent Spanish speaker. He took a keen interest not only in the social conditions of the migrants, but also in the future of Hispanic ministry and the formation of Hispanic priests.

Throughout the 1990s, we would see each other and talk at meetings of the National Catholic Council for Hispanic Ministry, the National Association of Hispanic Priests, and LaRed, the national Catholic network of youth ministers. These organizations were just beginning at the time, and then-Archbishop George's support and advocacy were vital for their growth and integration into the mainstream of Catholic ministry in this country.

He understood before many Church leaders that the Catholic profile and presence in America was becoming increasingly Latino, and that the pastoral challenge was to build up this community within the Church to prepare them to make their contribution to the moral and spiritual renewal of our society.

Much later, I had a conversation with Cardinal George. It was 2013, and I had just published my book, *Immigration and the Next America,* in which I chronicled the Latino roots of the Church in America, which stretch back two centuries before Thomas Jefferson wrote the Declaration of Independence, when missionaries from Spain, Franciscans and Dominicans, were preaching the Gospel from Florida to Texas to California.

Cardinal George complimented the book, kind words I treasure. He told me that he had always wanted to write something similar about the Jesuits from France who evangelized in New York and the American heartland, the missionaries who came upon the wide Mississippi and named it "The River of the Immaculate Conception."

It's a shame that he never got to write that, because he had deep awareness of America's immigrant roots and also the Christian spirit that animates our country's founding. He knew that the Church must reclaim that history, not as a distant memory, but as a legacy that we are responsible for.

As Michael Heinlein makes clear in this biography, Cardinal George was a man of faith and integrity, who was confident in the power of the Gospel and the Church's social doctrine to address the challenges of our age. He was a courageous defender of the Church's liberty in American society, a liberty that he felt was growing more restricted as our society grows increasingly secularized. His 2011 book, *God in Action*, remains a relevant and thoughtful examination of faith and American public life.

Heinlein is to be credited for recognizing Cardinal George's significance for the history of the American Church in our times. For me, his influence will always be more personal.

Cardinal George is a model for me as a bishop, and not only for me. He encouraged a whole generation of younger bishops. He was easy to talk to, a patient listener, and when he spoke, it was always from a pastoral heart, with a clarity and common sense that were refreshing and inspiring.

During the time when he served as president of the U.S. bishops' conference, I admired how he was able to foster dialogue, allowing bishops to speak their minds and voice different opinions, and how he used his leadership to promote unity among the bishops. When I assumed the role as president, many years later, I prayed to have some measure of his wisdom.

Heinlein's biography revealed a number of things that I did not know about my friend and mentor, notably his spiritual struggles while leading the Archdiocese of Chicago. The Cardinal's prayer and sacrifice and his love for the Church shine through in these pages. His honesty in confronting his challenges reminded me of something St. Paul said: "There is the daily pressure upon me of my anxiety for all the churches" (2 Cor 4:15).

Cardinal George's long trial with cancer is rendered beautifully by Heinlein. I had forgotten how bravely he had carried out his public ministry and how frank he was in discussing his illness in the media. In one of those interviews he said: "The Lord, in his goodness, prepares us to meet him face to face, by stripping away a lot of the accoutrements of life, desires, even good desires, so that in the end there is one thing necessary, that is the love of God."

To the end, Cardinal George was teaching, a last lesson in the meaning of Christian living and Christian dying.

Most Reverend José H. Gomez
Archbishop of Los Angeles
November 23, 2022
Memorial of Blessed Miguel Augustin Pro, Martyr

Preface

Though I was only eleven years old, living in the shadow of Chicago, I remember Francis George's arrival back in his hometown as its archbishop. My grandmother, knowing my interest in George even then, saved me clippings from the *Chicago Tribune*'s coverage of his appointment (undoubtedly that tells you something about what kind of child I was). I also remember getting up early in the morning to watch the consistory in which Pope John Paul II created Francis George a cardinal. As the years went by, George kept my attention. His wit, his foresight, his apparent virtue all made an impression — to me, he was magnetic. I was fortunate enough to meet George several times, mostly at our common alma mater in Washington, DC, The Catholic University of America. Never did I imagine I would one day write an accounting of his life.

But an experience in prayer before the Blessed Sacrament, not long after Cardinal George's death, left me with the distinct understanding that I needed to do whatever I could to help preserve and promote the cardinal's legacy. Though I did not know it at the time, this would come to mean that I would undertake this project, and more. As I began research for this book, I had no idea what to expect. Some aspects of compiling this manuscript went smoothly, while others were more challenging. Sometimes, I was not sure it would ever be seen by anyone other than myself. But whenever doors closed, God allowed others to open. Throughout, all I could do was continue to discern what God was asking of me. This book is the product of that discernment.

Cardinal George's life was a lot like yours or mine. He faced many struggles in his life, some public, some private. He endured a lot of suffering, even from an early age. For as much as he wanted to remain in the realm of ideas — he would often quip, "Don't tell me how you feel, tell me what you think!" — he certainly had a lot of feelings. He felt alone. He had resentments. He was almost always in pain.

But through it all, he stayed close to Christ the Lord. Even better, he brought others to Christ along the way. He still does.

I am humbled to be able to tell his story.

Michael R. Heinlein
May 7, 2022
25th Anniversary of Francis George's installation
as eighth archbishop of Chicago

A Note on Sources

Preparation of this manuscript relied on consultation of archives from Italy to Oregon: General Administration of Missionary Oblates of Mary Immaculate, Rome; United States Province of the Missionary Oblates of Mary Immaculate, Washington, DC; Archdiocese of Chicago; Archdiocese of Portland-in-Oregon; Diocese of Yakima; Tulane University, New Orleans; Pontifical Council for Culture, Rome. Correspondence cited in this manuscript is housed in these archives and, except for rare exception, referenced in the text only by date. Footnoted materials are from published materials and from unpublished, written manuscripts. Direct quotes not footnoted are from individuals — as the fruit of interviews — personal correspondence, or audio recordings.

Introduction

On April 12, 1992, then-Bishop Francis George of Yakima gave an interview to the *Yakima Herald-Republic* as part of the publication's "First Person" series — a regular Q&A spotlight that asked surface-level human interest questions and painted a picture of an individual within the community.

It was a fun little piece that offered nuggets of insight into George's life that typically were not explored by the media: His favorite foods were seafood and pasta; his favorite ice cream was chocolate; his favorite movie was *2001: A Space Odyssey*; his favorite childhood memory was being carried on his father's shoulders through the snow.

Among his answers to the interviewers' questions, which were attended to with George's usual careful thought and dry wit, three offered particular insight into the man whose biography you are currently holding. The answers are quintessential George, and in the years I spent on this work, I reflected on these responses quite often, coming to see in them the character and person of George himself. I believe they provide something of a roadmap for what readers will encounter in this book.

So what were these questions? 1) When asked who he would choose if he could be anybody famous for a while, George answered Aleksandr Solzhenitsyn, the Soviet dissident, author, and political prisoner. 2) When asked if he could have any three wishes granted, he answered greater love across racial and cultural boundaries and more conversation in families. (He gave away his third wish to the poorest person in Yakima County.) 3) And when asked what his dream job would be, he answered playing the timpani in a symphony orchestra.

I do not know exactly why George wanted to experience Solzhenitsyn's life, but my guess would be twofold: Solzhenitsyn knew what it meant to suffer for the sake of truth. A math major and captain in the Second World War, Solzhenitsyn was arrested in 1945 for writing private criticism of Joseph Stalin. He spent ten years in hard labor camps and was then exiled as a political prisoner. Secondly, it's possible that George saw in Solzhenitsyn, who boldly criticized the culture, both a prophet and a kindred spirit. Looking at Russia's tattered history, Solzhenitsyn, in 1983, proclaimed: "Men have forgotten God; that's why all this has happened." Did George see this as a foreshadowing of the future of his own country? Did he wish to learn from Solzhenitsyn's experience, his perspective, his well-formed conscience? George saw the shifts in our culture and our society. Did he see Solzhenitsyn, a prisoner from the East, as a prophet for the West today? As someone who could prepare us for the future?

George's two wishes relate directly to the priorities and concerns that weighed on him his entire life and ministry. One of George's main goals in ministry, both as a missionary and as a bishop, was unity — unity in Christ but also unity within the human race in Christ. He saw this as Bishop of Yakima, for instance, when there was strife between the Anglo and Hispanic communities. This strife, he knew, was a blockade to unity, a hindrance for two groups — all members of Christ's Body — that at times worked against each other and the building of God's kingdom. It was a lived experience, and it was something he worked hard to overcome as bishop there.

He also saw, as Pope John Paul II observed, that the way of humanity passes through the way of the family. He saw that families were breaking down, in large part because of trouble they had communicating with one another. They weren't unified themselves. He always spoke about the family as the basic building block of civilization, and he feared the government was no longer protecting the family. The consequences that would come from that, he knew, would be profound.

The easy-to-overlook fact that George gave his third wish to the poorest person in Yakima County reflected his vocation as a Missionary Oblate of Mary Immaculate (O.M.I.), a religious order that prioritizes having a heart for the poor. When he was considering selling his Chicago residence in 2002, he commented how he would like to live closer to the poor.

One final note on his wishes: George was not a selfish man. Notice that none of these things is about him, and that was how he lived his life. His wishes show his concern for others, his generous nature, his pastoral sensibility, and always, his closeness to the poor.

Finally, it was George's dream job to play timpani in a symphony orchestra. A set of four kettledrums, the timpani is an essential part of any orchestra. The timpani, which can roll in like thunder or fade into the background upon cue, is a leader — bold and resonant — but without domination. There can be a reticence to it, a hesitancy. Both factors were true for George's ministry as a bishop. He spoke when he needed to, but he feared sometimes he could be too desultory.

If I had to apply names to the drums of George's life and ministry, they would be "perseverant," "pastoral," "prophetic," and "discipleship." Amid the many struggles he faced, Cardinal George was a man of perseverance. He kept moving forward, no matter the roadblock he happened upon, because he knew God was alive and active. In a similar way, there's something enduring about the timpani. It reverberates, as George allowed Christ to reverberate in his life as he experienced the transformative power of suffering.

George was quintessentially pastoral. Far from a businessman, he was concerned about relationships and people, not careerism or advancement. He was attentive to the poor, to the margins, and he spent time with his flock. He often talked about how forming people was more important than money.

Cardinal George was also a prophetic voice for the Church — a man able to see things for how they are and from the point of view of the whole Church. He was able to use his gifts and talents to try to bring unity to his bishops and especially to his priests and flock in the Archdiocese of Chicago. As a leader, when he spoke, others listened. He proclaimed the truth, unifying the Church in Christ.

Finally, George was a disciple. He taught who Christ is, patterned his life on him, and brought him to others. He desired that we give God glory through our discipleship, our worship, and our witness. In short, as Archbishop Sartain said in the homily at George's funeral Mass, George was "so utterly a Christian."

Cardinal George had long attracted me with his wisdom, clarity, eloquence, orthodoxy, and objectivity. But as I got to know him more closely, I found someone who emerged a little differently, who suffered silently — and who allowed himself to be transformed by it. In this era of the Church, when there has been such a loss of trust and a lack of transparency, the Church needs role models of good and holy priests, as well as good and holy bishops. I believe with all my heart that Cardinal George was a good bishop and a good man. His own longtime confessor confided to me: "He was a saint."

We live in a time in which the Church is divided, and our mission is stymied because we find ourselves paralyzed from that division. Even the writing of this book manifested various difficulties that prove the truth of that unfortunate reality. George's way of articulating how we needed to move past the divisions — how we needed to be shaped by "simply Catholicism" and not get caught up in these weaponizing realities — is needed now just as much as when he was with us. In days when we look for authentic leadership in the Church, he gives an example of what it looks like: someone who can clearly articulate the Faith, who is committed to reform, who is honest and accountable, who is genuine and authentic, who is holy. We look for people who have the skills to be pastoral, to guide and connect with their people. We look for people to unite. We look for people who are defined by prayer, dedicated to Our Lady, devoted to the Eucharist. We look for shepherds. And an honest accounting of Cardinal George's life shows that these were his aims, guided by his episcopal motto, adopted from Saint Paul: "To Christ be Glory in the Church." Any close examination of his life makes clear that, above all else, glorifying Christ was Cardinal George's aim. May we learn from his example.

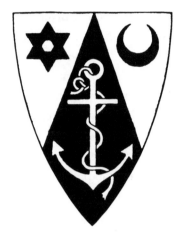

Chronology of the Life of Cardinal Francis E. George, O.M.I.

1937   Born on January 16, Chicago; baptized on February 14.

1950   Afflicted with poliomyelitis and suffered paralysis.

1951   Graduated eighth grade from St. Pascal School, Chicago; moved to Belleville to attend St. Henry's Seminary.

1957   Began novitiate in Godfrey, Illinois with Missionary Oblates of Mary Immaculate (O.M.I.).

1958   Professed First Vows as member of O.M.I. on August 15, Godfrey; moved to Our Lady of the Snows Scholasticate, Pass Christian, Mississippi.

1961   Professed final vows as member of O.M.I. on September 8.

1962   Moved to O.M.I. Scholasticate St. Joseph, Ottawa, Canada.

1963   Ordained a priest on December 21 by Bishop Raymond Hillinger at St. Pascal, Chicago.

1964   Began teaching philosophy at O.M.I. Our Lady of the Snows
        Scholasticate, Pass Christian.

1965   Graduated from The Catholic University of America,
        Washington, DC, with a Master of Arts degree in philosophy.

1966   Began doctoral studies at Tulane University, New Orleans; began
        residing part time in New Orleans.

1968   Taught courses at Tulane University.

1969   Began teaching philosophy at Creighton University, Omaha,
        Nebraska

1970   Graduated from Tulane University with doctorate in philosophy,
        concentrating on American philosophy.

1971   Completed master's in theology degree from University of
        Ottawa.

1972   Attended O.M.I. general chapter in Rome.

1973   Appointed provincial of O.M.I. Central Province, moved to
        St. Paul, Minnesota.

1974   Attended O.M.I. general chapter in Rome; elected vicar general.

1980   Reelected O.M.I. vicar general at general chapter in Rome.

1986   Concluded 12 years as O.M.I. vicar general.

1988   Completed doctorate in theology at Pontifical Urbaniana
        University, Rome; began role at Cambridge Center, Cambridge,
        Massachusetts.

1990   Appointed fifth bishop of Yakima by Pope John Paul II on July
        10; ordained a bishop on September 21, Yakima, Washington.

1994   Appointed to Synod of Bishops on Consecrated Life, Rome.

1996   Appointed ninth archbishop of Portland-in-Oregon on April 30;
        installed on May 27.

1997   Appointed eighth archbishop of Chicago on April 8; installed on
        May 7; appointed member of International Committee on
        English in the Liturgy (ICEL); appointed to Synod of Bishops on
        America, Rome.

1998   Nominated a Cardinal of the Holy Roman Church with the title
        of Cardinal Priest of *S. Bartholomaei in Insula* on January 18;

created a cardinal on February 21. Ordained first bishop (Joseph N. Perry) on June 29.

2001   Elected chairman of the Committee on Liturgy of the United States Conference of Catholic Bishops; preached Lenten retreat for Roman Curia; delegate to Synod of Bishops on Ministry of Bishops, Rome.

2002   Named member of the Mixed Commission established by the Holy See regarding the Essential Norms related to the United States Conference of Catholic Bishops' *Charter for the Protection of Children and Young People.*

2004   Elected vice president of the United States Conference of Catholic Bishops.

2005   Participated in conclave as cardinal-elector after the death of Pope John Paul II, which elected Pope Benedict XVI.

2006   Diagnosed with bladder cancer; underwent radical cystectomy.

2007   Elected president of the United States Conference of Catholic Bishops.

2008   Elected delegate to Synod of Bishops on the Word of God, Rome.

2010   Appointed to the Pontifical Commission for the Study of the Organizational and Economic Problems of the Holy See.

2012   Submitted retirement letter to Pope Benedict XVI upon turning mandatory retirement age of seventy-five. Bladder cancer returned in right kidney and liver, underwent treatment.

2013   Participated in conclave as cardinal-elector after the retirement of Pope Benedict XVI, which elected Pope Francis.

2014   Cancer returned; succession plan inaugurated. Retirement announced on September 20; became first archbishop of Chicago to retire, leaving office on November 18.

2015   Died on April 17 at historic Archbishop's Residence, Chicago; buried at All Saints Cemetery, Des Plaines, Illinois on April 23.

ONE
From the Beginning

The stone that the builders rejected has become the chief cornerstone. This is the Lord's *doing; it is marvelous in our eyes.*

Psalm 118:22–23 *(NRSV-CE)*

It was not improbable that, for the first time in more than 150 years, the Archdiocese of Chicago would receive a native Chicagoan as its archbishop. It was improbable, though, that the native Chicagoan would be Francis George. But on April 8, 1997, in what must have been possible only through God's providence, the sixty-year-old George was sent to his native see as its eighth archbishop.

As he faced the Chicago media for the first time, the city's new archbishop quoted this appropriate line from T. S. Eliot:

And the end of all our exploring
Will be to arrive where we started
And know the place for the first time.[1]

Francis George's explorations began after he left behind his Midwestern home at the age of fourteen, and they took him to places he would have never imagined, or even hoped, to go. As a young man, he had believed that God was calling him to the priesthood in Chicago. An unimaginable turn of events, however, would put an end to that dream. For this reason, the words he spoke to his new hometown flock on the day of his appointment as archbishop were — as if a line of divine poetry itself — what he had really hoped to say on the day of his ordination to the priesthood: "Now, I give the rest of my life to Chicago."[2]

"I certainly never imagined I'd be in this position," he said the day his return to Chicago was announced. "God has a sense of humor."[3]

If the Archdiocese of Chicago had its way, George would have never been a priest in the first place, having effectively barred him from ordination when he was fourteen years old. As a result, he turned elsewhere to answer the call to priesthood he had heard since he was very young — a decision that meant he was destined for places beyond his hometown. Like a true missionary, when he left his Chicago neighborhood, he did so fully prepared never to return.

But why did the archdiocese reject his application? As was the norm for anyone interested in becoming a diocesan priest during that era in Chicago, the candidate had to work his way through a system that began by attending Archbishop Quigley Preparatory Seminary, the archdiocesan seminary high school. "Frannie," as his friends and family called Francis George in his youth, had applied for admission to Quigley during his eighth-grade year — a year for serious vocational discernment in his day — and had been accepted. But things took a dramatic turn toward the end of 1950, when Frannie was stricken with poliomyelitis, or polio. That was a game-changer, and all bets were off regarding his future as a Chicago priest.

It must be said at this point that throughout his life, Francis George never liked to draw much attention to the disability that resulted from his bout with polio. It is not that he shied away from it; he was always attentive to persons with disabilities throughout his ministry, and he was not reticent about acknowledging his own physical limitations. But he was reluctant to put any spotlight on his own suffering and pain. If anything, he wanted to avoid being pitied or receiving any sympathy.

The same was true in his youth. While the effects of polio would have made getting downtown to the preparatory seminary via buses and trains a struggle, young Frannie, still on crutches at the time, was determined. He made the trek to Quigley, where the once-accepted applicant faced rejection. "They were very clear — very kind to me, but very clear," George recounted years later. "[The formators] said, 'You can come to school here … because you have a good record, and you're well recommended by your pastor, but you should know you will never be a priest in Chicago.'"

No reasons were given; they were only implied. One might think such a rejection would squash any priestly vocation. But the bleak pronouncement did not deter the young Frannie. "I thought about that for a day, and I said, 'Well, to heck with you guys.'"[4]

IN THE BEGINNING

It might be said that the odds were against Frannie from the very beginning. His mother had a difficult pregnancy, especially during its late stages, when the lives of both mother and child were in danger. He had to be delivered via caesarean section on January 16, 1937, a month before his due date. Margaret, his older sister and only sibling, recalled that he weighed about five pounds at birth, which necessitated his staying for over two weeks at St. Elizabeth Hospital in Chicago, where he had been born. After going home, baby Frannie spent the first several months of his life in a makeshift nursery in the family's large bathroom, something his sister said was arranged because it was the warmest spot in the house. At the time, the George family lived in a top-floor apartment at 905 N.

Leclaire Avenue, just around the corner from Our Lady Help of Christians Church in Chicago's Austin neighborhood. It was there that Fr. Patrick Hunter baptized the future cardinal on February 14, 1937.

Francis Eugene George was the second and last child of Francis J. George and Julia McCarthy. Francis, the father, was born and raised in Chicago, while Julia had moved there from her Kentucky birthplace when she was a young girl.[5] The couple met through mutual family and friends and were married at Epiphany Church in Chicago on August 11, 1929, on the cusp of the Great Depression. Margaret Mary was born six years before her brother. Young Frannie was named after his father and paternal grandfather, as well as his mother's older brother, Eugene McCarthy, who died at the age of thirteen and was buried back in Kentucky.

Margaret recalled leaving young Frannie at home in 1939 when she went with her mother and grandmother to take part in the funeral services of Cardinal George Mundelein, Chicago's first cardinal. Never would she have imagined that her kid brother would one day be Chicago's first native cardinal.

As a young boy, Frannie first caught sight of what would be his future home: the stately Archbishop's Residence on North State Parkway — home of cardinals in Chicago since Mundelein was given the red hat in 1924 by Pope Pius XI — situated at the edge of Chicago's Lincoln Park, about a block from Lake Michigan. He was on his way to the Lincoln Park Zoo with his mother and sister to see Bushman the Gorilla, a primate *Time* magazine claimed was "the best known and most popular civic figure in Chicago."[6] "Seeing Bushman was a highlight of my young life, and the cardinal's mansion was just a big house on my way to the zoo," Frannie recalled years later.[7]

For all intents and purposes, Frannie was 75 percent Irish and 25 percent German — the latter the ethnicity of his surname — and he came from a family of hard workers. Julia McCarthy's family traded their "old Kentucky home" in the rolling hills outside of Lexington for a place in the Windy City when she was a young girl. Her father, John Patrick McCarthy, was a metal worker. He died young and was buried back in

Kentucky alongside Frannie's uncle and namesake, although her mother is buried at the George family plot in Des Plaines, Illinois. Julia worked for an advertising company before having children. Her contentious Irish family went through bouts of not speaking with different family members. Once, when Frannie came home for a visit, his sister recalled him asking their mother, "Who are we not talking to this time?"

The George side of the family had been in Chicago for a couple of generations. Frannie's paternal grandfather, Jacob George, appears in Chicago city directories just after the city came of age when it hosted the World's Fair in 1893. He was of German ancestry and married an Irish girl, Mary Connelly. Her family had been in Chicago the longest of any of Frannie's ancestors and were parishioners at the historic Holy Family Church, one of only a few Catholic churches in Chicago that survived the Great Chicago Fire. Their son, Frannie's father Francis, had been baptized at Chicago's premiere German Catholic parish, St. Francis of Assisi Church.

Frannie's dad was taught by the Christian Brothers at Chicago's St. Mel High School and made a career working as an engineer at public education facilities, mostly for Chicago Public Schools. He worked his way up from performing basic janitorial duties to overseeing the physical plants of different institutions, and he retired from Northeastern Illinois University. He was the oldest child, and his father — a casket-maker — died young. Responsible and dedicated, Frannie's dad was tasked with looking after his mother.

Frannie's grasp of the importance of relationships began with his parents. He often commented on how much his parents understood each other, which he learned when his mother would take him shopping to buy clothes for his father. "She would take me by my hand," he recalled in 2009, "and I'd go through the men's shops with her and listen to her talking more to herself than to me."[8] He observed that as "she'd go along, looking at all the clothing that was available there," she would say things like, "Your father would never wear this ... Your father would never like this ... Your father will learn to like that." He learned that "she knew him better than he knew himself and he in turn, knew her mind and, most of all, her heart as well." Throughout his life he often spoke of this example of marital depth of understanding as a reference point for how our relationship should be with Christ.

It was clear that Frannie loved his parents and took seriously his Christian duty to honor them. Rare was the occasion when he did not send a greeting card for birthdays, anniversaries, or holidays, even when his vocation brought him to some of the farthest flung corners of the globe. When, years later, he was asked about his favorite childhood memory, he recalled an episode when his father carried him on his shoulders through the snow because he could not walk very well.

The George home cultivated in Frannie a true knowledge and love of the Lord and devotion to the Church. Julia George was a daily communicant. Everything was "centered around the Church," Margaret recalled. It was "really a very happy home," she said, also recalling that the family prayed the Rosary together each evening.

The Georges moved to a bungalow in the city's Portage Park neighborhood when Frannie was four years old. The family wanted to be close to the local parish, and their new home at 6121 W. Byron Street was just over a block away from St. Pascal Church. Their new spiritual home held a special place in Frannie's heart; it was "where I met the Lord and came to know who he is and his love," he said.[9] Many years later, on his last visit to the parish, he remarked, "Whenever I come to St. Pascal, this is sort of a shrine for me, of God's grace transforming my life, but transforming all our lives in many ways that are remarkable."[10]

Later on in life, George frequently referred to the importance of relationships and the ways in which they define who we truly are. He had a special relationship with his sister, Margaret, that continued throughout his life. As children, they were close, but, as she succinctly summed up their relationship, "I was his older sister." One of Margaret's favorite memories of their childhood together was listening to *The Cinnamon Bear*, a special children's radio program broadcast each night from Thanksgiving to Christmas. George recalled fondly, in a 2014 interview with Rich

Daniels of the City Lights Orchestra, that the show was "uncynical" — a characteristic that, as he aged, he lamented was lacking in most programming, even for children.

Christmas celebrations held a unique place in Frannie's childhood memories. He happily remembered how he loved to decorate the Christmas tree, especially the train set and its village, and how his mother would take him and his sister shopping downtown. He loved attending Midnight Mass with his family at St. Pascal — where he would often fall asleep — after which his mother would cook eggs and "marvelous sausage" sent by his Kentucky relatives. Frannie had extended family with whom he was close. Family vacations to a lake house or holiday gatherings often included aunts, uncles, and cousins. Frannie and his cousins enjoyed each other's company and had fun together, especially playing games like Monopoly and Pit. His cousins recalled how Frannie frequently won the games they played. One recalled Frannie was "undoubtedly the best player out of us all. We often accused him of cheating, but it has never been proven."[11]

Frannie fondly remembered the neighborhood as "a safe place." He added: "The streetcars turned around at Narragansett and Irving because that was the edge of the city ... and on the other side of Narragansett were cemeteries and truck farms, and on the other side of Harlem were real farms. We had the city to play in, and we had the prairies to play in. ... Our parents let us be free. ... We were taught to be resilient, to take care of ourselves, not to make excuses, be responsible, and it worked — at least I think it worked in my case, anyway."[12]

FAITHFUL AND FRIENDLY

Just before he went off to school at St. Pascal in 1944, his sister realized that Frannie had not learned the alphabet or his numbers. Margaret, who later became a teacher, took the initiative to teach him these, and he impressed her by how quickly he learned. The Franciscan Sisters of Mary Immaculate, who staffed St. Pascal school and taught young Frannie, later recalled how he stood out as the smart kid. He would recall them fondly over the years, once commenting how they taught him to love his patron saint.

Frannie could be reserved at times, and he loved to read. He once explained that he began reading as a child with interest not so much in books but in newspapers. Among the first things he remembered reading as a child was *Our Sunday Visitor*, the national Catholic weekly founded by Archbishop John F. Noll in 1912. In its pages, he found "the bringing together of reason and faith … for the first time" and learned what it means to give "reasons for the faith that is in you."[13] It's clear Frannie was an exceptional thinker from an early age. Also gregarious and outgoing, it seemed Frannie was everybody's friend. The boys on the block who hung out together were known as the "Byron Street Gang." Together, they would sit for hours at a local movie house, watching anything from westerns to science fiction for fifteen cents. They beat the pavement on their bikes, and Frannie's Irish Mail, a scooter-like bike he let friends take turns riding, was the envy of everyone. It was nicknamed the "Franarang." In the streets they played sixteen-inch softball, the sewer manholes standing in for the bases, or at Portage Park they played football. No matter the activity, many friends would remember Frannie for his stubborn determination to win — and to play by the rules no matter what.

Occasionally, Frannie and his friends would head downtown for adventures, like taking in the city's skyline from the Tribune Tower observation deck. He loved to head to Riverview Amusement Park on the days that rides cost only two cents apiece. "You had a dollar in your pocket. You could go to every ride as long as you didn't waste it buying cotton candy and frivolous food," he recalled years later.[14] The Byron Street Gang kept in touch throughout the years and remained a part of Frannie's life.

Young Frannie also struck up a lifelong friendship with Loretto Ryan, who was part of a group of students who walked to school early to attend daily Mass. She went on to become Sr. Frances Ryan, a vowed religious, and later held a professorship at DePaul University in Chicago. "He was someone you could talk to about ideas," she said.[15] "Like me, he loved books, and we would talk about them as we walked. He always wanted to become a priest and I wanted to be a Daughter of Charity." His integrity was clear to her as well. Frannie "was not goody-goody, but he always made the right decision. And he had a terrific sense of humor," she recalled.

A sense of duty, responsibility, and service was reinforced in Frannie through membership in Boy Scouts Troop 945. He received perfect scores on his inspections, and he learned to serve and protect others as a captain in the school safety patrol.

Frannie could have a mischievous streak. He used to place bugs on the tops of doors so they would fall onto Margaret's head as she passed through. Julia George, Margaret recalled, was known to tell her son, "You're the most stubborn child I've ever met." Perhaps that was just a high level of perseverance developing, something that would come to define Frannie's life in many ways — especially once afflicted with polio.

Julia George introduced her children to music, insisting on piano lessons and even taking them to the opera. She herself had a certificate to teach music. "She filled our lives with music," her son once remarked, "for which I was grateful, especially when I wasn't as active physically."[16] Frannie was also under the tutelage of Miss Janet O'Neill for piano lessons and performed at several recitals under her direction. At St. Pascal, he was a member of the choir — a compulsory service for all students in seventh and eighth grades — but he could hit all the high notes.

Frannie had a "beautiful voice," classmates remembered, which was particularly showcased during third grade, when he sang, without accompaniment, "Too-ra-loo-ra-loo-ra." The Irish lullaby had been brought back in vogue by Bing Crosby's portrayal of crooning priest Fr. Charles O'Malley in the 1944 film *Going My Way*. Frannie was also involved in the elite Paulist Choir in Chicago, directed at the time by the legendary Paulist Father Eugene O'Malley, the namesake and inspiration for Crosby's character in the film and its 1945 sequel *The Bells of St. Mary's*. At different times in their history, the group, based at Old St. Mary's Church in Chicago, sang for notables from presidents to popes. O'Malley was a strict perfectionist. Once he was reportedly so dissatisfied with Frannie's singing that, midway through a rehearsal, he sent the boy soprano and future cardinal packing for good.

SET ON THE PRIESTHOOD

Frannie's first-grade teacher, Sr. Rita McCabe, recognized the many talents of her prized pupil, recalling years later, "He was absolutely the brightest boy that ever passed through my class."[17] She saw more than intelligence, however. Even at Frannie's early age, Sister Rita found within him a strong faith and piety, evidenced by his attention and devotion to the liturgy and his reverence as an altar boy. In an effort to help his peers more fully understand the Mass, Sister Rita enlisted Frannie to stand before the class for a reenactment. "He was saying everything in Latin, and I was baffled," she said. "Seeing this little first-grader repeating these ancient words really surprised me. But I eventually got used to it. That's just Frannie."

Margaret recalled that her brother wanted to be a fireman when he was around two years old, but by age five, he made it clear that he wanted to be a priest. It was a common occurrence in the George home that Frannie would playact the Mass with his sister, she said, but after they almost set the house on fire, they were forbidden from using candles. Some of the neighborhood kids recalled how Frannie would set up a makeshift confessional in which he would hear confessions. He initially felt a tug at his heart toward the priesthood after receiving his First Holy Communion on May 6, 1945.

During his years in elementary school, Frannie was very close to Msgr. George Heimsath, the pastor of St. Pascal. As a head altar boy, Frannie was frequently found in the church helping Monsignor Heimsath with a variety of odd jobs, and his parents would often dispatch Margaret to bring her brother home for meals. Monsignor Heimsath was no-nonsense and considered strict by many — someone even George would, later in life, call "a curmudgeon"[18] at times. And he was frugal. He oversaw construction of St. Pascal Church during the Depression; he was known to wax the floors himself on Saturdays and mow the rectory lawn too. When Monsignor Heimsath made visits to the sick, he would take the city bus. And Monsignor Heimsath's influence on George's budding vocation was undeniable.

Sister Rita also recognized her first-grade student's vocation early on. Being a Franciscan herself, she arranged for Frannie to spend part of a summer with some Franciscan priests in Tennessee. She also recalled that Julia George "always felt [Frannie] would be someone special in the Church."[19] According to Margaret, their mother always thought Frannie would "go high" in the Church.

If he had not become a priest, Frannie could have gone down a variety of different paths. He had a razor-sharp mind and was a gifted artist and talented writer. He was editor of St. Pascal's new school newspaper, *Guard and Tackle*, during his eighth-grade year. In an editorial just before Thanksgiving, only a few weeks in advance of falling ill with the life-changing polio, Frannie wrote about the importance of gratitude: "So next Thanksgiving Day, when we bless ourselves to recite the Grace before and after meals, let us think of the simple words we recite and as we say them, be truly grateful to God who has given us so much."[20] The challenge of being thankful for all things would certainly be something for Frannie to ruminate on in the weeks ahead. It would also give him the ability to face an uncertain future and offer a valuable lens through which to make sense of a life that would see more than its fair share of suffering.

Everything changed for Frannie midway through eighth grade. Just before Christmas 1950, he was stricken with polio. Its origin was unclear, although his family speculated that he might have contracted it on a camping trip with the Boy Scouts. The disease, also known as infantile paralysis, was highly contagious and potentially fatal. The virus affected people differently, but for most it was asymptomatic. Polio could attack the central nervous system and leave victims' limbs withered and their muscles atrophied. By the time it hit Frannie, it had been a scourge on American public health for more than a half-century. Children were the disease's most frequent victims, and that year was one of the worst on record in Cook County, Illinois, where Frannie lived.

There was no immunization for polio until the mid-1950s, nor was there a cure. To make matters worse, its origins were difficult to trace. The stigma that victims came from "dirty homes" weighed heavily on the Georges, and Julia and Francis wondered all their lives why this had to happen. Frannie's disease also brought new financial burdens to the family, and for a time they received some assistance from the Cook County chapter of the National Foundation for Infantile Paralysis. By 1952, cases of this feared childhood illness had peaked in the United States; worldwide incidences of it dropped drastically a few years later after widespread distribution of the Salk vaccine.

The polio scared Frannie. At first, it seemed like he had the flu, until the paralysis began setting in. Frannie loved to draw, and suddenly he was unable to. The once-active boy could not even stand up without help. The polio symptoms had settled in his legs and right arm, and the Georges knew he needed to go to the hospital. Frannie was admitted for months as a patient at St. Francis Hospital in Evanston. His family came to visit him daily. Therapy and surgeries were required to help him battle the effects of the disease. "It was a horrible time," Margaret recalled. "We all cried and prayed."[21] As an adult, George would gratefully recall the compassionate care that he and so many other children with polio received from the nurses at St. Francis, and their efforts to bring some moments of enjoyment to their young patients during an extended hospital stay.

In 2003, George recalled some of the more trying moments he experienced as a hospital patient for polio in that era:

At that time, they brought patients on lorries into an amphitheater where all the medical students stared down at you. Your name was never mentioned; you were never introduced. Perhaps that small recognition of human subjectivity would have gotten in the way of the lessons that the doctors wanted to teach to medical students. But there was a sense in my own experience even at the time, young though I was, that something was radically wrong in that situation — that I'm more than an object for inspection by students and should be recognized as more. I'm more than somebody who is there in order to advance scientific knowledge.[22]

Despite the challenges, by all accounts Frannie's battle with polio taught him to understand suffering as redemptive — that it had a purpose. And it was a time in which he learned to trust that God's ways are better than our own.

A young girl who lived in Frannie's neighborhood came down with polio a few months before he did. Frannie had been friends with her brother. Their father came to visit Frannie in the hospital one day and gave him some advice that resonated to his core: "You'll be alright," his friend's father said. "Remember, there are people worse than you, so don't ever feel sorry for yourself."[23]

Years later, George would recall the great impact of that visit. "For a thirteen-year-old kid to hear that, especially when I was feeling sorry for myself, didn't know whether I could ever play ball again, didn't know what I could do. ... The assurance that the worst thing I could do is feel sorry for myself has stayed with me as the best advice I ever heard." He came to realize, he once said, that "the last thing you want to do is just come to self-pity." That does not mean it was easy and did not come at a personal cost, however. It is clear that Frannie battled resentment of his illness and its effects for the rest of his life, even if those closest to him never realized it. He recalled in 2009, "I resented the fact that I couldn't run anymore, and I couldn't play baseball. I had good help in the minor seminary where they led me through that and said, 'You have to stop being resentful against God, against everybody.'"[24]

Instead of letting the polio destroy him, Frannie let it shape him. A man who shared a hospital room with him would often engage Frannie in conversation. Margaret recalled he related to Julia that whenever Frannie fell silent, the man would look over and find his young roommate gazing at the crucifix on the wall. It is hard to know for sure, but it seems that perhaps this young boy whose future was uncertain — who was facing tremendous pain, fear, and suffering — was relying on Christ's cross as the means to make sense of it all. As he would say later in life, "Christianity without the cross is a false religion."[25]

Relatedly, many years later, as archbishop of Chicago, George began to sense something familiar as he was blessing newly installed Stations of the Cross at St. James the Greater Church in Sauk Village, Illinois, a parish in the Chicago archdiocese. He soon learned that the refurbished stations had formerly been in the chapel at St. Francis Hospital, and he revealed that he had gazed upon them in prayer for untold hours during his stay.[26] The story of his life would show how he understood that he could do anything through Christ his strength. Years later, as a cardinal of the Church, Frannie told a group of teens that the polio left him "a captive in my own body. I soon learned that self-pity got me nowhere. Faith was the way out, because in faith I was not alone, and good can come of something that appears bad at that time."[27]

The polio caused Frannie to miss months of school, and his illness hit his class hard. Classmate Loretto Ryan, later Sr. Frances Ryan, remarked, "He was there, and then he was just gone. No one was allowed to see him at all."[28] His peers in the eighth grade at St. Pascal sent letters of support and camaraderie just before Christmas.[29] One wrote, "We are all waiting for the smartest boy in our room to hurry back." Some students kept him abreast of all the gossip, including a budding romance between two classmates, how the patrol was getting along in frigid temperatures, and how the altar servers were faring without Frannie's leadership. Many letters tried to lighten Frannie's spirit with some jokes or silly stories. Some reassured him that he would get through this crisis because he had "such faith in God." A few letters mentioned how Frannie was seeking the intercession of St. Jude — patron of hopeless causes — perhaps an indication of how dire the situation might have seemed at the time. His "buddy" Boniface Wittenbrink instructed him, "Be sure to rub some of that St. Jude oil on your leg each day, it might help you get out of bed faster." More notes written by many peers in his graduation autograph book even expressed their desire that he not be discouraged from pursuing the priesthood despite the setbacks and difficulties he faced. Those who knew him best believed in him and reiterated his heart's longing. All his life, George kept a notebook filled with these letters of good wishes and cheer from his classmates.

Even throughout his illness, it appears that Frannie maintained his columns in the school newspaper, *Guard and Tackle*. In the final edition published by the class of 1951, Frannie wrote, "Throughout our entire life we can show our devotion and thanks by always doing what we know should be expected of us. And if we do this always, there will one day be a great reunion and this class of '51 shall once more be restored in the house of he who is King and Priest of God."[30] Despite his ordeal, Frannie's priorities — including his love of and faith in Jesus Christ — remained clear.

During Frannie's extended absence, the sisters from his school provided regular tutoring, and he managed to graduate at the top of his class despite having only returned to school for a few months before the end of the school year. For that accomplishment, he received a prized class ring — the one male among his peers so honored — at the graduation ceremony.

The effects of polio left Frannie permanently disabled, especially in his right leg, as well as constantly hurting. "He's always in pain," Frannie's sister, Margaret, would tell people as a key to understanding her brother. Classmates like Sister Ryan recalled how he never complained, and this became a common trait for George later as a priest and bishop as well.

As the summer of 1951 commenced, Frannie was still on crutches. His dream of attending Quigley — which would have meant navigating multiple public transportation transfers and several flights of stairs — was becoming as impossible for him physically as the leaders of the school posited his ordination as a priest would be. Though a letter from the rector of Quigley that was sent to Frannie's parents in early August 1951 indicated that their son had been accepted for admission in the fall, it had been made clear to Frannie earlier that summer that Quigley, a training ground for future priests in Chicago, effectively considered him unfit for Holy Orders on account of his disability.[31]

"When I signed up for Quigley, they told us clearly that ten percent would go on to ordained priesthood," he told Chicago priests in 2007. "They told me quickly: 'You will not be among them.'"

With his plans to attend Quigley quashed, we find ourselves back at Frannie's rhetorical, "Well, to heck with you guys." Frannie was introduced by a friend to the Missionary Oblates of Mary Immaculate, who operated a high school seminary in the downstate Illinois city of Belleville. Boniface Wittenbrink, the friend with the sage advice about the St. Jude oil, was planning to attend there, hoping to follow in the footsteps of his uncle and namesake who was an Oblate priest.

While sitting in the George family living room, Margaret recalled, an Oblate vocation director from Minnesota told Frannie that if he could walk across the room right then and there, he could be an Oblate priest. Frannie did so. It seemed as if his dream to pursue priesthood might be realized after all.

In that moment, a door was opened for Frannie. It was a door that allowed him to fulfill his dream, yes; but more significantly, it was a door that allowed his gifts and talents to be shared more than he could have ever imagined. And most importantly, that open door allowed Frannie to serve Christ, bring others to him, and bring him glory in his Church. Undoubtedly, at least in hindsight, Frannie would agree with his sister, Margaret, when she said, "It seemed the polio struck for a reason."[32]

TWO
Formation for Priesthood

Never let yourself be beaten down by difficulties.

SAINT EUGENE DE MAZENOD

In the summer of 1951, Frannie enrolled at St. Henry's Preparatory Seminary in Belleville, Illinois. Moving almost three hundred miles away from home was no easy task for a boy on crutches, especially just months after surviving a debilitating illness.

Given the difficulties that he faced, one might reasonably wonder what motivated such a young boy to pursue the priesthood. The Oblates of Mary Immaculate is a missionary religious congregation, and Frannie knew outright that life as a missionary, especially for someone who was disabled, would be no cake walk. He also knew that for a religious priest, especially in his day, there was no ecclesial ladder to climb. He

47

certainly was smart enough to succeed in many careers. While there were stereotypes and limitations facing persons with disabilities, it should be remembered that the highest office in American government had been occupied by a polio victim — President Franklin D. Roosevelt — when Frannie was born. Given the details of Frannie's story and the era in which it unfolded, there's no real explanation for the path Frannie chose other than his unshakable belief that he was called to it by God and motivated by his desire to love the Lord and his people as a priest.

In 2013, as he celebrated the fiftieth anniversary of his ordination to the priesthood, Cardinal George said he did not want to speak about doing things in spite of illness. Instead, he said, "You do things with those illnesses. Even illness can be a gift in some way."[1] The gift of his polio, in a strange way, was that it put him on the path to St. Henry's and the Oblates of Mary Immaculate — a decision that defined the rest of his life.

The Oblates had opened St. Henry's in 1926 at the request of its namesake and founder, Bishop Henry Althoff of Belleville. St. Henry's was operated by the Oblate Central Province, which was historically made up of Oblates with German ethnicity. More than three thousand students passed through this minor seminary in its sixty-year history, many of whom pursued priesthood with the Oblates or in a diocese. In its heyday, when Frannie attended, St. Henry's offered a six-year course of study, effectively a high school program followed by two years of college. Its beautiful campus was a paradise for young men in many ways, with fifty-four acres to explore, including two lakes. Of the many notable alumni who passed through the doors of St. Henry's, Frannie would one day be its most famous.

The Oblates of Mary Immaculate were founded in 1816 by French priest (later bishop) St. Eugene de Mazenod in the aftermath of the French Revolution. Guided by the motto "He has sent me to preach the Gospel to the poor," de Mazenod wanted the community to foster renewal in the life of the Church in France. Their successes at home in this missionary work quickly led to requests for similar service in foreign missions. Requests from around the globe for Oblate missionaries quickly began to flood the founder. The first North American home of the Oblates was in Canada, where they established themselves as a missionary *tour de force*, serving even in the far-flung outposts of the Canadian north. So pivotal to the expansion of the Church in Canada were the Oblates that authorities in Rome dubbed them the "Canadian Fathers."

Frannie had no obvious connections to the Oblates other than through his classmate at St. Pascal. Nonetheless, they had become well-established throughout the United States, with five provinces across the country at the time. But he did have a variety of providential connections with the Oblates' founder, Eugene de Mazenod. His name was Frannie's middle name, they shared an ordination anniversary, and, like Saint Eugene, Frannie would also become a bishop. They also shared a common branch in their episcopal genealogy and would both die of cancer. Before Frannie decided to attend St. Henry's, he attended the Oblate Vocation Workshop Week held there, and a handwritten addendum on his certificate of attendance notes that he took first place in the exam, presumably an entrance exam to attend St. Henry's.[2]

At St. Henry's, young Frannie would have heard and read about the fascinating and heroic work of Oblate missionaries throughout the world. Given his disability, and how the Chicago formators at Quigley turned him down when he pursued the priesthood there, Frannie was concerned about whether or not the congregation was the right place for him. During his teenage years, he underwent four orthopedic surgeries to help with the slight paralysis in his right leg. Wittenbrink recalled that sometime around their junior year of high school, one of those operations left Frannie in a half-body cast. The effects of polio also left Frannie feeling alone, and he said on a number of occasions that it had a bigger impact on him than he imagined at the time. There is no doubt the polio changed the course of Frannie's life, and the difficulties resulting from the illness meant life would not be easy for him. As a result, in his ministry as a priest and bishop — the former of which he was told he would never attain and the latter of which he would have never dreamed — Francis George had a special place in his heart for the abandoned and the marginalized.

The letter of acceptance to St. Henry's sent to Frannie's parents contained a postscript asking that the school be notified "immediately" if the recipients' son decided to go elsewhere. Some have said that Frannie planned to return to Chicago to prepare for the priesthood after he recovered a little from the immediate effects of polio. At least one person stated that sometime after Frannie completed high school, he again sought acceptance as a candidate for priesthood in the Archdiocese of Chicago, but was rejected once more. The ongoing effects of polio and the multiple rejections by his home diocese were opportunities for Frannie to take up the cross. Together they constituted a continual dying to self and a daily exercise in trusting God's providence. Answering God's call was already costing Frannie in ways of which many young aspirants to the priesthood would never dream. He just wanted to serve the Lord as a priest, and he resolutely remained on the path that had been opened to him by the Oblates.

The Oblates deserve praise for their decision to accept a student like Frannie. At that time, the Code of Canon Law, the law of the Church, contained particular prohibitions against ordaining candidates with certain disabilities, although polio was not one of them. Vocations to the priesthood were abundant in large dioceses like Chicago, resulting sometimes in candidates being told very close to their anticipated ordination that they would not be ordained because the diocese already had more than enough priests. Those times were much different than our own, and as a result, dioceses could be much more selective. Religious congregations were often more accepting, but welcoming and training a student with a disability such as Frannie's required increased flexibility by his formators and others in the Oblate community.

LIFE IN BELLEVILLE

St. Henry's had already demonstrated this openness and inclusivity a year earlier when it hired a lay teacher who himself suffered from the effects of polio. Paul Pichotta — affectionately called "Prof" by the generations of students he taught and mentored — was a legend at St. Henry's. He taught literature and also worked with administration of finances. His presence on the faculty no doubt helped support the cause of Francis George's acceptance to St. Henry's.[3]

Frannie's disability would be an opportunity to show his resolve; it demanded perseverance. He had to travel far from home, negotiating the Gulf, Mobile, and Ohio Railroads, often with some assistance from classmates from the upper Midwest who were also traveling back and forth to St. Henry's. During the first years after his affliction, he got around mostly on crutches. Because the school had no elevators, he was required to use crutches even on stairs, a skill that he mastered to the amazement of his colleagues and that he retained even later in life. Fellow students recalled that staff medical personnel would have to massage Frannie's legs at night in the hope of helping him regain greater muscle function. In those early days, it was unclear how long he would need to use the crutches. Eventually, he would transition to a cane and then begin to walk with only a slight limp. He was always pushing to gain more strength in his legs and be more self-sufficient.

While there were activities among the student body at St. Henry's, such as football games, in which Frannie could not participate because of his disability, the campus offered him other opportunities for outdoor recreation. Fishing was a hobby Frannie shared with his father throughout life, and St. Henry's had two lakes where he could enjoy the sport.

Frannie spent some of his leisure time reading and thinking. He loved to argue with his peers, especially about politics. Although weak physically, he could show his prowess intellectually. During these years he fell more in love with the intellectual life, having been inspired by one of his high school teachers to read *La Vie Intellectuelle* by Dominican Father Antonin-Gilbert Sertillanges. At the end of his life, George recalled the important role this text played in his own formation. "Unlike other books I had read, it didn't just report on something or offer explanations; rather, it opened up a vista, a horizon I would not have made explicit so early in my life without the help of the book and the advice of my teacher and brother."[4]

As a bishop years later, when George recalled how he loved living in community, Oblate confrere Fr. Allen Maes quipped in reply, "You loved living with people you could argue with!" He recalled how George used to tease him, "Stand up to me, Allen! Stand up to me!" George admired those who understood opposing viewpoints and engaged them because "one thinks more clearly when arguing with opponents."[5] For George, opponents were usually friends who just helped clarify his thinking by way of his vigorous engagement and debate.

In a Bible quiz at St. Henry's in 1952, sophomore Frannie earned the highest mark. His prize was a Bible, seemingly unnecessary given his achievement. In 1953, he was awarded the Charles Palmer Davis Medal for outstanding work in the field of current events. It was a prize awarded to secondary-school students, named for the founder of the student magazine *Weekly Reader*. Years later, these talents grew into a reputation for a deep understanding of the culture, and he was admired and respected across the globe for his ability to read the signs of the times, a gift especially valuable to the missionary activity of the Church.

Several of the extracurricular talents Frannie had brought with him from Chicago flourished during his years in Belleville. He quickly became involved with the school journal, *The Gleeman*.[6] Within a short time, he became its art editor and was also responsible for the publication's layout. Frannie's own artwork, much of which was religious in nature, was featured throughout the quarterly journal — including many covers, which the publication noted he made "more elaborate." When direction of art in *The Gleeman* was fully his, the editions included a written, detailed description of what the art expressed and why it was chosen.

Frannie's love for art during his years at St. Henry's also manifested itself in painting. He had nurtured an artistic bent since childhood, and it seems he might have picked up painting as a form of therapy as much as of enjoyment. His right arm and hand both needed to be strengthened after the polio, and painting was a good way to achieve this. Throughout the years, a portrait of the Holy Family that he painted has been featured in various places after he arrived back home as Chicago's archbishop.

He gave it to his sister, Margaret, and her husband, James Cain, on their wedding day in 1952. During his later years at St. Henry's, Frannie's artwork appeared on covers of *The Gleeman* as well as in its pages, each piece signed with the block letter initials "F.G." Another notable painting of his was a mural in the office of *The Gleeman*, a depiction of the journal's namesake mascot of sorts, which met its demise when the main St. Henry's building was demolished after its closure in 1984. The mural was featured in the journal's pages in 1957 with this written description by its artist:

> The gleeman of medieval ages was a storyteller who used to travel from castle to castle, singing and telling stories. He was one of the only means of communication in a world largely disjointed because of distances and lack of modern means of communication. He had to know how to read and write because of his profession. His coming was a cause of gladness and joy to the members of the community, just as the coming of well-written Catholic literature is a gladness and joy to the Christian community.

Frannie could be avant-garde and controversial, as often seen in his artistic written contributions to *The Gleeman*, which included everything from short poems and fiction to a philosophical analysis on "The New Warfare." In this 1955 piece, Frannie wrestled with classical just war theory and the morality of using the atomic bomb. His philosophically incisive mind — which would earn him a doctorate from Tulane University about a decade later — concluded with this frightful judgment on American pragmatism:

> With the exception of a small "radical" minority, everyone is "pretty well sold" on the use of nuclear weapons in all circumstances. And this is the greater disaster — far worse than any atomic or hydrogen bomb — that the conscience of so-called

Christian people is in so great a lethargic state that it fails to recognize evil as evil, that it sanctions national pragmatism and substitutes it for the moral order. This, more than the quickening advance of universal cataclysm, more than the collapse of international law, more than the New Warfare and the carnage and destruction it brings, is the greatest disaster of our atomic age.

Frannie also continued his musical training, often studying during summers with the Franciscan Sisters back home in Chicago at St. Pascal. In his last years at St. Henry's, Frannie served as organist and also as a member of the entertainment committee, which, among other things, put on school plays. He sang in the Belleville diocesan boys' choir and organized Christmas concerts at St. Henry's. While their peers played outdoors, Frannie and some of his classmates would play duets on the piano. And some of St. Henry's students, as *The Gleeman* put it, "decided to broaden their minds in the fields of music and art by taking piano lessons from that great maestro, Francis George."

For an occasional holiday away from the seminary, he liked to sneak away to St. Louis and attend the symphony or a play. Most of the things to which Frannie gave his time and attention were inside activities that did not require much physical strength, but he excelled at them because of his sharp mind and keen imagination. "One of the best parts of living in Belleville," George remembered, "was that four times a year we were allowed to come into St. Louis and to go to Powell Hall or Forest Park or to the new and also the old cathedrals and in that sense get to know the city and appreciate it in ways that I think are possible only for people who get to know a place when they are quite young."[7]

Frannie would return home from the seminary during summers and for some holidays. During some summers, he made profitable use of the love of and talent for music that had been instilled and nurtured in him by his mother by traveling to parishes on Chicago's north side to give some organists a vacation. One summer, he journeyed all the way to Salt Lake City, Utah, where his mother fulfilled a long-held desire to hear the

Mormon Tabernacle Choir perform. Frannie also used some of his summer vacation time to rehabilitate his muscles by joining the Chicago Polio Swim Club at the town hall of Chicago's Austin neighborhood, which provided helpful therapy to victims of paralysis. Dubbed the "city's most exclusive club," it offered an opportunity for polio victims of any age to swim in specially heated water to help them strengthen their muscles, and also provided them with social opportunities.

The intellectual capacity that Frannie began to display during his grade school years at St. Pascal blossomed at St. Henry's. In his first year, which would often be a time of struggle for most students who moved so far away from home, not to mention the special challenges it would present to persons with a disability, the monthly grade reports sent home to Frannie's parents show he received a B only once — in General Science. His grades on the rest of his curriculum were in the high 90s to 100, including the areas of "conduct" and "attitude to work."[8] In 1956, he received an exceptionally high IQ score of 146 on the California Test of Mental Maturity. *The Gleeman* described Frannie during his senior year of high school as "one of the lights of his class."

The faculty was almost unanimous in its praise of Frannie at the time of his graduation, describing him as a young man with "outstanding intelligence" and a "lively imagination" who was "responsible and resourceful," "purposeful," and "completely trustworthy." Similarly, they expressed a majority opinion that Frannie was "satisfactory" in his stamina and physical coordination, and were of one mind in describing him as "persevering."

At St. Henry's, Frannie found not only a community that welcomed him, but one where he could thrive. By the conclusion of his six years at the Belleville minor seminary, he had decided that he wanted to live the life of an Oblate of Mary Immaculate, so he applied for the novitiate and was accepted. It was clear by his application that Frannie remained concerned that he might have some difficulty because of his disability. He wrote, "Seven years ago I had an attack of spinal polio, which, although there was never any mortal danger, left my right leg slightly paralyzed. ...

This slight lameness has been no bother at St. Henry's, and the Fathers here have assured me it will be no impediment."

When he graduated from St. Henry's in 1957, Frannie was quoted in *The Gleeman* as having no special work in mind for his priestly life, only "whatever my superiors want me to do." By the time he completed the novitiate a year later, his formators included in his annual evaluations that for Frannie it was "not advisable to go to foreign missions." But Frannie was not discouraged. A well-worn prayer card found amid childhood items he kept all his life had printed on it a "Prayer for Courage," which seems like a guiding framework for the path ahead. It read, "God make me brave — let me strengthen after pain as a tree strengthens after the rain, shining lovely again. As the blown grass lifts, let me rise from sorrow with quiet eyes, knowing Thy way is wise. God make me brave — life brings such blinding things! Help me to keep my sight, help me to see aright — that out of dark — comes light."

Most religious orders require their members to profess three vows: those of poverty, chastity, and obedience. The Oblates, however, require a fourth vow — that of perseverance. His ability to excel so far from home and so quickly after his plans were thwarted by a debilitating disease revealed Frannie's extraordinary perseverance. It seemed the young Francis George had found himself in the right place after all.

MAKING AN OBLATION

"Oblate" comes from the Latin word *oblatio*, which means a sacrifice or offering. Frannie's life up to this point had been — and would continue to be — an oblation, whereby he learned more each day about the love that flows from redemptive suffering. As an Oblate of Mary Immaculate, he would offer his life at the service of his community, which took up missions to wherever the Church's needs were greatest. All of that would enable him to offer up his life for God's glory in imitation of the Lord. This life of oblation meant living for God and others. As he would say some years later, "The only thing you take with you is what you have given away."[9] With his entrance into the Oblates, Frannie set out on a path that presented continual opportunities for him to empty himself in ways never imagined for the Church, first as a priest and later as a bishop. Oblate Fr. David Kalert, who was a year behind Frannie in studies but attended novitiate with him, observed that "all his life" Frannie "gave himself 100 percent-plus to whatever he did."

Not very far from St. Henry's, in Godfrey, Illinois, the Immaculate Heart of Mary novitiate is situated high up on the bluffs overlooking the Mississippi River. The site was formerly a fruit farm that encompassed a Mediterranean-style summer home. Built in the 1920s by Charles Levis, a magnate of the glass industry from nearby Alton, the original main house had been modified and expanded to accommodate a novitiate after it came under Oblate possession. Frannie entered in August 1957, staying the canonically required one year and a day.

The life of a novice during Frannie's day was rather monastic, consisting mostly of study, work, and prayer. It was a time to learn the congregation's history and way of life, during which little to no contact with the outside world was permitted. To help fill their days, novices were directed to work on the two hundred acres of land around the novitiate. But Frannie would have had other indoor tasks assigned to him, including service as house organist and duties in the sacristy. There were also times of recreation, and while Frannie was not able to play sports, he would often cheer on and be present to his confreres from the sidelines.

His evaluation at the end of novitiate highlighted many characteristics for which Frannie would be known for the rest of his life and would become some of the reasons he rose to positions of leadership in the Church at an early age. His intellectual abilities were described as "outstanding," but he also possessed "good common sense." He displayed a "lively imagination" and a "talent for writing." He was found to be apt for teaching and was also noted to be a "very good speaker" with "good content and delivery." Frannie was described as having "good solid faith and piety" and fit well into the community: "docile and submissive, very sociable, shows good community spirit, gets along with fellow novices" and was "generous and helpful to others." He was "frank and open with

Superiors." And during the novitiate, he "made good progress in his spiritual life." As far as his future work in the congregation was concerned,
Frannie was found "capable of almost any work the Congregation has
to offer" but "not advised to do hard physical work." Again, it was noted
that Frannie "has not expressed any preferences" and was "determined to
become an Oblate priest."

His strengths and weaknesses were summed up in the description
of his character as "predominantly choleric with some sanguinic tendencies," according to the labels from the ancient temperament theory used
in such evaluations at the time. Extroverted and social, he was independent and ambitious, in the good sense. He exerted influence and was
found to possess "strong will power." But he had a positive effect on those
around him, and evaluations describe him as "usually calm and mild"
with "his temper under good control," and "very polite." And "although
inclined to pride," Frannie "worked hard to conquer it." In later years, he
described how he continually had to work on curbing his temper and
pride. Physically, the evaluation identified partial paralysis from Frannie's bout with polio, along with a "slight limp" that he retained the rest
of his life.

The conclusion: Francis George was recommended for first vows.
After unanimous approval from the provincial council, Frannie became
an Oblate of Mary Immaculate on August 15, 1958, when he took his first
vows in the congregation at the novitiate chapel in Godfrey. With those
vows, he embarked on a religious life of fifty-eight years. Brother Francis
Eugene George, O.M.I., then moved on to the next phase of his formation
at Our Lady of the Snows Scholasticate in Pass Christian, Mississippi.

Also known as "Pine Hills," after the name of the facility's first oc-
cupant, the scholasticate at Pass Christian was originally a short-lived,
five-story, 180-room resort hotel situated on twenty acres along Bay St.
Louis, near the Gulf of Mexico. Surrounded by southern Mississippi's
bayous and tall pines, its neighbors were vacation homes, hotels, and
small farms. The facility had been built by some New Orleans business-
men a few years before the Great Depression — the calamity that brought

about its demise. Pine Hills remained empty for nearly a decade until the United States military used it for training during the Second World War era. The Oblates took possession of the abandoned resort — legendarily painted a pink shade called "Savannah Peach" — in a sweetheart deal in 1953 and opened the scholasticate in the statewide Mississippi diocese of Natchez-Jackson. It would close by 1968.

The year that George arrived, the rector of Pine Hills was chosen for a special mission to oversee a revival of the Church's mission in Greenland. In 1962, Oblate Father John E. Taylor became the first American-born bishop to oversee a European diocese when he was nominated as bishop of Stockholm, Sweden. Little would George have imagined that he would follow in his footsteps one day as a successor of the Apostles and wear Taylor's own pectoral cross when he was ordained a bishop in 1990.

The scholasticate's plan of formation consisted of two years of philosophy and four of theology. During his studies at Pass Christian, Brother Francis truly began to emerge as a scholar, somewhat of a rarity in a community of rough-and-ready missionaries. Some professors believed the rare breed of students like Brother Francis was even more competent in their fields of study than they were; in fact, many were not even properly educated in their respective fields. Students like Brother Francis began to highlight a deficiency in the Oblate Central province's ability to operate an autonomous scholasticate, something he would help to change when he arrived on the faculty after priestly ordination.

It was during his time at Pine Hills, as photographs show, that Brother Francis began to lose his hair. He later said to Chicago priests in 2007 that, for him, "hair was a temporary aberration," as he had been bald from the time he was twenty-one or twenty-two.

Brother Francis' years of study at Our Lady of the Snows were important to many aspects of his formation. In some ways they allowed him to grow in humility, a virtue he needed to keep his self-professed pride in check. He also deepened his relationship with the Oblate community and truly grew to love his congregation and its mission. He gained a sense of the cultural disparities in America and became acquainted with the problems of racial injustice and the growing civil rights movement.

Toward the end of his time at Pine Hills, Brother Francis took on chairmanship of the Seminarians' Catholic Action Study of the South. As chairman, Brother Francis was responsible for leading the planning of the group's annual conference, which in 1962 was held at St. Joseph's Abbey near Covington, Louisiana. An August 26 letter written to his parents the night before the event sheds some light on the situation of life at an abbey for an Oblate of Mary Immaculate as well as gives a glimpse into Brother Francis's characteristic humor:

> Nice place — arrived here … last Friday night. Have been work-ing ever since. As I said, nice place — except the bell ringer should be shot — he wakes them up for Lauds at 4:20 — and rings the bells in the church tower for ten minutes — not that it matters too much, since we all have to be up for 5:00 a.m. Mass anyway. By the time 10:00 a.m. rolls around, you think it's the middle of the afternoon.

The title of the conference he helped arrange was "The Role of the Layman in the Growth of the Church" — a topic that was in some ways ahead of its time, since the conference was held just a few weeks before the official opening of the Second Vatican Council. Among the invited speakers was Archbishop John Cody of New Orleans, who would end up being one of Brother Francis's predecessors in Chicago.

The last few summers during his years at Pine Hills also afforded Brother Francis the opportunity to begin his pursuit of a master's degree in philosophy at The Catholic University of America in Washington, DC. While there, he stayed at Oblate College just across the street. During the summer of 1961, Frannie wrote a June 18 letter to his parents re-counting, with his typical humor and candor, a less-than-ideal train ride from Pine Hills to Washington. The reader of this letter can also hear his charity toward others, particularly in his concern for racial justice — the importance of which he had become more keenly aware after studying in Mississippi the previous few years. He tells how he walked into the dining car and sat down with a young Black couple who were riding to Washington for their honeymoon. As they were talking and eating, he looked out the window while passing through Greenville, South Carolina, and saw a newsboy holding a paper with the headline that read, "First Freedom Riders Arrive in South Carolina Without Demonstration." He quipped, "I thought: Could they have reported us to the press already?"

During one of his summers of study in Washington, Brother Francis became acquainted with Orlando Quevedo, a brother Oblate and native of the Philippines, who would eventually be ordained a bishop and, in 2014, be named the fifth Oblate cardinal, the next one after George. At the time of his confrere's death, Cardinal Quevedo recalled how Frannie was a "friend" with whom he "could chat and banter." He recalled, "What struck me about him were his sharp piercing eyes that looked at me as though I was the only person in the room with him. Those eyes were the windows of his mind and heart. He had a keen penetrating mind, whose grasp of culture, philosophy, and theology, even as a scholastic, would later unfold onto the public stage."

He also shared a funny instance of Frannie's "deep humanity" that occurred the night before their respective final exams at the university:

It was summer in Washington, DC, the eve of the final examinations at The Catholic University of America. Francis was doing a Master's in Philosophy. I was into European Diplomatic History. The other Oblate scholastics had gone up to their rooms to study. Francis and I stayed behind to watch the Miss Universe Contest on TV. It was a long, drawn-out event. I wanted to watch till the end because the Philippine beauty candidate was a semi-finalist. He also wanted to stay for the final result. At the end we both went to sleep around midnight without studying for the finals. Miss Universe first, summer studies second. But not really, for I am certain that he got grades of A for his Philosophy subjects that summer.[10]

While at Pine Hills, Brother Francis renewed temporary vows twice, received several of the minor orders, and professed perpetual vows on September 8, 1961, as he began his second year of theology. It was during that year that some of the faculty at Pine Hills began to discuss whether Brother Francis, whose intelligence and high academic abilities stood out to peers and faculty at the scholasticate, was being met with an appropriate academic challenge. Former professors noted that he excelled in no small part because of how hard he worked.

For a number of years, it was customary for the Central Province to send one or two standout students to the International Oblate Scholasticate in Rome. Oblate Fr. William Clarke, who was on the faculty of Pine Hills when Brother Francis was a scholastic, indicated that there were three criteria that were considered when choosing candidates to send to Rome: Did they have the right "head" — the intellectual capability to succeed at a Roman university? Did the candidate have the right "heart" — the emotional capacity to live in a foreign country and an international community? And did the candidate have the "stomach," which Father Clarke said was a code word for physical health and condition. Brother Francis would have had no problem with the first two, but that third one was the issue. Being a Roman scholastic would have involved a great deal of walking, largely on Rome's cobblestones, whether to participate in classes at the university, to visit historical sites and various Roman churches, to attend special events at the Vatican, or to take long hikes at the scholastics' summer residence in the Italian hill country at Roviano. It would all be too physically demanding for Brother Francis. But another plan was soon in motion.

Father Clarke wrote to the Assistant General of the congregation in Rome in a letter dated June 30, 1962:

> The faculty at Pine Hills, having discussed the matter, petitioned the provincial to transfer Brother Francis George to Saint Joseph Scholasticate to complete his Theological studies. Brother George is an outstanding scholastic from every point of view. It

is felt that wider opportunities for development which the atmosphere at Ottawa would afford could be used most profitably by this Brother. This would ultimately benefit not only the individual in question but the Province and the Congregation as well.

The transfer required permission from the Oblate Father General in Rome, which was given. With that approval, Brother Francis's time at Pine Hills ended after only four years. In yet another twist of providence, he was off to finish his preparations for priesthood in Canada.

THREE
A Priest of Jesus Christ

If you're going to be a priest, at least be a good one.

FRANCIS J. GEORGE

Brother Francis departed Pine Hills in 1962 with a Bachelor of Arts in philosophy. With ordination for the Archdiocese of Chicago off the table and study in Rome with the Oblates unadvisable, Brother Francis was sent off to Ottawa, Canada, to finish his theological studies. This next step in his formation followed a familiar — and almost undeniably providential — pattern. So many times in George's life, it seemed like doors were closing, but, in reality, they were only opening, albeit in unexpected ways. Always taking the next step in stride, Brother Francis left himself open to God's will.

Among other things, had he not gone to Ottawa, his path would not

65

have crossed Oblate Fr. Fernand Jetté at this formative stage. Father Jetté served on the faculty at the Oblates' St. Joseph Scholasticate in Ottawa from 1956 to 1965, teaching courses in missiology and theology. His particular area of interest was spirituality; he was an expert on the spirituality of St. Marie de l'Incarnation, the seventeenth-century pioneering missionary to Canada, educator, and foundress. Father Jetté was also well versed in the teachings and thought of Oblate founder St. Eugene de Mazenod, and de Mazenod figured prominently in the commentary and conferences Father Jetté offered as *magister spiritus*, or the Director of Spiritual Formation, at the St. Joseph Scholasticate. Father Jetté, who served as Brother Francis's spiritual director, was known for his wise counsel, but even more for his ability to listen and allow the Holy Spirit to work.

In February 1963, when Brother Francis would have been in his final year of formation in Ottawa before ordination to the priesthood, Jetté wrote this diary entry, praying for those in his spiritual care:

> Lord Jesus I entrust all those whom I have for direction to you. Soon it will be the time for many of them to make a definitive decision either for perpetual vows or for priesthood. Give them the necessary light and strength to act in accordance with your holy will. Give me the grace necessary to direct them and I ask this through the intercession of Mary Immaculate. ... At the present time I have much to suffer on behalf of some of those I have to direct and I have the impression that between now and the end of the year I shall have quite a lot of suffering on this point. May this suffering be for their good. Give me the grace of making a healthy discernment.[1]

Although the formation house in Ottawa during Brother Francis's time was known to be strict, those years were also transformative for the Oblates and their approach to formation. Along with the reforms and path of renewal adopted by the universal Church during the Second Vatican

Council, which opened in October 1962, the Oblates were examining possible changes to their community life and formation. The numbers of seminarians at the St. Joseph Scholasticate had begun to decline, and those who were there had become increasingly frustrated with what many regarded as overbearing regulation. This was a difficult time for faculty members like Father Jetté. The Oblate community as a whole would turn to him within a decade, though, to lead them through the turbulent times of change in the Church and in the world post-Vatican II.

Owing in part to his relationship with Father Jetté from these formative days, Francis George would be appointed Vicar General of the Oblates about a decade after his ordination, assisting Father Jetté after his election as the order's superior general. The formative role the priest had in George's life from his time in Ottawa is incalculable, and this bond would only continue to grow throughout the dozen years they together went on to guide the Oblate congregation.

Brother Francis's time in Ottawa also overlapped for a year with Oblate confrere Roger Schwietz — the future bishop of Duluth and archbishop of Anchorage — before the latter went on to Rome to continue his studies. Brother Francis was a few years ahead of Schwietz; the two had first met at Pine Hills some years previously. Brother Francis helped then-Brother Roger when he was having some doubts about his vocation, Archbishop Schwietz recalled. They went for a walk and, after a discussion with Francis, his doubts dissipated. "Already then he had this sense of insight that marked his whole life," Schwietz said.

It was in Ottawa that Schwietz really came to know George as an intellectual. "I knew Francis was the smartest person in the room, but he never let anyone know it," he recalled. He said Brother Francis was very patient with other people, taking time outside of class to assist those who were struggling with course material or concepts. "I never saw him embarrass anyone by correcting them," Schwietz said. Oblate Fr. William Woestman, who had even taught George in a seminar, agreed, and said George was "not an easy person to debate with because he is very intelligent and quick to point out where people are wrong … but he does it with great kindness."[2]

For Brother Francis, life in Ottawa was different from that in Pine Hills. He thrived in the more challenging academic environment. But he also faced greater restrictions. Students wore cassocks each day, ate their meals in silence, and were forbidden from having visitors in their rooms. Brother Francis lived on the fifth floor and was awakened each morning at 5:30 by the shouts of a confrere calling out, *Laudetur Jesus Christus* (Praised be Jesus Christ).[3]

Shortly after his arrival in Ottawa, Brother Francis wrote his provincial to thank him for the opportunity to study there and noted that he was happy with the decision. "The French is going to be something of a problem, but I hope that time and a little study will take care of it," Brother Francis wrote to his provincial on September 23, 1962. He had never studied French up until then, only Latin, Greek, Hebrew, and German. The courses in Ottawa were taught in Latin and not difficult to follow. In 2012, while receiving the Distinguished Alumnus Award from the University of Saint Paul, Cardinal George humorously recalled, "Living in Scholasticate Saint-Joseph imposed a certain French discipline that was necessary if one wanted to eat."

Mastering French proved immensely useful to Father George about a decade after ordination, when he assumed a role of international leadership in the congregation. When the French Ambassador to the United States visited Cardinal George years later in Chicago, he remarked, "His French is perfect."

The years of study and formation in Ottawa not only presented Brother Francis with a unique linguistic challenge but also planted in him an intense interest in cultures, which would become for him a focus of lifelong study. When Cardinal George was honored by St. Paul University as "Alumnus of the Year" in 2008, he reflected in his address on his time in Ottawa. He said then that the experience enabled him "to live in a milieu where the cultural differences were not only present but also discussed in such a way that everyone could be enriched. And I found that … there was perhaps a greater appreciation of the need for cultures to be in dialogue and certainly a much greater practice."[4]

Oblate scholastics during Brother Francis's time also were unable to listen to the radio or watch television. So, whenever Brother Francis got "nostalgic to hear English," he traveled "along the Rideau Canal to the Houses of Parliament and listened to the question period in the House of Commons … I heard [John] Diefenbaker and [Lester] Pearson argue back and forth."

"But the best, the one who really was a brilliant orator, was Tommy Douglas," George recalled. The former Baptist minister turned politician was a founding father of Canada's far left New Democrat Party and also the author of North America's first single-payer universal health care program as Premier of Saskatchewan. "Even though it was often more anti-American than not, that too was helpful in this meeting of cultures, this dialogue of cultures, that has served me in good stead all the years since I studied here," he said at the time. The idealistic George likely found Douglas's arguments appealing. For a time in the late 1960s and 1970s, George had been open to various forms of Marxist socialism. That all changed later during his global travels as Oblate Vicar General, when he encountered firsthand such systems of government and their effects on people.

The opportunities in Ottawa also enabled Brother Francis to develop a greater understanding of the Oblate founder, Eugene de Mazenod. He recalled at St. Paul's that he

> had been introduced to him at my own novitiate in Illinois, but it was an introduction at the second or third hand. Here there was a group of scholars who knew the founder because they took the time to study his writings which had not been translated into any other language at that time. … In the conferences we received as Oblate scholastics a deeper sense of who this man was.

To that end, George related a story that helps describe de Mazenod. Several years after his 1990 appointment as bishop of Yakima, Washington (incidentally, the place where the first Oblate priest was ordained in the United States), Francis George was transferred to Portland as its ninth archbishop. Portland's first archbishop, François Blanchet, who hailed from Montreal, Canada, was familiar with the Oblates and traveled to France to request Oblate missionaries for his vast new diocese in the American West. After meeting de Mazenod, Blanchet remarked, "I've seen Paul." Just as St. Paul is so influential for Christians, there is no question that de Mazenod's influence greatly formed Francis George's own mind and heart as an Oblate. Years later, his own missionary elan as a bishop would be very much an echo of de Mazenod's own ministry and vision.

In Ottawa, Brother Francis earned a master's degree in theology, although he did not complete it until some years after his 1963 ordination.[5]

A PRIEST FOREVER

Frannie's father was not so keen on the idea of his son becoming a priest. He never really spent much time around priests outside of Mass and thought some priests never did much else — that they led "lives too soft for their own good."[6] But he told his son that if he was going to be a priest, then he should be a good one. In the end, Frannie's father was proud of his son's notable accomplishments, which came one after another in his early years of priesthood. He always called him "Reverend." Not only was Frannie's mother supportive of the idea of his priesthood, but she knew his talents would take him far.

Brother Francis's two years in Ottawa encompassed his final preparation for ordination as well as his first few months as a priest. He was approved to receive major orders while in Ottawa and was ordained to the subdiaconate and diaconate there. The plan was for him to be ordained a priest there as well.

Naturally, Brother Francis would have wanted his friends and family to attend his ordination and be present for his first Mass. Hosting the event in Ottawa would have made it more difficult for many to attend, given its distance not only from his home in Chicago but also from his confreres in the Oblates' Central Province. God's providential hand, however, made it possible for him to be the first Oblate priest ordained in Chicago — and the first and only native son of St. Pascal to be ordained in his parish church (though the twenty-seventh native son to be ordained a priest).

George was approved for major orders early in 1963 by unanimous vote of the Scholasticate Directors' Council. The approval was only good for six months and was renewed in October of that year. An October 11, 1963, report of the scholasticate's superior, Oblate Fr. Maurice Gilbert, concluded, "We are very pleased with this Brother on every aspects (sic) of his religious life: psychological, intellectual and religious."

A letter written to his provincial in the United States on September 26, 1963, indicates that Brother Francis believed he would be ordained at the scholasticate, although the custom of his Canadian classmates was to be ordained in their home parishes. An ordination in January or February of 1964 was anticipated, but the scholasticate's superior declared that to be inopportune. That left George with three options: to be ordained with subdeacons and deacons just before Christmas at the Ottawa cathedral, which he likened to "getting ordained in the catacombs, since the Church would be practically empty"; to join one of his classmates in a different Canadian city; or to wait until mid-January so that he could be ordained with some scholastics in Montreal. "None of these possibilities would be very convenient for my parents," he observed.

So George proposed the idea of having his ordination in Chicago, though without much confidence it would be approved. He said in the letter that he "thought this would be out of the question" when he presented it to his superior at the Ottawa scholasticate. But in the end, "it turned out to be remarkably easy." George wrote for the provincial's permission, and St. Pascal offered to roll out the red carpet for its native son, he noted in his letter to the provincial. The reply he received from the parish promised to arrange for a choir, servers, "and even pay the Bishop." This development made George "very happy." The provincial wrote back on October 4 granting permission: "This will be good not only for you, but for the cause of the Oblates in the Archdiocese [of Chicago]," he wrote. "We are new there and need a little publicity to be better known."

George was ordained a priest at St. Pascal by Bishop Raymond Hillinger on December 21, 1963, in what the parish bulletin called "a colorful ceremony." It was a day of great pride and celebration for the people of St. Pascal when Francis George, who had once served Masses in that very sanctuary, prostrated himself on the floor, literally laying down his life in service of the Church as a priest of Jesus Christ. And the floor was especially cold that Saturday morning, since a subzero spell hovered over Chicago in those late December days. Fifty years later, as archbishop of Chicago, George recalled that he became a priest "because at a certain moment I realized by God's grace that it fits."[7]

He celebrated his first solemn Mass the following day, the Fourth Sunday of Advent. Many former classmates and brother Oblates assisted at the Mass. George ordered a silver gilt chalice from Trier, Germany, for the occasion. A dinner followed the first Mass, and Father George's parents hosted a parish-wide reception at the parish hall that night.

Bishop Hillinger, the ordaining prelate, was a Chicago native who served as bishop of Rockford, Illinois, for two years before his assignment as a Chicago auxiliary. Ill health caused his transfer back to Chicago, where he took up a pastorate as an auxiliary bishop until his 1968 retirement. Hillinger died in 1971.[8]

Father George was ordained during a time of immense change and turbulence in the United States and within the Church. President John F. Kennedy had been assassinated less than a month before. "I saw [Father George] break down into tears when we were in Ottawa," Schwietz said, recalling the assassination. "We went down to watch TV, and when they said he was dead, we both broke down into tears. He was very sensitive that way."

Cardinal George contextualized the significance of the event many years later: "I was ordained just after Kennedy was assassinated, and I didn't realize the impact of that on the collective psyche of the American people because I was living in Canada." He recalled that the proximity of his ordination to the assassination made him suddenly "realize that I'm beginning my priestly life among a people who are collectively mourning and dealing with an event that leaves permanent wounds." He reflected on how priests "were trained to deal with individuals and their difficulties, but to realize that the whole people can suffer in that way was a very sobering way to begin my priesthood."[9]

Brother Francis had asked permission to have Brother Schwietz serve as commentator at his ordination Mass, and so the two traveled together to Chicago in December 1963. According to George, "He was a great help to my mother in getting the house in order." Years later, when George told his sister about Schwietz's appointment as bishop, Margaret remarked, "But he's the one who cleaned the bathroom of our house on Byron Street." "So are great men remembered," George quipped in reply.

A few years later, in the summer of 1968, Father George preached the homily at the "ceremonial first Mass" of Father Schwietz after he returned home from studies in Rome, where he had been ordained a priest on December 20, 1967. Father George offered in that sermon something of a commentary on the priesthood vis-à-vis the signs of the times, observing that the priest "is a mediator, a communicator, a celebrator." He continued:

> [The priest] is a source of discomfort for those who have settled for a false reconciliation, for those who think it possible to reconcile men through violence or force ... a stumbling block for those who would settle in our own country for a reconciliation among men based on long-established patterns of social injustice or prejudice. For such people, [he] is an obstacle, because they are not able to celebrate the memory of Christ ... for them [he] is an embarrassment, a sign which proclaims Christ and makes him present in a society or a place where he is not welcome.[10]

Although each Oblate belongs to a province and is under obedience to its provincial for assignments in ministry, the first assignment — itself called an "obedience" — is given directly by the Father General in Rome. This obedience can be given anywhere in the world where Oblates serve, and not necessarily in one's own province, as is the most likely case for future obediences.

In a letter to Father General Léo Deschâtelets, the Oblate Provincial of the then-Central US province, Fr. William Coovert, described newly ordained Fr. Francis George as "sensitive, energetic, strong willed, calm, and frank" and "very intelligent." He called George a man of "solid faith" and a "good community man." And he said he was a "very good" preacher and an "excellent" teacher. Father Coovert's recommendation that Father George teach in the Central Province's scholasticate was made on January 14, 1964, as he was "just what Pine Hills needs."

On February 5, Father George was invited to write a letter expressing the same preference to Father General Deschâtelets. After expressing his desire to "always be a good Oblate priest in the service to the Church," Father George said he would like to teach in the scholasticate in the Central Province at Pine Hills. But he was also open to working in Newman clubs at universities and expressed an interest in retreat work. He added: "For several reasons, both psychological and physical, I do not feel that I have a vocation to the missions, neither Scandinavia nor Brazil."

Father George also expressed an openness to return to the scholasticate in Ottawa to help offset the shortage of English-speaking professors, but was candid in his preferences: "I find the climate in Ottawa a little difficult, and right now I very much want to have the opportunity of doing somewhat more pastoral work than would seem to be possible for a professor here," he wrote. Oblate Father William Woestman recalled that the Ottawa Scholasticate had wanted George to join their faculty.

Father General Deschâtelets listened to the recommendations, assigning Father George to the Central Province and, more specifically, to Pine Hills. In Father George's letter of appointment, Father Coovert wrote on May 28, "Your contribution of intelligent zeal and hard work for the Church of God will be a considerable help."

Prior to beginning his first obedience, Father George spent the summer in Washington, DC, studying at The Catholic University of America, followed by a few weeks at home in Chicago with his family. At the start of the 1964–1965 academic year, Father George returned to the Pine Hills seminary, this time as a teacher. His subjects included history of philosophy, metaphysics, epistemology, and American and contemporary philosophy. He was also put in charge of the seminary's music department. Father George would serve at Pine Hills for four years, while at the same time finishing two masters' theses — in theology and philosophy — and beginning doctoral work at Tulane University in New Orleans.

In some ways, Francis George was a product of his times. He thoroughly embraced the Second Vatican Council. He recognized the need to reimagine much of how the Church operated, and he was known to wear a suit and tie as the Sixties came to a close. At the same time, he was hesitant to relinquish the Church's traditions, and he was not fond of liturgical experimentation. One former student even remembered a perturbed Father George scouring the sacristy before Mass in the late 1960s in search of a maniple to wear.

Those were busy years for both Father George and the universal Church. During George's time on the faculty at Pine Hills, the Second Vatican Council came to a conclusion. At the same time, men were leaving the seminary and priesthood in sizable numbers, and others were rethinking how they lived their lives and even what they believed. Father George would spend the rest of his ministry working to advance a proper understanding and implementation of the council. Later, as a bishop and cardinal, George was able to help the Church cling to the truths that Vatican II had underscored and illuminated. But that same desire was also present in him as a young priest.

When Father George was named eighth archbishop of Chicago three decades later, the front page of the *Chicago Tribune* declared that his beliefs had taken "a right turn in Rome."[11] But what such a claim fails to observe is that George had the astute ability to think outside the box during a time of reform and renewal, while also refusing to be ruled by an ideology. A good deal of George's contribution to the Church's life and mission came from his prowess in balancing the swinging pendulum of extremes adopted in the name of renewal or in reaction to it.

In a 1966 homily given by Father George at Pine Hills, subsequently published in the seminary's newsletter, the young priest tackled the shifting meaning of the priesthood after Vatican II, which in the minds of many seemed up for grabs. "Along with everything else in the Church, the priesthood too is subject to new scrutiny, to new attempts at a redefinition," he said. "If the meaning of the priesthood is no longer evident, if the priest's image is blurred and confused, it affects all of us."

Such a statement illustrated his ability to cut through the cacophony of debates and get to the heart of a matter — and to the truth. But it also illustrated his ability to play things out logically and understand where an idea or event could lead.

With characteristic clarity, Father George addressed the ambiguity regarding the priesthood that was emerging and circulating in the wake of Vatican II's articulation of the lay apostolate, at a time when distinctions between priests and laity were often blurred. Some advocated for a theology of priesthood that minimized any distinction or difference between ordained priesthood and the priesthood of the baptized. Ordained for almost three years, Father George was able to find the middle ground that occupies the space between clericalism and anticlericalism and see the priesthood as it really is.

While it might come across as strange to us today, George made a point that was vital to the time: Priests can do any task — i.e., teach philosophy, do social work, or serve as a building contractor — but, in the end, those tasks are not priestly and can in effect be done by anyone. George was concerned that the true meaning of priesthood was being lost, and he did not want it to devolve into something it never was. If the priest was set apart, it was because of "his unique role as privileged worshiper and instrument of God in the sacramental system."

"A priest who insists he is only a brother Christian is simply wrong," he said. "A priest who never dispenses the sacraments is not functioning as a priest; a priest who abdicates his responsibilities as a teacher of divine truth and a ruler of God's people is changing the meaning of the priesthood itself, not just its realization in our age."

"If you want to be just like any other man, with the same privileges and rights and responsibilities and opportunities, if you don't want a life lived in anticipation of an event not yet fully realized and a life, therefore, in some ways incomplete and unfulfilled, then, for God's sake and your own — don't become a priest," he said. "Personal intimacy with God must be ours if God is to act through us in a meaningful way. Otherwise, we are not living witnesses, but living lies." Taking his father's counsel one step further, George not only wanted to be a good priest; he wanted to help the Church have good priests too. And he would spend much of the rest of his life with this desire as a central focus of his ministry.

FOUR

Priest, Philosopher, and Professor

What better way to thank God again for the gifts we have received in Christ than by sharing them more widely?[1]

CARDINAL FRANCIS E. GEORGE, O.M.I.

The image of priesthood that Francis George illustrated for the seminarians at Pine Hills in 1966 was especially interesting in light of the direction his life as a priest was taking. It was clear from his earliest days of priesthood that he was destined for a path in academia. And yet, he knew that academia was only worthy of pursuit because the community needed professors. Being a professor was not an end in itself for Father George. Rather, he saw himself as simply one cog in the wheel of his missionary order, responsible for the specific task of educating more missionaries and enabling them to serve the Church through proclamation of the Good News to the poor.

Father George was a member of the faculty of Pine Hills in Pass Christian, Mississippi, from 1964 to 1967, when his academic path required the pursuit of doctoral studies. The priest and his provincial decided it would be best for him to pursue a doctorate in philosophy at Tulane University in New Orleans "because it was near the seminary where I was teaching, and I could continue to teach part-time while beginning my graduate studies," George recalled at a 2007 gathering with Chicago priests.[2]

Getting accepted by Tulane, however, was a challenge.

"They were very skeptical of my coming to Tulane, not eager to have me enter their philosophy department," George said in 2007. In 2005 he recalled, "The project of a Catholic intellectual life that tries to bring the faith to bear upon any form of the intellectual life is not something that is very welcome."[3] He went on: "When I interviewed at Tulane University as a very young priest to be accepted into their graduate Department of Philosophy, they were very clear about that. They had never admitted priests to their Philosophy Department and they were very clear why not. They said priests are not free to think!"

"So, finally, I talked around and talked and talked and talked," George recalled. "What you had to do was beat them at their own game, and if you could do that, then they were at ease. And eventually I did it enough to get a degree out of them. But to do that, I had to live in a very self-consciously secularist milieu. They told me I couldn't bring a collar into a classroom because they didn't want religious authority symbols in their classrooms. When they invited me to teach, finally, at the end, the same rule applied. The idea was that this is a university, and faith and church might be OK to comfort people but they don't make any truth claims that we have to listen to and, therefore, on an intellectual level there can be no conversation between faith and reason in the strict sense." In 2005, Tulane University awarded Cardinal George its Distinguished Alumnus Award.

In 2007, George, when talking to the Chicago presbyterate, discussed the effects of the clergy sex abuse crisis on Catholics. He posited that it would prompt some Catholics to ask, "Why believe in God at all?"[4] This, he noted at the 2007 priests' gathering, would cause a dichotomy to arise between those Catholics who would grow stronger in their faith as opposed to those who were more Catholic in name only — what he often referred to as "cultural Catholics."

In that vein, he began to talk extemporaneously about the experience with his professors at Tulane, most of whom he described as agnostics or atheist Jews. He related a story at the 2007 gathering about one professor in particular, who began to value George as a colleague while he was teaching undergraduates during his doctoral studies, which helps to illustrate how George internalized his experiences and related them back to faith and vocation:

> I remember one question that was raised in speaking to Professor Karl Hamburg ... [he] was a profoundly searching man, but a disturbed man. Once he sat down when we were going over something to prepare for a class and said, "What is it like for you, who believe in a God who is provident, to get into an airplane that is different from someone like me getting on that plane when I don't believe there is a God at all?" A series of conversations followed. Our own faith life, particularly faith in a provident God who loves us and gives us the ability to love each other and to love our people, is a world very different from the world a lot of other people live in. And it's hard to move from their world into ours. It's hard if we have deep faith to go from our world into theirs, but we have to live in both worlds I think, as priests, to convert the world and shore up the faith of Catholics so that they will know the truth of who God is. I never succeeded with Professor Hamburg, although we kept up in writing until, finally, he developed heart trouble ... and effectively wanted to die. And he did. He died alone.

And I thought to myself, "Did I fail some way? Should I have tried to be more friendly with him, although I couldn't keep up that friendship from a distance?" ... But I pray for him still. As I know you still pray for the people you feel you failed at times in your own ministry.[5]

George concluded: "No matter what the world thinks of us, no matter how our position in society might shift, we are at the center for God's plan for the whole world. And what we do in celebrating the Eucharist is the most important thing that happens in this world. ... Every time the Mass is celebrated the center of the universe is on this altar, and that's what keeps us all going."

At Tulane, George studied American philosophy. He often mentioned to others that he "studied enough of it to know he didn't like it." An old course catalogue from Tulane notes this field was "the specialty of the [philosophy] department."

In a 1965 essay titled "Socrates in the Seminary," George reiterated the value and vital role of philosophy in seminary formation. "All philosophizing is done in a cultural context," he writes, "and this can be a religious context. But genuine philosophy begins with a clean slate, without any presuppositions other than the philosopher himself and his experience in reality."[6]

George's dissertation director, Dr. Andrew Reck, noted in a 1999 interview that at the time George was studying American philosophy, most American universities had turned their backs on the subject. Tulane ended up serving "as a magnet for people like Father George" because their philosophy department was particularly strong in that area. George greatly impressed professors like Dr. Reck for choosing "the unique and innovative field of social philosophy before it came in vogue a decade or so later." In addition, Dr. Reck described his "short, thin, balding, amiable" former student as "very intelligent" and "a superior student in a group of superior students."[7]

As much as George's years in New Orleans and at Tulane were a chaotic time for the Church, they were for society, too. Catholics were wrestling with Vatican II and its implementation, the nation was debating the Vietnam War, and Robert F. Kennedy and Martin Luther King, Jr. were assassinated. "It was a very much unsettled time," George recalled in 1999. "But I don't remember it as being unsettled for me. Those were happy years [at Tulane]."[8]

George's research and dissertation consisted of filtering through the thought of three giants of American philosophy: Harvard professor Josiah Royce, an absolute idealist and promoter of a communitarian theory of society; University of Chicago professor George Herbert Mead, the pragmatist and founder of a school of social psychology and the theory of the individual self; and University of Michigan professor Roy Wood Sellars, a celebrated naturalist and realist, who proposed a vision of a democratic and socialist society.

George defended his dissertation at Tulane on the Tuesday before Thanksgiving in 1969 and graduated the following year. Titled "Society and Experience: A Critical Examination of the Social Philosophies of Royce, Mead, and Sellars," George's dissertation addresses the problem: How can norms be derived from experience?

He answered the question, briefly, in his paper's abstract:

Social experience is identified as value experience and becomes normative — not because of some difference specific to social experience, but because social experience intensifies all component elements of experience as such. ... Avoiding both unexperienced absolutes and individual caprice, a determined natural law or hypothetical social contract, a metaphysics of experience can provide a base or context in which social experience becomes normative for future experience and furnishes at least general directives for social reform.[9]

LIFE IN NEW ORLEANS

When George began studies at Tulane, the idea was that he would commute from Pine Hills to New Orleans, a journey of a little over an hour by car, so that he could work on the doctorate while also fulfilling his role at the seminary and continuing to live with his religious community. It was necessary to maintain some residence in New Orleans, however, due to the demands of being a full-time doctoral student. So for a time, George lived at Our Lady of Lourdes Church in New Orleans — an experience that would further expose him to the systemic racism in American society.

The pastor of Our Lady of Lourdes at the time was Msgr. Lucien J. Caillouet, a vicar general of the Archdiocese of New Orleans and brother of an auxiliary bishop. Despite Archbishop Joseph Rummel's efforts to desegregate Catholic worship in New Orleans as far back as the late 1940s, Monsignor Caillouet resisted full implementation. After the parish school was desegregated together with all archdiocesan schools in 1962, "white flight" caused the number of parishioners and students to drop. The once affluent parish began to struggle. By the late 1960s, when George was living at the parish, the majority of its members were Black. The pastor, who had been reluctant to adjust to the demographic shift, retired in 1968.

George's living accommodations at Our Lady of Lourdes allowed him to study at Tulane and still continue pastoral ministry, but it was unclear how permanent they might be. For some time previously, George had taken a room in the backyard carriage house of Mrs. Evabelle Baudean, a widow known to the Oblates since she owned a vacation house near the Pass Christian seminary.

The carriage house of "Mrs. B." functioned as a rent-free hostel of sorts for young Catholic men studying in New Orleans. Their payment came in the form of doing chores. The situation, as George described it in a July 27, 1967, letter to his provincial, had "distinct advantages of location, finances, etc.," but had "disadvantages of lack of space and several other inconveniences — none of them impossible." Regardless, it was not meant to be a permanent arrangement.

George's desk was a piece of plywood that rested on a sink. He shared the modest housing arrangement with two Loyola University pre-med students, one of whom was Dr. Joseph Garcia-Prats, a longtime neonatologist in Houston. In an interview with the *Chicago Tribune* at the time of George's installation as archbishop of Chicago, Garcia-Prats recalled George as intelligent but not pretentious. "We might get into some philosophical discussions, but you had to be careful when you got into that because you were with one of the experts," he said.[10]

George explained in the July 27 letter to his provincial that he found the situation at Our Lady of Lourdes in many ways "inferior to Mrs. B.'s," but, he noted, it had "the great advantage of allowing me to have some hand in priestly work to a greater extent." George's stay at the Our Lady of Lourdes rectory thoroughly gave him the experience of parish life, as did his first years of priesthood in Mississippi when he provided sacramental ministry to small-town, rural parishes around Pine Hills. The presence of assistant priests and a pastor who understood his situation meant that he was not in danger of being overworked at the parish in New Orleans.

One significant difficulty with living at the parish was that it required use of a car, which he did not have after another confrere was reassigned elsewhere. The commute from Our Lady of Lourdes to Tulane would have only been possible by walking some distance to the streetcar — not exactly a simple hurdle given his post-polio handicap. George's father, he explained in the same letter to his provincial, had even apparently offered to advance "a couple of hundred [of dollars] or whatever it takes to get a used car with automatic transmission." A subsequent letter from the provincial said getting the car was no problem.

George's health suffered, even in these years of prime adulthood, from the effects of polio. Around Thanksgiving of 1967, he wound up in traction after surgery at New Orleans' Baptist Hospital, where he also assisted as a chaplain. "I have the now standard ruptured disc, aggravated by my unbalanced manner of walking," he wrote in a letter to his provincial on November 28. "I am keeping up on reading and assignments at Tulane, so I shouldn't lose any time there," he added.

FACING CHANGES

Ordained for approximately five years, George was becoming something of a rising star in his Oblate community. He freely offered advice, which appeared to be appreciated and at times sought. Widely respected among his confreres, he was nominated to various community positions and appointed to sit on various committees, including in the role of acting chair of the province's committee on religious life.

In November 1967, Father George was a featured speaker at the first province-wide congress held at King's House in Belleville, Illinois, where he spoke on authority in the Church and religious life. George related to his provincial in the November 28 letter how that gathering was "the best thing that's happened to me in my time as an Oblate." He added, "When I went up to Fr. Simon to tell him I appreciated his talk — which I did very much, although I disagree with much of it — he told me in parting, 'Be orthodox!' I will."

Francis George made it clear early in his priesthood, even while still in formation, that he was not afraid of change or reform. Unbeholden to what he perceived to be an outdated, outmoded way of living, Father George was enthusiastic about the reforms of Vatican II. At the same time, he was not going to abandon truth, tradition, or orthodoxy. He represented some of the best fresh thinking in those postconciliar days, keeping a balance between a certain willingness to move forward under a new paradigm and the desire of maintaining the tradition of the Faith. This balance would be more and more striking as time went on.

As it happens, Francis George did not return to Pine Hills with a doctorate, as was the plan when he began studies at Tulane. In fact, he did not return to Pine Hills at all, as it closed permanently in 1968. Running an independent seminary for the province resulted in certain deficiencies. There was no one on the faculty with a doctorate. Several faculty members acknowledged that the seminary needed more teachers who did not find themselves intellectually inferior to their students — Francis George included. In his classes, it was clear that he was usually the most versed on a topic. These challenges created an institutional problem and made it particularly difficult for the school to obtain accreditation. There were also concerns that the seminary's location prohibited a truly well-rounded education.

Before the Second Vatican Council, a guiding principle of seminary formation, especially for religious communities such as the Oblates, was *fuga mundi*. By "fleeing the world," it was commonly believed that candidates for ordination, particularly those under religious vows, were able to shun worldly allures and temptations and instead focus their attention on the things that matter most. Many began to perceive this, particularly in light of the teachings of Vatican II, as antithetical to the embrace of culture demanded of those expected to minister in the Church's name. Over time, expectations shifted, and eventually the former approach was considered abnormal, even a distraction to those in formation from understanding those to whom they were expected to proclaim the Gospel.

The Oblates, once characterized as "country Jesuits," might have had educational apostolates included in their missions, but they were not regarded exclusively as an intellectual community. The community was instead more focused on mission work and evangelization. In certain parts of the world, Oblates preached the Gospel for the first time. Pope Pius XI commended the Oblates in a September 14, 1932, audience for their fidelity "to the beautiful, glorious, and holy specialty by which you devote every effort, talent, and your life to the most abandoned souls in the most difficult missions." At the same time, the Oblates did not shy away from attending to the intellectual gifts of their members more inclined to the intellectual life. Many were sent to study in Washington, DC, Rome, or Ottawa, for example, to further their educations.

With the closing of Pine Hills, the scholastics in theology were sent to the Oblate College of the Southwest in San Antonio, Texas. With the theologate relocated there, the philosophy program also needed a new home, and the plan was for it to be established at the Jesuit-run Creighton University in Omaha, Nebraska. It was believed that students would benefit from a university community in which they could attend classes with lay students their own age and be more involved in the world. This experience, the Oblates hoped, would help them to better understand those to whom they would minister.

In a letter to his provincial, George mentioned his reservations about moving the Oblate scholasticate from Pine Hills to Creighton, recommending instead that the new Oblate philosophy program be located closer to one of the three metropolitan areas within the province. However, the move to Creighton was finalized — and along with the students transferred to the new Oblate House of Philosophy went a supply of philosophy professors. Father George, in the summer of 1969, was one of them. It appears, just as the provincial had said in recommending George for the position at Pine Hills — "He is exactly what Pine Hills needs" — that George was looked upon as one of the forces for change who would solidify a more scholarly faculty of philosophy at Creighton and help bring about some internal reforms.

George was encouraged to apply for a faculty position at the university, which he was eventually offered. His provincial wrote in a May 7, 1968, letter, upon the appointment:

> You have been a great help at Pine Hills in forming young Oblates, in making them mature religious men with sound principles of spirituality. I am sure you will continue being an asset to the Oblate House in this way. To help the young Oblates grow in spirituality will be a challenge, requiring much wisdom and patience, but most of all love and concern for their development.

Francis George responded in a May 10 letter with appreciation for this "vote of confidence," saying that examples of such "have the same function in community that renewal of vows has in the relationship that obtains between God and ourselves."

Before moving to Omaha with the other Oblates who began the house of studies there, however, Father George required one more year in New Orleans to finish up his doctoral work. During the late summer of 1968, he spent time in Chicago consulting the papers of George Herbert

Mead in preparation for writing his dissertation. During his final year at Tulane, when he was not conducting research for his dissertation, he was teaching as a graduate fellow in the university's philosophy department — a fact that is somewhat ironic given that only a few years before they did not want to accept him as a student. George was a team player and worked hard to get enough of the work done on his dissertation so that he would be able to move to Omaha for the start of their second academic year at Creighton.

During his final few months in New Orleans, Father George lived at Cody House, an archdiocesan residence for retired priests located across from the New Orleans seminary. It was operated by the retired Monsignor Caillouet at the former home of Coadjutor Archbishop John Cody, who had been appointed to Chicago that year. This was the first of two times Francis George would occupy a former residence of John Cody — the second being when he moved into the residence of the archbishop of Chicago.

THE PROFESSOR PRIEST

For three years, Father George — now called Frank by some (a short-lived nickname of uncertain origin) — taught philosophy at Creighton University. He began as an Assistant Professor and departed as Department Chair, an astonishing accomplishment for someone just thirty-four years old. While there, Father George also served as spiritual director to some of the scholastics at the Oblate formation house. He was popular among his undergraduate students and esteemed by his colleagues in the small philosophy department. Servants of Mary Sr. Mary Alice Haley, who taught with George during his time at Creighton, remembered him as "notably sharp, intelligent, out front and to the point, a great conversationalist." He was approachable and had the ability to "make things work," which she attributed to the pragmatist American philosophers he studied at Tulane. Another colleague, Eugene Selk, recalled in a 1997 interview with the *National Catholic Reporter* that George had a "mind packed with ideas."[11] Selk was always pushed and challenged by his conversations with George and often rushed to jot down notes afterward. "He would have so many interesting angles," Selk said, calling him "a fascinating man." George and Selk kept up a correspondence throughout the years, especially during the years George would live in Rome. Selk even visited there at a time when their former colleague, Sister Haley, was living in Rome as her congregation's superior general.

Illustrating how Father George excelled at both the professional and the pastoral, Haley recalled how he "knew how to treat people and deal with people, even difficult personalities." She recalled a former colleague of theirs who had made it his life's ambition to become chair of the philosophy department. "His personality was such that he could push pretty hard. But George was not intimidated or manipulated by him." As for George's accomplishments, in what turned out as a brief tenure at Creighton, Haley said, "He did what he promised to do." Haley recalled also that, when at the end of her first year she received a letter from the dean stating she would not have her contract renewed, George went to bat for her. "No, this is not going to happen. I will not accept the chairmanship of the department. If you go, I go," she recalled George saying. "Integrity was his middle name."

George's colleagues and former students enjoyed his sense of humor and great, hearty laugh. The seminarians who lived with him then remembered George in his third-floor room "pounding on a typewriter and laughing out loud." They nicknamed him "the screeching eagle."[12] His sense of humor was not the only thing appealing to the students. His brilliance was respected, even if at times it was hard to understand. Sometimes his lectures were so heady that he would call upon a particularly bright student to interpret what he was saying. He enjoyed calling out students for weak arguments in papers. Many times — as several students recalled — he did not hesitate to mark papers with a rubber stamp given to him by a student, on which was emblazoned "Bullshit!"

Fr. Thomas Singer, a former colleague at the Oblate House of Studies at Creighton, whose parents were friends with George's in Chicago, also recalled George as "kind of iconoclastic," making him particularly popular among college-age students. Creighton — like the Church, nation, and world at the time — was in a bit of turmoil during George's years at the university. George weighed in on a variety of issues, employing characteristic philosophical methodology to figure out answers to complex problems, and was not shy about the conclusions he reached. He was not quiet about his opposition to the Vietnam War, he stood in support of Catholic conscientious objectors, and he was not uncritical of President Richard Nixon. George was a board member of the Omaha Association of Clergy and Laity for Peace. Then-Fr. Roger Schwietz, who served at Creighton with George for a time, recalled that George was "not necessarily an activist, but he thought it was a great mistake to be involved in that war."

George incorporated current events and public figures into his philosophy lectures, papers, and exams. He wanted students to think through important issues of the day in his philosophy classes, like when some Black cheerleaders for Creighton's basketball team refused to stand for the national anthem in the early 1970s. One of his final exam questions read:

> Problem: You are a cheerleader for an unnamed midwestern University's basketball team. Some of the squad cannot in conscience stand during the singing of the National Anthem before each game. You have no individual objections to standing during the Anthem, but the squad as a group has decided to modify the traditional role of cheerleader by absenting themselves from the floor during the Anthem.[13]
>
> Questions: a) How many conflicts of roles are present in the situation? b) How might the notion of "unbounded rationality," which Emmet discusses in her last chapter (Living with Organization Man), help in solving these role conflicts?

As a member of the university community, George tried to bring about unity and consensus around such controversial topics. He penned the following proposal and submitted it to university administrators:

> Resolved: It should be a matter of Creighton policy to refrain from the playing and singing of the National Anthem before sporting events hosted by the University.
>
> I. Civil religion is a type of exaggerated nationalism in which citizenship, the relation to one's country, becomes the dominant relationship in a person's life; the State becomes the object of ultimate concern, i.e., becomes effectively an object of religious worship; and the right of the State to enter into every facet of human experience is taken for granted. Civil religion, in a Judeo-Christian context, is an inversion of religious values. One who practices civil religion is practicing a false religion.
>
> II. The singing of the National Anthem is not in itself an act of civil religion. It is an important value statement, an identification of self with the American people and their ideals. But what is at issue in the resolution is not the singing of the Anthem, but its being sung at sporting events. Although the present practice in this country is to play the Anthem before sporting events, a public profession of citizenship would seem to be out of proportion to the event that follows, i.e. playing a game has nothing to do with one's citizenship or loyalties. Sports should not be used to elicit political sentiments or value statements from those playing or attending. If we insist that a sporting event should be such an occasion, it may be because loyalty to the State is a matter of ultimate concern to us, and we have not properly distinguished civil loyalties from religious imperatives.
>
> III. Part of Creighton University's distinctiveness lies in its addressing itself to value questions and especially to questions of religious values. We publicly define ourselves as an institution dedicated to academic excellence and to the supreme importance of religious values in human life. There is in this issue a clear opportunity for Creighton to state its value priorities.

Other major instruments of value education in the city (e.g. The World-Herald, TV shows and UNO) either will not or can not raise this question. Admittedly, this is a difficult educational issue. But that's what we're about.[14]

In the middle of George's first semester on campus, during a time of great racial strife across the country, university president Fr. Henry Linn, SJ, wrote a letter to the entire Creighton community, prompted by "verbal abuse, non-acceptance, and ostracism."[15] He saw at Creighton a local manifestation of what he described as "our deadliest national malady — racism."[16] Linn was forthright, saying at a university convocation, "Racial bigotry exists at Creighton." In his estimation, it was clear that "students display a white racism which is intolerable at a Christian university." Father Linn died a month later, with the stress of campus tension no doubt playing a role in his health.

By January, some Black students were discussing the possibility of having their own college at the university and demanding a portion of seats on the student council. A series of Black Studies courses was added to the curriculum, and an interim university president announced a university-wide seminar on racial injustice.

Around that time, George wrote an op-ed for *The Creightonian* university newspaper in which he attempted to cut through the rhetoric and reorient the conversation on racism, a skill that he would rely on throughout his life as a leader in the Church.

He wrote of his experience at a faculty seminar on the topic of the Black student's experience at Creighton:

> Some faculty looked on the presence of black students at Creighton as a problem of assimilation of a minority to the standards traditionally established by the white majority. This reaction brings into question neither the white American value system nor the purpose of the university itself.
>
> Others, however, recognized the presence of the black stu-

dent at Creighton not as a challenge for someone else to tell him who he is or should become, but as an opportunity for those of us who are non-black to discover who we are.

To do this it would seem necessary to create a university community which is supple enough to respond to the needs of all its members and broad enough to be the medium for the creation of a new self-awareness.

How should a university organize itself? Into schools and departments and societies and clubs so jealous of their own baggage that each would prefer to miss the train rather than chance storing its luggage in a common compartment?

Is a university worthy of the name if it cannot incorporate and communicate the experience of any of its members to any other?

This is not to destroy specialization and academic standards; it is merely to recognize that the refinement and criticism and intellectual honing which is the task of a university community must have as its object the shared experience of all the members of the university.

Anyone … who isn't willing to bear the burden of his own self-consciousness, to lay his opinions and values on the line and to criticize as well as defend them, does not belong at a great university.[17]

George was similarly outspoken in response to the Supreme Court's 1973 *Roe v. Wade* decision legalizing abortion nationwide. In a 2010 address at Brigham Young University in Salt Lake City, Utah, George recalled how he was surprised at the Supreme Court's decision and how, when he attempted to share his opinion in the local newspaper, it was not published. "I saw right away — when I wrote an op-ed piece for the *Omaha World-Herald* — that unless you defended that decision, you weren't going to be published, you weren't going to be heard in the public press. At least there."

Just as relevant today as then — with no small amount of prophecy — the letter reads:

Elaine Wells' many reasons for legal abortion ("Another Point of View," *Omaha World-Herald*, Feb. 17) are persuasive only if you share her assumption that the only rights in the abortion question are those of the mother. She argues that an infant's worth depends entirely upon its being wanted. Evidently, if a woman wants a new car rather than a child, the car is automatically more valuable. She argues that only wanted children will be loved. But wanting isn't loving. No one is born loved; we all learn to love each other.

Ms. Wells locates the issue very well when she contrasts quality of life with right to life. Certainly there are times when the quality of life becomes so oppressive (e.g., in a concentration camp) that a person might be better off dead. But who is finally to decide when the quality of life is such that the right to life, especially of someone else, ceases? The right to life of a human fetus at any stage in its development is not legally of little importance relative to the quality of life of its mother. What about other cases in which quality of life and right to life clash? What of the right to life of senile parents who are a financial and psychological burden to the independent lifestyle of their adult children? Since lives are no longer equal before the law but are valued according to their quality or style, are all lifestyles equal? What of the quality of life of Jewish people, of black people, of Polish people, of hippies, of people on welfare, of the chronically ill or the blind? Are we now to judge legally the relative qualitative value of these lifestyles? Why not?

Ms. Wells admits that abortion is a moral issue, but her morality seems to admit only one principle: self-determination of his/her own lifestyle by a competent adult. This is a principle of great importance, but when it becomes the only principle, morality degenerates into rugged individualism. Then value comes from competence alone and the weak have no rights. No single group, religious or otherwise, has insisted on society's protecting those unable to protect themselves; rather, this insistence has been part of our common legal heritage. It is so no longer. Now we are all to be fully self-reliant. To be protected by our legal system, even an unborn child will have to be able to stand on its own feet.[18]

Despite his own youth and disability, George was proving to be an intellectual powerhouse in the university community and a clear leader in his own religious congregation. At the age of thirty-five, he was elected as a representative of his province to the historic General Chapter in Rome for the election of a new superior general.

Just before he left, some of his Creighton students penned a surprise tribute to their beloved professor, who would be gone for at least the next month.

> You told us he was process,
> You said that it was good.
> We thought he was substance,
> We thought we always would.
> But now you've gone and changed him,
> We don't know what to do.
> And so, Fr. George, we sing these words to you!

> You done stomped on our God,
> And you mashed that sucker flat!
> You so neatly — confused me completely!
> You started philosophizing,
> I knew that I was dead.
> 'Cuz every word ya spoke,
> Sailed right over my head!

I only hope that someday
You get them low down blues.
And maybe at the General Chapter,
You'll look down at your shoes.
And you'll think about that God of mine,
You crushed beneath your soles,
Between you, Aquinas and Teilhard,
You shot my God all full of holes.[19]

Sr. Mary Alice Healy remembered that just before George's departure, he called members of the philosophy department faculty together for a meeting in which he stated clearly that, should he be asked to serve the congregation in some capacity, he would say "yes." It seems he had an idea of what might be coming.

FIVE
Oblate Leadership

He had a way of letting go and putting himself in God's hands.

ARCHBISHOP ROGER L. SCHWIETZ, O.M.I.

In a sign of the times, 1972 brought with it the first time that an Oblate superior general resigned from what had previously been understood as a position for life. The vacancy came in the midst of the 1972 General Chapter, at a time when the superior general recognized his limitation of advanced age and the need for fresh leadership in the wake of the changes and challenges of Vatican II, including the flight of massive numbers of missionaries.

At only thirty-five, Father George was one of the youngest capitulants, or participants, at the lengthy chapter, which, at six weeks, was the longest in the congregation's history. Because of the unexpected resignation, the election of a superior general had been added to the agenda. Age was something that Father George pondered rather frequently during the chapter sessions; he had been surprised, upon his arrival in Rome, to encounter what "seemed to be a very old group."[1] After the chapter elected Fr. Richard Hanley, an American just six years older than himself as superior general, George noted with his characteristic candor: "At the election of the General and his team that mentality again surfaced in the idea that a 41-year-old man could be considered an extremely young person. I think this can only be true in ecclesiastical circles; nowhere else would a forty-one-year-old be considered out of the ordinary."

At the chapter, Father George gained a greater understanding of the congregation, noting his appreciation of "the broadening of the horizons that has taken place in my own mind as a result of talking with people here." George was known for speaking his mind and apparently was appreciated for it. He was nearly elected a member of the order's administration in Rome as general councilor from the United States.

George was able to help the congregation begin to articulate how to move beyond the crises afflicting the Church at the time. The post-Vatican II years left many religious communities in a state of confusion and struggling to maintain a faithful yet relevant identity. George had a gift for cutting through any rancor or division, getting to the heart of an issue, and bringing unity out of an ideologically driven division. It was clear in the minds of many capitulants that George could help the Oblates move forward with a vision for the future, grounded in good sense and with a true spirit of their vocation and zeal for mission. And he had an appealing combination of youth and wisdom beyond his years.

A report Father George gave at the chapter illustrated his ability to give solid and steady leadership to the community at a time when it was sorely needed. George offered an honest appraisal of his confreres' concerns back home: "Basically, we are worried about the Congregation's ability to serve mankind. Are we helping to keep man in touch with God and are we helping man in his spiritual life?"[2] He questioned whether or not the Congregation, as it was currently set up, was as effective as it should have been.

Religious practice has radically changed, and in some places has almost disappeared. Tension in the community, and frustration in the apostolate, both tend to breed conservatism. To return to the past is too simple a solution, and is not enough. Courage to face the future is there indeed but we seem to lack a sense of direction in the way we direct our work. Many of the American Oblates demand from the Chapter something more than generalities or just mere business decisions. We need something to galvanize our Oblates to make greater efforts to spread the Gospel of the Lord and the kingdom of God.

In shades of a common theme he would take up in the future, especially as a bishop, he asked, "How can the kingdom of God be made present here and now? While we are Americans and must as such respect the culture of our country, when do we say no longer can the Oblate fit himself into the culture and that hence he must change the culture?"

Reflecting privately on his intervention later, he questioned if he had been "too negative in tone," perhaps giving "a false impression" that the Oblates in the United States were "falling apart."[3] He also wrote privately at the time, "This Chapter is forcing me to come to terms with my own commitment to the Oblates." He also observed to himself criticism of the spirit of poverty espoused by the Oblates at the time: "Everyone wears old clothes to the Chapter meetings and good clothes to go out!"[4]

Electing the first American as superior general was a historic moment for the Oblates. Fr. Richard Hanley came to the office from the former Western Province of the United States. Fr. William Woestman, a capitulant in the 1972 chapter, recalled that Father Hanley had stated several times at the meeting that he should not be elected. His confreres, however, had other plans. The election of Father Hanley would change the direction of the community.

Hanley, George noted to himself, "respects people tremendously and includes them all," adding that "it is a tribute to Hanley that the unification of the Congregation which cannot be accomplished on the levels of ideas can be done through the force of his personality." However, Father George also expressed privately some dissatisfaction regarding Father Hanley based on what George had heard during a Mass just days after Hanley's election, writing simply: "Hanley doesn't believe in purgatory." Over the next two years it would become clear to many of his collaborators in Rome that Hanley held a variety of problematic and heterodox theological views — including temporary ordinations, the ordination of women, and the return of married priests to active ministry.[5]

PROVINCIAL

At the conclusion of the 1972 chapter, George returned to his life and work at Creighton for another year. The following spring, on May 29, 1973, after the customary consultation, George was appointed Provincial of the Oblate Central Province in the United States, requiring a move to the provincial house in St. Paul, Minnesota. At just thirty-six years old, George became the youngest individual to hold such an office in American Oblate history.

Father Hanley expressed in a May 30, 1973, letter how he and the General Council were "delighted" with the appointment. "We all realize we are asking a great sacrifice of you, Francis, giving up much of the work you love and do so well for an unknown venture," he wrote, thanking George for accepting the post. "At the same time, it is evident that you have a tremendous vote of confidence from the Oblates from the Province, and that is the first requisite for leadership. Some men will cause you pain, it is all part of the Paschal mystery, but we are confident that you are big enough to weather such storms," Hanley told the new provincial. And he gave George a boost of confidence, saying that what was wanted by the men now in his care are things he was already giving them "in large doses," including openness, participation, and leadership.

George hoped as provincial that he would bring leadership necessary to clarify common purpose and overcome plurality among the Oblates that only served to stifle mission. And he did so, considering that he would serve in this position for about a year and a half. As a leader,

George was looked upon by his confreres in the province as a good religious, someone who could articulate a vision for ministry and lead the province through what remained troubled times, and always with a bit of good humor. In his first province newsletter in July 1973, after recounting his first month in the position, the short priest noted self-deprecatingly: "Final Preliminary Observation on The State of Things: what this province needs is more short albs."[6]

Advancing into leadership at such a young age meant that George was diverted from the academic path he had envisioned for himself and that his gifts and talents would be put to use in other ways. A priest for just ten years, George was now responsible for nearly 250 confreres, the Oblate priests and brothers throughout nine midwestern states, plus dozens of other Oblates from the province missioned to foreign territories throughout the world. He worked to bring unity and consensus in the province and, as he explained in the July newsletter, he relied on the collaboration of a provincial council, which by his own design would "compensate for my own weaknesses" and "be fairly representative of a broad spectrum of opinion within the Province." Within the first few months, he visited the ministries of the various Oblate installations in the province and met with the bishops of the dioceses where Oblates served. He also traveled abroad to missions of the Central Province, including Brazil, Greenland, and Scandinavia, and he shared his experiences and perspective with his confreres. "If the Brazilian mission constantly reminds us of the urgency of the needs of the oppressed, the Scandinavian mission reminds us of the hollowness of physical well-being in a life that has lost all meaning," he wrote in the December 1973 province newsletter. "The poor are the favored of the kingdom, but this is so only because the kingdom is the kingdom of God. We in the US need the overseas delegations more than they need us. We need them to be ourselves," he added.

These global experiences shaped George's worldview. They helped him to begin seeing the bigger picture, and process what he learned amid firsthand experiences with God's people. Seeing the poverty in Brazil amid much national corruption and oppression, George gained new appreciation for American civil liberties. But he also began to wonder as an American, as he wrote in the February 1974 province newsletter, "How much of our prosperity is bought at the price of misery?"

In his first letter to Oblates of the Central Province, written on June 10, 1973, George's own honesty, integrity, and humility were obvious and proved to be characteristic of his style of governance throughout the years ahead. "I have a lot to learn about the Province, its personnel and its ministries," he wrote. "In order to learn well, I shall have to ask many questions, and I hope that no one will be offended by my doing that. I shall try to be totally honest with all of you; in turn, I ask you to be honest and frank with me. I ask also for your prayers and your patience. I pledge to do the best I can to serve you and the people we all serve."

The asking of questions, as off-putting as it might have been to some, would be an important feature of George's governance style in the years ahead, and his communiques with members of the province were thought-provoking and honest. As George grew into his role of provincial, he was eager to learn from his confreres about their general well-being and about the fit of their assignments. He preferred to keep lines of communication open.

Only a month on the job, in a July 1973 letter to Oblates of his province, George began wondering — clearly out of his great love for the congregation — if Oblates were men with a future. Pointing out the dichotomy of what the next year represented, after mentioning plans to observe the fiftieth anniversary of the province, he quipped, "It's a good thing we have something to celebrate next year, because we will have no fourth theologians. This is a sobering statistic. What does it tell us about ourselves?" He explained that the good news was that Oblates are "what we are because we want to be; we know we can do otherwise." Then he began to examine some basic facts, including that almost twenty priests had requested dispensation from vows in the past few years. This, though, was not a phenomenon unique to their congregation. "The Church's changed self-understanding, the recasting of the role of priest and religious, swift shifts in society at large, the upward mobility of the American Catholic people, the loss of credibility" were among the reasons he listed for the change. He also questioned how much the problem was brought to prayer. "We used to pray for vocations each day after lunch in our houses." At the end of his reflection, George admitted that he did not want to be caught up in a numbers game — but he added that, even so, "a kind of death wish can operate in individuals and groups when they are sufficiently demoralized." He did not pull punches: "Because we are a voluntary society, we can choose to be the last generation of Oblates," adding, "we can refuse to take ordinary means needed for our own survival. Such a choice, I am convinced, would be sinful."

To mark the province's fiftieth anniversary, George requested in December 1973 that each Oblate observe a day of prayer, fasting, and abstinence in advance of the celebration. "Thus prepared spiritually," he said, "we have every reason to hope God's blessing will be with us."

As provincial, George helped the Central Province articulate and outline the vision for their ministry in a mission statement: "Missionary Outlook of the Central US Province." Although completed after he left the position, George's fingerprints can be found throughout the brief text.

In his many years in Church leadership, not only did George work hard to be an effective and faithful priest, but he made it a priority to help other priests also live as authentically as possible in their own vocations — all with an eye toward the good of God's people. In George's brief tenure as provincial, he tried to help identify the hidden and often mishandled addiction to alcohol, with which some of the clergy struggled. When a confrere once raised the subtle challenge that the province had twenty alcoholics who had yet to be identified, George established the province's Alcoholism Education Committee. About a year later, with help from George's successor as provincial, approximately twenty Oblates from the province were seeking treatment for alcohol abuse.

A CRISIS OF LEADERSHIP

Despite whatever gifts and talents Father Hanley may have brought to the community as superior general, he was unable to navigate the polarization in the Church that was also permeating Oblate life. As George described it in a 1975 interview, "Hanley had a vision of the future not shared by a large number in the congregation."[7]

The truth of this statement was made evident by Father Hanley's resignation — not just from his position of authority but from the congregation altogether. Described publicly as "for personal reasons," Hanley's departure was mostly linked to the fact that he had fallen in love with a Sisters of the Cenacle woman religious, which in the minds of many may explain why Hanley appealed not to be elected at the 1972 chapter. Hanley ended up resigning after just two years in the position, thereby giving up his unsustainable double life. George said in a July 4, 1974, letter to Oblates of his province that the news of Hanley's resignation was "painful" and a source of personal "regret." In terms of what it meant for the congregation as a whole, George wrote:

> The resignation gives us the chance once again to submit ourselves to a divine purpose which is always larger and more mysterious than our own projects and concerns. It seems to me of great importance that we accept this event in the life of the Congregation in a spirit of fraternal love and of deep Christian faith, giving way neither to demoralization on the one hand nor smug superiority on the other. I can only do what any religious leader should do in a time of crisis — ask you to keep your eyes and hearts firmly fixed on the mystery of Christ's suffering, death and resurrection and on the demands of the Gospel in our common life.

During a speech at a 2013 Oblate jubilee celebration, George reflected on this time as a "huge crisis," when it "wasn't clear whether [the Oblates] would dissolve or not," adding, "there was a deep sense of betrayal, but also a sense of anger" in the congregation.[8] At the time, if an order's superior general resigned, the Holy See presumed there must be problems with the congregation as a whole. So Hanley's resignation even prompted the delay of the beatification of the congregation's founder, Eugene de Mazenod. Fr. Fernand Jetté — the former spiritual formation director at George's scholasticate in Ottawa and Hanley's vicar general in Rome at the time — set the tone for an atmosphere of honesty and integrity: "It is God who guides both history and individual men — and he does so by paths known to him alone. We must believe that on God's part everything is grace."[9]

Hanley's departure required another General Chapter to convene in 1974. Before departing, George wrote in a November 8, 1974, letter to encourage Oblate pastors in his province to cooperate with vocation directors to address the order's declining numbers. He asked pastors to take active steps to invite young men to consider their way of life and make it obvious that they were serious about having others join them. "God will send us candidates if we provide a milieu in which religious dedication can deepen and holiness can develop," he wrote. "If we create prayerful communities of poor and chaste men, obedient to the Lord and to each other and dedicated to preaching the Gospel to the poor, God will fill our ranks. If not, all the programs, projects, formation committees, meetings and letters will remain a futile dance." He added, "Let us pray together for the grace of personal conversion and for the spiritual reform of the Congregation." This invitation to his province would be one George was soon able to share with the entire Oblate congregation. And he could do so because it was also his personal objective.

1974 CHAPTER

The resignation of the superior general was a source of frustration and challenge for the whole congregation. And the timing was downright miserable. Father Hanley's departure came as the meaning of the priesthood and religious life was malleable in many minds during the post-Vatican II years, and misinterpretations of the Council added to much internal confusion among the Oblates. The congregation was no different than the many other religious communities that were witnessing large numbers of men and women leave the priesthood and religious vows. From

1969 through mid-1974, 305 Oblate priests (or around 4 percent) were laicized. In the same timeframe, 454 Oblates left the congregation while under temporary vows, 112 left while in perpetual vows, and 406 died.

With new constitutions drafted after the council, and a rethinking of the missionary vocation in general, the Oblates needed clear direction to maintain their identity. While Hanley's motivations for leaving were not widely known at the time, it was understood that the congregation needed leaders who lived the life and could help the congregation live it too. Leadership needed to help overcome divisions within the congregation, which were in many ways a microcosm of the divisions in the Church as a whole. The new leadership would need to right the ship and, even more so, help the order cling to its founder's charism and authentically live the Oblate calling in a post-Vatican II, modern world.

It might have been reasonable to expect that the 1974 chapter would be much simpler than the chapter two years earlier, since it seemed only a new superior would need to be elected. Other issues slated for discussion would include fundamental values, administrative structures, and a better definition of what was expected of the superior general. In a letter to Oblates of the Central Province, George expressed his desire for an open, frank chapter. "An election is a political affair, in the sense that it is concerned with public policy," he wrote to his province confreres on July 4. "We have a choice of secret or uninformed political activity on the one hand or open and informed political activity on the other. I prefer the latter."

The permanent position of vicar general had been created at the 1972 chapter and was held by Canadian Oblate Fr. Fernand Jetté. Given Father Jetté's reserved, reflective, and introverted traits, he was not widely expected to be elected the superior general. That changed, however, when he gave an opening address to the chapter.[10] He was candid about the declining membership of the order, which he related to a lack of focus on mission and the need for the spiritual renewal of religious life. It became clear that Father Jetté offered the chapter capitulants the vision and authenticity needed in their new leader. Jetté was a lifelong student of Eugene de Mazenod and was able to issue a *cri de coeur* for a renewal of Oblate life and mission, offering an examination of conscience of sorts for the congregation to live anew, according to the mind of the founder. He concluded by recalling what Cardinal Leo J. Suenens once observed: "The times are hard on unselfish vocations," adding, "It is perhaps even truer today and more than ever the world has need of such vocations." That could, perhaps, be a fine summary of what it means to be an Oblate: one who unselfishly offers his life in the service of proclaiming the Gospel.

While it became clear that Father Jetté had many of the answers needed to help steer the Oblates through their present crisis, it was also clear that the runner-up for the top position was Francis George. Both Fathers Jetté and George were on the ballot for the position of superior general and, as such, each had the task of explaining to capitulants why the other might be better suited.

Father Jetté explained:

> Many, especially among the young Oblates, would like to find in the next General the visible incarnation of Father Hanley's spontaneity, dynamism, and drive towards the future. With me as Superior General, you would have a rather difficult image to sell to them. I am not a man who has mixed a lot with people, all the dynamism that I possess is hidden, and I have managed to control the spontaneity I have. Normally, it takes time to get to know me, and the outside image is never very exciting.

He also noted "a certain lack of preparation for international travel" and "the lack of personal experience in missionary work properly speaking. … I have worked mainly in teaching, giving retreats and spiritual direction with some administration thrown in."

Father Jetté requested that, if elected, the capitulars give him "as a permanent team in Rome, a strong group which can, bit by bit, impress the Congregation by its competence in the domain of Spiritual Life, Mission and Formation." This step, he said, was "an essential element" in order to maintain and develop unity within the congregation.

More to the point, Father Jetté explained that the Congregation needed a vision of "the Oblate as an apostolic man." He went on:

> Father de Mazenod, when he founded the Congregation, knew what he wanted: men who would put themselves at the service of the poor, yes, but men endowed with a special quality, men who would be authentic disciples and descendants of the first Apostles. This has not been sufficiently insisted upon, in the actual effort towards renewal in the Congregation. It is however from there that unity in the Congregation will come. If we continue to look for it in outside activities, whatever kind they may be, we shall never get it. We shall just manage to become more divided than ever.

George delivered a passionate talk, explaining to capitulants that he did not find himself "prepared to be Superior General."[11] He explained this was not the result of "a false humility but from a practical point of view." He offered as reasons his limited knowledge about the government of the Congregation in Rome, saying, "I am not at ease here." And he explained limitations regarding linguistic ability and age. "I do not feel prepared or spiritually mature to undergo the type of suffering that the next Superior General will have to face. With the serious differences that exist among us, the next Superior General will have to act decisively in a changing world and Congregation."

In a nod to Father Jetté, whom he considered the candidate that possessed the skills to succeed in the midst of such a challenge, George said he hoped the next superior general "will have courage enough to lead us in a genuine spiritual renewal and reform. Without a real evangelistic spirit, religious life is an empty formula. We shall have to live more and more a life of poor men. The leadership is ours in this Chapter, and we must show it."

In the election for superior general, George placed second behind Father Jetté. As the new superior general, Father Jetté presided over the nominations committee for the position of vicar general. George was at the top of a list of three proposed candidates, with six additional names added to the ballot. On November 27, 1974, at age thirty-seven, George was elected vicar general out of nine total candidates, winning seventy-six of the ninety-nine votes cast on the first ballot. Because the position was so new, George would be able to shape and define it. As vicar general, he would exercise the same ordinary powers as the superior general, aside from what was restricted to the latter in law. Back home, upon receiving the news of George's election, his sister, Margaret, quipped to their mother, "Why did he open his mouth?" In his diary, Father Jetté wrote, "Father George has been elected Vicar General. I am glad. We can, I hope, become truly friends."[12] George ended up in Rome after all: He would serve as vicar general for the next twelve years. His Oblate confrere, then-Fr. Roger Schwietz, was not entirely surprised. "He had vision," he said of George. "He saw different things others did not see."

MOVING TO ROME

At the start of 1975, a few weeks after the conclusion of the chapter that changed George's trajectory yet again, Father George wrote in a January 1, 1975, letter to his confreres back home in St. Paul:

> I leave the Province at this time with great personal regret, not only because the whole Roman scene is unknown to me and therefore somewhat fearsome, but also because I remain highly appreciative of our personnel, constantly edified by our ministry and thoroughly convinced that this Province has a significant role to play in the US region and the Congregation at large. I expected to return to the Province after the Chapter, and there are now a number of unfinished projects ... I hope you will all forgive the mistakes I have made.

Shortly after his election as vicar general, George expressed his hopes for the reform of the congregation. He indicated the temptations to which religious orders often fall prey, particularly taking on the life of the culture around them. Religious orders needed "to become far more authentically Gospel people than we seem right now," George said.[13] And, in parting comments in a January 12, 1975, letter to the provincial council on the newly adopted province mission statement, he honed in on what he believed to be the key to it all: poverty.

> Here, I can go on and on … I think we've got a good start on religious renewal (prayer, community, etc.) and on personnel development (alcoholism program, continuing education, etc.). But on poverty, I feel most of the Province doesn't even know what I've very gingerly been trying to begin discussing. I think we've simply lost any recognizable spirit of poverty. The danger, of course, is that we become only a pious association of professional people. Historically, any authentic religious renewal has been associated with poverty and the acceptance of a life style drastically more simple than ours. If we have everything we need, the question of poverty will always remain what it is now, a joke (Where can I get some of that poverty, as the bum says).

On George's election, Oblate Fr. Thomas Singer, involved in Central Province administration, wrote in the December 1974 province newsletter, "Well-meaning friends stressed that the province's loss was the congregation's gain. Bishop [Bernard] Law [then of Springfield-Cape Girardeau] called and in his quiet Southern way assured me that 'it's good for the Church.'" Singer added: "I can't think of a better man for the job: a happy combination of super-intelligence with lots of heart and humor."

SIX

Oblate Vicar General

*When I was a young man, I prayed that I might live in such a
way that God's will for the world's salvation might be realized.*[1]

CARDINAL FRANCIS E. GEORGE, O.M.I.

At the start of 1975, Father George was back in the United States preparing for his move to Rome and the new task that awaited him. He faced the challenge of setting aside the work he had begun at the local level to concentrate on strengthening the congregation at the universal level. And he still needed to learn the language.

George's twelve-year stint as vicar general (in two six-year terms) resulted in his second longest assignment, aside from his tenure as archbishop of Chicago. The nature of his own formation and the ministries to which he had been assigned had brought about a host of moves for Father George since arriving in Belleville to begin high school. Such is the life of a missionary. But frequent changes do not equal easy changes. In a January 13 letter to Father Jetté, Father George wrote, "Saying all these farewells is becoming a bit depressing, so I think I'll be ready to get into the work at Rome soon." To Bishop Albert Zuroweste of Belleville, with whom he collaborated frequently as provincial, he wrote on February 18, "I am sure that, with God's help, everything will work out for the best."

Together, Fathers Jetté and George made a good team, and their work to renew Oblate life manifested itself in myriad ways. For Jetté, George was honest, open, trustworthy, collaborative, and effective as he helped govern the congregation. As vicar general serving in Rome, George would share in the same authority of the superior general in the ordinary administration of the Oblate congregation, with focused oversight of day-to-day operations at the General House in Rome and direct collaboration with the Holy See. This, in principle, freed up the superior general for global travel and overall animation of the congregation. That meant George helped oversee almost 6,500 Oblates throughout the world.

Jetté profoundly informed George's own style and vision. At a 2013 gathering with Oblates, George himself described the "quiet, unassuming" Jetté as the Oblate who "most shaped me in every way, but especially as an Oblate."[2] George greatly appreciated Jetté's governance style, which he called "an exercise in discernment." George said Jetté taught him "an enormous lesson of how to govern with one eye on the people and with one eye on the heart of the Lord." Calling him "a rock," George admired Jetté as "someone you could rely upon always … who guided indirectly often, and liked to persuade rather than command."

Living at the Oblate General House in Rome provided Father George with a truly global experience. The international house received members of the hierarchy and dignitaries from all around the world, affording George a unique perspective on international affairs, both secular and religious. The role also exposed George to the inner workings of the Roman Curia, which positioned him to be more directly of service to two congregations of the Holy See: the Congregation for the Evangelization of Peoples, which directs the Church's missionary activity, and the Congregation for Institutes of Consecrated Life and Societies of Apostolic Life.

As an administrator of a large religious congregation, George took the view that leadership was not authoritative. Rather, he saw that one more effectively leads by example, sharing experience, and expertise.

There was no doubt in the minds of friends, colleagues, and even many who knew him only from afar that George was a man of passionate convictions. He possessed the rare ability to quickly draw accurate conclusions and an equally acute long-ranging vision. Those who knew him best have often commented that his mind was generally the sharpest in the room and that he was always many steps ahead of others in his thought processes. All these character traits were gifts to be shared with his congregation and with the Church. But they also could be a cross, especially when dealing with those who might have had trouble understanding his point of view. Because George was grounded by an understanding of who Christ is and propelled by an abiding desire to make him known, those who knew him best trusted that his priorities were in the best interest of the congregation and the Church.

George's outgoing, inquisitive, and loquacious style complemented Father Jetté's introversion. Although Jetté committed himself to several tours throughout the global Oblate missions, George did too, visiting dozens of countries. He went to each mission as a brother and lived according to the local cultures. The experiences gave him a unique perspective of what it means to be a truly "catholic" Church.

During the two terms Father George served as Oblate vicar general, he was an effective leader who, along with Father Jetté, stabilized the congregation and established a clearer vision for it that was in accord with both the founder's vision and the reforms necessitated by Vatican II. Other Oblates assisted the two leaders in the General Administration, including Frs. Rene Motte, Marcello Zago, and James Cooke, who served as assistant generals.

Life as an administrator in Rome was certainly different for George.

Within his first year, the academically inclined, cerebral George lamented in a letter to a friend that there was "not enough time to read." In 1977,
almost three years into the job and after participating in a thirty-day
Ignatian retreat outside of Toronto, George composed a personal evaluation exercise.[3] He was characteristically hard on himself, but he was not
falsely modest. He recognized some of the tasks he was good at, but, at
the same time, he struggled to see himself as useful and effective in his
position. His idealism, paired with his expansive mind, could identify all
the flaws in how the General Administration functioned, but at times he
felt powerless to change anything about it. This was a lifelong struggle
for George, who often found himself boxed in by systemic inadequacies
and frustrated that he could not bring others to his position effectively
enough. "I don't think any of us is easily persuadable," he said privately of
the members of the General Council at the time. It was not that he was
unable to rally people to his views; rather, George's frustrations stemmed
from the congregation's difficulty in finding a common purpose, which
was additionally bogged down by the tendency of leadership to be a "bit
self-righteous and moralistic." He added: "I would like to see more of an
attitude of prayerful discernment."

George also struggled at the time with the loneliness of living in
Rome. Within his community, he found good men but superficial relationships. His residence at the General House in Rome, as he expressed
in an August 17, 1977, personal assessment of his position, was "not very
conducive to community life" as he would have liked to live it. He noted
how he thought himself to be misunderstood. Possessing the self-image of "a very moderate man, sometimes a bit liberal but sometimes also
truly conservative," he continued, George found others perceived him at
the General House community as "quite liberal," to which he wondered,
"Either my own self-image is askew, or the community is slightly to the
right of Louis XIV." Nonetheless, he said he felt "at ease with everybody in
the House; there is no one I don't talk to or am afraid of."

The Oblates have a longstanding relationship with the Sisters of the
Holy Family of Bordeaux, members of a French association of laity, re-

ligious, and clergy. During his time in Rome, George regularly celebrated Mass at the generalate of the Holy Family sisters, and through that association with the community became very close friends with their superior general, Sr. Mary Slaven. The two would often share a day in the city, taking in everything Rome and the surrounding area had to offer by way of historical sites, museums, and eateries. During his time in Rome, George also became lasting friends with then-Msgr. J. Basil Meeking, a priest and later bishop of Christchurch, New Zealand, who worked at the time for the Holy See's Pontifical Council for Promoting Christian Unity. Years later in Chicago, George called upon Bishop Meeking's many intellectual and pastoral gifts. For several years, Meeking assisted George with many projects while living with him and others at the archbishop's residence. Friends from home also came to visit George in Rome, like then-Fr. Roger Schwietz, who recalled George driving around in his tiny, green Fiat Cinquecento. "He was a wild driver," Schwietz remembered. "He really picked up from the Italians how to zoom around, and I would just hold on."

George described himself in the 1977 personal assessment exercise as being "content" in his vocation, although living in Rome made him feel "like a seminarian again or a kind of participant in a floating seminar." His description in the document described his priestly life as having "taken on new importance" and that he was "more than ever committed to Oblate life even as I see ever more clearly both the bad and good of the Congregation." He saw his life then as "more than ever a life of faith," in which his prayer "deepened" as well as his "personal desire for union with the Lord."

STRENGTHEN THE CONGREGATION

The Missionary Oblates of Mary Immaculate were not immune to the high attrition rates of religious orders in the late 1960s. Some of George's correspondence from the mid-1970s evidences a great deal of laicization requests, similar to what so many other congregations and dioceses were dealing with at the time. As vicar general, George turned his attention to identifying the roots of the crisis, and he became a strong voice in the *ressourcement* of religious institutes called for by Vatican II.

In the turbulent postconciliar years, religious congregations were not just shrinking in number. The renewal of religious congregations was sometimes equated with a hard restart, which resulted all too often in their abandonment of their past. But thinkers like George understood that, much like with the implementation of the council itself, there was a need to maintain continuity with the past. A vital aspect of the renewal and reform of religious communities was the need to revisit how the founder's charism was — or should be — alive in the congregation. Toward the end of George's first year as vicar general, the Oblate congregation embraced this challenge, encountering their founder Eugene de Mazenod anew. George and Jetté both recognized the importance of the Oblate founder's witness in the renewal of religious life of the congregation, and George articulated that well for the Oblates throughout his tenure as vicar general. George had first begun to encounter de Mazenod in a most profound way during the spiritual conferences of Jetté while he was a seminarian in Ottawa. Regarding the delay in de Mazenod's beatification, George recalled in 2013 that he and Jetté both received a call from Pope Paul VI about the matter, who asked, "Do you want your founder beatified? Are you going to continue as a religious congregation?"[4] George credited Jetté, who spoke from his heart about the importance of the beatification of the Oblate founder, with saving the beatification of de Mazenod.

Vatican II's Decree on Religious Life, *Perfectae Caritatis*, articulated the identification of the "original inspiration behind a community"[5] as a central principle driving such an effort. George discussed the significance of this for the Oblates in a 1976 talk given in Rome on the Oblate charism, which was subsequently published as an essay in the journal *Review for Religious*.[6]

In his exploration of how best to keep alive the founder's charism in a religious community, what he described as "founderology," George asked:

Each religious foundation began with a group who shared a common spirit. This spirit, rooted in grace, enabled them to lead a common life and attempt a common task. How can a religious institute today know if it still has this original spirit? Is there a method which can help a religious community get in touch with the founder's spirit and live it authentically?

After identifying two extremes by which a congregation can keep alive the founder's vision and charism, George proposed a middle way "which neither copies a founder nor replaces him but rather interprets him for our time and for generations of religious yet to come." By stressing the need to resituate the founder's hopes and motives at the center of Oblate life, George helped the congregation find a unifying, life-giving source of animation for their common life as professed religious priests and brothers. To achieve this, George was put in charge of ongoing formation for the congregation, which helped this effort to be successful, allowing for greater mission and service to the Church.

The General Chapters of 1972 and 1974 gave mandates to achieve this goal. "On a deeper level, ongoing formation challenges us both individually and as a Congregation to clarify the bases of our hope," George wrote in 1975[7]. "In any society, the rich and the established place their hope in a continuation of things as they are. The very suggestion of change must come as a threat. The poor, on the other hand, place their hope in change, since they have nothing to lose." George maintained that the chapters' desire for the development of an ongoing formation plan "is an admission of our own poverty, of our hope for something more, something better, something new."

He continued: "Ongoing formation now is meaningless without the poor man's hope for something better in the future. Whatever the future holds — a truly renewed Church, a society run by and for the poor — we will be part of it to the extent that we are renewed people, able to lead others in the following of a Christ who 'makes all things new.'" He also kept his finger on the pulse of the formation of Oblate scholastics, recognizing how vital proper formation is in order to truly live the Oblate vows.

In a 1977 letter to a confrere, George, lamenting recurring themes he saw in men leaving the congregation and being granted laicization, said, "The Congregation demands a unity of commitment, not of thought nor of motives of making the commitment, which change as men develop and circumstances shift." Later that year, in another letter, George noted the example of one particular Oblate requesting laicization. In it, he identified what he saw as a root problem that he had sought to correct:

> He always spoke in terms of devotion to ministry, to a function, rather than to Christ as a person. I've tried to go over that with some of the scholastics here — the consecration is first of all to a Person, not to a particular job or role or cause. As the laicization requests come in, it's clear that something was lacking in the understanding of commitment of some of them. It doesn't matter whether their ideas are of the left or the right (and we have cases on each side): what matters is if their love was for a Person, Christ as Lord and Savior, rather than for an idea (which turns out to be their own anyway) or a role or status or even a service (ministry).

As a means to revitalize the congregation amid the aftermath of Vatican II, and to strengthen its bond to the mission of the founder, George was responsible for overseeing a revamping of the congregation's constitutions and rules. The original rule dated back to 1818 and had been revised at different times throughout the congregation's existence. The most recent revision had been made in 1966, and many Oblates found the result inadequate. The task before the committee overseeing the constitutions, which was chaired by George, was to restore a more unified animation to the vowed Oblate life and mission. The new constitutions were approved in the 1980 General Chapter — the same Chapter that reelected George as vicar general.

A year later, in a talk in South Africa in which he drew attention to the distinction made in the new constitutions regarding three titles found in Oblate life — priest, religious, and missionary — George cautioned against the temptation to see only one of these realities as the exclusive interpretation of Oblate life.[8] Oblates are priests, George said, who are "called to a mission in the Church ... a pastor in the Church." Oblates are religious men, he said, who are "called to a mission to the Church ... to be a reminder, even to the Church, of a way of life and of love that is now the object of our faith and of our hope." And lastly, Oblates are missionaries "called to a mission for the Church, to go to places and peoples where the Church is hardly or not at all present." For George, the Oblates, and thus himself, belonged to "a corps of men with a mission: in the Church, to the Church and for the Church."

Prayer was another means of achieving greater unity in the congregation. "If," George wrote in a 1988 talk on Oblate spirituality, "a common prayer life unites a group, [then] the certitude that all share the same love makes it easier to accept the differences of opinion in the group. No matter their particular ideas, they all continue to share a common affective stance."[9] While in Rome, George served as general editor of *Oblate Prayer*, which was published at the end of his tenure as vicar general by the General Administration in Rome. The book is a treasury of prayer and a type of spiritual directory, which, as George described it, was meant to form "a new incarnation of the Founder's spirit and charism." The work was compiled to promote common identity in prayer among the Oblates, George said, including traditional Oblate daily prayers and practices, resources pertinent to Oblate feast days and ceremonies, and a treasury of prayers in Latin for international gatherings. George described the spirituality of the book as rooted in a threefold foundation, which expressed "a qualitative Oblate movement towards union with God": "a sense of personal consecration to God's will; a life in union with Mary; and a communal life marked by love and affection." It was George's desire that invoking the Oblate tradition of prayer would "form Oblate communities sure of their identity and more deeply rooted in the Congregation's mission." He added that, without an instrument like the book, "Oblate spirituality itself might become just a subject to be studied rather than a common way to holiness." Once, George recalled how when he joined the congregation, a prayer for Oblate vocations was prayed every day at lunchtime. Eventually it was removed from common usage — a move that left George wondering if the Oblates lacked concern for their future. "Oblate spirituality," he explained, "is a path to be trod together, talking while we walk, telling each other what we are to do, what we believe in and, in community prayer, what we love."

Such observations remain relevant today and are indicative of George's keen ability to identify the problems in ecclesial life, not to mention identify their cure. But even more, they are descriptors of himself — of how he lived and exercised his ministry. All of this would define the next phase of his life as a bishop as well, bringing the riches of his experience as an Oblate to the wider Church in America and abroad.

MINISTRY TO THE WORLD

With George's developed global perspective and the expansive reach of the Oblates throughout the world, he knew the congregation was in a unique position to evangelize the cultures in which they found themselves. He elucidated on his vision in a 1984 talk on modern religious life, in which he considered: Does religious life "have something to say in and to the world today?"[10] The talk is a kind of synthesis of his convictions that religious life could function as "a transforming agent" in modern culture, so it offers a roadmap for how it might. He turned to the witness and authenticity of Oblate life first, asking how it could be "more clearly prophetic and more effectively mediating in today's secularized societies?" George challenged the Oblates to be "sufficiently open to the groups composing the societies in which we live" and to foster a "theological culture deep enough" among Oblates to "intrigue secularized people willing to talk with those who live out of an explicitly evangelical vision." He saw the need for more self-denial and penance, a necessary tool for witnessing to "freedom, justice and truth," so as to attract the secularized who search for those same values. Can such people, George asked, find such values expressed in public prayer? And he also wondered aloud if the Oblates had enough opportunities for communal prayer, inviting a reexamination of communal prayer practices as an "essential dimension of religious life [that] speaks to the culture." George stressed the importance that, as religious, Oblates' lives must be marked by living under God's providence "in the conviction that he makes use of our efforts and of historical events so that, in his time, all might be renewed in Christ." In challenging religious to speak a word of hope to the world, he said, "Those who do not believe in him often find themselves without real hope, and they can only listen in wonder or even anger to those who, without naïveté or false innocence, nonetheless speak of hope. ... To the extent that our very lives 'speak' of Christ, they will be words of hope in today's culture."

With as much relevance to his day as in any age, George said in 1978, "Justice is a concern today to the extent that it is absent from our world."[11] In his tenure as vicar general, George oversaw Oblate efforts regarding peace and justice, helping Oblates ground the terms in the context of faith, rather than politics or ideology. "Action for justice as integral to evangelizing becomes problematic when evangelizers are seen to take political positions in the name of faith," he wrote in an internal memo to the Oblate General Council.

To this role, George brought his characteristic nuanced thinking, candor, and ability to synthesize many diverging opinions to bring unity in the light of the Gospel. His main task was to help foster consensus amid many differing views. He facilitated congregation-wide conversations on injustice throughout the world, including its causes, effects, and solutions. He strongly challenged the thinking of some Oblates who had become sympathetic to Marxist explanations, particularly in Latin America, for the causes of injustice — and many of them were at odds with George because of it. He also had a nuanced take on liberation theology, which he described as something that "makes dialogue in the Church extremely difficult." He had a talent for exposing such proposals as inadequate, while at the same time remaining sympathetic to the help they provided. In a 1978 internal memo to the members of the Oblate Justice and Peace network, noting the difficulties in finding a path of cooperation congregation-wide, George proposed five areas for collaboration: continuing a congregation-wide self-examination, assisting in the development of peoples, community organization, capital transfer, and consciousness raising.

George's insights and efforts toward reform were invaluable in this regard because of what could be described as a crisis in ministry for priests. George made it clear that the Church needed religious men, not social workers — men who were faithful to the Gospel and not co-opted by any government or political movement. This was also a common theme during his time as a bishop.

These were significant issues for the Oblate congregation during George's tenure in Rome, whose members vowed to serve and evangelize the poor. In 1978, Oblate Fr. Heinz Hunke was expelled from the African country of Namibia for speaking the truth about institutionalized torture. And their confrere Fr. Michel Lynde was forced from Laos, then a closed society intolerant of ideological differences and freedom of thought and expression. George supported both men. He noted in the letter to members of the committee in 1978, "The Christian prophet not only denounces injustice, he shows who Christ is and points people to where He can be found. Often he does this far more by what he suffers than by how he acts or what he says."

On many occasions throughout his life, George spoke about the unique aspect of suffering in the life of priests and religious. In one particular example, he recalled his friend and former Ottawa classmate Fr. Raynald Beauregard, who served in the kingdom of Lesotho in Southern Africa. George recounted Father Beauregard's story on several occasions, including the 2009 homily at the ordination of Chicago priests, in which he held up Father Beauregard as a model of priestly ministry. His friend, George said, "told the people, as priests do, who Christ truly is and how Christ had conquered the spirits in which they had believed and which they believed were out to punish them. He told them they don't have to be afraid, for God is love."[12] George continued:

> Some of his new converts, his own parishioners who had not yet understood the new life given by Christ, took up knives and killed Father Beauregard on the twenty-third of December, 1976. They admired his great physical strength, and they thought they would share in that strength if they killed him. Before he died, and it took him about twenty-four hours to die, he said that he had been in the hands of the Blessed Virgin Mary for a long time and that he surrendered his life to God. Life was a gift, and he gave it back. Twice he said that he forgave those who had attacked and killed him. His was a beautiful death, but a disturbing witness to life in Christ. While Fr. Beauregard's self-sacrifice might be extraordinary, nonetheless it bears resemblance to our own call to leave everything in order to follow Christ and, in Christ, to find the fulfillment of everything that we erroneously thought we could possess on our own.

Another Oblate about whom George spoke on several occasions, including during the same 2009 ordination homily, was Fr. Lawrence Rosebaugh, a missionary among the poor who often lived on the streets and even spent time in jail. George highlighted the example of the "quiet, soft-spoken" Rosebaugh as an effective Gospel witness. "Blessed are the poor, Christ said, and Father Larry Rosebaugh believed him," George explained. "Go, sell what you have, give it to the poor and come follow me, Christ taught, and Fr. Larry took Christ at his word." In the early 1970s, Rosebaugh approached George, his Oblate provincial, and asked to be removed from the congregation's health insurance because he wanted to evangelize the poor as an equal. George could not approve the request because, as provincial, he was responsible for his well-being.

George continued: "A man who had nothing of his own was shot and killed by robbers a week ago on a stretch of road in Guatemala. The robbers, if that is who they really were, took almost nothing, because Fr. Rosebaugh had next to nothing materially, in life and in death."

SAYING GOODBYE

Despite living abroad for so long, George kept in close contact with his family through postcards and letters sent from the destinations of his international travels. In a letter to a friend — written just before he left for Rome, after packing and finishing up business in St. Paul at the provincial headquarters in 1974 — George wrote, "Thanks very much for notifying my parents about my arrival in Chicago. My mother likes nothing better than greeting planes, so she would have been disappointed if she hadn't been there when I got in." During his time in Rome, George brought his parents across the Atlantic for a grand European tour.

Whenever he was in North America, he made time for a visit to Chicago, which his mother especially welcomed after his father's health began to decline. She loved when he could take her out in the car for shopping. Before then, George tried to prioritize fishing trips to Michigan with his father, which coincided with visits to see George's sister, Margaret, and her family in Grand Rapids.

He did his best to maintain these familial connections, even while thousands of miles away and immersed in responsibilities.[13] For one Father's Day, he sent a postcard home depicting the creation of Eve from St. Mark's Basilica in Venice. "Dear Pop," he wrote, "this is not a women's lib card — it shows God the Father creating Eve from Adam's side." On one birthday card to his mother, George wrote, "Take care of yourself. You're the only mother I've got." In another, he apologized for sending a Mother's Day card instead of a birthday card because "Lesotho doesn't have a great selection of cards." Father Jetté wrote to George's parents on July 23, 1979, for the occasion of their fiftieth wedding anniversary, noting that their marriage "has been a blessing for the Oblates: in fact, it is the cause of Father Francis's presence among us, and furthermore as Vicar General of the Congregation!" In 1985, George was in Grand Rapids, preparing to celebrate his nephew's wedding. "It's like producing a Broadway play," he later wrote Father Jetté. "They've added all kinds to the ceremony since I last performed a wedding, almost fourteen years ago. Everything went well, thank God."

George was abroad when his mother suddenly and unexpectedly died on January 29, 1983. Summoned home, George stayed with his father, who had been in failing health for a few years already, for about a month. George would often celebrate Mass with him on the family's dining room table. "It's strange living here without my mother," George wrote to Father Jetté on February 8. "It's like living inside her mind, since so much is arranged as she planned it — even the food we're still eating." George wrote a friend about two months later: "It's as if there's a big hole somewhere in the center of things; it doesn't go away, but I'm getting used to it. … She was a woman of great faith, and the Lord will be good to her. But I still miss her — or miss looking forward to seeing her again as I used to look forward to seeing her when it got near time for a trip home."

Decisions regarding his father's future care were taken seriously, as George indicated in the letter to Father Jetté. "I don't want my dad to lose his wife, his friends, his house and his belongings all at once," he wrote. But it was clear more care was needed, and so his father was moved nearer to Margaret in Grand Rapids, Michigan. About eighteen months later, George was able to arrive in Grand Rapids just before his father's death on June 9, 1984. It seems as if the father was waiting to say farewell to the son. "My dad is certainly happier than he has been for the last couple of years," George wrote Father Jetté on June 18. George celebrated the funeral Masses of both of his parents at the family's home parish, St. Pascal in Chicago.

A MISSIONARY TAKES FLIGHT

As a means to being more effective in his role as vicar general, George took upon himself an increased load of travels. There is no small irony to this, considering the concerns that had once been expressed to him about his potential commute to Quigley in downtown Chicago. George embarked on several multinational trips during each year of his two terms as vicar general in order to survey various Oblate installations through-out the world, better understand their needs, and determine how they could best live out their mission. While there is no complete, comprehensive list of the places George visited in his dozen years as vicar general, what is known is impressive. He visited the United States and Canada, including the Inuit (Eskimos) in the Arctic circle. He visited most of the countries in Europe, a half-dozen in Africa and South America, a dozen or more in Asia, plus Australia and Tahiti. He encountered native peoples, often amid great poverty. He stayed in huts and traveled down rivers on canoes. He contended with forces of nature, including two solid weeks of rain while on a 1980 trip to northern France and Holland, and swarms of mosquitoes in upper Canada.

On one trip to visit an Oblate missionary friend in Zambia, George learned about the mission and the flock that his friend served along the banks of the Zambesi River, which he recounted in a talk given at the 2000 Eucharistic Congress in Rome.[14] "His ministry was a great comfort to him, especially when he was able to celebrate the Eucharist with the people, both in the small mission church and in the villages," George recalled. "His heart was often troubled, however, by the problems of the people, not only as individuals or in families, but also, in the society as a whole. Zambia had not adjusted well to the new global economic order. The people he served lived, for the most part, by subsistence farming. A whole generation of young parents was dying of AIDS. The indebtedness of the country meant that education and health care were being curtailed." And George experienced this first-hand:

> After Mass one morning, [the man] returned to the priest's house and I went to the bank of the river to thank God for the natural beauty of this troubled country. Four men came out of the bush and approached me to ask where they could find the priest. I indicated the house alongside the chapel and three of them went to the door. The fourth stayed with me and we began to talk. I did not speak his language, unfortunately, but he

spoke some English. When I asked about his family and work, he repeated many of the difficulties that my friend had already shared with me. Then I asked him why he and his companions had come to speak to the priest. He explained that many stories were heard in his small village, and some of them were about Jesus and the Gospel and the Church. They had come to ask the priest for information about his religion. I then asked him why he was not with his three companions, talking to the priest. He responded, "Oh, I've thought about what we've heard, even while I was walking here, and I've decided it's not for me. It makes no sense when I look at my life — that God would love us, that God would sacrifice himself for us, that God is stronger than the spirits who harm us. I don't believe it. It's too good to be true."

Each trip George took was followed by a detailed report on the socioeconomic, political, and cultural circumstances of the given region, as well as a diagnostic report on the health of the local Oblate community. George became allergic to the nationalism he encountered throughout the various mission fields he visited, including in America. "How does the faith, once expressed from within a cultural tradition, then criticize that tradition, demonstrate its inadequacy as a vehicle of God's love, universalize and liberate believers from the demonic constraints of their own culture?" he wondered in a September 17, 1977, internal memo to council members of the General Administration. "I take nationalism to be a demonic expression of a culture," he continued. "We adapt the faith within a culture, but a culture totally closed in on itself becomes 'nationalistic,' no longer open to other cultures, exalting the nation as the ultimate object of devotion. Nationalism, in the sense I am referring to it, is a form of idolatry." He was particularly concerned about the use of national symbols, such as the flag, in sanctuaries. "This mixing of religious and national symbols is dangerous, since there are times when the cross demands one course of action from us and the flag another."

Given the international character of the congregation and their missionary outposts, the various visits George made throughout the globe had their international flair, much like life at the General House in Rome. Once in Indonesia in 1979, a dinner was hosted for George with Oblates from Germany, France, Italy, Ireland, and Australia. Six Oblates were speaking four different native tongues while gathered in a Chinese restaurant in Indonesia drinking Australian wine.

These adventures, while enlightening and educational, also featured moments that were harrowing and difficult. One such event occurred in May 1975, on a day that George later recalled as the "worst" of his life. "After having a difficult time negotiating at the border between Germany and Czechoslovakia, I was dogged for a day by security," he said in an interview in 1991.[15] He revealed in the same interview that his "most embarrassing moment" had been in June 1982 "when I was deported in India."

Sometimes George found himself within a comedy of errors, like the time when he was traveling from the Philippines to Indonesia in November 1978. The trip went on "not without some mishap," he wrote Father Jetté, "since Philippine Airlines had booked me on a flight that does not exist." Other times, George did things he never imagined he would do, especially regarding cuisine. As the Oblates were one with their people, George always jumped right into the local culture. This meant at times eating dog, as he did with Oblates in northern Borneo, or seal blubber, as he did with Eskimos in northern Canada, or crocodile, as he did in French Guiana.

That same year, a trip to Poland left a lasting impression, as he communicated in a letter to the Polish ambassador in Rome. He appreciated the nation's natural beauty and the chance to make an eyewitness survey of the horrors of destruction from World War II, as well as the unique history of the Faith in Poland and the contemporary significance of it. This was less than four months before Polish son Karol Wojtyła would be elected pope, an event that would change the course of George's life in many ways. Eugene de Mazenod desired the Oblates to be "men of the pope," and George was in Rome for 1978, the "year of three popes," when

St. Paul VI and John Paul I died less than two months apart, and St. John Paul II was elected.

By the start of 1986, George had returned from his fifth trip to Sri Lanka, third to Hong Kong, and second to Thailand. He had also traveled throughout Africa exhaustively. In 2012, he reflected on his many travels and placed them in context, in which he described …[16]

> being abandoned in an Eskimo fishing village in Greenland; being caught in an exchange of gunfire between guerillas and the Filipino army in Mindanao; being part of a manifestation and attacked by the forces of order in 'La Grande Place' in Brussels; walking through the squatter camps in Santiago, Chile, with the Vicariate of Solidarity under the Pinochet regime; being bombed in Jaffna, Sri Lanka, at the start of that country's long civil war; bargaining for passage and perhaps for life, with soldiers who controlled the crossroads in the interior of the Congo; being refused entry to apartheid South Africa and deported helplessly from India, living in the indignities and shadows of Communist control in the lands of Eastern Europe. I learned I was not in control, and I also experienced personally what the Psalmist chanted long ago: "Put not your trust in princes."

Amid his increased traveling, the difficulties associated with George's post-polio disease gradually worsened. Over the years he had three orthopedic operations, which he believed always brought about a decrease in muscular ability. For a long period of his life, since the early 1960s, George went every five years to the Mayo Clinic in Rochester, Minnesota, for a complete physical. This arrangement had a mutual benefit for George and the medical research community, since they followed the effects of his childhood polio. When he was thirty-five, George said years later, doctors explained, "You have a stressful job, and you're the first generation of polio patients who will grow old with the disease. You're also the last, because of the effectiveness of the Salk vaccine. We'll follow you until you get the disease that will kill you."

Just after his father's death in 1984, George received a good health report — including very low cholesterol, which he attributed, in a July 4 letter to Father Jetté, to "the good effects of vino Italiano" — but his leg weakened by polio needed attention. Worn cartilage and stretched ligaments in the knee were causing pain, and the surgeon recommended either an operation or a brace. "That choice was easy for me," George wrote to Jetté. And so it was at that time that George was fitted with the brace he would wear the rest of his life — the same brace with which he was eventually buried. "I have an animus against orthopedic surgeons," he continued. "They always treat you like a slab of meat." At the end of that August, George wrote to another Oblate confrere that he had already had three adjustments to the brace. This course of treatment would be a regular occurrence for the next thirty years.

After having served six years as vicar general, George was overwhelmingly reelected to his second term during the 1980 Chapter. In a homily at the gathering, George turned his attention, as he so often did, to the endgame of Christian life: holiness.[17] He cited St. Paul's explanation that true holiness is a life "hidden in God." While George was busy during his years as vicar general, and even at times wrestled with how much he actually accomplished, he was a man of faith who trusted in God's plan, even when he struggled to comprehend it. "This true life remains hidden, even to the believer," he said in the homily. "Faith is not a set of answers to the riddle of existence. Faith is rather a belief that the fullness of our life remains always hidden to us but known to the Father." His own life bore witness to this, as he continued to live in trust and obedience as he neared the end of this phase of his life and looked to God for what was to come next.

SEVEN
Returning to America

*Culture is the object of our evangelization and not just the
sea in which we swim. To form Gospel-shaped people, the
Church must work to create Gospel-friendly cultures.*[1]

CARDINAL FRANCIS E. GEORGE, O.M.I.

Among the American friends Francis George kept up with over the
years was Bernard Law, who had been bishop of Springfield-Cape
Girardeau, Missouri. Pope John Paul II appointed Law as archbishop of
Boston in 1984, and created him a cardinal the following year. Because
George was living at the seminary in Pass Christian, Mississippi, while
Law was a priest of the statewide diocese of Natchez-Jackson, the two
had known each other for decades.

To describe Cardinal Law's legacy as complex is an understatement to say the least. It tells the story of a zealous evangelist and activist, as well as that of a bishop who spent his life in service to the Church and clearly taught the Faith. Law was the motivating force behind the publication of the *Catechism of the Catholic Church*. And yet the memory of these accomplishments is indelibly tainted by the gross mishandling of the clergy sexual abuse crisis in his archdiocese. This came about, in part, because he delegated far too much oversight to others on one hand, and ambitiously gave more attention to national and international affairs on the other, allowing administration of his archdiocese to slip from his hands. Long before the scandals in Boston that tarnished Law's name and strained George's friendship with him, Law was a vocal force for racial justice. As editor of the *Mississippi Register* — the diocesan newspaper of which he served as editor — Law took an unapologetically pro-integration stance. This forceful support of civil rights resulted in the loss of many subscribers, among other things, and made him the recipient of death threats. It was around the struggle for civil rights that George and Law found commonality in those early days.

George and Law kept in touch throughout the years, meeting during the time George lived in Rome. When Law became a bishop, George's correspondence with him often included George's own analyses and opinions on current affairs, especially his commentary regarding various documents written in that era by the National Council of Catholic Bishops (NCCB, later the United States Conference of Catholic Bishops). In one series of letters, George wrote not just to Law but also to his future predecessor in Chicago, then-Archbishop Joseph Bernardin, president of the episcopal conference from 1974 to 1977, to express certain hesitations regarding an impending document on nuclear disarmament. He followed up with a more familiar letter to Law, in which he noted in more detail the flaws he identified in the NCCB document's rhetoric.

Law's friendly relationship with the Oblates continued into his time as a diocesan bishop in Missouri, where the Oblates operated a minor seminary. As early as 1981, Law was attempting to establish a think tank and wanted George to be a part of it. That initiative would have to wait until George finished up his second mandate as vicar general, and it would not take shape until Law had moved to Boston. If George was to become involved in this project, he would need to avoid election as the next superior general at the 1986 General Chapter.

George was not elected, though — a conclusion that he had happily anticipated. Since Father Jetté had concluded two terms as superior general, he was not eligible for reelection to the post. George was likewise not elected to fill Jetté's shoes because religious congregations typically will not elect someone who has been so intimately involved in the general administration on the heels of two consecutive terms of the same superior. George wrote his provincial on February 5, 1986, "I'm looking forward to getting back to America after the Chapter, with help of God and remaining always open to the whisperings of the Spirit. I have prepared a speech for the Chapter, however, which should guarantee me a ticket out of here (joke — in part)." Looking back, on January 23, 1987, George wrote his successor as Oblate vicar general, then Fr. Giles Cazabon, "As I recall, it would be hard to judge if, during my twelve years in Rome, the moments of light were ever more numerous than the moments of darkness!"

RETURNING HOME

George knew he wanted to head back to the United States, but it was not entirely clear where he would make his home. Upon returning stateside, a sabbatical was in order, although George was hesitant about it. "It seems embarrassing to come back to the Province and immediately ask for time off!" he wrote his provincial on February 5, 1986. Given Law's invitation to assist with his new center in the Archdiocese of Boston, George decided to take his sabbatical there, deeming it wise to spend six months listening and relating to lay Catholics on a regular ministerial basis and see what they expected of their priests. First, though, he enjoyed a month-long homecoming tour of his home province, where he reunited with his Oblate confreres throughout the Midwest. He also reserved some time to spend with his family. After visiting his sister, Margaret, and her family in Grand Rapids, George rejoiced in his January letter to Cazabon, "I slept ten hours a night for two weeks at my sister's house, and I feel better rested than I have for several years."

George seemed ready for a change. He wrote a friend in a July 13, 1986, letter, just before the 1986 Chapter:

> After fourteen years in Oblate administration, much of that time with dying provinces, I have some convictions about what gives life and what brings death. There are places of life and places of death in the Congregation and the Church. Perhaps it's selfish, but I don't want to spend a lot more time with those who are dying, or sometimes killing themselves, and who keep insisting they are the wave of the future.

George long had a concern for ideological divisions in the Church in America, particularly among religious, even fearing how he would have to enter the fray and be bound to speak in certain circumstances. "I had hoped to keep my mouth shut to avoid being caught up in polarizations," he wrote in the July letter. Admitting that was unlikely, he explained, "Maybe that is impossible for me to do anyway, but I was convincing myself I could do it." He concluded: "So my plans are shot."

George could not escape being pigeonholed, despite his best efforts to avoid it. A 1997 article described his beliefs as having taken "a right turn" during his fourteen years in the Eternal City, in no small part due to the influence of the more traditional and spiritually insightful Father Jetté.[2] Many confreres have indeed noted the profound impact of Jetté's witness on George's outlook. For his part, Jetté proposed, "You know, if he became more prudent or more conservative in Rome, it might be because he had a chance to see the world firsthand. ... He saw the reality of all the things that he was idealistic about."

In other words, it was in Rome that George was able to experience Catholicism in all its breadth and fullness, which expanded his mind and heart more than his own experience of Catholicism in America had done to that point.

George also understood that it is typically an American trait to characterize religion by attaching political labels (i.e., "left" and "right"), and he challenged this practice time and again as polarization in the Church continued to fester, especially in the United States. Referencing a piece he submitted to *America* magazine but which was not accepted for publication, he wrote to Cazabon on December 20, 1988:

> It sets out, in broad outline, what I think of the political life in the United States right now and why I have in recent years become more critical of liberal programs. A number of men here interpret this to mean that I have become politically conservative, and that is a fair interpretation only if one has the two choices — liberal and conservative. The goal should be to change the conversation so that public life has more than the present two choices.

During George's return tour of Oblate missions around his province, he observed similar politicization within his congregation. What he encountered left him somewhat troubled. At the time he had moved to Rome, he was considered by many of his confreres as edgy, provocative, and even progressive — traits that were synonymous at the time with the more "liberal" trends in the Church. One confrere stated, "When he went to Rome he was one of us." At the time of his return to America, however, George had developed in his thinking. He wrote to a confrere in Rome on February 8, 1987, "When we invite a young man to be an Oblate, is there anything to join? The polarization that hurts the Church here [in the United States] is present among us as well, and this has resulted in avoiding some crucial questions. The Church seems healthy enough in parishes and among ordinary people. It's the religious professionals who are divided and, often, alienated."

As for his own future, George described this period to Father Cazabon, in the January 1987 letter, as a "watershed moment in my life." He explained, "Right now I don't yet see clearly where the call of the Lord might lead, but I trust him and am happy to wait a few months and finish immediate projects." Chief among those was completing his second dissertation, which George had begun researching at the Pontifical Urban University in Rome while still serving as vicar general. George finished the draft of this dissertation during his six-month quasi-sabbatical in Boston, even as he reacquainted himself with American society and got settled in his new home.

George's dissertation — *Inculturation and Ecclesial Communion: Culture and Church in the Teaching of Pope John Paul II* — examined the sainted pope's teaching on culture and ecclesial communion.[3] As the means of interpretation, George relied on the philosophical anthropology of Karol Wojtyła (the future Pope St. John Paul II), which integrated modern philosophical anthropology with the classical theological vision of the human person's nature and destiny. The dissertation, which he described in a proposal as "an exercise in ecclesial self-consciousness," aimed to offer a unique theological contribution extending from the teaching of the Second Vatican Council. It incorporated a significant focus on the theological topic of inculturation, then (and still) hotly debated, which he said is ultimately "judged by the fullness of Catholic communion." To these themes he turned again on many occasions throughout his life. He successfully defended his dissertation in November 1987, earning his second doctorate, this one in sacred theology. The two terminal degrees George earned were the same two that John Paul II earned, one apiece in philosophy and theology.

After years of administration, much of which he never particularly relished, George longed to immerse himself again in a life of study, research, and teaching. Aside from the Boston offer, other options were on the table, including a professorship at the Urbanianum in Rome, a theological fellowship at Yale University, and an invitation to become a visiting scholar in the Harvard philosophy department. Despite not having much apparent interest in a position in the Roman Curia, George was interviewed for one by then-Archbishop Alberto Bavone, who served as secretary for the Congregation for the Doctrine of the Faith under prefect

Cardinal Joseph Ratzinger.

In his own words, George described in his January 1987 letter to Cazabon his current status: *"Je marche plus dans les ténèbres que la lumière,"* French for "I walk more in the darkness than in the light." But, he added, *"Avec confiance cependant,"* meaning "However, with confidence." It seemed George had his misgivings about joining the Cambridge Center. "The Church is much more polarized here than I had expected, and we don't need one more source of tension." But he admitted in the same letter, "I feel I owe it to Cardinal Law to look into the possibility of setting up this think tank. I'd promised him I'd help. Please pray that I'll do what's best for the Church."

The Cambridge Center for the Study of Faith and Culture in Boston, where George was headed, was the brainchild of Cardinal Bernard Law. Cardinal Law was also instrumental in the growth of the Pope John XXIII Medical-Moral Research and Education Center, now known as the National Catholic Bioethics Center. Law was a mission-driven leader, remembered for a panoply of new initiatives in the Boston archdiocese and beyond. Respected then for his pastoral skills and vision, Law had become a figure of national prominence and leadership within the American Church.

George committed himself to the work of the Cambridge Center for almost three years with the permission and support of his provincial, under whose authority the former vicar general had been returned by new Oblate superior general Marcello Zago. In many ways, George was an ideal candidate to help guide the center from its inception. Not only had he obtained his doctorate in American philosophy from Tulane in New Orleans, which enabled him to more accurately read American culture by identifying its pragmatic philosophical underpinnings, but he was also just completing his second doctorate. The topic of this second dissertation was just as relevant as his first to the focus of the Cambridge Center.

George settled into his new Boston home, a house on the edge of Boston College, about a half-mile from Cardinal Law's residence in

Brighton. In the area also lived Holy Cross Sr. Madonna Murphy, who coordinated the center, and others, such as Philadelphia priest and scholar Msgr. Richard Malone, who participated in its work. The latter recalled that George was considered by Law as a perfect example of what the American hierarchy needed.

The vision Law set forth for the Cambridge Center came from, according to a descriptive pamphlet on the center, a recognition that America's unique perspective on the human person arose from "a tangle of old values, new spiritual hungers and dramatic developments in science, law and communications." The center's self-described *raison d'etre* was to help "make the Gospel message about redeemed humanity a force today, in this culture, in words it will understand, with scholarship it must respect." Law had hoped, according to the pamphlet, that the center would allow Catholic scholars to "study and learn from trends in contemporary American culture, while developing ways in which the Church might better humanize the culture's development." The think tank was also meant to have a collegial spirit, facilitating common prayer and personal study among the scholars and giving them opportunities for publication, in addition to offering regular seminars.

At the heart of the center was the Circle of Fellows, chaired by George, comprised of scholars intrigued by identifying points of convergence between the culture and Catholic Faith, while simultaneously evangelizing and transforming the friction points of those two entities. The center grounded itself in the unique character of Pope St. John Paul II's Christian anthropology, proposing that this thinking was the doorway to modern dialogue between faith and culture. George's fellows were charged to "work with others to transform the culture, so that the Gospel of Christ will influence tendencies in the arts and in communications, in the care of the dying and the healing of the living, in education and economics."

While at the center, George began contributing to noteworthy American Catholic publications by writing a variety of semi-popular pieces, as well as making significant contributions to different scholarly journals.

Fr. General Zago wrote, on November 18, 1989, "Continue to write, you have a gift! I am convinced we can extend our mission through writings." George also contributed to the life of the local Church in Boston through participation in various committees and by giving talks.

At the center, George was working on a project called "American Mission — an investigation for American purpose from the perspective of the theology of history." He hoped this initiative would give rise to a public discussion "about what it means to be both American and Catholic." Plans were underway to organize symposia as well. Unfortunately, though, the center encountered a number of setbacks early on which kept it from accomplishing its task. A variety of factors, including lack of collegiality and poor funding, prevented it from ever successfully getting off the ground. This was a source of frustration and disappointment for George.

An Oblate who lived with George at the time, Fr. Charles Breault, attributed the center's difficulties to a lack of intellectual curiosity, which undoubtedly contributed further to George's frustration. During a 1997 interview, in what seems to be a common mischaracterization and fundamental misunderstanding of George's positions, Breault criticized George's inability to entertain certain questions — even those on which the pope had spoken authoritatively.[4] "I know the pope said we can't ordain women. But how do you stop thinking about the issue?" Breault said. "What bothers me is that there is a certain area where [George's] mind won't let him go."

As far as George was concerned, however, "all priestly virtue is a habit of surrendering oneself to Christ for the sake of his people," as he explained in a 2003 address at Mount St. Mary's Seminary.[5] He argued that "in the virtue of faith, which is a virtue that is infused and also one that grows as we come to study and understand the contents of the act of faith in a more explicit fashion, there is a surrender of one's mind." He regarded it "a great tragedy when the Creed, which is a great proclamation of praise and thanksgiving because God has revealed the truth that makes us free, is interpreted as a loyalty oath." That means, he said, "that some don't understand the connection between freedom and truth."

While living in Boston, George celebrated the twenty-fifth anniversary of his ordination to the priesthood. He enjoyed assisting at parishes around Boston, including St. Camillus in Arlington and St. Patrick in Brockton. He revealed in a March 25, 1988, letter to Father General Zago, "Perhaps I'm most enjoying the pastoral work in a parish not too far from the center. ... At least once a month I also have Sunday liturgy for a group of refugees from Haiti who want Mass in French. I'm happy to have that kind of pastoral work."

Years later, after George's death, Fr. Roger Landry of the Diocese of Fall River, Massachusetts, recalled George's ministry at St. Paul's Church near Harvard.[6] Landry, who was an undergraduate at Harvard, recalled that George regularly celebrated Masses for students. Landry captured George's unassuming, pastoral presence:

> Those of us who were daily Mass goers were fortunate to have so many fine priests and great preachers at and around St. Paul's at the time helping out with Masses. Four of them went on to become bishops, another to become a provincial and others to head up major departments for Dioceses or Universities. The quality of pastoral care was so high that — I'm embarrassed to say — I took for granted "Father George," the diminutive giant of a priest who would celebrate about once a week. His deep, somewhat academic homilies were a testimony to how much he knew and how much my fellow students and I needed to learn.
>
> When I came back for my junior year, he was no longer on the schedule and I didn't know what had happened to him until one Sunday I read in the bulletin before Mass a note from the pastor welcoming back to St. Paul's "Bishop Francis George of Yakima, Washington, who helped at daily Masses at St. Paul's from 1987–1990." I was bewildered that I couldn't recall any priest whose first name was Francis or last name was George during that time. But as we stood for the Opening Hymn, I saw "Father George" with

his familiar limp, a result of childhood polio, ambling toward the altar, this time with a zucchetto on his smooth crown. Once I got over my confusion that I had always thought his last name was his first, I was left stunned in my juvenile, ecclesiastical myopia that they had made him a bishop, since he always seemed more like my professors than like any bishops I knew. Thanks be to God, Pope John Paul II and his advisors saw what I was missing!

LEAVING BOSTON

In a November 8, 1989, letter, George wrote to Father General Zago that it would be his final year in Boston. "The province is asking me to direct the setting up of structures and programs for the Oblate-lay collaboration [and] … I am happy to get into this." George added: "I will leave Boston with some regret, mostly because this Center is not solidly established, and I hate to leave something in a precarious state. My own work here has been a source of some satisfaction to me, and I have especially enjoyed the ministry I've done in several of the parishes and on the diocesan level, in committees, but the structures of the Center are still in flux and its financial status is precarious." Ultimately, regarding the center, he explained in a November 5, 1989, letter to his provincial, "The idea is good, the institutionalization is defective, and I am coming to believe other means could be more effective in serving the faith/culture dialogue in the Church. Finally it's that service which counts."

The Cambridge Center eventually dissolved after being transferred and subsumed into a similar effort already underway at The Catholic University of America in Washington, DC. And its demise might have been hastened by George's departure. In 1990, as the center was struggling to get off the ground and obtain the support and interest it needed, a figure like George was a key to keeping things afloat. Many letters went back and forth between George's Oblate provincial, Fr. James Deegan, and Cardinal Law. The province made its case to Law time and again that George's involvement at the center would need to come to an end, as they determined needs for George to fulfill within the wider Oblate ministerial efforts in the United States. Law repeatedly asked for an extension of George's permission to serve the center, but it was ultimately rejected by the Oblates. In early 1990, the Oblates also turned down an invitation for George to take up a position with the philosophy department at The Catholic University of America. The provincial informed George in a June 6, 1990, letter, "In the last two years, Francis, I have had more requests for your services than I have received for any other Oblate."

The final correspondence between Cardinal Law and George's Oblate provincial was in August 1989. The provincial had kindly informed Cardinal Law that George would be assigned to the central province on July 1, 1990. He was destined for Belleville, Illinois, once again, this time to direct a program overseeing Oblate collaboration with and animation of lay ministry. George wrote to Zago in a March 14, 1990, letter, "I think I'm ready for a bit more activity. One problem will be to remain intellectually alive."

As he prepared for the new role coordinating Oblate collaboration with the laity, George said in his November 5 letter to his provincial, "I think I should spend the first year giving talks and really listening, especially to lay people. I'll have to have some help in figuring out how we should go about doing this. It will help if I learn to keep my mouth shut for longer periods of time." Slated to assist him on the board that would oversee this effort was his Oblate confrere from the Ottawa scholasticate Fr. Roger Schwietz. That collaboration never came to fruition, however, since Schwietz was named bishop of Duluth, Minnesota, in December 1989.

George was hoping to live at an Oblate formation house near Saint Louis University, which would afford him opportunities for research and to foster the intellectual life. He indicated not much worry on his part in a November 5 letter to his provincial: "Provided I can get a good mattress and some bookcases I'll be alright." There was some consideration that he might live with the Oblate community in Belleville, but that seemed to be put on hold, as he learned that "I frighten people — me, the most mild-mannered of men." A straw ballot of Oblates in his province showed George was a contender to be the next provincial, and he had been named to the provincial council.

As his superiors debated George's next assignment, the correspondence with his provincial shows that he was nothing but open to whatever they deemed best for the mission of the congregation. His own preferences, if any were mentioned, were usually identified in a subsequent letter, reiterating his obedience to the needs of the community. He was perfectly content with moving to Belleville and taking on the new post, even writing a Canadian Oblate in mid-June to communicate his upcoming change of address to Illinois.

Sometime at the end of June, however, just as George was preparing for the move to Belleville, things abruptly changed. George received a phone call from the apostolic nunciature in Washington, DC, informing him that Pope John Paul II had appointed him the fifth bishop of Yakima, Washington. Cardinal Law had intervened.

A NEW MISSION

Once he had been appointed to Boston and received the red hat, Cardinal Bernard Francis Law, Archbishop of Boston, became a major power player in the American hierarchy. He knew talent when he saw it, and he did his best to serve the Church's interests by seeing to it that such talent was used well.

Law was regularly consulted on episcopal appointments by Cardinal John J. O'Connor of New York and by Cardinal William W. Baum, who was then serving as Major Penitentiary, or head, of the Apostolic Penitentiary, the dicastery of the Roman Curia responsible for the granting of indulgences and related matters. Baum was a longtime friend and mentor to Law, his predecessor as bishop of Springfield-Cape Girardeau and the former archbishop of Washington, DC. At the time of George's appointment as a bishop, both O'Connor and Baum served as members of the Holy See's Congregation for Bishops. After O'Connor's death in 2000, Law himself assumed this most consequential post, in which he exercised a decisive role in the nomination of candidates for the episcopate in the United States — a position often dubbed "kingmaker."

In George's case, Law seems to have helped render the final word to the Oblates in reply to taking George away from his center. Law saw the potential of underusing George's talent, no doubt, and put him forward as a candidate for the episcopacy. And for good reason.

Father George was not so sure. "Does the Holy Father realize I don't even know where Yakima is?" George replied to the nuncio upon receiving the call that informed him Pope John Paul II desired him to lead a diocese in central Washington state.[7] George was against the idea of being named a bishop and did not relish a potential move to the Diocese of Yakima. The night before the Fourth of July holiday, George went to Washington, DC, on a mission. According to the Oblate confrere Fr. Thomas Singer, who picked him up at the train station that evening, George intended to go to the nunciature after the holiday and decline the appointment in person.

True to his word, on July 5, George articulated his concerns to the *chargés d'affaires* at the nunciature, admitting he was ignorant of the situation in central Washington and asserting that he believed someone else, such as a priest of Yakima, would be better suited for the post. In return, George was reminded that he was a member of a missionary congregation and had promised to go where he was sent. How could he say no? As an Oblate, he was one of de Mazenod's "men of the pope." He could not turn against everything that he was trained and had promised to do. Upon receiving this reply, George accepted the nomination, returned to Boston, and wrote to Cazabon in a July 18 letter, "I'll have to change my style now and become less argumentative. That sacramental grace had better be pretty powerful." On a more serious note, he added, "I regret that I won't be as directly involved [with the Oblate congregation] as I might have been; and I deeply regret that I won't be able to go back and live like a brother among the Oblates I grew up with." Nevertheless, he concluded with acceptance. "This is a strange turn of events, Gilles, but I take it as God's will."

Despite George's initial reluctance to accept the post, he would grow to love the Yakima Valley and its people to such a great degree that, almost six years later upon his departure for Portland, he was dubbed "the Good Bishop" by the Yakima newspaper.

But first, he had to get there. Within the next few days, after he consented to the appointment, George prepared for a trip to Yakima during which he would be hosted under the guise of "Father George," a special guest who had come to give a talk to chancery staff. He left a note on the desk of the religious brother who oversaw his Boston religious house, informing him of the impending appointment and asking for his secrecy.

The path on which George set out when he entered St. Henry's Preparatory Seminary in Belleville and on which he continued when he made first vows with the Oblates of Mary Immaculate at the novitiate in Godfrey did not, at that time, set him on the path to climb the ecclesiastical ladder. So it was no small irony that up that ladder he advanced.

Yakima seemed to be the perfect fit in many ways. At this point in his life, culture was George's game. Having helped lead a major congregation of missionaries for over a decade, he was a natural leader for a diocese imbued with a missionary spirit and an outreach to several divergent cultures. Never mind, as he admitted in 1991, that he was "beginning to suspect that Yakima doesn't really have 300 days of sunshine every year."[8]

EIGHT
A Missionary Bishop

*The bishop is the center of unity, visible unity — the Holy Spirit
is the center of invisible unity in the Church — so you try to
keep people together for the sake of the mission. Whatever
is necessary for that purpose is what I've tried to do.[1]*

CARDINAL FRANCIS GEORGE, O.M.I.

Francis George arrived in Washington's Yakima Valley on July 9, 1990. His new diocese and its see city gained its name from the Yakima people, the original inhabitants of the region. In 1855, the US government created the Yakima Indian Reservation, the existence of which itself caused strife and violence for nearly two decades. The region offers a smorgasbord of natural beauty, encompassing a beautiful display of mountains, rivers, and other majesties of the natural world. The climate and nutrient-rich landscape lend themselves — with the assistance of irrigation — to extensive production of fruits, vegetables, and other agricultural goods. George quickly grew fond of the gorgeous, scenic hills surrounding the valley.

At the time George arrived, the Yakima diocese was just under forty years old, having been established by Pope Pius XII in 1951 from territory belonging to the Seattle and Spokane dioceses. The Catholic population within the diocese hovered at around 12 percent.

The lifelong missionary had his work cut out for him as the diocese's new bishop. The day before his appointment as fifth bishop of Yakima became official, word in the chancery was that an overly educated northeasterner might not be the best fit. But in short order, George's quick wit and sense of humor both impressed and disarmed. His instructions on the phone for the priests meeting him at the airport were, "I'm short, bald, and lame." About two weeks after his appointment, in a July 23 letter, George wrote the chancery to expect forty boxes of books he had just packed up. "Perhaps we had better rent space at the library at Yakima. It's a bit embarrassing to find oneself with all these books, but I don't know what else to do with them but bring them."[2]

George made his home in a small apartment on the third floor of the school at St. Paul's Cathedral and insisted on having a chapel installed before he moved in. He often concelebrated daily Masses with the cathedral's legendary rector, Msgr. John Ecker, who had been pastor there for several decades and wore many hats in the diocesan curia. At one point, George considered moving into a house, but he decided against it ultimately because he preferred, instead, to solicit funds for schools and other projects. He encouraged Monsignor Ecker to have common meals prepared at the cathedral rectory for the priests, accustomed to community life as he was — although Ecker noted that when he started to try that, George was on the road most of the time. The plans were scrapped, although they still regularly shared meals together at local restaurants.

As George got settled into his new environment, he was busy attending to the details that are part of any episcopal ordination. George designed his coat of arms to resemble that of then-Blessed Eugene de Mazenod, founder of the Oblates. George had also requested that his congregation's founder be added to the Litany of the Saints during the ordination rite, along with the names of then-Blessed Kateri Tekakwitha (the first Native American to be beatified), St. John Neumann (the first and only American bishop to have been canonized), and St. Martin de Porres (a mixed-race Dominican friar and patron of racial harmony). He wanted the liturgy to be an expression of diversity, and he sought to incorporate as many cultures in various ministries within the liturgy as possible. George requested that a woman religious proclaim one of the readings and that one of the local farmers carry up an apple or two in the offertory procession.

As a religious and an intellectual, George had a learning curve ahead of him when it came to shepherding the Diocese of Yakima. Not only had he never been a full-time pastor, but the majority of his new fold was Spanish-speaking. An immersion course in Spanish was quickly arranged, during which George spent a month in Cuernavaca, Mexico, prior to his ordination and installation on September 21, 1990. The language instructor recalled to a member of George's chancery staff a few years later that she never had a student pick up the language so quickly. His ability was no doubt enhanced by the fluency in Italian he had acquired after twelve years of living in Italy.

George's nearly two-and-a-half-hour-long bilingual ordination liturgy was held at the large Holy Family Church in Yakima in order to accommodate crowds the city's St. Paul Cathedral could not. The night before, a celebration of Evening Prayer was held at the cathedral, during which the symbols of George's office were blessed and he was blessed by all the priests of the diocese while kneeling in the center of the sanctuary. At a dinner in his honor afterward, George recalled a passage from the Second Book of Kings in which Elisha cursed boys who mocked the prophet's baldness and two bears came from the woods to destroy them. He joked that some friends suggested he adopt that passage as his episcopal motto. Later, George admitted in an interview that he tried very hard to hide the fact that he liked being bald. That made it all the funnier when, at one staff Christmas party in Yakima, George was saddled with a hairdryer from the white elephant gift table.

At the ordination Mass, Bishop George was described in Pope John Paul II's letter of appointment as "a man truly worthy and prepared to sustain" the task of serving Yakima on account of his "priestly virtues and outstanding human qualities." The pope poignantly instructed George, drawing from the theme of his disability, to assist the flock entrusted to his care "so that they may walk without difficulty as healthy sheep, that the infirm may recuperate from their ills, that the wandering, having heard your voice calling them, may return to the sheepfold from which they strayed inadvisably."

During the Mass, an argument took place between the master of ceremonies, Monsignor Ecker, and the apostolic nuncio. "This was going on over my head just as the nuncio was supposed to be putting his hands on that head, and it didn't serve to reinforce the confidence in the work of the Holy Spirit that I was trying to stir up in my own heart," George recalled years later.[3]

At the end of the Mass, as reported in the newsletter of his native Oblate province, George told his flock, "Now that I'm your bishop, my life is yours." During these final remarks, George endeared himself to the people of the diocese by making reference to a theme he would mention at different points throughout his tenure in Yakima. Detailing the physical limitations caused by his bout with childhood polio, George explained he was prone to falls.[4] "I get around fairly well," he said, "but occasionally, two or three times a year, if the way is slippery or I'm not watching my step, I fall. ... So if this happens when I'm visiting you, don't get excited; just reach down and pick me up, and we'll go on together." After roaring applause, George went on:

> What concerns me ... is that I still might fail in other ways. That
> I might fail from a lack of patience to listen carefully to what you
> tell me is on your mind and in your heart; that I will fail to lack

the wisdom to understand what I must do and what we must do together so that the Church may grow and the Gospel may be reaching forth ... that I will make a mistake in judgment and someone will be hurt; that I will forget a fact, a name, a place, a face that you have the right to expect me to remember. ... If any of this happens, when it happens, don't get excited, just reach down and pick me up, and we'll go on together.

The apostolic nuncio, then-Archbishop Agostino Cacciavillan, was chosen by George to be the principal celebrant of the Mass, a bit unusual given the custom of having the metropolitan archbishop preside at an episcopal ordination within his province. At the time, however, tensions that had arisen first more than a decade before still persisted between the Holy See and Archbishop Raymond Hunthausen of Seattle, Yakima's metropolitan. A Holy See-directed visitation of Hunthausen had been provoked by his many controversial stances, including the refusal to pay half of his income taxes because of federal stockpiling of nuclear weapons in his archdiocese. The investigation concluded, among other things, that Hunthausen was doctrinally weak in certain areas. The situation dissipated soon after George's ordination when Hunthausen's early resignation was accepted by the pope.

Hunthausen did help lead George to the cathedral during the installation Mass in his new diocese. George's friend and Oblate confrere Roger Schwietz, who had been ordained a bishop about six months previously, was one of the co-consecrators, as was George's Yakima predecessor Bishop William Skylstad. Skylstad's whirlwind departure from Yakima for Spokane — brought about by scandals related to his predecessor's alcoholism, and, it would emerge later, sexual misconduct — meant that George's own episcopal ministry, from its earliest days, had as a backdrop the various scandals surrounding bishops and priests that would later absorb much of his episcopal tenure. It was amid the early days of this crisis of the clergy that George would provide clarity and leadership throughout his ministry as a bishop. Skylstad was installed in Spokane a record ten days after his appointment. And nationally, on the same day George was named a bishop, Atlanta archbishop Eugene Marino's resignation was accepted. Marino, who had been the nation's first Black archbishop, retired to take on "spiritual renewal, psychological therapy and medical supervision" after revelations that he had been involved in a longtime affair with a female Church employee whom he had secretly married two years previously.

Gayle Miller, secretary to Skylstad and, under George, the first female vice-chancellor of the diocese, recalled the devastation at hearing Skylstad was leaving Yakima, a small, rural diocese of about 60,000 Catholics at the time, a majority of whom spoke Spanish. "This man is coming to Yakima, what on earth?" Miller recalled wondering about George's arrival. But she quickly came to love her new boss. "He could relate to everybody," she said. "He wasn't a climber."

George hired Michele Schumacher as director of social justice ministry and of the family life office, which George established in Yakima. Schumacher recalled how personable George was. "For all of his intelligence and all of the positions that he held, he was very down to earth and very real," she said. "His intelligence was such that he was never intimidated. He had no problem always saying what he thought. You always knew where you stood with him."

George got right to work, and visiting parishes every weekend was a top priority. He made his way around the diocese to help lead parish anniversaries, celebrate confirmations, and even sometimes fill in for a pastor who was away. Given the vastness of the desert diocese and the lengthy distances between parishes, George would often stay the night in the parish's rectory. As he approached two years in office, though, and as other duties increased locally and nationally, George became concerned he was not getting enough time with parish communities. He made it clear that he wanted to come to know what was on the hearts and minds of the people in his flock, what fears and concerns they had and in what context they lived their faith. To address these concerns, he began extended parish visitations, during which he spent several days in a parish, meeting with all concerned constituencies, celebrating daily Mass, and getting to know the people of his flock more intimately.

"The people really got to love him, especially the Hispanic people, and he had a special love for them," recalled Msgr. Perron Auve, George's first chancellor in Yakima. Schumacher recalled, "He was a very educated man who knew how to meet simple people. ... He was comfortable with it, he loved it, and they loved him. And he spoke their language, which was amazing to me, because he was such an intellectual. He knew how to address people where they were at." On one of his trips across the state, George, who was known to stay awake late into the night working or reading, fell asleep at the wheel and totaled his car. He was fortunate to walk away from the crash without an injury. From then on, he often had a driver accompanying him, especially for events at night.

Monsignor Auve also noted that George had a special place in his heart for the diocese's poorer parishes. "I think he had a special kind of understanding of poverty probably because of his vows. This diocese is poor. I mean, we don't have very much money at all, and he didn't want us to pack up a lot of money either." In the late 1960s, the Yakima diocese was in deep financial trouble, and Cardinal James McIntyre and the Archdiocese of Los Angeles helped oversee a plan to save the diocese from financial disaster. The diocese continued to rely on the generosity of many others throughout the country, including grants from the Catholic Extension Society based in Chicago. Bishop Skylstad worked to overcome further financial woes, and George finally retired the diocesan debts. When George arrived in Yakima, he found that the diocese had no savings in reserve, which left it virtually unable to help parishes in need. As a mission diocese, Yakima's needs were greater than what its people could provide for themselves. It troubled George, shortly after he arrived, that he had to deny a parish financial help to replace a church roof because the diocese had insufficient funds. So George put in place various structures to help set the diocese on a more solid financial footing.

In Yakima, after a close examination of Catholic social teaching, George proposed to chancery staff that the diocese should pay a family

wage, not just an individual wage. "So I redid the wage scales according
to the number of children for which people were responsible," George
recalled in 2003. "In other words, I was paying people for their relationships rather than for their production and the lawyers immediately told
me, 'You don't dare do that because that contradicts equal pay for equal
work and you will be put in jail if you try to do it.'"[5]

"As you know," George wrote on July 18, 1990, to Fr. Gilles Cazabon, his successor as Oblate vicar general, "it's better to have good people
and no money than the reverse." Once asked what three wishes he would
want granted if given the opportunity, George answered, "1. Greater love
across racial and cultural boundaries; 2. More conversation in families; 3.
The third wish I'd give to the poorest person in Yakima County."[6] George
could also be generous from his own resources, a fact that was not widely known. On one occasion, when a member of his chancery staff was
buying a home and had trouble making ends meet — especially in light
of the low salary paid to an employee of a mission diocese — George
offered a private loan. After he moved away, he forgave the unpaid debt
in an off-hand comment he made after his installation in the Archdiocese of Portland. "That's just the kind of guy he was," his former staffer
recalled.

For George, the material was much less important than the theological and spiritual, and the people of his diocese understood that. As a
rule, they knew what George believed. He stated the Catholic Faith very
clearly and succinctly in his homilies and talks throughout the diocese, as
well as in his bimonthly column in the diocesan newspaper, the *Central
Washington Catholic*. George not only shared the timeless truths of the
Faith with ease and eloquence, but also related them to the challenges
and situations of the day with characteristic clarity and candor. Gayle
Miller recalled that working for George was an on-the-job course in
Church teaching. "My faith deepened. I learned so much about my faith
from him," she said.

While working for George, Michele Schumacher quickly came to
find him as a man who "knew the truth," adding, "there was a strength

to be had in that ... so masculine, such certitude and strength. He was a fortress." Schumacher also recalled that George was "a perfectionist," particularly when it came to writing letters. Monsignor Auve called him "a real wordsmith." George could also sometimes be irascible. Though he did not talk about it, he was in a lot of pain as the effects of his post-polio disease advanced in different ways. In general, George's health struggles remained relatively stable, aside from a fall here or there, during his time in Yakima. In the fall of 1995, he had to undergo an operation for continued problems in his right leg. Although no bone operation was needed, he had internal bleeding above the knee, which necessitated cauterization of torn muscles as well as veins. His brace, which had been putting strain on his muscles, was corrected as well.

George is remembered also for the good rapport he had with his staff in Yakima. When he hired Ree Kearns as his diocesan director of religious education, she learned that she was not his first choice, so she confronted him about it. He said he was hoping for someone with more formal theological training, but in the end it did not work out that way. The two hit it off well, nonetheless, and Kearns found him to be a great role model. "He and I always joked about the challenge that our relationship with Christ isn't just about the head knowledge, but the heart knowledge," she recalled, observing that "most people that knew him thought of him only as a head person." That made her "sad," though, since she knew "he just had a big heart and showed it to me in many, many ways."

Despite occasional disagreements, Kearns recalled how George challenged her positively "to pretty much back up what I was saying, maybe about a particular issue or whatever and how to articulate the faith effectively." George, Kearns said, was "willing to listen to your opinions, your thoughts or your suggestions, but you had to have reasons for them." Miller recalled the same response from George when she once approached him about a teaching on the Church with which she did not agree. "You always had to defend your position," she said. Schumacher recalled George's convictions as "very strong," adding, "he was not a pushover in any way. If he felt strongly about an issue, he would not back down in any way. He possessed a real confidence. That man, when he took a position, he knew he was right. He was absolutely convinced this is the truth and nothing is going to change about it."

BUILDING UP THE LOCAL CHURCH

There was a poetic and providential connection between George and the earliest seeds of faith planted in the Yakima Valley. In 1847, three Oblate brothers from France arrived there and established what is now referred to as the Ahtanum Mission, just a few miles to the west of the city.

Fr. Charles Pandosy, one of those three original Oblates in the Pacific Northwest, was ordained a priest the following year — the first known ordination in what is now the American state of Washington. Emblematic of the poverty to which Father Pandosy was committed in ministry, his nightshirt functioned as his alb. As wars between the US Army and the Native Americans raged on, the Oblates were driven out of the area for suspected support of the Indians, and their mission was burned to the ground in 1855. It was later rebuilt in 1867. Given the threat posed to their safety by the US government, the Oblates retreated to British Columbia, Canada. In God's providence, through George's appointment, an Oblate became bishop of the area from which they were once tossed out — and it came just three years after the US Army formally apologized to the Church in the presence of Bishop Skylstad for burning the mission and treating the Oblates so badly. As the fifth bishop of Yakima, George assumed the mantle of his predecessors and those early Oblate missionaries who helped establish the Church in central Washington. It is quite apropos, then, that George was naturally at home in Yakima. "He loved Yakima," Schumacher recalled. "I found it so intriguing how he was in his element. I guess it corresponds to the mission that he found with the Oblates. He was truly a missionary priest, a man made for evangelization."

When he is first appointed, each bishop chooses an episcopal motto, a phrase which reflects his heart and mind and indicates his pastoral priorities. George chose as his *Christo gloria in Ecclesia* (To Christ be Glory in the Church), taken from St. Paul's Letter to the Ephesians (3:21) as a scriptural form of the traditional greeting *Laudetur Jesus Christus*, commonly used in religious communities like the Oblates. He chose Latin instead of English or Spanish to build a unifying bridge between Yakima's two cultures. The motto expressed the Good News of Jesus Christ, which George announced to the Church and society through his ministry. It also set the stage for the task that lay before him: to unite the Church and, as a bishop, to bring many disparate parts of Christ's Body together to give God praise and glory. It can be seen as the foundation for his approach to ministry and his priorities and plans. "If a priest loves his people, if a deacon loves his service to the Church, a parish flourishes, no matter the deficiencies of the ordained minister," he wrote to his clergy on July 3, 1992. "If the priest is too concerned about his own agenda, his own preferences, if he withholds his love because of fear or insecurity or selfishness, the people withdraw and the parish withers," he observed. "Ministry is a joy to the extent it is a form of loving."

George did not have to reinvent the wheel in Yakima, but he employed his own gifts and talents to augment the work of renewal begun by Bishop Skylstad. George began with a focus on the renewal of priestly life in the diocese, writing to the presbyterate on December 12, 1991, "Priests cannot call the people to renewal unless we have first begun to be an instrument of renewal ourselves." In one of his columns in the diocesan newspaper, he encouraged the faithful to inquire among their priests about their renewal program and to pray for their priests. In a letter on the Solemnity of the Sacred Heart of Jesus in 1994, George implored his priests, "As you mention my name after our Holy Father's in each Mass in our diocese, I ask you to make it a true prayer that I may become a saint in my ministry to you and, with you, to our people." One year he gave Thomas à Kempis's devotional *The Imitation of Christ* to his priests as a Christmas gift.

George was not entirely well-received by the priests of the diocese, at least not at first. Some were a little leery of him being an outsider, a religious, and an academic. He was met with resistance early on from members of the presbyterate when he wanted to move away from using general absolution at communal penance services. "I hope discussion can take place in a spirit of detachment, discernment and openness to God's will in this matter," he wrote to the priests of the diocese about the situation in a November 1, 1990, letter. "If we are internally divided, Christ cannot easily use us to unite his people and the world," he said. Some of his priests advised him to take his time in applying this change. While he followed their advice and moved more slowly than he had first intended, he eventually implemented the change. At the same time, he published a pastoral letter on the Sacrament of Reconciliation. He was deeply concerned about the diminished liturgical reverence he saw on visits to the parishes, and other sacramental and liturgical guidelines were forthcoming regularly during his tenure.

Despite the tensions at times, George loved his priests in Yakima. His letters to them were geared to help them be effective pastors, to read the signs of the time and guide their flock amid ecclesial and societal changes and challenges. He gave them wise spiritual counsel, had great candor, and was open and honest, keeping them abreast of his own life and sharing his challenges and concerns. Often the letters he wrote to his priests were familial in tone and read like his communications to Oblate confreres.

George also challenged his people and their priests to respond to Church teaching more robustly. He initiated diocesan facilitation of natural family planning courses and repeatedly worked to promote it during his tenure. When only two couples showed up to the first diocesan-sponsored class early in his tenure, George wrote to his priests in a March 18, 1992, letter and asked them to be more deliberate about promoting the program. Situating artificial contraception in the cultural situation, he said that ignoring it as a product of "our American penchant for seeing all laws as external imposition of individual freedom, is directly related to the high rates of divorce, promiscuity, abortion, child abuse, spousal abuse and teenage pregnancy." He added: "If we do not preach the Gospel, we cannot pastor the Church."

In 1995, on the Solemnity of the Sacred Heart of Jesus, in what turned out to be his last letter to Yakima's priests, George wrote: "I thank God for the priests of the Yakima diocese daily. But I also pray that the good will and fraternity we enjoy together may translate ever more effectively into a common will to work together, to model for the faithful the unity that Christ wills for his Church."

In his first year, George began listening sessions with priests as well as other groups, such as deacons, women religious, and laity. He kept such lines of communication open and welcomed conversation and feedback. By the time he left Yakima, the priests had gained much respect for his open and honest approach and for his ability to listen and keep open paths for dialogue. On his part, George took personal interest in the formation of priests, making regular trips with his vocation director to Mount Angel Seminary near Portland for the seminarians' evaluations. And he took special interest in helping seminary administrators and faculty overhaul the seminary curriculum.

Beginning in the 1980s, as more cases came to light, the American bishops began discussing the need to address the problem of clergy sexual abuse. By the early 1990s, many bishops were beginning to formulate their own protocols for handling this scourge, and George was no exception. Within his first six months in Yakima, he planned a workshop for priests and lay diocesan employees on "celibacy, sexuality, and sexual misconduct." He wrote to Yakima's priests on April 22, 1991, explaining, "As representatives and employees of the Church, it is essential that we are both well informed and highly responsible in this most sensitive area." In 1993, George produced the diocese's first formal policy regarding sexual misconduct.

On Holy Thursday 1993, he addressed the clergy scandals in a letter to his priests. "Celibacy, if embraced, can release great spiritual and psychological energies. If only half-heartedly accepted, celibacy can create a void, as it should, which might not be filled with God's love but with our own compulsions, as it should not. Then celibacy, while always a dangerous undertaking, becomes spiritually menacing," he wrote. More to the point, he said, "The Church is a scandal to the worldly when she is faithful to her Lord in her teaching and her acts. The Church is a scandal to the faithful when her members and her ministers dissent from teaching and excuse themselves from her prescriptions. The first scandal is our mission, the second is our shame." George invited the priests to recommit themselves to the mission received from Christ and called them to renewed conformity of mind and action to the demands of Christ and the instructions of the Church. "Then we will grow holy together," George instructed.

One of Yakima's more notorious abusers reportedly received a letter from George responding to the abuser's complaints of unfair treatment. George took him to task over his poor attitude. By today's standards, more might be expected, but at the time, George was working within what Church law permitted and expected him to do. At the same time, he engaged in no cover-ups of abuse, and any clergy who abused minors that George had to deal with had already been handled by his predecessor.

IN THE ARENA

George's arrival in the state of Washington coincided with two upcoming referenda on important life issues related to abortion and euthanasia, proposals that were emblematic of the Northwest region's libertarian individualism, a characteristic of both liberals and conservatives there. "Since people are often uneasy with arguments from principles," he wrote to Yakima's clergy on February 15, 1991, "public discussion is often limited now to comparing examples in order to prove a point and carry the day. Whoever can find the worst-case scenario wins the day, but laws based on this kind of reasoning are deficient. No matter what happens, the truth is the truth, and we have to keep finding ways to preach it and model it, kindly and persistently."

On October 1, 1991, George wrote to the faithful asking them to "take up their rosaries in order to ask Our Blessed Mother to protect us from a modern assault on human life." He continued: "Since life is a gift from God, it does not have to be strong and independent in order to be valuable. A human being in a civilized society does not have to be 'wanted' by anyone in order to merit legal protection." The move for further legal protections for abortion and the legalization of euthanasia, George said, will one day be seen for what it is: "public policy destructive of our lives and our society." He argued, "This may take years, just as it took several generations and a civil war to outlaw slavery in this country and long decades for Marxism to collapse in the Soviet Union." A week previously, George also supplied his priests with preaching notes to explain the seriousness of the issues facing the citizens of Washington, saying, in part, "When we preach about morality, it seems to me to be good to always explain why the Church teaches a particular action is immoral and not just state a conclusion. Above all, we must always hold out hope to all people."

George was vocal on life issues throughout his time as a bishop, particularly as they were brought up for public debate and considered for protection by law. In addition to his collaboration with the efforts of the Washington State Catholic Conference, George used his column in the diocesan paper to address the issues clearly and succinctly, explaining the Church's teaching to help form the consciences and intellects of his flock. The *Catechism of the Catholic Church* was promulgated by Pope John Paul II during George's time in Yakima, and George made the volume central to his teaching ministry.

In 1994, the Washington State Catholic Conference advocated against proposed ballot initiatives that would discriminate against homosexual persons, arguing that as they stood they might foster discrimination against homosexual persons and were, therefore, "morally wrong." The initiatives were eventually defeated. The same argument was used to denounce a bill proposing a new legal category for homosexuals and bisexuals based on their orientation.

As bishop of Yakima, George was regularly in the arena publicly commenting on issues of the day, and not infrequently via the "letter to the editor" department of various newspapers. As the Washington state bishops were assailed for their criticism of the bill, George wrote an op-ed for the *Seattle Post-Intelligencer*.[7] "This category is a mistake," George wrote, "and it misuses civil rights legislation. Civil rights categories protect individuals." They should not, he argued, be used to cover behavior. George expressed the concern of the state's bishops: that the law would prevent distinction of sexual orientation from behavior, which itself prohibits others from, among other things, raising children according to their own standards. For instance, he said, what would parents do if a teacher was living in an open same-sex relationship? "Parents have the right to insist that a teacher not model immoral behavior," George argued. He concluded: "It's not 'enlightened' to saddle Washington State with bad laws."

A follow-up letter to the editor expressed the author's surprise that the outlet ran an op-ed from a Catholic bishop, which he found "oh, so hopeful." Another letter to the editor from a different reader opined that George's op-ed failed to hide his bigotry, which could not have been further from the truth.

That same year, in a letter to the editor printed in Seattle's archdiocesan paper, *The Catholic Northwest Progress*, George took issue with the outlet's coverage of a talk on implications of Pope John Paul II's 1993 encyclical *Veritatis Splendor*, which he gave to the local St. Thomas More Society.[8] "Since the talk was technical, your reporter and I informally agreed to meet after the conference in order to clear up any points and assure an accurate story. I am sorry that conversation never took place. Now I have to say that what appeared in *The Progress* seemed garbled to me," George wrote. "The way your presentation of my talk ends, however, I seem to espouse the very point I was arguing against. A premise in a long argument turns up as its conclusion!" George disavowed what was reported of his talk, respectfully asked that his letter be printed in the paper, and expressed his deep regret that the "misleading article will probably make it even more difficult to be understood in the future."

Along with other significant Catholic scholars, such as then-Fr. Avery Dulles, Fr. Richard John Neuhaus, and George Weigel, George was a signatory of the 1994 ecumenical document "Evangelicals and Catholics Together: The Christian Mission in the Third Millennium." The text's foundation rested in the reality that the "two communities in world Christianity that are most evangelistically assertive and most rapidly growing are Evangelicals and Catholics." It offers a common testimony on the need for mainline Protestants and Catholics to achieve more unity through common witness to a world desperately needing it, particularly in practice of everyday, spiritual ecumenism. In his own assessment, George thought Catholics and Evangelicals had much to learn from each other. He thought Catholics could learn more about evangelization methods and practice. And he proposed that Evangelicals could learn a bit more from Catholics regarding church-state relations. Writing in an Oblate ecumenism newsletter about the document, George said that "watching the US become an increasingly immoral society brings into turmoil Evangelicals' sense of God's kingdom."[9] He continued: "It doesn't have the same effect on Catholics, because we know this country is not God's kingdom and is not destined to last forever. We can watch it fall apart with greater equanimity." Overall, George reiterated that Catholics should "be nice to Evangelicals and even Fundamentalists. Often to our surprise and theirs, we have more in common than we had once thought."

In 1992, George had written a letter to the *Yakima Herald-Republic* to set the record straight on misconceptions recently presented in its pages about why the Catholic Church does not ordain women to the priesthood.[10] "Catholic doctrine, like that of other churches, has to be understood on its own terms, not those borrowed from other sources, whether religious or civil," George wrote. "Catholicism, however, is not a religious club but a public church; so conversation about its life and beliefs and their relationship to civil society and to other religious communities is important."

A major concern for George in Yakima was the relationship between the two language groups: those who spoke English and those whose native tongue was Spanish. Cultural, economic, and ecclesial divisions were resulting in the Hispanic community's desertion of Catholicism for Evangelical churches. George was adamant about reversing this trend and planned to be deliberate in his approach to the issue, according to a letter he wrote to his priests on June 21, 1991:

In the Church, we go beyond civic tolerance to a state of mind in which we cherish the differences, because each difference tells us something about Christ: how He can take on flesh today as an American, an Indian, an African, a Mexican, a Canadian, etc. Without the differences, we know Christ less completely. This will be a constant refrain in the years to come, and I hope we can help the people come to see how their faith presents this vision of human relationships. It will be a credible message, of course, to the extent that the presbyterate and the deacon community model, among themselves, this vision of cherishing differences.

George believed, as he wrote to his priests on March 7, 1995, that "if we cannot model a community which is able to show our unity in Christ while enjoying our cultural differences which enrich the Body of Christ, we have nothing to say to society at large." As he began the process of helping parishes worship together, healing and harmony came about. By the time he left, churches were again filled, and Mass schedules needed to be expanded to accommodate the Hispanic communities of the diocese.

The unique cultural situation in Yakima was primarily brought about by the massive influx of Mexican migrant workers who came to labor in the fields, vineyards, and orchards of the predominantly agricultural region. The wages and conditions afforded to the migrant workers were issues of social concern and justice. George entered into the contentious situation by speaking the truth with charity, advocating publicly for the rights and dignity of all involved. When he addressed the Yakima Rotary Club in 1994, he noted that the Latin word *hospes* was the root of two very different English words.[11] "Hostility," which means guests are received as enemies, or "hospitality," which means that they are received as friends.

"The ecologists remind us that we are all guests on this planet," George continued. "How much are we willing to change this community to be truly participatory? How do we treat our fellow guests, and can we truly make Yakima a hospitable place for all who live here?" George noted that the tensions ran deep, with fear on both sides. He argued, "We have to do more talking along class lines. … Have we stopped to talk to the people we want to rescue from their present plight? They need to be invited into a new way of belonging."

In 1993, a group of farm workers asked George to help them form a union, as a neutral intermediary in that effort that both sides could trust. George wrote to his priests, "Welcoming is not just an obligation of politeness or tolerance, it is a religious act. Welcoming a stranger is an act of faith. It shows that even someone we don't really know is recognized as a brother or sister in Christ." Gayle Miller recalled that when George spoke up for the migrant farm workers, some farmers were very upset with him. They called George in for a meeting, but he was "afraid of no one," Miller recalled. At the end, "they all walked out laughing and chatting."

George recalled that the hard labor situation of the migrant workers in Yakima was demanding a lot of his time and attention. George observed the workers' living conditions, particularly worse in winter, with their families living in uninsulated shacks built for summer occupancy. George knew the workers had more than enough reasons to be upset, but he also asked them to share in their own words why they wanted to start a union. He learned wages were not the biggest issue. They replied, "Bishop, they don't respect us."[12]

What George observed could be learned from this was that "when questions of the relationship between labor and capital begin not with economic issues but with a sense of shared humanity, the deeper nature of human work begins to surface."[13] He believed this to be an example of the reality that if unity and charity were to be found among divided people, "it must be totally respectful of the dignity of all those involved, no matter at which end of the gifts — giving or receiving — they find themselves."[14]

George was respected by both sides of the discussion. He knew the employers were not evil, mostly seeing themselves as giving workers a job when they looked for one. In George's assessment, the crux was a fundamental disagreement on this point because "the workers saw themselves first as persons deserving of respect, and people demand respect more than they demand wages."[15]

The local community felt deeply the loss of the last Catholic high school in Yakima; the closure created a great deal of tension among area Catholics. The diocese, amid its own financial problems in the late 1980s, could no longer financially support the school. Not long after his arrival, George was approached about what could be done to remedy the situation. He recognized the need for a Catholic high school and decided to come up with an outside-the-box solution. Drawing on his network of contacts from his years in Rome, George contacted the De La Salle Christian Brothers and invited them to open a new high school in Yakima, seeing their involvement as crucial. The aim of the school, in addition to providing a quality Catholic education for students, would be an exercise in unity — bringing together the ethnically diverse Catholic community in Yakima and providing a more stable environment for the economically struggling students by giving them the resources to move beyond their poverty and receive a decent education.

The school came about "only by providence," according to one of the school's founders and longtime president, Timothy McGree. George initially said starting the school was contingent upon the establishment of a $5 million endowment, noting that the closure of the last high school in Yakima had wounded and fractured the community. The endowment would ensure that this school did not close. "It cannot close," George said. After the Christian Brothers agreed to sponsor the school, George removed that obligation. "There would be no Catholic high school in Yakima today without that connection George made with the Christian Brothers and without his own vision," McGree said.

Another condition George placed on his support of the school, from which he did not waver, was that the school must accept any student wanting to go there who could not afford it. "He did not want students to be turned away because they didn't have money for tuition. That has been a guiding principle for us," McGree said. On George's final visit to Yakima in 2014, the school's gymnasium was dedicated in his honor. And George bestowed a medal for educational excellence on McGree. The success of the school is one of the legacies of George's time in Yakima. In 2019, 63 percent of the student body received more than $1 million in financial assistance. Since 2008, La Salle High School of Yakima has boasted a 100 percent college acceptance rate among graduating seniors.

George's concern for the youth and the challenges they faced manifested in a variety of other ways. He enhanced and strengthened the diocese's youth ministry as a place to help unite the community. He sent some of his priests to Los Angeles to learn how the archdiocese approached problems related to gangs in the Hispanic community. The then-publisher of the *Yakima Herald-Republic*, James Barnhill, remarked in 1996, "I was so impressed with him that I invited him to come in to speak to our senior management people and all the folks in the editorial department. Here was a guy who was here just a few years and he had a better handle on the understanding of the Hispanic family than perhaps a lot of us had."[16]

RISING STAR

George's unique talents put him on the map nationally and internationally during his early tenure as a bishop. He was seen as something of a rising star, and many in Yakima wondered when he might be promoted somewhere else. During his time in Yakima, George served on several important committees for the United States Conference of Catholic Bishops, including doctrine, evangelization, and Hispanic affairs. And he chaired another committee that facilitated the bonds between scholars and bishops. In 1993, he was appointed to the board of trustees at The Catholic University of America in Washington, DC, his alma mater. George was also named the episcopal moderator of the National Catholic Partnership on Disability, a position to which he brought many insights, having spent the majority of his life as a disabled man. George was also a much sought-after speaker and writer. In 1994, he was appointed by Pope John Paul II as a member of the Ordinary Synod of Bishops on Consecrated Life.

One day, while on a sick call at Yakima's St. Elizabeth Hospital, George saw two young men walk past the chapel, one remarking to the other as he looked through the glass doors at the sanctuary, "I really like that cross with Christ on it." The other young man asked, "Why? You're not Catholic." The first young man responded, "No, but it sure reminds me of what he did for us." This got George thinking. He believed that the faithful needed the same reminder, and he planned for the installation of a noticeable and elegant crucifix at St. Paul's Cathedral in Yakima. "Christ, glorified on the cross fulfilling the Father's will, is the central icon of our religion," he explained in a September 14, 1995, letter to members of the cathedral parish. George commissioned Benedictine Br. Claude Lane of Mount Angel Abbey in Oregon to craft an iconic crucifix for the cathedral. Unwilling to solicit more funds for the project from the faithful, George used funds from his own parents' estate. "Ever since their deaths, my sister and I have talked about a memorial for them, and a crucifix in the Yakima Cathedral is appropriate. Had they been alive when I was made bishop here, they would certainly have wanted to give a gift." With no indication of a future outside of Yakima, George modestly said, "The crucifix will be their gift to our diocese and its cathedral." Of course, it seemed to the people that their son was really that gift. Yet in the end, what remains is that crucifix, an icon of George's own tenure as the bishop of Yakima, an appropriate and fitting reminder of his service.

About a year after its installation in the cathedral, George would celebrate his last public Mass as bishop of Yakima beneath the crucifix dedicated in memory of his parents. On April 30, 1996, George was appointed the ninth archbishop of Portland in Oregon. A week before the change was announced, he related the news that Perron Auve and John Ecker, two of his closest collaborators during his time in Yakima, had been designated as monsignors by the pope. Their investiture occurred at George's Mass of Thanksgiving, which concluded his time in Yakima four days before his installation in Portland.

The *Yakima Herald-Republic* editorialized that George's leaving was a "tough act to follow."[17] Noting his impact on "not only the Diocese of Yakima, but the entire Central Washington community," they argued his departure "can be measured by the depth of disappointment and regret that he is leaving." The editors opined, "we join the entire community, Catholic and non-Catholic alike, in saluting him and the realization that Yakima's loss is Portland's gain."

Gayle Miller remembers many of the staff crying at George's final Mass in the diocese. His final words, the famous phrase "all shall be well" from Julian of Norwich, was a comfort to her and others. The outpouring of love for George rolled in from all over the diocese. Many noted how much he loved the community and how people felt heard and understood when speaking with him about concerns. He is still remembered there as a unifier and bridge-builder.

George wrote his Yakima flock: "Leaving this diocese is hard, because these have been among the happiest years of my life; but each of us lives under obedience, first to God and then to those whom God has placed over us, and so I go gladly, knowing that this is God's Will for me and for our diocese."[18] He beckoned his flock to "lift high the cross that Fr. Pandosy first erected here 150 years ago" and in doing so urged them to be "a people so in love with Christ that you will be constantly looking for ways to share your faith with others."

Monsignor Ecker said he would miss George, despite sometimes arguing and often disagreeing. That's because he "always respected [George] as an understanding, faithful, compassionate, and loyal servant of the Church and of his people." Dominican Sr. Maria Ybarra, who worked in the diocesan office for Hispanic ministry during George's tenure in Yakima, wrote a poem describing George's departure as leaving "a trail of broken hearts."[19]

PORTLAND

The Archdiocese of Portland covers the western third of Oregon, claiming in 1996 nearly 270,000 souls in its fold, over four times the Catholic population of the Yakima diocese. As its archbishop, George was also metropolitan of the other Catholic diocese in Oregon, Baker, as well as dioceses in Idaho and Montana. It is the second-oldest American see to

have been elevated to the status of an archdiocese, having been so designated in 1846. His arrival in 1996 meant George led the archdiocese in
celebrating its sesquicentennial. He also welcomed the US bishops' conference to Portland for their annual spring assembly at that time.

In many ways, George's new archdiocese was similar culturally to
central Washington, perhaps being even more emblematic of the Pacific
Northwest's libertine spirit. The retired archbishop of Portland, Corne-
lius Power, himself a former bishop of Yakima, said someone asked him
if anything good can come from Yakima. He replied, "The same question
was asked about 2,000 years ago. Can anyone good come from Nazareth?
And he turned out very well."[20] George added with a smile, "He got crucified, though." Had George been in Oregon longer than he was, there
might have been a variety of reasons many would, indeed, have called for
his crucifixion.

When George arrived, he immediately faced questions about the
debt he inherited from his predecessor in Portland, then-Archbishop
William Levada, who had been transferred to San Francisco. When asked
how he planned to repay the more than $3.5 million cost for a remodel of
the archdiocesan St. Mary's Cathedral, George quipped, "First, I have to
find out who we owe it to." As for his plans, "A bishop has to respect the
nature of the local church he serves," he said. "Before I have goals, I would
want to talk to a lot of people."

The year ahead would prove to be busy. George made evangelization
a top priority and began planning for an overhaul of archdiocesan administrative structures. Meanwhile, he guided the Catholic response in
the state as it wrestled with abortion and euthanasia proposals and dealt
head on with a court case involving direct government violation of the
seal of confession.

George called euthanasia "a sign of spiritual bankruptcy, as much for
the society which allows it as for the individual who requests it."[21] And
he pleaded for the life of a death row convict. "Execution denies the possibility for conversion, reconciliation and reparation for the evil done. It
takes another life — violently — out of the hands of a merciful God who

is the giver of all life."[22]

In coming to Portland, George called for "a new springtime for the Gospel" in the largely unchurched state of Oregon.[23] As part of his response to this call, he was very open and receptive to various new ecclesial movements. Through a connection in Yakima, George had been advising a small group of men belonging to the fledgling People of Praise movement, who desired to live an active life bound by the evangelical counsels of chastity, poverty, and obedience, and who also wanted to pursue the priesthood. George drafted various Oblates to assist the group in establishing the proper canonical structures needed by a society of apostolic life. Still in Yakima at the time, George advised the group to find an archbishop of a major see who would welcome them and support their study in preparation for service as priests. After one possibility did not materialize, they decided to ask George about establishing themselves in Yakima in the spring of 1996. One of those young men — now Bishop Peter Smith, auxiliary bishop of Portland — recalled that George said something to the effect of, "I would set you up tomorrow, but there's something that I need to take care of first." Two days later George was named to Portland, where he welcomed them.

George was installed as ninth archbishop of Portland on Memorial Day, May 30, 1996, at St. Mary's Cathedral. In a state where the majority of the population supported abortion and euthanasia, George pledged to oppose such violations of life's sanctity, no matter how much the culture might find them acceptable. "The moral law is not negotiated like a trade treaty," he said in his homily.[24] "The Church has lived with the barbarism of the ignorant and the outcast. ... The Church lives with the barbarism of the well-educated and well-scrubbed, which is far more frightening." One attendee was quoted in the archdiocesan newspaper: "It was important for him to come out strong against abortion and euthanasia ... I think we've been too quiet." George also made an appeal in his inaugural homily for recognizing the sanctity of life in the disabled. "A final note of thanks to those whom I cherish as especially my own — the disabled and handicapped who are present here," George concluded. "Each member of the Church has a charism, a gift which God gives to build up the Church. One of these charisms is to make visible vulnerability and weakness. Scripture tells us that strength is made perfect in weakness," George said. Finally, George revealed his program to his new flock in two short sentences, saying, "A bishop's job is never to point to himself. It is always to point to Jesus Christ." Those in Portland saw too, that, while known for his own orthodoxy regarding the Faith, George was also pastorally open to discussion and dialogue — particularly with controversial groups aimed at changing Church teaching and practice. With clarity and kindness, George managed the unique tensions of such circumstances.

A letter of appointment by Pope John Paul II read at George's installation described the desirable traits of an archbishop as "a watchful administrator and skilled teacher." It continued: "Your previous work and the heavenly strength of the Lord himself will help as well as sustain you." At the end of that June, George and a contingent of faithful from Portland and Yakima, as well as family and friends, traveled to Rome, where George received from Pope John Paul II the pallium, a white woolen vestment worn over the shoulders of a metropolitan archbishop to signify his unity with the See of Peter. Before returning home, George made a pilgrimage to the Marian shrine at Lourdes, France, the site of the 1858 apparitions of the Blessed Virgin Mary to St. Bernadette Soubirous and the related miraculous healing spring. "I have never been to Lourdes," wrote George in Portland's archdiocesan newspaper, "and I want to go now to ask the Blessed Mother for health sufficient to do a good job as archbishop of Portland."[25] Upon his return, he wrote:

> The most beautiful part of the ceremony for me was the procession of the sick with the Blessed Sacrament in the afternoon. Hundreds of people on stretchers and in wheelchairs go ahead of Christ in the Blessed Sacrament; immediately behind the Blessed Sacrament walk the bishops who are present that day. Isn't that the way it should be everywhere? The sick lead the way and the bishops follow them and the Lord.[26]

George's brief tenure in Portland occurred at a time when the archdiocese was embroiled in litigation after a major violation of the seal of confession, an event that made waves even in the halls of the Vatican. Eight days before George's appointment to Portland was announced, Portland priest Fr. Timothy Mockaitis, while visiting the Lane County Jail in Eugene, Oregon, heard the confession of Conan Hale, an inmate who was suspected of murdering three teenagers in 1995. The confession had been recorded on tape by jail personnel, as discovered by a local newspaper reporter just three days after George's appointment.[27] The district attorney and a US District Court judge refused to destroy the tape at the archdiocese's request, and it was unclear if it would be used in the murder trial. "If this tape is used in court, our relationship to the state will be different from what we had believed it to be. Use of the tape will have a chilling effect on our religious life," George wrote to his new flock.[28]

As soon as George arrived in Portland, Mockaitis was "very impressed with how well he was acquainted with the case," noting that "he immediately jumped into the action." In Mockaitis's view, George was very supportive and was keenly aware that all eyes were on what would be a precedent-setting case with regard to religious freedom. He also supported the idea that Mockaitis must continue his work in the parish while the archdiocese moved the case along. According to Mockaitis, George said the case was "the most important issue in the archdiocese."

The archdiocese and its legal team handled the case, which began to work its way through the federal court system. All involved knew the stakes were incredibly high. As George explained to the faithful of the archdiocese, "Historically, even the civil law has recognized and respected the absolute confidentiality of the Sacrament. Now, for the first time in a free country, the legal respect given to the Sacrament has been breached by the secret tape recording of the encounter."[29] George vowed to go as far as the US Supreme Court if needed to make right the desecration. "This taping of a sacramental confession should have never happened in the United States of America," he said. In their plenary gathering that November, the US bishops expressed their united agreement and publicized a statement of support.

In the midst of the crisis, George was adamant about reiterating the importance of sacramental confession and chose to use what he saw as a direct affront to the integrity of the Church's freedom to celebrate the sacrament as an opportunity to foster a deeper understanding and appreciation of it. As a public witness of the sacrament's importance, George celebrated a communal penance service in the middle of the summer at Mockaitis's parish in Eugene.[30] Mockaitis reported that, from the pulpit, George exclaimed, "The tape must be destroyed. It was wrong to make it and it was wrong to play it." George also noted the importance of mercy in this situation, and said, according to Mockaitis, "The Church must forgive the moral wrong that has been committed. We must forgive." Mockaitis recalled his great gratitude for George's presence and leadership. "I admired him for his tenacity and his willingness to be directly involved and present in all the court hearings," Mockaitis said. "He took a personal interest in the case."

The recording was ruled unconstitutional by the US Ninth Circuit Court of Appeals in early 1997. The ruling was given by a panel of judges — one Catholic, one Protestant, one Jewish. The prosecutor who ordered the recording of the confession reiterated that he would not use the tape for any reason, and it was ordered sealed by the Lane County circuit court judge. It was never given to the archdiocese and has never been known to have been destroyed.

With George's move to Portland, it seemed as if his presence in the Pacific Northwest was cemented. Instead, his tenure was destined to be short-lived: He stayed just eleven months. Fewer than six months after George's installation in Portland, Cardinal Joseph L. Bernardin, archbishop of Chicago, succumbed to pancreatic cancer at the age of sixty-eight. In his archdiocesan newspaper column at the end of November, George wrote that Bernardin's "dying was a witness to the world."[31] Little did he know upon writing those words that he would be Bernardin's successor.

George's name had not been widely floated as the next archbishop of

Chicago. In fact, had bets been placed on who was to fill that role, good money would not have even had George as a contender. He was a long shot. Presumably, Cardinal Bernardin had discussed his successor with John Paul II during the former's last trip to Rome two months before his death. The *Chicago Tribune* presented a list of candidates the day after his death.[32] Archbishop Daniel Pilarczyk, Bernardin's own successor in Cincinnati, was included as "the most obvious choice in the list of likely candidates."[33] He was considered a moderate like Bernardin, a former president of the episcopal conference whose Polish heritage would afford him a warm reception in Chicago, which has a very large number of Polish residents. Also topping the list were then-Archbishop Justin Rigali of St. Louis and then-Bishop Donald Wuerl of Pittsburgh. Other names floated were Archbishop James Keleher of Kansas City and then-Bishop Edward Egan of Bridgeport — both Chicago natives — as well as Theodore McCarrick, then-archbishop of Newark and now-laicized former cardinal. In the Holy See's *Report* on the McCarrick affair, released in the wake of the sordid episcopal tenure of the former cardinal, it appears that the rumors circulating about McCarrick even at the time prevented his appointment to Chicago. There had been particular sensitivity given to the fact that the recently deceased Cardinal Bernardin had been accused of misconduct himself just a few years before his death. Cardinal John O'Connor of New York, in a meeting about the Chicago appointment for the Congregation for Bishops, expressed some concern that McCarrick might not be the right fit for Chicago, lacking what he saw as the "firmness necessary to 'compensate' for the prevailing permissiveness" in response to the Bernardin years.[34] Moreover, it looks like, given Bernardin's own past accusation, the congregation was keen to see appointed someone highly reputable, without a whiff of scandal. As the report indicates, McCarrick had ultimately been passed by because of the rumors that swirled about his own misconduct, even if unproven at the time, because "in the flammable Chicago environment it would be risky for him to be exposed [right] now."[35]

Rumors began swirling after George took an unannounced flight

to Chicago on April 7, 1997, following the installation of Archbishop
Charles J. Chaput in Denver. George had been expected to stay the night.
Portland had barely come to know George, and he was already being
sent off. According to several individuals who spoke with George about
the process, he tried at first to encourage the appointment of another
candidate to Chicago. He did not think it was fair to the Archdiocese
of Portland to leave so soon after arriving because he took seriously the
bond of a bishop to his flock, as bridegroom and bride. He had even
chosen his place of burial, though many in Portland had a sense George
would not be there long. One priest remarked upon George's departure
that although "short in stature, he is a giant."[36]

George received the call to go to Chicago on Monday of Holy Week,
responding to the nuncio at first, "Are you sure the Holy Father has considered all the options?"[37] George privately told others that he made
known his position that moving him so soon from Portland was not a
good decision for that local Church, since two interregnums in as many
years would mean less than optimal governance. He admitted he would
leave Portland with "a heavy heart" and would always remember in his
prayers the flock he had shepherded for less than a year.[38] At his farewell
Mass in Portland, he said that he felt like he was "saying hello and goodbye in the same breath. Perhaps the Archdiocese of Portland trains its
archbishops too well."[39]

As George's second successor in Portland, Archbishop Alexander
Sample, observed, the people in the Pacific Northwest "really appreciated
his pastor's heart." He continued, "Even after twenty-one years, and such
a short time [in Portland], his name will still come up. He definitely left a
mark in the hearts of the people here."

Mike McCarthy, a turf grass grower and Catholic father of three
from western Oregon, shared a story in an interview after George's transfer from Portland.[40] He sat next to George on his return trip to Portland
following the announcement in Chicago and quickly came to see his
warm, charismatic style, as well as his wit and wisdom. "I can understand
why he was chosen to go to Chicago," he said. "I don't think he's at all

concerned about meeting the new demands; he's a capable and confident person. I think he's more concerned about what his mission in life is than any titles or any fanfare," McCarthy observed. "They're going to have him going from daylight to dark — he might as well be a dairy farmer now."

When George died in 2015, his former chancellor in Portland, Mary Jo Tully, recalled how his impact in Portland "far exceeds the short time he was here." She added: "His concern for us followed him to Chicago. Years after he left, he still asked about specific parishes and priests. ... He inquired about situations that were unresolved when he left."[41]

Jay Levine, a television journalist with the local CBS affiliate in Chicago, broke the news on the eve of his appointment that the city's next archbishop would be the homegrown Francis George of Portland. Meanwhile, at her home in Michigan, George's sister, Margaret, awaited the official announcement with joy, having been told confidentially of the transfer during a visit with her brother in Portland about a week earlier. As she waited, she thought about how the unimaginable was now very real. Her little brother, whose hopes of being a priest for his hometown diocese had been dashed by polio — the boy who could start down the path to priesthood because he could walk across the living room floor, and who later traveled the globe as a missionary — was, in God's providence, returning to lead the very archdiocese that had told him he could not be ordained as one of its priests. In less than a year, he would also be named Chicago's first native-born cardinal.

NINE
Getting to Know the Place

The bishop as pastor is a sign of hope for the world, therefore, if his own life is transparently conformed to Christ, if his ministry unites minds and heals hearts, and if his particular church points clearly to Christ as the source of eternal life. Then, in his life of availability to his people and his ministry in their service, the bishop is truly joined as Christ's agent in the battle against evil.[1]

CARDINAL FRANCIS E. GEORGE, O.M.I.

When Francis George returned home to Chicago in 1997 as its first native-born archbishop and recited T. S. Eliot's poem "Little Gidding," it was clear he was set on getting "to know the place." The most emotional moment of his homecoming as archbishop happened not during his announcement or installation but about a month later, at the first Mass he celebrated as archbishop of his home archdiocese at his home parish, St. Pascal.

Phones began ringing off the hook in his old neighborhood on April 7 with the exciting rumors that George would be coming home. Back at St. Pascal a few months later, George acknowledged it was "very moving" to return to his home parish that day.[2] It was the place of his first Communion. The place where he first heard God's call to be a priest. The place where he had served and attended Mass so dutifully. It was home to the school from which he graduated and where he had come down with the polio that changed the course of his life. And it was the church where he was ordained a priest and from where he buried each of his parents.

With his usual sense of humor, he told the overflow crowd that day, "I never expected, as one going to Mass here, to stand here as archbishop. So it better be God's will or else we're all in trouble."

He spoke in depth about the will of God, stressing the importance of living a life so closely attuned to God that we can discern if our activities are fitting into his purpose for our lives. "Do they contribute to God's reign?" he asked. "We must pray to see God's purpose in our lives and in our archdiocese so that together we can be a sign of God's kingdom."

Only 306 days had passed between George's installation in Portland and his nomination to Chicago. Though he was moving from smaller dioceses to one of the country's largest, his experience in overseeing the global Oblate congregation had prepared him in many ways. Asked the difference between Chicago and Portland, he quipped, "Chicago is huge. But people in the parishes are really the same."[3]

Being archbishop of Chicago — the nation's third-largest diocese — meant George was now pastor to over one-third of a city that was roughly 40 percent Catholic. With 2.3 million Catholics on the books, the archdiocese was as diverse ideologically as it was ethnically, with no small amount of tensions dividing both society and the Catholic community. As ideologues argued about the path forward and how to account for the decline in priests and religious in the years after Vatican II, George steered the Church of Chicago — and, quite often, the Church in the

United States, as evidenced by his own reach and influence over the years — through a time of sharp disagreements about whether there had been too many changes in the Church or too few. Chicago had a reputation for its progressivism, but it also faced problems common to the life of the Church in other large urban centers, such as declining Mass attendance and a shrinking institutional footprint.

Given his advancement in the American hierarchy from relative obscurity, George was hard to define. This did not prevent the local and national media and Church pundits from giving it their best shot, usually in a way that incorrectly pigeonholed him. The front page of the *New York Times* immediately branded him as a "conservative intellectual," trying to put him at odds with his predecessor, Cardinal Joseph Bernardin.[4] With a personable, unpretentious demeanor and razor-sharp wit, George was quite a contrast with the genteel Bernardin. When asked how he differed from his predecessor, George said, "[The Cardinal] was a southern gentleman; I'm a Chicagoan."

At the press conference announcing his appointment in Chicago on April 8, 1997, George intuited the reality of how he was being portrayed and also the danger in it — a theme he revisited many times over the remainder of his ministry as a bishop. "The bishop is a symbol of unity; he's to be a point of reference. The faith isn't liberal or conservative," he said. "The faith is true and I will preach the faith."[5] In a radio interview a few months into the job, George observed, "The image of archbishop here is somewhat at odds with my self-understanding and the Church's understanding of who I am."[6] One day, though, he hoped to be remembered as "a good archbishop [who] is primarily a pastor who's also a teacher, who's also a priest." Then he joked that no other archbishop of Chicago had lived past seventy-five years old, when he would be able to retire, saying, "I'd like to beat those odds." More than seventeen years later, George would indeed be the first archbishop of Chicago to retire.

In the assessment of the *Times*, George was "a man like Pope John Paul II … an intellectual committed to defending traditional Catholic teaching but also interested in issues of social justice for the poor and others."[7]

Scott Appleby of the University of Notre Dame remarked in an interview at the time that George was "theologically right in line with the papacy, but socially progressive," while cautioning that labeling George as liberal or conservative should take a back seat on account of his "pastoral gift and intelligence." Commentator and Jesuit priest Fr. Thomas Reese said George's appointment to a major see like Chicago showed that John Paul II's papacy was "looking for bishops who are prominent as teachers, perhaps more than as pastors." But in George, as is consistent with the teachings of the Church, it is unclear how such a distinction between the two is possible.

Fr. Matthew Lamb, who lived and taught in Boston around the same time as George, noted in an interview that George "combines the mind and heart."[8] Dominican Fr. Romanus Cessario, who also knew George while in Boston, noted when George was named to Chicago he possessed "three indispensable qualities" that he believed to define great bishops: "He is a doctor of the faith; he is an apostle; he loves the poor." Jude Dougherty, the longtime dean of philosophy at The Catholic University of America, observed then that he was "a man of intellectual courage, with experience in the secular and religious worlds, and a kind of global outlook."[9] He added: "He isn't afraid to take a minority position and isn't afraid to challenge. He'll defend the faith."

One of George's most important goals was to evangelize. This is not unique to the episcopal office per se, yet he knew that proclaiming the Gospel in a culture so desperately in need of it was an urgent and pressing task. And he also knew that divisions within the Church were deleterious to that mission. "Only if we are truly one in Christ will the world believe," George said. "A divided Church lacks the energy and creativity to preach the Gospel."[10]

In his exercise of episcopal ministry, George was far from an autocrat and was not focused on a top-down approach. He saw things more providentially than most, and he trusted those who were given certain duties, even if it might cost him — as it sometimes did. George regarded the bishop as the man at the center, the one who gathers all in Christ and helps them to be holy. He never had any desire to climb an ecclesiastical ladder, much less to become a bishop. George made that point quite clear in a gathering with young professionals, when one asked him about his own ambition: "I understand there are two kinds of priests, those who want to become bishops and those who don't. Which kind are you?" With charity and tact, George explained, according to longtime Executive Assistant Mary FioRito, that when he chose to enter the Oblates of Mary Immaculate on account of his disability, he was keenly aware of two things: that it was tantamount in his day to rejecting a life of any careerism in the Church — since in those days religious priests very rarely became bishops — and that he would never again live in Chicago.

George established a lasting legacy of evangelization during his time in Chicago. Yet his efforts at evangelization, as successful as they may have been, came more or less in fits and starts. So much of his attention during his time in office ended up being absorbed by the clergy sexual abuse crisis that rocked the Catholic Church in the United States and the world. As the crisis unfolded, George became a pivotal player, providing credible, steady leadership in Chicago and beyond. Even amid the crisis, George found ways to proclaim the truth of Christ and the Gospel, albeit against a backdrop no one would have ever imagined. He understood the damage done by the crisis and how its effects knew no bounds. Grappling with the various tentacles of such a monster tested George's mettle. His response to crises both public and private revealed the virtue of his character and his attentiveness to God's will. Although he took a great deal of heat, especially because he was the figure at the top, no evidence has ever been offered that suggests George was complicit in any abuse coverups.

Dealing with abuse cases especially showed George how lonely leadership could be. He inherited an overgrown archdiocese in which operations and communication were not fully functional; its many layers of bureaucracy left him feeling powerless or at odds with his flock at times. Popes John Paul II and Benedict XVI both described the same phenomenon. When some believed him to be hesitant to act decisively and openly about a predatory Austrian cardinal, John Paul II stated that he would like to do more but "they won't let me."[11] Pope Benedict once remarked, pointing at the threshold of his private apartment, "My authority ends at that door."[12] The system that George inherited in Chicago could often be a source of pain and suffering. But ultimately, he knew that Christ was risen from the grave, and he moved forward in faith, determined to obediently perform the tasks God entrusted to him as a bishop.

GOVERNING CHICAGO

George's installation in Chicago occurred on May 7, 1997, a sunny spring day, and it was a grand affair. More than 130 bishops attended, including eight American cardinals. In addition to large numbers of laity, religious, and clergy, representatives of the various Christian communities and religions observed by Chicagoans attended, as did political leaders such as the mayor and governor. In his installation Mass homily, George hinted at the unlikely reality that he was now Chicago's archbishop: "If surprise is a sign of God's presence, then God is with us in force today."[13]

George was both perplexed and perhaps frustrated by the media's eagerness to know what his plans were for the archdiocese. He commented on this in 1999:

> When I first came to Chicago, the press were very eager to know, "What is your program?", as if I were a CEO, as if that were my job: to be president of a modern religious corporation with a lot of assets. … There was some consternation in the Chicago press when I said, "My job is to teach the Gospel as the Church has handed it down to us from apostolic times. My job is to be a priest, to make holy the people by seeing that the sacraments are available to them. My job is to be a shepherd, a pastor who will call people together in Christ so that we can live the way that he gives us." It's all in canon law and it's utterly predictable; but if it's utterly predictable it doesn't make a great story. So the *Chicago Tribune* talked about me as a "reluctant archbishop." … I was just saying that I don't come in with a program. I come in with the mission that the Church gives every bishop, and that is

to love the people as Christ loves them, to make that love visible
through teaching, through sanctifying, through governing and
then to allow the Spirit the freedom to do what the Spirit wants
to do with all of us, bishop and people together.[14]

This was all bound up in George's own episcopal motto, which George
once wrote, "says that I believe the Church exists, first of all and above all,
to glorify Christ, to make his grace visible to the world in the Church's
ministries and mission. If people look at the Church and see Jesus Christ,
then everything else will fall into place."[15]

Practically speaking, George's initial plan was to follow a group of
priorities that he inherited from Cardinal Bernardin, known as the *Decisions* document, which was the product of a long, expansive consultative
process in the archdiocese that had been completed before Bernardin's
death. George wanted to respect that process, a plan focused on three
priorities for ministries within the archdiocese: First, to become an evangelizing Church. Second, to strengthen efforts to hand on Catholic Faith
in schools and catechetical programs. And third, to improve formation
of candidates to priesthood, diaconate, and lay ministries. Years later, in
a 2006 gathering with Chicago priests, George argued, "We don't need to
plan. We don't need five-year plans. If I had a five-year plan — and I did
in a sense, but it all went haywire — but maybe that's good. It is finally
God who's in charge."[16]

George's time was rarely his own as archbishop of Chicago. On week-
days, unless he was scheduled to celebrate Mass elsewhere on a given day,
George began the day by celebrating Mass with everyone who lived at his
Residence. Also attending would be the Albertine Sisters whom George
invited to oversee his household and any guests who may have been invited to attend before a morning meeting. Immediately after Mass, George
had breakfast, prepared by the sisters. If meeting guests were not present,
the archbishop would often look over the newspapers.

Following breakfast, George made his way to the archdiocesan offices
for appointments and meetings. If George was in the office at lunchtime,

he would eat at his desk, often a brown-bag lunch he had brought from home, but if he was at home, the Sisters would serve lunch at noon. The Sisters were always gracious about accommodating "surprise" guests for lunch, since, if the archbishop had an appointment at home that ran right up to noon, he would frequently invite his guests to join him for lunch. Afternoons frequently continued with more meetings. These could be with individuals, such as "courtesy visits" with visiting religious superiors, diplomats, or dignitaries, or they could be diocesan committee meetings. In between appointments, he would attend to mail, sign letters, and answer correspondence. Office time typically wrapped up around 5:00 p.m., followed by dinner at home an hour later. Evening appointments and functions were more common than not. Sometimes he would have private appointments with priests in the evening at the Residence. When he met with survivors of sexual abuse, these too were normally held at the Residence, because he wanted to protect their privacy and help them to understand that he was welcoming them into his home.

If there were no evening appointments, which was rare, or else after them, George would work on his mail. This task often began in the car, on the way to or from events, when he famously would throw the mail into the back seat. Once, when accompanying him for a trip, Sr. Mary Paul McCaughey, archdiocesan superintendent of schools, found this out when she started getting pelted with mail after George forgot she was there. He read all of his mail — the staff would simply sort it into what was reading material, what was correspondence of a general nature, and what required his personal attention. Sometimes attending to his mail occupied him late into the night. George was a night owl more than a morning person and was frequently up until midnight or later. He prayed his breviary throughout the day, sometimes in the car, but it was most often late in the evening that he would spend time before the Blessed Sacrament.

Wednesdays were typically George's day off, during which he would stay home and work, read, or prepare talks. This would also be the day for family members, personal friends, or his confessor to visit. But the one thing that did not stop was the mail. He preferred to go through it rather than leave it all for Thursday and be swamped.

On the weekends, Mass would be celebrated at the Residence's chapel at 7:30 a.m. Saturdays could be filled with appointments at his home or occasionally at the pastoral center. Saturday mornings and early afternoons were also often an optimal time for him to meet with priests and/ or with abuse survivors. Saturday afternoons and evenings were often filled with Mass at a parish, or an event, reception, or dinner at a major diocesan conference or hosted by another group. Sunday mornings and afternoons most frequently meant public Masses, either as part of a parish visit or at another event. It was not uncommon to have at least two such public commitments on a Sunday, sometimes three.

George made it his goal to be the first Chicago archbishop to make a pastoral visit to every one of the archdiocese's then 378 parishes. He accomplished this, visiting many more than once. Many of those who met him in those parish visits have recalled that George was usually the last to leave. He would stay and speak with anyone who wanted to shake his hand or take a photograph, as he knew that for many people it would likely be the one time in their life they would meet their archbishop. As much as his schedule allowed, he would celebrate the midday Mass on First Fridays at Holy Name Cathedral, and after Mass would stand near one of the cathedral's side entrances to greet anyone who wished to speak with him. He extended the same personal, pastoral presence in non-church settings as well. In downtown hotels, while attending high-end functions that demanded his presence, he frequently greeted waitstaff, doormen, and other hotel employees, often speaking with them in Spanish, the language of a large portion of Chicago's hospitality workers. On occasion he even made his way into the kitchen to do this, sometimes even eating his meal there after an event. He was known to stop by a hospital at the end of a long day of appointments and events to visit the sick, or at a funeral home to console a family at a wake. He was a man of the people, relating with them in quiet, unassuming ways, often out of sight of the media. He loved being a pastor, spending himself for his flock without counting the cost.

After arriving in Chicago, George also wanted "to work toward shaping a staff at the Pastoral Center which would be transparent in its operations and would be directed in every department and agency toward the mission of the Archdiocese."[17] At first, this meant that George's idea of an organizational flow chart for chancery operations had all positions with a direct line to himself. In a behemoth operation like the Chicago archdiocesan pastoral center, though, that was quickly proven untenable. Early on, George brought in Jimmy Lago as an informal chief of staff to help him develop a chain of command that suited him and was also manageable. Lago was viewed as an indispensable collaborator, and he was eventually named the first layman to serve as chancellor of the archdiocese. With his assistance and that of others, George oversaw the consolidation of the archdiocesan offices, some of which were scattered among various parish campuses, into two principal centers. His goals were to break down "silos" and encourage greater collaboration among various chancery offices, and also to locate one of these centers on the south side of the city for the first time. In accomplishing this, George, who understood and valued Chicago's architectural heritage, also preserved and repurposed two buildings important to the history of the archdiocese.

George's sense of management was itself an exercise in evangelization, and he bristled at the notion of the Church as a business. He was known to quip that when he died, St. Peter would not be asking him how much money was in the checking account. George knew his duty was to be a good steward, and he responded to that responsibility from the priority of mission. George remarked once about a boyhood friend who said to him on the day of his 1997 installation, "You may think that what just happened has something to do with Jesus or the Gospel, but it doesn't. Being archbishop of Chicago is all about finances, real estate, and political clout."[18] George elaborated on that, thinking:

A statement like that, however, says less about the Church than it says about the assumptions that habitually govern our thinking. It says something about a corrupt culture. When people take it for granted, and even take morbid satisfaction in believing that, to accomplish almost anything at all in life, they have to play a game that destroys their own integrity and that of our institutions, corruption touches us all.

George displayed the antithesis to that job description in his approach to his ministry as a bishop. While he knew that such administrative realities were part of his position, he did not allow himself to be defined by them. Most of his meetings with politicians took place behind closed doors, and he rarely allowed his photograph to be taken with them, lest it be misused as a sign of support or to help garner votes during a campaign. As a good steward, he relied upon the counsel and direction of informed clergy and lay collaborators.

He greatly bristled at the thinking that made a bishop of the Church equivalent to the CEO of a business. "Since there are more CEOs than there are bishops, many tend to look at the bishop in this light," he wrote.[19] "We are a commercial republic, and business metaphors are the prism through which we see much of reality, including the Church and her bishops. When we think of the Church using only a business corporation as a model, we forget that our ties to Christ and to one another in his Body are closer than our ties to our blood family or to any corporate or civil association. Those who hear the Word of God and keep it are Jesus' mother and brothers and sisters. Through Baptism and Eucharist, the life of the Blessed Trinity courses through our veins."

Likewise, George was concerned about the failures of the business approach to managing dioceses and parishes. Upon returning to the United States in 1987, he observed on several occasions how the Church was destined for a period of institutional decline. In many ways, it was simply a question of numbers. During his time in the unchurched Pacific Northwest, George experienced what it meant for the Church to be a minority, even sometimes an insignificant one. This was not something the Church in Chicago had experienced for more than a century. As if the forces of secularization were not enough, the clergy sexual abuse crisis further complicated matters, and throughout his time in Chicago, George would reiterate that the current model was untenable.

But George made it clear that the need to advance the Church's mission was more important than any desire to preserve the Church's institutions. In 2005, referencing the recent release of Mundelein professor Denis McNamara's book *Heavenly City: The Architectural Tradition of Catholic Chicago* — which features an extensive review of the artistic patrimony visible in Chicago's churches — George noted that the publication was a reminder that the "burden of maintaining these buildings we have inherited and of sustaining so many other works of the Archdiocese is falling on fewer practicing Catholics. This is a situation which cannot be sustained in the long run. Either one fills institutions or one closes them."[20]

As he said at a gathering of Chicago priests in 2014:

> The Church, after all, as we all know, was born without any institutions at all, including no parishes, no universities, no hospitals, no newspapers, nothing. The Church was born with a set of relationships, to Christ through the Twelve. And inspired and given life by the Holy Spirit, it's those relationships that are at the heart of who we are. And if everything else disappears, that's enough, we'll be the Church.[21]

Although George closed a number of parishes and schools, he hesitated about doing so as part of a massive overhaul of the local Church. "I don't think it's a good idea to put out a huge closure plan, like you were Napoleon redrawing the map of Europe. Because it just invites a lot of opposition," he said at the 2014 gathering. "You do it in ones and twos, and you do it responsibly, in such a way that in the end you've got what you need to remain solvent, but you haven't come out as if you were God Almighty saying this is the way we've planned from on top." George believed his approach was respectful of people first and foremost and was not as alienating as other alternatives.

In George's 1997 installation homily, discussing the gifts that Christ gives us, George remarked that those we encounter have a right to ask where the gifts are whenever we show up. "If we cannot show them, share them, make them public, we betray our Lord," he said. As far as the Church's mission was concerned, George gave clarity to the Church's teachings and advocated unequivocally against the threats to her freedom and the secularism that threatened its mission.

HEALTH CRISES

Without question, suffering defined much of George's life. There was the physical debilitation, manifested in his limping gait and those occasional falls to which he alerted the people of Yakima. Bishop Robert Barron recalled one of those occasions in Chicago when George, in full episcopal regalia, fell flat on the floor, miter going one way, crosier the other. But he got up and carried on with a characteristic, "I'm alright, I'm alright."

Then there were the two bouts with cancer, the first of which resulted in the loss of his bladder and made life more difficult and complicated. Rarely, however, did he complain or even speak about his health woes aside from when asked. At times during his cancer treatment, he curtailed his schedule because of compromised immunity, for which he apologized because he could not be as available to others as he wanted to be. On other occasions he appeared pale or ashen, causing gossip to swirl. But aside from all this suffering, which was mostly interiorized, he experienced silent suffering that people knew little to nothing about.

George's first bout with cancer came in the summer of 2006, on the heels of a very ugly episode of clergy sexual abuse in Chicago, the result of which was the laicization of the notorious predator Daniel McCormack. Many of George's close collaborators believed the stress of the scandal weighed on him so much that he took on the suffering in a physical way. There is a relationship between cancer and stress, just as there is also a high rate of cancer among polio survivors. Regardless of its origins, he discovered blood in his urine, which led to the discovery of a tumor on his bladder. And it was quite serious: His personal doctor at the time, Jesuit Fr. Myles Sheehan, said George would have died within a few months without action. Doctors recommended a radical cystectomy (the removal of the bladder and the reconstruction of an artificial bladder). Father Sheehan noted, "One should not underestimate the word *radical*," pertaining to the kind of operation George had, explaining that, literally, his "insides were rearranged." The operation at Loyola University Medical Center led to several complications as well. During recovery, he began to bleed internally, which required emergency surgery to repair. "It was frightening," Father Sheehan recalled. "I don't think he was worried much about dying. He didn't like being uncomfortable, though." But "he wasn't nasty about it," Sheehan said, and George was always grateful, even in face of so many setbacks.

The stress of serious medical complications and the suffering that accompanies an illness and its treatment reveal a person's character. George embraced his suffering with perseverance and peace, according to Sheehan. In such circumstances, "you see people's character refined and come out more clearly," Sheehan said. George was "not a complainer," Sheehan remembered, saying, "During the recovery, like anybody, he needed reassurance. But he also prayed through the experience. It was a very difficult time, and it was a privilege for me to accompany him through that." George often asked for the assistance of prayers from others, also hoping irregular Mass-goers would go to pray for him. He noted he would seek the intercession of two saintly bishops whose influence had been great in his life and in whom he had great trust: Eugene de Mazenod and Pope John Paul II.[22] He relied on their protection and assistance to see God's will in the midst of illness.

George also kept a sense of humor throughout his health crises, Sheehan recalled. During the 2006 ordeal, George let out a belly laugh, according to Sheehan, when he was told some of Sheehan's medical students were inquisitive about visiting bishops, who they described as "the priests coming to visit the cardinal wearing bling — big crosses on chains like rappers." Or how, when George was released and a gaggle of reporters stood outside the hospital, his pants fell down — due to having lost weight in the hospital — while Sheehan was helping him from his wheelchair. Sheehan remembered that George just laughed and said, "And now the cardinal archbishop of Chicago prepares to meet the press."

Sheehan knew George had a life of pain and suffering because of the polio. The new aches and pains could be "scary" at times for George, but Sheehan noted that he "would have been crazy not to be unsettled." George's doctor also recalled how the nurses who took care of George in the ICU "talked about how he was easy to care for" and that "he didn't throw himself around" or seek special attention on account of his position.

George did not want his suffering to go to waste. He had spent his life knowing and embracing suffering as redemptive. He observed in 2006 that "sharing in the sufferings of Christ is part of our call to be his disciples."[23] And he commented about the good he hoped to accomplish by offering up his suffering, intending it to "bring peace in the Holy Land and the Middle East and be useful, as well, for the healing of the wounds of the sexual abuse crisis and the strengthening of the Catholic faith. I am not looking forward to life without a bladder, but even that loss can be a grace."

As he announced his diagnosis with cancer, George reflected on his motto: "To Christ be Glory in the Church":

> There are many ways the Church gives glory to Christ: in her worship, in her works, and in the way that Christ uses the Church to give witness to the power of his grace. We can see Christ at work in miracles, when the rules of fallen nature are set aside for a moment and we see the glory of God shining through our human weakness. But if God's goodness is made visible in miracles, God's compassion and forgiveness are made present in suffering. If we always cooperate with God's grace, then the Church gives glory to Christ in all circumstances, good and bad. That is our vocation and our joy.

On Holy Saturday of the following year, George took a fall when he slipped on holy water as he participated in the traditional Polish blessing of Easter baskets. When Father Sheehan caught news reports on television, which prematurely and inaccurately stated George hit his head and was unconscious, he rushed to meet George at the emergency room. He recalled George was worried that he may have broken his hip, given that he had hurt the leg that had long suffered the effects of polio. He ended up having much more wrong with his shoulder and arm than he initially realized, something few knew about. Upon arriving at the emergency room, Sheehan found George and tried to lighten the mood of the moment as he inquired about the reported head injury: "You didn't hit your head and you weren't knocked unconscious?" Sheehan asked. George insisted not. "But you said all those things about how you endorsed women's ordination," Sheehan jested. "He looked at me and said, 'Myles, I hate you,'" Sheehan recalled with laughter.

George's cancer returned in 2012, and he wrestled with it for more than two years before it took his life. Sheehan was "not shocked" the cancer had come back but, thinking it had been beaten after six years, he was "unpleasantly surprised at the recurrence." Ultimately, his cancer surgery in 2006 gained George eight more years of life. Two years after fighting cancer the first time, George wrote privately, "I am more 'spent' than tired — arthritis makes it hard to walk."[24]

PASTORING PRIESTS

At the time of George's installation in Chicago, in an analysis for *Our Sunday Visitor*, Russell Shaw noted George's interest in British prime minister Benjamin Disraeli, who served under Queen Victoria in the latter half of the nineteenth century. Disraeli, Shaw recalled in the words of a biographer, had "determination, a courage and a parliamentary genius seldom surpassed."[25] As Shaw observed, George's appointment to a place like Chicago meant he "may need all the determination, courage and even parliamentary genius he can muster."

George's philosophical mind resulted in his being portrayed as argumentative at times, especially because of his characteristic knack for asking many questions. He admitted as much quite often, especially to his priests — including during his homily at the celebration of Evening

Prayer with them the night before his installation. "Sometimes people assume that if I question something, I am against it," he explained.[26] He apologized for any concern associated with his inquisitive nature, but gave a defense as well: "the cost of not asking questions is to live in ignorance and, possibly, to mess up many people's lives."

George's style greatly impressed the legendary, progressive Chicago priest, sociologist, and author Fr. Andrew Greeley, who commented after the appointment that George "was articulate, self-confident, and clearly very, very intelligent."[27] Later, he would comment that George was "75 percent Irish and has 200 percent Irish wit and charm."[28] Greeley's enthusiasm for George was no minor point, given that he had the reputation for almost never holding back from criticizing his superiors. He called one of George's predecessors, the late Cardinal John Cody, "one of the most truly evil men I have ever known," and he was often at odds, too, with Cardinal Bernardin. Greeley became a friend to George, despite their many differences. They were an intellectually odd couple who even occasionally attended the opera together.

Greeley, who lived in a condominium in Chicago's towering John Hancock Center and long held a faculty position at the University of Chicago, was quite a character and a rogue in many ways. He advocated for ideas George took no interest whatsoever in supporting, such as the ordination of women. He also sharply criticized Pope St. Paul VI's encyclical *Humanae Vitae*. Greeley's vision of faith could occasionally be clouded by his undying and fierce loyalty to the Democratic Party. But Greeley also loved the priesthood, regarded himself as a parish priest at heart, and defended priestly celibacy. He wrote a collection of novels, some of which were regarded by many as highly risqué. George, however, understood Greeley's purpose in them. "Greeley has given great attention to the role of imagination in the life of faith," George observed in 1999.[29] "What he is doing is re-evangelizing the imagination, using fiction to express the faith and the mysteries of the faith. That's an extraordinarily significant project. Pope John Paul talks about faith creating culture. Using fiction is one way to do that." But, he cautioned, "How well he's doing it is for someone else to judge." Perhaps most notably, Greeley was one of the first Catholics to blow the whistle about the clergy sexual abuse crisis in the 1980s, when cases were being ignored and bishops were covering up abuse.

George's experience in overseeing large numbers of priests began in the Midwest as an Oblate provincial and then continued in Rome, where as vicar general he lived in a community with fifty other Oblates. He also helped oversee nearly six thousand priests in the forty-eight Oblate provinces throughout the world and lived and met with them during his visits. "I like priests," he told the priests of Chicago as he preached during vespers on the eve of his installation in 1997. "Catholic priests are good people, faithful to God and worthy of people's trust." He shared how he had only met five or six "real rogues" in his time and, he noted, "the rest of us often make mistakes, sometimes horrifying and seriously sinful mistakes, and some of our sins have terrible consequences for their victims, whose forgiveness we must seek, and for the Church."[30]

The Chicago presbyterate included a host of quiet, dedicated pastors who collaborated with George in the service of God's people. But many of the crosses he bore as archbishop came from the same presbyterate, albeit a much smaller contingency. Difficulties with Chicago priests began shortly after George's arrival and carried on for quite some time. These challenges were especially aggravated by the clergy sexual abuse crisis. Collaboration with the presbyterate was not optional; rather, it was constitutive to his very vocation and key to any successful governance in Chicago. About ten days before his installation, George welcomed the priests of Chicago to his residence, where nearly seven hundred waited in line for over an hour. *"Mi casa es su casa,"* he told them.[31] It was a symbolic gesture that endeared him to some priests, many of whom had never been in the archbishop's residence at all. This meeting led to a series of regular informal gatherings with priests, which George would host one Sunday evening nearly every month during his years as archbishop. A small group of priests of different ages and backgrounds would be invited to the residence, and there was no preset agenda. They were welcome to discuss any topic at all, and he was eager to understand what was on their minds and those of the people to whom they ministered.

As the years pressed on, a variety of problems arose in the diocesan presbyterate that made George's role challenging. Just weeks after George's installation, Fr. Daniel Montalbano reportedly died at age fifty in an extremely improper and sexually compromising situation, with homosexually explicit material stacked up in his rectory. There were several other similar stories. It had been rumored widely that some in the Chicago presbyterate were engaged in active sexual relationships, both heterosexual and homosexual in nature. Some of these stories served as the content for novels penned by Father Greeley, who maintained that a powerful lobby in the Chicago presbyterate exercised a great deal of influence and external authority in the archdiocese. Greeley referred to them as "the ring of predators," who were "a dangerous group."[32] Even more shocking, he said, "There is reason to believe that they are responsible for at least one murder and may perhaps have been involved in the murder of the murderer." Adding that they are "clever" and "cover their tracks," he warned that "should they slip, should they get caught, the previous scandals will seem trivial." Chicago priests also had a history of not always being in sync with their archbishop. In 1966, some of them had organized into a quasi-union, a group now called the Association of Chicago Priests and Deacons, to protect their rights under George's authoritarian predecessor Cardinal John Cody.

One of Greeley's mentors, Msgr. John Egan — himself a legendary Chicago priest and social activist who was now to serve his sixth archbishop — opined very highly of George upon his arrival. "He struck me as a man who listens and is open. I think he's honest and will tell the truth. I also feel he's a no-nonsense man. I think he will be fair."[33] He added: "He strikes me as a man with common sense. That's all we need in an archbishop." But not all priests were looking for transparency and common sense.

Greeley acknowledged in 1998 that George was the best archbishop Chicago had ever had, noting that he was "one of the most brilliant and erudite men I have ever met."[34] Yet later that year, he said that whether

George could:

> administer the large, complex, and since Cardinal Cody, disori-
> ented Archdiocese remains to be seen. If he can't, then no one
> can. Whether he will be able to build a competent staff also re-
> mains to be seen, especially since ... he doesn't have much of a
> bench. Finally, it remains to be seen whether those priests of the
> Archdiocese who are intimidated by his brilliance and quickness
> will learn how to argue back.

Greeley's comments were prompted by an event that occurred five
months into George's tenure in Chicago. Former president of the Association of Chicago Priests and then-cathedral rector Fr. Robert Mc-
Laughlin rallied a sizable group of priests called the Pastors' Forum.
They formed this quite different sort of "McLaughlin Group" shortly
after George's arrival to voice complaints about George to the apostolic nuncio. The aim of the group, which identified itself by a letter with
forty-three signatories (out of just over 900 archdiocesan priests), was to
put the new archbishop in his place. The letter made national headlines.
They admitted their complaints were fueled by rumors after Bernardin's
death that "the Vatican intended to appoint a new archbishop who would
shape up this wild group."[35] If even Christ was thrown out of his own
town for speaking the truth, why should George be any exception? In a
2012 report to the Holy See, George said that many Chicago priests prid-
ed themselves on "a 'mythic' past, when Chicago led the nation in many
ecclesial reforms. Unfortunately, some of them believed that Vatican II
could be implemented only in opposition to episcopal authority."

In the memorandum from the Pastors' Forum, George was pejora-
tively dubbed "Francis the Corrector." It seemed to some that George had
not acted quickly or diligently enough to fulfill his promise to Chicago's
priests on the eve of his installation. Unlike Cardinal Bernardin's legendary self-introduction as "Joseph, your brother," George said, "I am
your bishop." But, he added, "I will work very, very hard to become your

brother." Although the issues they complained about fell properly within his duties of office, these priests objected to a variety of things about George's leadership, including how he wanted kneelers reinstalled in a Mundelein Seminary chapel, or his request that a high school change its theology textbooks to something more in conformity with Catholic doctrine, or his insistence that lay ministers receive Communion at the proper time. They also objected to George's opposition to suburban Oak Park's proposed ordinance on domestic partnerships and to his intention to welcome into the archdiocese priests from other countries and cultures. And they did their best to remind George that he had no experience as a parish pastor in his curriculum vitae. Regarding the liturgical abuses, while it is true that George, during his parish visits, would address pastors about liturgical aberrations, he did so not to embarrass or reprimand but to foster unity — one of his principal objectives as archbishop. He wrote in 2004, "Where there are aberrations in Eucharistic practice, there are most probably more general difficulties in ecclesiastical discipline and, eventually, there will be problems in professing the apostolic faith."[36] At the same time, George saw these kinds of things as unnecessary distractions to the Church's mission. "Preach the Gospel, go and make disciples, baptize, teach. Instead, we are arguing about where the furniture should be in the sanctuary. I get a little bit distracted by that or a little bit impatient with that at times," he said in an interview just before his installation in Chicago.[37]

Another major point of contention for many in Chicago's presbyterate was familiar to George from his years in Yakima: the use of general absolution, which he found to be unwarranted, especially in the contexts in which it was most commonly employed. It took him many years to overcome the obstacles being proffered by priests, but he eventually put an end to the practice, adopting a stance on the issue much more in accord with the Church's norms. As George said, "The Catholic faith shapes a Church with a lot of room for differences in pastoral approach."[38] But none of the approaches, he stressed, should separate us from what the Church asks us to do in order to achieve communion among believers.

Over the years, George supported a variety of initiatives to underscore this reality, particularly in the sphere of prayer and liturgy.

Not long after his arrival in Chicago, George was introduced to a sizable group of likeminded men at St. John Cantius Parish who were interested in discerning a vocation to the priesthood. The one-time struggling, dilapidated inner-city parish was experiencing a renaissance in its mission of "restoration of the sacred." George suggested that, under the leadership of the parish pastor Fr. C. Frank Phillips, CR, the men form an institute of consecrated life dedicated to advancing their mission, which would "make available to the people of God, the heritage and gifts of the universal Church in all their forms and all their splendor."[39] It was providential that George was bishop at the time, since he had a decisive role in revamping the constitutions of the Oblates of Mary Immaculate while serving as their vicar general. As George helped the group establish itself, he also took keen interest in the formulation of their constitutions. The Canons Regular of St. John Cantius were formally established in 1998, the first religious community of men founded in the Archdiocese of Chicago. The Canons' mission is to restore the sacred "in the context of parish ministry through solemn liturgies, devotions, sacred art and music, instruction in Church heritage, Catholic culture, and catechesis." Their apostolate is a living, breathing embodiment of Pope Benedict's call for a hermeneutic of continuity — something to which George committed himself as a bishop — with the Church's tradition post-Vatican II. Their ministry has also responded to the mission of Christian unity, particularly in their early days, when George asked them to oversee facilitating communion with Rome among small communities who rejected parts or all of Vatican II and adhered exclusively to worship using the 1962 Roman Missal. Elevating the sacred in all things also has a great evangelizing effect, found in, among other things, leading large numbers of young people to embrace the Catholic Faith. The Canons have found success in bringing many to Christ in the neighborhood around the parish, including young atheists. Father Phillips recalled that their founding archbishop would often tell the Canons, "I want you to grow. I want this to succeed. Live your constitutions. Be men of prayer."

George held in great esteem the contemplative communities in the archdiocese, understanding them as a pivotal, life-giving force in the Church. In 1998, George invited the Poor Clares to reestablish a foundation in the Archdiocese of Chicago, and the Monastery of the Immaculate Conception in Palos Park became a reality two years later. For them, George was a beloved patron, and with them, George maintained a close relationship. The same could be said of the contemplative Carmelite Monastery in Des Plaines, where George spent time regularly with its consecrated women. George's understanding that the contemplative dimension of the Church's life and work is vital was closely linked to his efforts to promote Eucharistic Adoration throughout the archdiocese. He reiterated the importance of the practice's development over the centuries and responded to the call of recent popes for a revitalization of the Church through it. The largely lay-led effort was, in George's view, indicative of "a thirst for holiness" among the faithful of the archdiocese.[40] He faced opposition to this emphasis on Eucharistic Adoration from some priests who trivialized the practice to their people as "cookie worship." While some may have viewed the institution of some of these practices as a return to an outdated tradition — or emblematic of a certain conservatism — in George's logic, it was merely a means to continually tether the archdiocese to the Church's own life force. He believed that when the Church is united in belief and in practice, she will be united in mission and holiness.

George celebrated the universal call to holiness as "one of the most important truths of the faith restated during the Second Vatican Council." He often reiterated how the council taught that holiness is the calling of all the baptized. "If all are called to holiness, then the Church should recognize that holy people are found in all walks of life. As I've often said in the parishes, one of the great joys in being archbishop lies in meeting so many people in whom the grace of God has worked."

In early 2002, about five years after his arrival in Chicago, the *Chicago Sun-Times* conducted a survey of pastors that revealed a 90 percent approval rating by 142 pastors across the 378 archdiocesan parishes.[41] A separate *CBS-2/Sun-Times* poll of laity in the archdiocese found three-quarters giving George marks of "good" or "excellent." This was particularly noteworthy given that confidence in episcopal leadership was dropping drastically across the nation on account of the clergy sexual abuse crisis. And the survey noted that, although priests initially balked at a major capital campaign launched by George in 2000 to assist archdiocesan parishes and schools, many considered it ultimately to be "a blessing." One Chicago priest commented in the survey, "He could have just looked at the finances and said we don't have any money and that's that. But he did what needed to be done."

Likewise, the survey observed that although George's arrival put Chicago priests on pins and needles, given his "reputation as a Vatican hard-liner," it quickly became clear that those fears "were largely unfounded." While George "began flexing his muscles" on certain rules pertaining to the celebration of Mass or the Sacrament of Penance, one priest said, "He is absolutely certain that the rules are correct, and he follows them." Another said, "I'm a liberal, and it's hard to say he's not doing what he's supposed to be doing as a leader of the Catholic Church." One pastor said George "doesn't have a pastoral bone in his body," while another said plainly, "I don't think Jesus himself could meet the expectation of the Chicago Catholic Church."

McLaughlin's group told George in 1997 that his actions upon entering the archdiocese "left damage."[42] At the same time, the Pastors' Forum leader insisted the letter was not an expression of "displeasure with the archbishop," just a communication of a "somewhat painful" transition. In one of his regular *Chicago Sun-Times* columns, Father Greeley addressed the motives of the Pastors' Forum and the reaction of George and the archdiocese. He connected it to "a recklessness that comes from near despair [recalling] the quixotic tyranny of the Cardinal Cody years."[43] Greeley praised George's response, especially how George "did not feel attacked," and said he was impressed that a bishop admitted he "might have to change his style." Greeley criticized George's advisors, whom he maintained should have "insisted that [George] meet with the priests who wrote the letter and then have a press conference with them to clear the air before he left for the synod of bishops in Rome" that fall. Since that had not happened, Greeley lamented that "the icon of 'Francis the Corrector' lingers in the atmosphere, a poisonous and apparently false image."

George accepted whatever faults of his that had contributed to the tension that resulted in the letter from McLaughlin and his group. While he did not see the letter as "a crisis," he did acknowledge that perhaps he felt "a little more relaxed than I ought to be" as a Chicago native.[44] He insisted some of the claims were "misinformed" but was also concerned about their criticism of his "style." He said, "I have to take that seriously. … These are important members of the presbyterate."

In 2012, in his quinquennial report to the Holy See, George stated that his ministry brought "practicing Catholics together around Christ (General Absolution services have been abolished; first confessions are heard before first communion, lay preaching at Mass has been eliminated, with an occasional abuse in some parishes, etc.)." He was also able to advance mission at the same time, citing a redefinition of discipleship based on evangelization and stewardship, new initiatives in the media, and engaging in public debate about the day's most important issues.

George thought, as he observed in his homily on the eve of his installation in 1997, that the postconciliar years caused the Church to be "stuck in an endless argument between devotion and liturgy, or in a constant dispute between charity and justice. I think this when devotion is treated as the enemy of liturgy and charity as the betrayer of justice, or when liturgy is reduced to private devotion and justice not recognized as constitutive of the Gospel of Jesus Christ."[45] How did he hope the situation would be resolved? "In a Church filled with devotions of all sorts and active in its liturgical participation; in a Church able to give in charity and desirous also to work for justice. In short, in an evangelizing Church that reaches out to transform society into a civilization of love."

George saw his role in governance as a means to bring all together in Christ. His apostolic mandate from Pope John Paul II said as much directly: "By virtue of his prudence in judgments and his experience in ecclesial matters, he will know, equally in turn, how to govern effectively and advantageously." He understood that the Church's teaching was a source of unification, as were the Church's liturgical rubrics or even our postures at prayer. He saw his job not as correcting, but as uniting.

In order to be an effective bishop, George regularly asked his flock to pray for him. In 1999, he wrote:

> One is called by God to this vocation and is sustained in it by the prayers of the people. Every bishop is grateful for his vocation, but every bishop also recognizes how fragile his own cooperation with Father, Son, and Spirit may be. The Church encourages prayers for the Pope and other bishops because without them the risk is great that the bishop might begin to go his own way and forsake the saving embrace of Father, Son, and Holy Spirit.[46]

The 1997 memo from the disgruntled priests came around the anniversary of Bernardin's death, and it certainly made the transition more difficult, particularly in a city where priests had been mostly left unmanaged for decades. Progressive Notre Dame theologian Fr. Richard McBrien characterized George's appointment to Chicago as a time of excitement for conservatives. "They want him to come in and clean up the mess," he told the *National Catholic Reporter*.[47] Russell Shaw, in the same piece, said in perhaps the most accurate assessment at the time of George's appointment, "As orthodox as he is, I don't think he's going to prove to be an inquisitor or crackdown sort of guy. He's going to act on his own convictions and try to bring people along rather than shove them along."

A colleague of George's from the Cambridge Center, Msgr Richard Malone, observed that when George arrived in Chicago "he discovered no one had really been an active archbishop; they had been national figures. Chicago had been left to itself. He thought his job was to govern. And I think that meant that he was going to run into trouble from the start."

TEN

Governing and Suffering in Crisis

The day I became a bishop, a burden was laid on my shoulders for which it will be no easy task to render an account. ... To be honest with you, my obligations involve me in so much turmoil that I feel as though I were tossed by storms on a great ocean.

SAINT AUGUSTINE

Given his extensive background in ecclesiastical governance and his lengthy résumé, Cardinal George was asked in 2013 by Chicago CBS 2's Jay Levine, "What's the best assignment you've ever had?" With his characteristic smile, George responded, "Well, archbishop of Chicago, of course." Levine followed up by asking, "What's the most challenging assignment you've ever had?" George replied instantly, "Archbishop of

Chicago, beyond any doubt!"

George had already been warned about the difficulties of being archbishop of Chicago — most notably by his predecessor, Cardinal Joseph Bernardin. One night in Rome — at the North American College, where they were both staying as participants in the 1994 synod on consecrated life — Bernardin discussed the deep divisions in the Archdiocese of Chicago over a late-night glass of milk with the man who would, unbeknownst to them, succeed him in less than three years. When George expressed his disconcert, Bernardin smiled at him and said, "Well, you know, Francis, Chicago is sometimes ungovernable."[1]

Once in office, George would come to find that "Chicago is locked into patterns of self-destruction that I am powerless to change," as he wrote privately in 2004. Yet George believed that a "crisis of authority in the Church cannot be resolved if bishops don't act like bishops."[2] In order for bishops to govern well, they need, most of all, the cooperation of their priests. The biggest question of George's governance in Chicago was how to bring that about.

Another point of frustration for George was that he was often the last to know about things. As he noted in a 2006 internal memo to all archdiocesan employees, "I was puzzled by a 'system' that almost systematically seemed to exclude the office of Archbishop from information, especially from bad news. Sometimes it seemed motivated by a protective concern not to burden the Archbishop; sometimes by a conviction that it was really none of his business. But in too many areas, the byword seemed to be, 'Don't tell the Cardinal.'" George argued, "The quality of governance depends upon the flow of information; information in any office, except in the case of health or finance records in some instances, is not something to be guarded rather than shared."[3]

These struggles within the archdiocese were all the more painful for George, as he had arrived at his new assignment intending to focus on local governance. Despite his eventual rise to national leadership, George had not planned to immerse himself in national policy as had his predecessor. "I had no intention of trying to be a competitor with Cardinal

Bernardin," George said at a gathering with priests in 2006.[4]

> I have very little interest in national policy for many reasons. I
> have no intention of trying to fill his shoes. And I still don't. I
> think that each of us brings something and none of us replaces
> anybody else. But I knew that to some extent you did have to get
> used to somebody with a slightly lower profile, as I would have
> hoped, a much quieter one, because I'm much more at ease with
> that.

George's mindset was grounded in his understanding of his own vocation as a bishop. He argued his "deep conviction" at that same 2006
gathering: While central and important, "bishops are not the Church."
He added: "Both the liberals and conservatives put too much emphasis
on the bishops. So the idea of being in some sense a guru, of being some
kind of mythic figure — that's not who I am then or now in my understanding of who I am."

Some of the idea that bishop was equal to Church stemmed from
an Illinois state law created decades before — a practice not uncommon
throughout the United States, but legendarily effective in Chicago. The
law legally classified the archbishop as "corporation sole" — a system of
organization whereby the diocesan ordinary solely manages all assets of
the diocese. The name of Chicago's archbishop, therefore, is on the title
for every parish, school, and all other entities under the auspices of the
archdiocese. This legal reality dated back to the great institutional builder
of Catholic Chicago, Cardinal George Mundelein, who helped the local
faithful emerge from a minority status and take on greater roles and responsibilities in society, and utilized corporation sole to build a massive
institutional structure in Chicago. George explained to Chicago priests at
a 2006 gathering that he saw the existence of corporation sole in Chicago as a "myth," or something ironically opposed to the reality of the job.
"Whatever it means, it was simply designed as a way to protect the assets
of the Church civilly while we govern according to the code in which ev-

ery parish is a corporation, a public juridic person in the code."[5] Instead, it ended up meaning that laypeople considered the ordinary to be fully in control, all-knowing, and all-powerful. George lamented how far this was from the truth and admitted that this style of governance was "very isolating" because it sustained the appearance of "all kinds of trappings and very little substance." It also gave, he said to the priests in 2006, "little sense of accountability, on my part to others or others to me, be it the chancery office or parishes."

It was difficult for George to get his footing in Chicago. "The job puzzled me quite a bit. And I'm a man who has had a lot of jobs and have done them fairly well," he explained at the 2006 gathering. "I have a sense of my limitations, but I'm not falsely modest. I've done a lot of things around the world in the Church. So I came here with that expectation it would take me a while, but eventually we'll get the hang of it. And I have a very hard time working into it."

The reality was that large parts of the Chicago presbyterate can be very much influenced by a political model, as if each parish was something like a precinct or ward. As George put it, such a large archdiocese can, "paradoxically, be quite provincial because it has many resources." Once a pastor got his turf, he and no one else was often the one in control. One of the psychosocial aspects of this paradigm is that everyone looks out for himself and his own but the one at the top is often treated with suspicion — a suspicion that is mutual. This mindset was influenced by politics and reinforced by Cardinal John Cody, Chicago's archbishop from 1965 to 1982, whose governance many described as despotic. His successor, Cardinal Bernardin, had to work hard not only to regain the priests' trust but also to de-escalate a considerable amount of tension between the archbishop and the presbyterate. Bernardin's administrative style was to be more or less hands-off. Many priests have argued, including Fr. Andrew Greeley, that when George arrived and wanted to exercise a more hands-on form of governance — in a good sense — some priests had a flashback to the Cody era. Countless priests have said that as they got to know George, they believed he loved them and that he was their brother despite any disagreements they might have.

In his 2012 quinquennial report to the Holy See, George under-scored the provincial realities of the Chicago presbyterate, regretting that in such a large archdiocese, "some priests come to almost nothing outside of their own parish." He also said that the priests "as a whole trust me" but acknowledged that "there is a small group who would be opposed to me personally." He observed also in the report that the reality of Chica-go's long history of "strong presbyteral leadership and relatively detached episcopal leadership" was changing. One of the reasons, he argued, was George's great reliance on the auxiliary bishops to assist him in gover-nance, in addition to the reality that "economic constraints are forcing more inter-parochial cooperation."

As the clergy sexual abuse crisis ground on in the first decade of the new millennium, the priests' bond with George grew somewhat stronger. The scandal exacerbated the difficulties he experienced in governing and absorbed a great deal of his time and attention, but it also raised his na-tional profile as one of the handful of significant voices at the time. Just weeks before the highly anticipated June 2002 meeting of US bishops in Dallas, which yielded a "zero tolerance policy" for offending priests and deacons — a policy of which George was initially skeptical before later becoming a defender at the Church's highest levels — the *Chicago Tribune* took a shot at George.[6] In an editorial titled "A Challenge to Cardinal George," it argued that Chicago Catholics had great difficulty completing this sentence: "My cardinal gets the loss of confidence in the hierarchy, and he says we really have to ..."

George publicly replied to the *Tribune* in his biweekly column pub-lished in the archdiocesan newspaper, the *Catholic New World*. He noted that "a bishop who doesn't get the loss of confidence in the hierarchy today must be comatose. But bishops cannot address that loss outside of the context of faith which creates the Church as Church."[7] In completing the *Tribune*'s prompt himself, George not only got to the heart of how to proceed through the clergy sexual abuse crisis but also, more to the point, explained his primary role as a bishop: "My cardinal gets the loss of confidence in the hierarchy, and he says we really have to ask for the grace to be more faithful disciples, in what we believe and in how we act, bishops and people together around Jesus Christ." As he wrote his flock that summer, "A crisis of authority in the Church cannot be resolved if bishops don't act like bishops."[8]

As the clergy sexual abuse crisis broke into the open early in 2002, George often addressed the concerns, anxieties, hurt, and shame of his flock, as he would throughout the rest of his tenure. He was especially troubled that nearly 10 percent of weekly Mass goers disappeared after the 2002 abuse and cover-up stories emerged from Boston and beyond, from which he also indicated the archdiocese never quite rebounded. In a Mother's Day column that year, George reflected on how he thought his parents would react to the scandal by explaining what they had taught him about the Church: that the Church is a mother who gives us "the life of grace and brings us to salvation in Christ."[9] This was in contrast, he argued, to contemporary descriptions employed to describe the Church — such as organization, institution, corporation, personal club, or state — which "dominate an imagination not shaped by Catholic faith." These perceptions of the Church have actually contributed to the crisis.

Knowing that his flock's faith in the Church weakened as the clergy sexual abuse crisis gained steam and dominated headlines around the world, George reminded them:

> Your mother is always your mother; and the current crisis surrounding those who are 'fathers' in the Church cannot weaken the attachment of her true children to our holy mother, the Church. The Church remains as the creed describes her: one, holy, catholic and apostolic. She is fully visible in the communion of all those who gather with and under the Bishop of Rome. Finally, with repentance for sin and purified for mission, her children will continue to rejoice in her.

George also regretted how a diminished priestly identity contributed to the crisis, particularly as it became more fashionable to no longer define priestly identity on Christ's terms and the priest's exercise of ministry on the Church's terms. If a priest takes on celibacy as a means to ordination, he will likely experience resentment, George argued. And the result, as George put it, will be that "resentment will destroy the Church as well as the priest."[10]

As George tackled the clergy sexual abuse crisis, he simultaneously worked to implement a robust lay ecclesial ministry. This was not only because lay ecclesial ministry was rooted in and emphasized by the teachings of the Second Vatican Council, but also because it was equally part of the Church's own baptismal faith. In the reemergence of lay leadership in the Church, George saw an antidote to clericalism, which he described as "a sinful attitude that removes a person from being accountable."[11] Reflecting on what he had encountered in leadership positions immediately after Vatican II, he supported the importance of lay leadership in the Church, saying that "to limit leadership solely to bishops and priests is clericalism, which is a sin."[12] But he also cautioned that "we cannot make the opposite error, however, and say that ordained pastoral leadership is not intrinsic to the very nature of the Church."

THE RYAN AFFAIR

As the metropolitan archbishop of Chicago, with jurisdiction over an ecclesiastical province that encompassed all the dioceses in the state of Illinois, George was directed by the Holy See to investigate allegations of a bishop's own misconduct and abuse, which dragged him into the sordid tale of Daniel L. Ryan, bishop of Springfield in Illinois. Accusations had been leveled against Ryan by a group of laity in that diocese who obfuscated their argument with a lack of detailed accounts from victims and also by intermingling their allegations of misconduct with a variety of ideological, theological, and liturgical complaints against the bishop. The group had contacted the apostolic nuncio, who in turn asked George to investigate the situation.

Meanwhile, as Ryan was trying to head off a crisis, he admitted preemptively in 1997 to the nuncio that he had a problem with alcohol and occasionally blacked out, arguing that because of this he was not responsible for the acts of which he was being accused, which consisted mostly of drunkenness and homosexual activities with male prostitutes and other members of the clergy. George was informally tasked with looking into these allegations on behalf of the nuncio.

George charged a highly credible lay member of his staff, Jimmy Lago — who had a background in child welfare investigations — to oversee this investigation on his behalf. This was a move ahead of its time, as it was quite irregular then to delegate a layperson to oversee the investigation of a bishop. A lengthy process ensued — involving conversations with alleged victims and informants — in which details were not always easily forthcoming and mixed information was offered. After the investigation's conclusion, George received a full, detailed report. Determining the credibility of the victims was difficult at times, because they were often troubled youth who were addicted to drugs and in jail, and their allegations were often tied to demands for money. While the investigation showed how hard it was to ascertain the truth with a "smoking gun" level of precision, it is clear that something unusual and seismic happened behind the scenes, given that the Holy See eventually asked Ryan to resign from his position. Such a result, at that time, was not the typical operating procedure. Many involved with the case and its aftermath credit George for quietly but forcefully pushing for that outcome, which is something he regularly did in a variety of situations, though few ever knew it. Claims have been made, however, that allege that George tried to silence the group that exposed Ryan's misdeeds to the hierarchy so they would not go public. Given the end result, however, these allegations might be more realistically understood as an entreaty to a collaboration that would result in what both parties wanted: the removal of Ryan without publicly forcing the Holy See to circle the wagons.

Years later, George refused to attend a retired bishop's annual Christmas party when he learned that Ryan, in retirement, would be present. Given George's own record, it is clear he had little respect for such a person. Dealing with individuals and situations like this was just one aspect of the hidden suffering that George faced as a bishop.

SUFFERING AND ISOLATION

At a 2012 gathering of youth and young adults from the Archdiocese of Chicago, George was asked about his patron saint, St. Francis of Assisi. Describing Saint Francis as "a man who was very, very close to Christ," George added that "he even had the stigmata, the wounds, the last eight months of his life." George may have felt an ever-closer bond with his patron due to the personal suffering that he experienced throughout his life, particularly as governing archbishop in Chicago.

The difficulties with the Chicago presbyterate, in addition to the clergy sexual abuse crisis as it unfolded locally and nationally, were clearly an enduring source of anxiety for George and added a further dimension to his private suffering. Many who knew George for any length of time could observe the physical toll the years in Chicago had taken on him. Friends from Yakima remarked that it seemed like he had less joy. For George, serving as archbishop of Chicago was not so much a position to relish as it was a cross to bear.

In August 2004, George privately wrote that he found himself "deeply depressed" after the death of his auxiliary Bishop Edwin Conway, also his vicar general, because he was greatly dependent on Conway for strengthening his relationship with the Chicago presbyterate. Conway was a well-liked and well-known priest in Chicago, an honest and trustworthy collaborator who helped George navigate the waters of the archdiocese. Conway's death meant for George, in his own private words, "the end of my hope for a truly effective government." He was bothered by "mundane" efforts of evangelization in the archdiocese. He lamented that "the city is against me, as is popular opinion." He also struggled with his relationship with Chicago and Cook County's political life.

In 2012, George added his own description of Chicago politics, which so much shaped the life of the local Church, to his quinquennial report to the Holy See, saying, "Chicago is governed very like a Leninist one-party state and has a very long history of engrained civic corruption." He explained, too, that since the Democratic Party controlled the state, county, and city governments, "there is tension around some issues, especially at the moment the question of 'gay rights.'" He often joked with some friends that the difficulty with Chicago politicians was that they were all Jesuit educated, a joke only another religious could make.

In 2001, George wrote privately of how he felt "isolated" in Chicago, "unable to move or influence." George's great lament in his efforts to govern was how difficult it was "without cooperation of the priests," which he added, "I can't get."[13] Nonetheless, he made himself available to priests at all times, as those who lived and worked with him attest. If a priest needed to see him, it was George's clear expectation that their request was to be prioritized.

George found frustration with a culture of "lying in Chicago," and he wrote privately in 2004 that he saw his existence in Chicago "like being drawn into a web of evil," even calling it "a 'prison.'" As he agonized interiorly over his desire to be "well-accepted," he also knew he must do his job as a bishop. That same year, he wrote privately, "I have been Archbishop of Chicago for 7 years — they have not been happy years — I have held back, I have been full of resentment. ... But it is I who must accept — surrender to the role here and let Christ act as He wills ... I am fully ready to do that."

The clergy sexual abuse crisis only exacerbated the frustrations George experienced in Chicago, which he already found plagued by scandal in many ways. He wrote privately about his regret that the Chicago priests had lost their way, and he was deeply burdened as "its sexual and financial sins are being exposed" along with "its arrogance, etc." He acknowledged to himself, as he wrote privately, "I need to lead, but I am fearful. I wait for God, but as a *Deus ex machina*, not a God who shapes us slowly."

Australian Cardinal George Pell, the former archbishop of Sydney and inaugural Prefect for the Holy See's Secretariat for the Economy from 2014 to 2019, was a longtime friend and admirer of George. From

2019 to 2020, Pell spent a year in solitary confinement after a wrongful conviction for sexual abuse of minors. Pell was sympathetic to George's description that it was like "a prison" in Chicago. "I've got no doubt that my life in jail, in solitary confinement — I was completely safe there, undisturbed, was boring, of course — was much easier than life as Archbishop of Chicago," Pell explained, adding, admittedly with some modicum of hyperbole, "being archbishop of Chicago might even be more difficult than being pope." Pell added: "Chicago is a great diocese [but] it's not an easy diocese."

The cross George bore in leading a difficult archdiocese and presbyterate also motivated his personal interest in reshaping Mundelein Seminary, the major seminary of the archdiocese. George knew that reforming the presbyterate in Chicago was a long game. He was much more present at the seminary than any of his predecessors, addressing the student body each semester and regularly hosting classes of Chicago seminarians for dinner. He was interested in having a relationship with them. While many of his priests would have been happier had he left them alone and let them do as they pleased, George wanted to build a culture of priests tethered to their archbishop in unity of mission. And many of Chicago's priests, particularly the young priests he accompanied through formation and subsequently ordained, came to truly love him as a father. Some of these seminarians did not hesitate to request a personal appointment with him to seek his counsel, and he was always willing to meet with them. A good number of them served as pallbearers at his funeral ceremonies in 2015. In total, George ordained 222 priests during his time in Chicago. In his 2012 report to the Holy See, he noted, "As a whole [the priests] trust me, even when they disagree with me; and I trust them."

The challenges posed by the clergy sexual abuse crisis and a difficult archdiocese had ramifications on George's own psyche and spiritual life. "Perhaps I have lost hope, even in God," he wrote privately in 2004.[14] For the most part, he carried this spiritual darkness, this profound share in the cross that came about from his office, interiorly. George pushed on despite the difficult times, maintaining a jam-packed schedule until the latest hours of each day. In response to the selfishness and sins of others that often burdened him, George offered himself for the good of others.

George's hidden life of suffering began, of course, with his own childhood polio. The effects of the disease had shaped his life, and he wrote privately in 2001 of his "resentments" — what he acknowledged as a spiritual distraction. "I resent my illness at 13, of my parents' deaths, my appointment to Chicago," he wrote privately. He feared he was not loving his flock enough, and he longed for more unity with the Lord. He urged himself in response: "Conversion … talk to God, not think about him."

Often, in these circumstances, it was clear that he saw the grace from Christ in the sacraments as the strength he needed most. He wrote privately in 2008, acknowledging his dependency upon the Lord: "What a lonely world it would be without the Eucharist." On more than one occasion, he resolved, amid the struggles he faced, to go to confession, and at least once he mentioned fasting from the Eucharist, which, he wrote privately in 2001, "forces me back to the *mysterium iniquitatis* and my cooperation in it." Though this is an uncommon spiritual practice, it is one that is sometimes embraced by those who possess a very deep interior life and have reached an elevated state in the spiritual life.

George constantly seemed dissatisfied with himself and his leadership in Chicago. In 2002, he wrote privately about a "fear of surrendering totally." The next year, he worried about not loving the people enough and not using his public role well. "Is my great uneasiness with being a public figure because of resentment long ago of shame of polio?" he wrote privately. In 2004 he wrote privately about the duties of his position, which he found both "spiritually dangerous" and "physically debilitating." He believed he was not cut out for "the lifestyle of the Cardinal Archbishop of Chicago, an endless round of benefits and banquets, of parties and receptions."

As a shepherd, he knew his faithfulness to the Lord was measured by his service to the flock. "I often think that death would be a liberation, and yet I must encourage them," he wrote privately in the same year. He lamented never having enough time to dedicate himself to the tasks at hand in any adequate way, but he reminded himself that "five loaves and two fish are enough if Christ uses them."

The drama of the clergy sexual abuse crisis also made George anxious. In 2013, he admitted in an interview that "I used to have perhaps an idealism that couldn't imagine a priest doing terrible things like this. Now I know a few priests … that have done things like this, and they are terrible things."[15] In the same interview, George commented that "seeing the results [of abuse], you live with the consequences." He added: "It affects my prayer life. It affects my prayer for priests and victims as well. It's a permanent sorrow that's always there." George wrote privately in 2004, observing how he saw "the Church despoiled and the faith eroding" in the wake of the crisis, but in the end he knew "there is only Christ and his will that count."[16] At a gathering of Chicago priests in 2006, he acknowledged the stress put on Catholics because of the crisis. "In the end they know why they're Catholics and they know better what it means to be Catholic."[17] But he observed that it would mean a lot of long-term changes for the Church and her members:

> We live in a society that has had cultural Catholicism — and that's not a bad thing. But I think [the crisis has] called for a more intentional Catholicism now, and it has to be or else it won't go on. Maybe that's what the Lord wants us to talk about. Not only the intentional relations of accountability among ourselves, to the Lord most of all, but also the way in which we make the lives of the baptized much more intentional. I think we will have a Catholic Church in the next generation or two that's going to be a creative minority.

George had a large number of clergy abuse cases to handle in his tenure in Chicago. In 2002, he removed from ministry several priests who had been allowed to remain in some kind of ministry by Cardinal Bernardin, even in the wake of credible abuse allegations. In a 2012 gathering with

Chicago priests, George remarked that even among the 6,000 priests he helped oversee as Oblate vicar general "we didn't have anything like the numbers [of abusers] that I looked at here."[18]

In 2008, George wrote privately that the sexual abuse crisis is "like a target — unable to escape."[19] The cases of abuse that emerged under his tenure in Chicago, for the most part, were past problems that he inherited, often concerning priests who were already retired or deceased. George was both lauded and criticized for his response as such cases came forward. But no criticism that he faced could compare in its magnitude to the case of Chicago priest Daniel McCormack. In January 2006, McCormack was removed from ministry after being arrested for the second time. The complex case first came to George's attention in September 2005, after McCormack's first arrest for suspected sexual abuse of a minor.

In a striking example of George's concern that the archbishop of Chicago was sometimes the last to know about things, he was not told about the arrest until three days after it happened. At that time, he was informed by a vicar for priests that McCormack had been quickly released after his arrest. George later apologized for thinking that McCormack's release meant that he was not a danger to children.

When George arrived in Chicago, McCormack had been serving on a seminary faculty — a position of trust, as George put it. At the time of his arrest, McCormack headed a parish and had recently been appointed as a dean. He was a popular, energetic young pastor who served poverty-stricken inner-city parishes that welcomed mostly minority families.

It is now known that McCormack was living a double life and, in fact, had been involved in sexual misconduct since his days as a seminarian. According to a 2007 interview in the *Chicago Sun-Times*, Bishop Gerald F. Kicanas, the former rector of Mundelein Seminary who in that capacity had recommended McCormack for ordination by Cardinal Joseph Bernardin in 1994, said he had been aware of "sexual improprieties" on McCormack's part — two involving adults and one involving a minor.[20] This alleged behavior, which McCormack reportedly admitted, occurred mostly during his years in college-level formation for the priesthood, according to Kicanas, although it only came to the attention of formators during his time at Mundelein. Kicanas said in the same interview, however, that "it would have been grossly unfair not to have ordained him," adding, "there was a sense that his activity was part of the developmental process and that he had learned from the experience."

Kicanas said he considered the bigger threat to be McCormack's problem with alcohol abuse. "We sent him to counseling for that," Kicanas said. "I don't think there was anything I could have done differently." In a 2010 interview with the *National Catholic Register*, Kicanas responded to the *Sun-Times'* story, saying that it "does not accurately reflect what I said and was put into a context that is not accurate."[21] He went on to say that he "would never defend endorsing McCormack's ordination if I had had any knowledge or concern that he might be a danger to anyone, and I had no such knowledge or concern." He further added that "at no time while McCormack was a seminarian at Mundelein did I receive any allegation of pedophilia or child molestation against him."

A 2006 internal archdiocesan audit determined, according to then-Mundelein Vice Rector Fr. John Canary, that the incidents of misconduct on the part of McCormack had been noted in his seminary file. Auditors, however, could not find any such notations. Said the report:

> Audit review of Fr. McCormack's seminarian files failed to locate any documentation of allegations of sexual misconduct or allegations of sexual abuse on the part of Fr. McCormack, however, the interview of the former Vice Rector of the seminary identified three (3) distinct allegations of sexual misconduct of both adults and of a minor on the part of Fr. McCormack that were brought to the attention of the seminarian officials in the spring quarter of 1992. The former Vice Rector recalled that these allegations were documented to Fr. McCormack's file.[22]

Part of the problem in Chicago regarding proper transmission of information in the McCormack case was the practice of keeping a priest's seminary file separate from the personnel file that the archdiocese maintained on him after ordination. George corrected this practice in the wake of this tragic episode.

When McCormack was being vetted for his appointment as head of a deanery, just before his first arrest, two vicars for priests recommended against it. Their reasoning, given in response to a question about suitability for the position from George's vicar general, stemmed from a letter in McCormack's file that indicated the archdiocese had received a phone call from a concerned parishioner saying McCormack frequently had boys with him in the rectory. The vicar general, soon-to-be-appointed Chicago auxiliary bishop George Rassas, recommended to George nonetheless that McCormack's nomination as a dean proceed. It later surfaced that McCormack had also been suspected of abuse in 1999, but this was not appropriately reported to either state or archdiocesan authorities. Archdiocesan school personnel had also fielded a number of complaints about McCormack from 1999 to December 2005, but according to an external investigator authorized by the archdiocese after the McCormack scandal, the allegations were not reported to competent authorities.

After McCormack's first arrest, the archdiocese had a difficult time constructing a case to put before the review board. At that time, the US bishops' *Charter for the Protection of Children and Young People* and the Church's code of canon law provided that a priest could be removed only when an accusation had been found credible. The police and the state were not sharing information from their own investigations, and, as far as George knew, no victim who was willing to cooperate with a thorough investigation had come forward to the archdiocese.

Over time, a systemic breakdown had taken place within archdiocesan administration for many reasons: in part because people in various parts of the system operated in "silos"; in part because of competing personal interests and an ineffective sharing of information; in part because of a system developed and more accustomed to handling the investigation of historical cases of abuse rather than current ones; and in part because state officials did not cooperate effectively with the archdiocese.

The Charter is specifically designed to prohibit the diocesan bishop from interfering with an investigation against a priest or deacon of the diocese accused of sexual abuse of a minor, and in this case, that rule worked against George. When the archdiocesan review board recommended in the fall of 2005 that McCormack be removed from ministry, they did so without conclusive evidence. George, striving to balance "zero tolerance" with the rights of priests, objected, knowing that a removal without proper grounds would be a violation of Church law, would cause undue damage if the allegation ended up being false, and could potentially be reversed if the priest appealed to the Holy See. It turns out, however, that George's desire to follow established norms and procedures, on account of his concern for justice and fairness for all parties, also came at a great cost. He would later say, "I wish that I had followed [the review board's recommendation] with all my heart."[23]

After learning of McCormack's 2005 arrest, George had been told that a priest-monitor had been assigned to McCormack — which was then part of standard archdiocesan protocol for accused priests while they were under investigation. But the system, as George put it, "was sorely inadequate," and it fell apart. Monitoring was sporadic and dependent at times on what information the accused was willing to share. McCormack abused again, and more than one child suffered. After his final arrest in January 2006, a conviction followed a guilty plea of five counts against him.

The McCormack case — including the failures of the archdiocesan response — is arguably the ugliest chapter of Chicago's clergy sexual abuse crisis, and George could not escape it. But, as evidence shows, he did not downplay it or cover it up. He was not protecting another member of an exclusive clergy all-boys club, nor was he, as a bishop, trying to cover up for one of his priests. And his response to the case was not motivated by fear of losing ecclesiastical assets. At this point in the Church's history, however, someone had to stand in the breach and try to do right by all parties, and that's where George placed himself. "We are sometimes asked to choose between the accuser and the accused," said George in Dallas in 2002.[24] "But of course, precisely as bishops, let alone as disciples of the Lord, we cannot choose one or the other; we have to choose both. We have to love both."

George believed every allegation needed to be taken seriously because, in his own experience, more often than not the allegations are true. George also understood that if a priest was removed because of a false allegation, his life could be ruined and great damage could be done to the spiritual lives of many other priests and of the people they served. In at least one such case, George invited the falsely accused priest to concelebrate Mass with him at Holy Name Cathedral and publicly did all he could to clear this priest's name of any wrongdoing.

In the McCormack case, George, as the head of the archdiocese, took the fall for everyone and apologized. He did not call out any particular individuals who were more at fault than others. He did, however, place a disciplinary letter in the personnel file of his vicar general — ordained an auxiliary bishop just weeks after McCormack's second arrest — as well as the vicar for priests. In 2012, after the archdiocese paid out a settlement of more than $12 million to abuse victims, including McCormack's, George said, "In the sense I'm responsible for this archdiocese, I have to accept the blame."[25] It was later reported that the archdiocese of Chicago has acknowledged thirty "substantiated" claims of abuse related to McCormack and, as of 2021, has paid out $10 million in settlements related to his abuse alone.

In the aftermath of the case, George was concerned for the health of the archdiocese. "The sins of priests and bishops destroy the Church, and I pray that our Archdiocese will not be harmed," George wrote to his flock.[26] He worried about the Church being despoiled of her patrimony. "What happens to me in all of this is of small importance; what happens to the Archdiocese is of great importance," he wrote. "It is not God's will that this Archdiocese be torn apart; but God depends upon our cooperation to prevent its being harmed and to make it stronger."

Above all, George needed cooperation from his priests. In early 2006, after McCormack's second arrest and removal from ministry, George made an urgent and bold plea in a private memo to priests that if any of them were engaged in nefarious activity they should make themselves known.

> To be honest with you, I often feel like I am walking on quick-sand here. There is so much that I remain unaware of, yet I am, in the end, responsible for it all. I want to say now that if there is any priest who is leading a double life, who is engaged in dishonest or sinful practices that destroy the Church, he should, for the sake of the Church, come forward. If a priest cannot change and convert anew, he should leave his sacred office in the Church. People rightly have high standards for us, the standards the Church herself gives us and which each of us has freely accepted. All of us are sinners, but there are types of perversion that are completely incompatible with the calling of ordained priesthood.[27]

In subsequent weeks and months, there were many priests who, to their credit, went to George, admitted their failings, and left public ministry as a result.

George also asked his priests, in the same letter, to find a way to constructively move forward. "If we can lay aside our competitiveness and work together for the mission of the Church, if we can develop fraternity and lay aside bravado and cynicism, anger and duplicity, we can together be the effective instruments the Holy Spirit needs for a genuine spiritual renewal of the Archdiocese," he said. "This is what gives meaning to our own lives and hope for the future." In response to the systemic failures in the archdiocese related to the McCormack scandal, George called for a thorough, independent investigation, something of a first in any American diocese. He put chancellor Jimmy Lago in charge of providing for a more comprehensive, effective, and prompt archdiocesan response to clergy sexual abuse. George yet again depended on Lago's background serving as a child-abuse investigator and child-protective services administrator and then on the Ethics Commission of the Office of the Inspector General of the Illinois Department of Children and Family Services, to help the archdiocese be of better service to abuse survivors. But he was also depending on the father of children for this vital role.

Lago was instrumental in bringing about a report, commissioned by the archdiocese and conducted by former FBI agent Danny Defenbaugh, that detailed a litany of deficiencies in the archdiocese's process of investigating claims of sexual abuse against minors. This is believed to be a first for any American diocese. At a 2012 gathering with Chicago priests, George spoke about his disappointment in getting the truth out about the McCormack case. While admitting that the system fell apart on his watch, he regretted how much public perception of the case "is paralyzing the mission and I take it — as I get older more and more — to heart, because that's going to be my reputation. And I accept it, if that's the will of the Lord. But it's really, from my perspective at least, not justified, it's not fair." He regarded it as "fair," however, when he could tell his people "that there is nobody [in ministry] who has ever abused a minor child at any point in his life as an ordained priest."[28]

Reiterating George's own concerns, Defenbaugh's report identified as a major deficiency the poor flow of communication within the chancery, with George often being the last to receive critical information. In an attempt to correct this, especially regarding the sensitive topic of sexual abuse of minors, George wrote in a memo to archdiocesan employees in the wake of the McCormack fiasco, "In the case of anything related to the sexual abuse of minors, I ask you with insistence to come forward directly to me or to someone who will immediately inform me." George also wrote to the director of the Illinois Department of Children and Family Services (DCFS), asking that this agency also begin to share information with the archdiocese gleaned from their own investigations of those accused of sexually abusing minors — something that did not happen in McCormack's case. For example, the archdiocese, including George, had no knowledge that the DCFS had "found credible evidence of child abuse/neglect" against McCormack. McCormack was informed by DCFS of this finding in a December 14, 2005, letter, but this crucial document was not shared with the archdiocese until after the priest's second arrest. "With all my heart, I wish they had given me this on December the 14th," George stated in a deposition on the case in 2008 upon seeing the letter for the first time.[29] "They gave it to Dan McCormack. Had they given it to me, he would have been out immediately." George wrote to his priests, "There is more than irony in the claim that going only to the State will result in immediate action, when quite the contrary happened here." As he told Chicago priests in 2012, "If there's any coverup with McCormack, it's with the civil authorities."

In a drafted letter to the editors of the *Chicago Tribune* — amid great criticism against the archdiocese and its archbishop, and in an attempt to set the record straight on the McCormack case — George noted that the case had revealed a flaw in the Dallas Charter. Because of the ugly episode, the Charter, at George's instigation, was amended to provide for the temporary removal of a priest while he was under investigation. "In that sense, some good has come out of this evil story," George wrote.

During his time in Chicago, in relation to legal settlements with survivors of clergy sexual abuse, George twice released the names of accused priests, along with their personnel files. "Painful though publicly reviewing the past can be, it is part of the accountability and transparency to which the Archdiocese is committed," George wrote ahead of the release of the list for the second time, just weeks before his 2014 retirement.[30] Around the same time, George commented in an interview that he believed when the full, true story was written about how clergy sexual abuse was handled in Chicago, at least from the early 1990s onward, it would be rather different than what might be found nationally. He reiterated that since reforms had been put in place during the latter years of Cardinal Bernardin's tenure in Chicago, the police often knew more than the archdiocese did, and that there had been no cover-ups on his watch. He also stated clearly that he had never transferred a priest he knew to be an abuser in Chicago or anywhere else.

Writing to Cardinal George on February 20, 2006, Father Greeley acknowledged that "the Bernardin plan" worked, but the McCormack episode suggested that "there are some eventualities it does not cover."[31] Noting that "no human system is mistake proof," Greeley — who it must be remembered was one of the first public voices about the gravity of the clergy sexual abuse crisis — said to George, "if a mistake is found, it should be fixed so that it doesn't happen again. All this seems unexceptional. So why the rage?" As far as critics were concerned, Greeley told George, "Some folks, we both know their names, would like to wrest the Archdiocese away from you. They don't know what they're asking for."

In January 2006, George wrote about how both the year of evangelization then underway and the scandal then absorbing him and the archdiocese presented an opportunity for conversion. He commented in a column that year, "I have begun to add some extra time in prayer before the Blessed Sacrament to my own daily schedule in order to ask God's forgiveness for the sin of sexual abuse of minors. In this time before the Lord, I try to bring to mind, besides the many victims I have personally met and prayed with in recent years, all those who might not have yet come forward and the many more victims who are suffering silently in our society."[32] A year later, he wrote privately resolving to "pray for troubled priests more regularly" as a means to let go of his "anger and sense of betrayal."[33]

BRINGING HEALING

George regularly met with survivors of clergy sexual abuse, and his honesty and candor in the wake of this scourge on the Church earned him the admiration of many. "Beyond the physical, emotional, psychological and social damage that is done by sexual abuse, there is a deep spiritual wound, rooted in a profound betrayal of trust," George observed, and he invited his flock to take up the work of spiritual reparation for the abuses and sins committed by clergy.[34] He called upon Saint Paul's instruction to the Colossians: "Now I rejoice in my sufferings for your sake, and in my flesh I am filling up what is lacking in the afflictions of Christ on behalf of his body, which is the church … to bring to completion for you the word of God, 26 the mystery hidden from ages and from generations past" (Col 1:24–26).

George continued:

> In the Body of Christ, we profit from other people's virtues and
> we suffer from other people's sins. All the saints did penance
> for the sins of others. They did so because their souls were at-
> tuned to the movements of the Holy Spirit in the Church and
> the world. Many who are most attuned to the demands of social
> justice recognize that the exploitation of another human being
> is the consequence of sin and the root of injustice. People with
> well-developed spiritual antennae can see and hear a world cre-
> ated in love, fallen in sin yet set free now by Christ. Believing
> this, we can take upon ourselves the spiritual work of reparation
> for sin, including the sin of the sexual abuse of children.[35]

George relied on prayer as a means to move through the crises he faced,
even while admitting publicly and privately at times that it could be difficult to pray or that he could not pray as he believed he ought. "Prayer
for our own complete conversion to Christ and for the conversion of
the world" is a vital tool in healing and rebuilding, he said.[36] Those who
worked closely and lived with him also recall George's regular private
fasting and penances, the purpose of which, Pope St. John Paul II taught,
"is to overcome evil, which under different forms lies dormant in man"
and "to strengthen goodness both in man himself and in his relationships
with others and especially with God."[37] In a 2006 gathering with Chicago priests about the crisis, George stated, "The Lord wants us to move
through this, I'm more and more convinced of that. And I'm more and
more convinced each day we will be stronger because of this. John Paul
II talked about a purification. Purification is very painful. There were
nights — and I'm sure there will be again — where I didn't sleep very
well."[38]

In 2019, four years after George's death, an international summit on
clergy sexual abuse was held at the Vatican in the wake of another wave
of scandals and cover-ups. To open the gathering, five survivors of abuse

were invited to share their experiences with the 190 participants, including Pope Francis. In the historic and important testimonies offered by survivors to key members of the hierarchy, George was the only bishop mentioned by name, held up as a model of leadership amid the sex scandals plaguing the Church. The survivor from the United States stated:

> One of my finest memories of Francis Cardinal George is when he spoke about the difficulties of fellow priests who have abused, and I considered those words, coming from a man in his position, even though they must be really hard for him to say, they were the right and proper thing to say.
>
> I thought that was leadership at the time, and I think it's leadership now. And I thought if he could put himself out there, and lead by example, then I could put myself out there and I think other survivors and other Catholics and faithful people can put themselves out there, to work for resolution, and work for healing, and work for a better Church.
>
> So we respond to leadership, we look to our bishops for leadership, I would ask the bishops to show leadership.

That survivor was Michael Hoffman, who shared his abuse story with the archdiocese in 2006. Hoffman, who later became active in ministry to other survivors of clergy sexual abuse, was asked if he would like to meet with George, an offer extended to all victims who came forward under his tenure. At their meeting, Hoffman was greatly impressed by George, who accepted what he had to say with a pastor's heart. George, Hoffman said, was authentic and human, and their conversation consisted of "two broken hearts, basically, trying to repair each other on this terrible topic." Hoffman said that as a result of his meeting with George, he was "comfortable continuing practicing my faith."

Hoffman's meeting with George inspired the Archdiocese of Chicago's Healing Garden, which was dedicated by George at Holy Family Church in Chicago in 2011. The archdiocese intended the garden to be for abuse survivors a place to heal, to pray for healing, and to move forward to a future with less anxiety and embarrassment.

Hoffman was inspired and encouraged in his work with clergy abuse survivors by George's honesty about abusers in the clergy. Hoffman said George "acknowledged there was a disconnect in abusers ... living a kind of a double life." He found George's honesty refreshing and risky, acknowledging that "there would be a cost to him to say something about his beloved priests ... and he did that." Hoffman thought, "If he can take a risk, I can take a risk," and he decided to begin his ministry among other survivors, outlined in his 2013 book, *Acts of Recovery*. Looking back on his interactions with George, Hoffman said, "I consider him an inspiration."

George also supported the work of many clergy sexual abuse survivors who sought to help bring healing to the long-term effects of abuse in the lives of other survivors, such as Teresa Pitt Green. Green co-founded Spirit Fire ministry as a means to strengthen and support survivors of abuse by Church leaders. George asked his staff to read Green's first book, *Restoring Sanctuary*, in which she tells her own story and reminds other Catholic survivors of clergy sexual abuse that "healing and forgiveness really do exist." It also challenges them to respond to the call to discipleship in seeking restorative justice. George did not just pay lip service to the media in speaking about the clergy sexual abuse crisis; rather, he actively sought ways to bring about needed reforms and foster genuine healing.

OTHER PRIESTLY PROBLEMS

For generations, it was the norm for Chicago pastors to be left in their own parishes for a long period of time — sometimes decades. A pastor was regarded as the spiritual father of a parish community and, as such, often remained in a parish until retirement or death. Eventually, to ensure that parish life did not become stagnant or captive to the pastor's whims, term limits were set for pastors, noting that they would not ordinarily stay in one parish for longer than two consecutive six-year terms. This policy, approved by the Presbyteral Council during the Bernardin era, was reaffirmed at various times during George's tenure but existed as a source of contention among a number priests nonetheless. The personnel board was insistent on preventing two classes of priests from developing: those who could be moved and those who could not. The policy provided for exceptions, and a priest could plead his case for remaining where he was, but ultimately the archdiocese did not want the good of the parish to compete with the good of the local Church. As George once wrote in reference to this matter, every parish, just as every Catholic, has three pastors: pope, bishop, and priest. When Fr. Robert McLaughlin was moved in 2002 after reaching his term limit as pastor of Holy Name Cathedral, George explained this reality in a letter to Cathedral parishioners as "Catholic communion called out of every particularism," adding that "a change of pope, a change of bishop, a change of parish pastor, even if painful, can be an occasion for growth in the faith."

When it came right down to it, clergy and the faithful alike had two choices when faced with new assignments — or, really, with any life change at all, something with which George certainly had acquired plenty of experience: "We can either respond to an unwanted change, even one we consider unjust, by surrendering ourselves anew to the Lord in the hope he will bring good out of evil; or we can give ourselves to a kind of resentment which poisons our life and feeds our anger."

Enforcing term limits in Chicago could at times be difficult, especially when pastors developed a certain cult of personality, as did priests such as Father McLaughlin, Fr. Patrick Brennan, or Fr. Michael Pfleger, among others. Chicago has had a long line of priests rooted in a strong sense of social justice, and George was happy and willing to work with them to transform the society into a civilization of love, although he had concerns at times that some of these leaders could fall into the trap of being more community organizers than priests. Father Pfleger, the white pastor of the largely Black St. Sabina Church on the southside of Chicago, is something of an iconic example. Ordained in 1975, Pfleger has spent his entire priesthood at St. Sabina, transforming the neighborhood, guided by Dr. Martin Luther King Jr.'s idea of "the beloved community." Father

Pfleger contended that doing this was the work of a lifetime, not just one or two terms as pastor.

At times, though, Pfleger's own persona, agenda, and disobedience put him at odds with the Church as well as his archbishop. This conflict surfaced at different times throughout the years and during the tenures of each archbishop under whom he served. Among the sources of conflict have been his own adoption of children, in defiance of the protocol for Catholic priests; aberrant liturgical practices; and the invitations he has extended to pro-abortion politicians and to non-Catholics — such as Rev. Jesse Jackson, Rev. Al Sharpton, and Louis Farrakhan — to preach from his pulpit. In the case of Sharpton's appearance, a statement from the archdiocese expressed George's belief "that making a case of this invitation at this time would be a futile gesture and a waste of effort." While George supported Pfleger's good work in his community, he also recognized that the parish had become a place unto itself, so any hasty moves would further wound ecclesial unity and, given the personalities involved, could potentially bring about a small schism centered in the parish.

George found it necessary to suspend Pfleger twice, although, as he told the priest in a 2011 letter, he had "consistently supported [his] work for social justice and admired [his] passion for ministry." The first suspension came after Pfleger took on Hillary Clinton by name during the Democratic Party's 2008 primary, in which he mocked her race (though Pfleger, too, is white). This occurred in the pulpit at Trinity United Church of Christ in Chicago, the spiritual home of Clinton's opponent, Barack Obama, led by the controversial pastor Rev. Jeremiah Wright. Just after video surfaced of Pfleger's outburst, the media confronted George as he made his way from his car into St. John Cantius Church for an ordination of priests. He was unable to comment since he had not had a chance yet to review what had happened. After the Mass, George looked at one of the newly ordained, Fr. Batholomew Juncer, and, clearly in reference to the Pfleger fiasco, reminded him that as a priest he now represented the whole Church, so prudence and obedience were essential.

Though Pfleger was no stranger to media coverage, this particular story made national headlines. George's office was flooded with calls, letters, and emails demanding he "do something" with Pfleger (as was often the case when Pfleger was the subject of media coverage), and many callers were unpleasant and rude to George's staff. "The Catholic Church does not endorse political candidates," George said in his statement about the Clinton ordeal. "Consequently, while a priest must speak to political issues that are also moral, he may not endorse candidates nor engage in partisan campaigning." Believing that "politics divide and the faith unites,"[39] George had written in a 1976 internal Oblates memo, "a churchman's opinions about politics have the same value as a politician's opinions about the Bible."

In 2011, George suspended Pfleger — who had been known to say things from his pulpit like "I don't need no cardinal" — a second time when he publicly claimed George was "removing" him from St. Sabina, contrary to their private conversations about a potential move. "Our private conversation was misrepresented publicly as an attempt to 'remove' you from Saint Sabina's," George wrote to Pfleger in an April 27 letter. "You know that priests in the Archdiocese are 'removed' only because they have been found to have sexually abused a minor child or are guilty of financial malfeasance."

When in media interviews at the time Pfleger threatened to leave the Catholic Church, George replied to him in the April 27 letter as he would have to any priest in such a position:

> If that is truly your attitude, you have already left the Catholic Church and are therefore not able to pastor a Catholic parish. A Catholic priest's inner life is governed by his promises, motivated by faith in love, to live chastely as a celibate man and to obey his bishop. Breaking either promise destroys his vocation and wounds the Church. Bishops are held responsible for their priests on the assumption that priests obey them.

After learning that Pfleger also threatened to "start his own church" after George had asked him to consider a new assignment, Executive Assistant Mary FioRito recalled George remarking to his personal staff, "What? Start his own church? He's going to die and rise from the dead again?"

Pfleger returned some weeks after his second suspension after publicly recognizing his commitment to both the priesthood and the archbishop and offering an apology for the harm he had caused. The following year, George and Pfleger worked out a succession plan that eventually resulted in Pfleger serving at St. Sabina as "senior pastor," while Fr. Thulani Magwaza was assigned as pastor. At that time, George also named Pfleger as archdiocesan spokesperson on the scourge of gun violence facing the city and appointed him temporary administrator of another parish.

GIVING CHRIST GLORY

In 2007, George marked his tenth anniversary in Chicago, but rather than it being a joyful occasion, he was reeling from the many challenges he continued to face and from the human suffering that resulted. The clergy sexual abuse scandal, particularly the McCormack case, had derailed his vision and plans for spiritually advancing the archdiocese. He had been diagnosed with cancer in 2006 and recently broken his right femur in a fall. Ironically, this same year, George was elected president of the US bishops' conference — a position demanding even more of his time and energy. Yet those who knew him best, and his own public work and writings, clearly attest that despite his interior sufferings, George confidently and consistently continued his work of proclaiming Christ in word and deed.

During this time, George reflected in a column on an experience of St. Teresa of Ávila. The devil came to her once, the story goes, disguised as the risen Christ. But she immediately refused to worship him. Before he left, though, he asked how she knew he was not really Jesus. She answered, "Because you have no wounds." There is a phenomenon that can happen with the written word — that what is penned comes straight from the heart as an exposition of what is carried by our soul. It could be well argued that this is what happened with George as he processed his suffering and its meaning. And despite it all — really, because of it all — he knew the Lord and made Christ's life his own. And yet, George remained hard on himself. He thought often of de Mazenod, who described himself as "heart" more than "head." The Sulpician method of spirituality, observed by the Oblates, speaks of "Jesus as my head; Jesus as my heart; Jesus as my hands." George struggled, as he wrote privately in 2008, "I seldom get past the 'head' part."[40]

The spiritual darkness George experienced interiorly is not uncommon and appears in the lives of many of the Church's greatest saints. It defined St. Teresa of Calcutta's own spiritual life in reaction to the faces of evil she saw in the poverty, destitution, and disease to which she responded each day. Though their suffering was different, as they had unique charisms and missions, it is of note that as George's hidden suffering endured — and as he began to emerge from a period of a few years of great trials — he wrote frequently about those experiences of Mother Teresa and also about martyrdom and its role in the life of the Church. In 2008, he wrote:

> Considering the toll of evil and suffering in the world, some deny God's existence. … Others come to regard God as real but ineffectual or powerless to shape the course of human events. But if God is not provident, then worship becomes meaningless. A merely cosmic principle is cold comfort.
>
> Part of a response to the problem of evil points to the fact of human freedom. … God permits evil because he respects our freedom.
>
> There are evils, however, that are not just permitted by God but, in a certain sense, caused by him. …
>
> In the spiritual lives of very holy men and women, union with God begins, like every loving relationship, with consolation and joy. In order to live habitually with God, however, the

sins that separate us from him and from one another have to be abandoned. This purification of one's life ... brings its own suffering.[41]

This theme of suffering and martyrdom was at the forefront of George's tenure in Chicago from the beginning. In June 1997, George received his second pallium in as many years from Pope John Paul II. This woolen band, worn over the neck and shoulders, indicates an archbishop's bond to the successor of St. Peter. In God's providence, Mother Teresa was present as a special guest at the Mass during which the pallium was imposed on the archbishops. There, George heard John Paul II preach about the enduring model of Saints Peter and Paul, whose pastoral leadership shone forth even amid sufferings and difficulties. The pope observed in his homily that it was necessary for the faith of the Apostles to be "crowned with the supreme test of martyrdom," adding that their faith enabled them to know that "what to the eyes of the world seemed a defeat, was in fact the beginning of the fulfillment of God's plan."[42] Reflecting on the pope's message that day, George said that "the pope reminded us how Peter and Paul sustained one another in their mission, even though it was difficult, and that we, too, will be able to do the mission Christ calls us to if, in fact, we sustain each other in Catholic communion."[43]

In his wisdom, George knew how important it was to seek heavenly assistance in the wake of the scourge of the clergy sexual abuse crisis. On December 8, 2004, the Solemnity of the Immaculate Conception, George consecrated the Archdiocese of Chicago to the Immaculate Heart of Mary. He wrote to the faithful of the archdiocese, "With God's help and Mary's prayers, the coming celebration of the 150th anniversary of the dogma of the Immaculate Conception will re-awaken in the Archdiocese a sense of the primacy of grace and help us to live together in peace. That is my prayer, and I hope it will be yours."[44]

George accepted the cross of his cancer diagnosis as a means of not only his own sanctification but as an opportunity to offer penance for the healing of the Church. In 2008, he again made a pilgrimage to Lourdes,

France, to seek the healing brought to pilgrims through the intercession of the Blessed Virgin Mary. Oblate of Mary Immaculate that he was, George knew turning to Mary at this crucial time was greatly needed. In a different column, written some months before the pilgrimage, George wrote, "The work of salvation entailed Mary's emptying herself to be filled with God's purpose for her, in imitation of Jesus' self-emptying of his divinity in order to become Savior of the world. Mary is free of all sin so that God is entirely free to work in and through her." And so, turning to Mary, George asked, "What will we pray for at Lourdes? ... For healing."[45] And what topped his long list of items that needed to be healed? "The lives of those who have been sexually abused and for the healing of the wound to the Church that such abuse has inflicted."

"To Christ be Glory in the Church" was an apt motto for George. A vocal defender of the Second Vatican Council and an attentive student of its teachings, George knew what it meant to be a bishop according to the mind of Christ. As a successor of the Apostles, George was motivated with a concern to deepen and inform the faith of his flock. But more than that, he desired the souls he shepherded to become the saints God called them to be. That, after all, is the primary means by which Christ is glorified in the Church.

Years later, George tied martyrdom to his episcopal motto on the occasion of his tenth anniversary in Chicago. He wrote:

> The privileged way of giving glory to Christ in the Church is to suffer martyrdom. ... Not yet called to bloody martyrdom, we in this Archdiocese need to become ever clearer and more intentional about how we are to witness to the Lord and give him glory through the offering of our lives, the joining of our self-sacrifice to his. One of the joys of being Archbishop here is to come to know, personally or through correspondence, so many who are faithful disciples of Jesus Christ, often in the midst of great personal suffering. To them, especially, I am grateful.[46]

The red worn by George and other members of the College of Cardinals signifies, in a spiritual sense, their readiness to spill their blood in defense of the Catholic Faith and the pope. "In a sense the fancy dress, the red color, means that a cardinal is a marked man," George told those gathered at Chicago's cathedral for his first public Mass back home as a cardinal in 1998.[47] "He is rather someone who reminds people that they must, with everything that is in them, surrender themselves entirely to God." But as George's life shows, suffering's purpose can be understood in multifaceted ways and can come from varied sources. Yes, suffering can be embraced for the good of the individual and for the good of the Church. But it can also come about, at times, because of those within the Church. Theologian Hans Urs von Balthasar once observed, "In the midst of the official Church, sanctity agonizes."[48]

In presenting the vision of the Church arising from the texts of Vatican II, George called the Church to deeper communion, to the fullness of relationship in Christ. This meant a separation from the "ideology of individualism," which he saw and understood as fracturing the communion that Christians ought to be building as members of Christ's Body. Not only did he think, speak, and write about this, but he lived it. He thoroughly understood and frequently emphasized that our bonds with each other should take priority, since we are incorporated at birth into relationships that define us as someone's son or daughter, brother or sister, and so on — long before we are aware of who we are. Since all men and women are created by God, in his image, we all have the ability to move beyond ourselves. Made in God's image, humanity can transcend individuality and move to "harmony and peace, mutual love and love of God," George taught. "Our mission is to call people to that level, which isn't only higher, but also more global. It is universal."[49] In the end, as he said on various occasions, "the Church is where you go when you want to be free."[50]

In 2013, while looking back on his fifty years as a priest, George was asked if he would do anything differently. He responded, "What I would try to do is avoid mistakes I've made; but in terms of what I've done, it's been what I've been told to do and I did it. ... I've tried to be obedient to the Lord's will as expressed by the Church."[51]

Bishop Robert Barron, given his proximity as a part-time resident at the cardinal's house for many years, observed George's spirit of sacrifice close up. "His was a life of ... constant activity and obligation. Public speeches, gatherings, conferences, individual conversations, liturgies — morning, noon, and night, pretty much Sunday through Sunday." What stuck out most to Barron was that in seven years of living on and off at George's residence and observing his life and duties, "never once, in all the years I lived with him, did I ever hear Cardinal George complain about what he was obliged to do. He simply went ahead, not grimly but with a sense of purpose."

He proceeded, in the face of whatever came his way, according to the logic of Saint Paul: "We also boast in our sufferings, knowing that suffering produces endurance, and endurance produces character, and character produces hope, and hope does not disappoint us, because God's love has been poured into our hearts through the Holy Spirit that has been given to us" (Rom 5:3–5 NRSV-CE).

Many have spoken about the possibility that, at least once, George was offered a position in the Roman Curia. George graciously replied to such a notion that he believed it would be too physically onerous and that he was more useful to the pope in Chicago and the United States. George saw his suffering as a share in the cross that contained purpose — for his own sanctification and also for the good of those in his charge. In 2001, he commented during an interview with the *Chicago Tribune*, "I hope to die in Chicago. Much to the chagrin of a few folks."[52]

As if his illness had been preparing him all his life for the struggles he faced as a bishop, George knew how to rely on God's grace and love to see him through. "Surrender to Christ!!! (again!) as he surrendered to [the] Father's will,"[53] George once wrote privately on retreat in 2004. Another year, he wrote privately, "Lord, weaken my defenses so you may do with me as you will."

In 2010, he wrote privately reflecting upon how he was "afraid to even pray 'Thy will be done'" and that he was "afraid to love." Amid these struggles, while he feared losing his intimacy with Christ, he still expressed his heart's desire to give his all to Christ, imploring him, "Lord, grant that I may love you as you want me to love you."

"If you tell the truth," he preached at an ordination Mass in 2009, "you may be killed by those whose position you threaten. If you give your life to people for the love of God, they may betray you. It is all part of priestly life. You know this; your formation has prepared you to live this life. Now it is your life."[54]

This reality, which George keenly understood, formed a backdrop for his comments in a 2006 address in the Diocese of Corner Brook, Canada. In the midst of the clergy sexual abuse crisis, he asked aloud, "Why in the midst of this suffering, we ask, has this happened? Did I do something and now God is angry with me? Am I being punished and why is this happening to me? Does God still love me? God seems to have forsaken me."[55]

George acknowledged that when suffering is constant, we must ask, "How does suffering become Christian martyrdom?" He stated that "martyrdom in the Christian sense is a free surrender of our lives — not suicide, we don't take our lives — someone else takes them but we give our lives for Christ. We lose our very selves because of the love of Jesus Christ." Suffering then becomes "fully accepted," as George said, "when you participate in the work of Christ for the salvation of the world." He continued: "Why should we freely accept suffering? Because there is a sense of the depth of God's love for us." All suffering is a loss, "the loss of one's very self."

But, in George's view, there exists also "the fear that whatever would be left at the end of my suffering, it will not be me, I will be changed, I won't be suffering, I will be something else. The loss itself can become the source of new life in Christ when we freely surrender our very selves to him." Turning suffering into martyrdom meant "to embrace the suffering and the death that comes while trusting in God's love that whatever comes next, God will be pleased. And that is enough for us." George seemed to know this all too well.

The following year, after Pope Benedict XVI opened the Year for Priests that extended from June 2009 to June 2010, George began surfacing names of holy Chicago priests who might be investigated for canonization. The name of Fr. Augustus Tolton stood out among the rest. Born a slave and ostracized all his life for the color of his skin, even within the Church and by his brothers in the priesthood, Tolton was the first identifiably Black man ordained a priest from the United States. He was known for a life of suffering and, as the investigative process that documented Tolton's life concluded, a life of heroic virtue. George presided over the ceremony in which this documentation was sealed and prepared for shipment to the Holy See's Congregation for the Causes of Saints. He observed in his homily at the 2014 liturgy marking the end of the archdiocesan phase of Father Tolton's cause that introducing it was "one of the most important, if not the most important" ecclesiastical action he had taken in his more than seventeen years as archbishop of Chicago. That was likely because George understood the scandals plaguing the Church to be spiritual crises. And he knew that through the proclamation of the Gospel, the sacramental gifts of Christ, the prayers of the Blessed Mother, and the witness of the saints, the Church would find what she needed to survive.

When George's retirement was announced in 2014, the *Chicago Tribune* ran a piece on September 21 with the headline, "George led in tumultuous times." To him, that may have been an understatement. But in all that he faced, he consistently gave of himself. "Hopeless sinner though I am, Lord," he wrote privately in 2007, "make me a saint for the sake of your people!"[56]

ELEVEN
A Good Neighbor

We live in the world as well as in the Church, and
the line is porous between them. It must be so, for the
function of the Church is to love the world and proclaim
within the world that Jesus Christ is the leaven, the
communion, within the solidarity among peoples.[1]

CARDINAL FRANCIS E. GEORGE, O.M.I.

In a deliberate play off of his predecessor Cardinal Joseph Bernardin's legendary self-introduction to Chicago as "Joseph, your brother," Francis George introduced himself to the same archdiocese at his May 7, 1997, installation Mass by saying, "I am Francis, your neighbor."[2] With this, George drew attention to his new territory's well-known status as a city of neighborhoods. He explained that "Christians are to look on everyone as a potential neighbor." He cited George Herbert Mead, the University of Chicago professor whom George researched in connection to his first doctorate, who said Jesus "generalized neighborliness."

By identifying himself as their "neighbor," George demonstrated his unity with Chicagoans on a level that mattered most. The city is made up of seventy-seven neighborhoods that define residents not just by real estate but by ethnicity, socioeconomic status, or culture. Northeast Illinois is also the most religiously diverse region in the United States. And while the Catholic Church is the largest religious body in the Chicago metropolitan area, making up roughly 40 percent of the citizenry, it is not the religious majority. In fact, there is none.

At his installation, George reflected on what role the bishop plays in the neighborhood. "In any place, at any time, the bishop must see to it that the whole Church makes visible the gifts Christ wants his people to enjoy," he said. "Christ's love, his forgiveness and healing, the salvation won by him, the Gospel, and the sacrifice of Christ himself — the Church makes all of these visible in words and sacrament and action so that they can be shared. The Church exists where the gifts of Christ are shared."[3]

George's self-description as "Francis, your neighbor" also meant that his role in the city was for all the people in Chicago, not just those entrusted to his care as archbishop. While George wore many hats as a leader of the Church in Chicago — most notably the cardinal's red biretta — he was also a key leader in the city. George constantly challenged others to a greater concern for the poor, the marginalized, and the abandoned, and he was eager to support initiatives with the same goal.

Responding to the teaching of the Second Vatican Council and striving to be a good disciple who builds up God's kingdom, George worked especially hard to form relationships across religious boundaries. He saw it as a calling. Convinced of who he was and who Christ is, George clearly gave positive witness to Christ. He recognized the vital role religion played in building up society's culture, and so he engaged in ecumenical and interfaith dialogue, which he once described to a friend as "taking another's point of view." His aim was to gain broader understanding of his neighbors and to clarify his own thinking as he worked to build up God's kingdom. This was, of course, consistent not only with who George was but also what Catholics believe. To be Catholic, George said in a 2012 interview with Salt and Light Television, "doesn't mean to be sectarian." He continued: "We are not an enclave. We're not a little group that's shouting at the wind. Nor does it mean that we're simply chaplains to the status quo." Simply, he explained, it "means you know who Christ is, and you know who you are in relationship to Christ and relation to all his friends, all the saints in the communion of saints, our family here, the family of God which is the Church. And then we know what the world is, because we're in it, we're not separated. How do you make that world a bit more like the kingdom of God? How is the Church a sacrament of that kingdom? Not to be co-opted or isolated."

Dialogue with others was integral to George's public ministry. His world travel as an Oblate exposed him to a wide array of cultures and religions, and he knew that "otherness, plurality and diversity are richness, not threat, because our faith tells us that every other, every person, is made in God's image and likeness," adding, "this is the basis for both generosity and for dialogue, for giving to others what they need and for sharing with others what is most important to us."[4] More than that, it flowed from the very identity of the Church, according to the teaching of Vatican II, as the sacrament of the unity of the human race,[5] a definition of the Church George said we do not think about often enough. George knew that the Church's ecclesiology of communion — "a network of relationships based on sharing of gifts from Christ" — exists "to be a catalyst or a leaven for the solidarity of the human race."[6] His ministry as a bishop was an example of how ecclesial communion works with human solidarity as "partners in mission as the Church finds her way in a new relationship to the world that Christ died to save." George argued that this new relationship was necessarily encouraged by Vatican II, because "the Church was in danger of becoming a museum." His relationships with an expansive network put into practice the council's intention that we might all live in the peace of Christ.

George was also effective as a "neighbor" in helping bring unity to all men and women because he was, quite simply and in the logic of St. Irenaeus of Lyons, a human being fully alive who magnified the glory of God. Bishop Robert Barron has described such a person as one who "holds up Christ — human freedom and divine truth in perfect harmony — and [he] says 'behold humanity; behold the best you can be.'" It is clear that many across religious and cultural boundaries saw George in this light. As a mark of his authenticity, George quickly gained trust and developed a great chain of relationships and friendships with civic and religious leaders throughout Chicago. In 1995, George wrote that the ideal bishop is "a center of unity, a man of contacts, around whom all can gather who want to gather in Christ, a man of dialogue who rejects no one and is respectful of all opinions."[7]

Among the various commemorations at the time of George's funeral rites in 2015 was an ecumenical and interreligious observance at which leaders gathered from the religious spectrum of metropolitan Chicago. Expressions of gratitude for Cardinal George's engagement and collaboration were offered by those from different churches and religious communities who were touched by Cardinal George's friendship and leadership. As Fr. Thomas Baima, George's vicar for ecumenical and interreligious affairs, observed — recognizing the universal respect he maintained among Chicagoans — "Although he might not have been their archbishop, he was their cardinal."

ECUMENICAL AND INTERRELIGIOUS DIALOGUE

George worked together with leaders of many religious communities in Chicago in areas of common concern and for the common good. He partnered with the Muslim community on common issues pertaining to the family and sympathized with their plight amid anti-immigration attitudes. He wanted to encourage and support Muslim communities in metropolitan Chicago, and he was especially attentive to the fact that they faced many of the prejudices that had confronted Catholic immigrants from Europe in the previous century. He was a regular guest at Islamic

Iftar meals during Ramadan. George worked diligently to strengthen relations between Catholics and Muslims, something he saw as "the most important conversation in the next hundred years," because "if we can come together without the defensiveness of the past and the bloodshed of a thousand years when Islam was a great threat to Christendom, we might be able to envision together a world which will be a better home for the human race."[8]

George was a close friend and advisor to the Jewish Federation of Chicago. In one conversation with their leadership, when asked how they could return the favor and help him with an issue on his heart, George expressed his concern for Christians in the Holy Land who were forced from their homes due to lack of employment. The leaders of the Jewish Federation, taking seriously the first time that Chicago's archbishop expressed to them something they could help him with as a response to their mutual friendship, offered a proposal. Working together, the federation and the archdiocese would jointly fund a computer literacy center in the all-Christian village of Fassuta in Israel.

George's relationships with other Christians were also inspired by Vatican II's ecumenical mission. As George advocated for ecumenical dialogue, he noted that Christian denominations "are not enemies but family: a fractured family, but still family."[9] And he worked to ensure that Catholics in Chicago worked with other Christians not only on "common projects for social transformation" but also toward "complete unity in faith." In a column on ecumenism, George commented that as we enter into the third millennium, visiting the Church of the Holy Sepulchre in Jerusalem shows "what we have made of the Body of Christ in the last thousand years," since the place of Christ's Resurrection is divided among various groups of Christians.[10] "We ask the Lord to forgive us and to lead us, in his way and in his time, to the full communion he wants us to enjoy," he added. In 1999, George embarked on the "Pilgrimage of Love" to Constantinople and Rome with the Greek Orthodox patriarch of Chicago, Metropolitan Iakovos. As "brothers in the episcopate" and members of their respective dioceses, the two religious leaders were a visible, concrete example of George's desire to walk with his Christian brothers and sisters toward the Lord. Together they prayed at important religious sites in the holy cities and met with both Orthodox Ecumenical Patriarch Bartholomew of Constantinople and Pope John Paul II, pledging to continue working for the unity Christ wills for his Church.

George often facilitated greater collaboration among other Christians and non-Christians in human solidarity and advocacy for religious freedom throughout the Chicagoland area. In 2013, Mayor Rahm Emanuel and surrogates in the Chicago city council planned to end the exemption from water bills for the city's not-for-profit institutions. The move would have resulted in an additional $20 million in annual revenue for the city. But not only would such a decision have negatively affected small Christian congregations, it especially would have hurt small nonprofits, particularly those who served the poor, such as homeless shelters, daycare centers, and community clinics. Many would have likely been forced to shut down. George stood side by side with a wide array of religious leaders and other nonprofit heads from Chicago, none of them with the same reach or visibility as the archdiocese, and advocated with and for them to be given a more reasonable solution. Practically speaking, many of these institutions served the poor in ways that subsidized what the city might need to offer if such faith-based social services were no longer available. But George also saw the situation as further evidence of the decline of religion's importance in the public square. "We've had a society that up until this point in time has thought of religion as a social good. As a kind of a glue that keeps people together. And that's what we're saying in this case," he said.[11] Knowing that governments were "not the ultimate forum for human experience," George argued that nonprofits did not "want to face them around this particular issue at this particular time because we simply can't afford it." Noting that Lake Michigan belongs to no one but is "a gift from God," George remarked that "we feel sometimes maybe we should charge the city for using our water." George's leadership on these efforts paved the way for the city to offer a sliding-scale compromise that allowed these organizations to keep their doors open.

A HEART FOR THE POOR

As an Oblate of Mary Immaculate, George had a heart for the poor. Because of that, he was greatly drawn to and deeply proud of the work the archdiocese did to serve the less fortunate. "Sometimes the allegation is made in a rather spiteful way," George said in a wide-ranging interview in 2013, "that we're willing to sacrifice our service to the poor for the sake of our so-called doctrine. Doctrine aside, what I'd like to say is that one of the great things about being the archbishop of Chicago is precisely the way in which this diocese has put most of its efforts toward serving the poor."[12]

George frequently noted, with both concern and gratitude, that one out of every three persons in Chicago received help from Catholic Charities of the Archdiocese of Chicago. Msgr. Michael Boland, who led Chicago's Catholic Charities during George's tenure as archbishop, recalled George as "a strong voice for the poor." He saw this up-close when accompanying George on visits across Catholic Charities' 280 sites in the archdiocese, which George made a priority, or on the occasions when he helped unload Christmas gifts donated by Chicago Fire Department members, or when he helped serve the hungry or homeless at dinners. Boland remembered George for being "comfortable talking to a donor, a staff person or a little child as if they were the most important person in the world." Bishop Joseph Perry, ordained an auxiliary bishop of Chicago in 1998 — the first bishop George himself ordained — recalled visiting one of the twenty-eight towers comprising the Robert Taylor Homes, one of the high-rise urban housing projects wherein many poor Blacks lived on Chicago's southside. While visiting one resident's family and hearing her story, Perry recalled that George got up from his chair and, visibly moved, walked across the room to hug her. "You could see the sympathy, the empathy that poured out of him towards her. And he asked her what he could possibly do for her, for her situation."

Also during George's time in Chicago, Catholic Charities built eighteen residences for low income seniors, two assisted living facilities, a nursing home, a priest retirement home, and a home for homeless veterans — the first built in the country. Boland recalled not only George's personal interest in each of these projects but also his presiding at their dedications. So it is understandable that George once commented about "very hurtful" letters claiming the Church lacked attention to the plight of the poor, which angered him. George also observed that in contemporary American society, the poor and the defenseless in the womb are synonymous: "The common good can never be adequately incarnated in any society when those waiting to be born can be legally killed at choice."[13]

George's desire for the poor to know that the Church had not abandoned them was also made manifest in the Mission of Our Lady of the Angels, situated in the West Humboldt Park neighborhood on Chicago's west side, one of the city's poorest areas. In 2005, George invited Franciscan Friar of the Renewal then-Fr. Robert Lombardo to oversee the revitalization of the shuttered Our Lady of the Angels church and school properties, a site well known in Chicago and beyond for a 1958 fire at the school that resulted in the tragic deaths of ninety-two children and three religious sisters. A mission was established to tend to the spiritual and material needs of the local, inner-city poor. Its reach and focus have grown in the years since its founding, and in 2021 alone, the mission's food pantry provided more than 35,000 households more than 2 million pounds of food, according to an August 2022 newsletter from now-Bishop Lombardo. The Franciscans of the Eucharist of Chicago, a religious community of men and women founded at the mission, is overseen by Lombardo. George supported the community's foundation and canonically approved the new religious congregation's way of life in 2010.

In American ecclesiastical culture, bishops customarily receive honoraria — monetary gifts offered in gratitude for services uncharged — for speaking engagements and pastoral visitations. In some cases, such as the egregious examples of former cardinal Theodore McCarrick and Bishop Michael Bransfield, it has come to light that such money has been squandered and misused. In contrast, and as a way of maintaining the vow of poverty he had taken as an Oblate, George deposited the honoraria that he received into a fund that could be drawn upon to respond to some of the numerous charitable requests he received, a common practice among bishops. To be transparent and ensure the funds were used prudently, George entrusted a committee of his staff to vet the requests and recommend how to allocate those funds.

George often expressed his admiration for Mother Teresa's dedication to the poor. In 2000, he observed that she was known all over the world because of "her single-minded pursuit of one idea: that Jesus Christ is present in those who are most in need."[14] In his own ministry, although very different from Mother Teresa's, George was attentive to the poor. This stemmed, of course, from the Gospel mandate. But it also arose out of his own background as a member of a missionary congregation and a compassion motivated by his own personal suffering. As George was known to tell rooms full of donors, "The poor need you to draw them out of poverty, and you need the poor to keep you out of Hell." In 2003, George said to the US bishops, "The middle class exists in order to set people free, including the poor; but if wealth is not dedicated to the well-being of the poor, then it becomes a road to condemnation."[15] When asked by the *New York Times* at his time of retirement how he might like to be remembered, George said, "I tried to be present in the life of the poor."[16]

When George was visiting parishes, he often came into contact with individuals cast aside by society. If they asked for a moment with him, he would make himself available. Monsignor James Moroney, the longtime executive director of the U.S. bishops' Committee on the Liturgy, regularly traveled to Chicago to meet with George, who as chairman of the committee was overseeing revisions that were being made to the English translation of the Roman Missal. During one of those meetings, he recalled that George's private phone line rang. And as Moroney recounted on his blog at the time of George's death, "He looked at his watch and excused himself, saying this would probably take a while. He then greeted someone on the phone, telling his caller how glad he was to hear from her. The next twenty minutes consisted of questions about how she was doing, quietly listening to her stories and strong interjections reminding her to 'take her meds.'"[17] Moroney recounted that, after returning to their meeting, George told him the caller was a parishioner he had met at a confirmation years ago who had been "diagnosed as a schizophrenic and had so enjoyed his gentle and patient listening to her that she asked for his private number, which he gave to her, with the agreement that she would call him only once a month on a given day." Moroney was highly impressed that the cardinal archbishop of Chicago himself would take the call. He "sat there like the good priest he was," he recalled, "and listened to her struggles, encouraging and shepherding her in the model of Christ the Priest and Shepherd into whose image he had been molded."

A HEART FOR THE SICK AND SUFFERING

George once recalled that upon his arrival in Chicago, chancery advisors wanted him to close forty schools. "I said, 'I can't do that the first year, I may as well go somewhere else,'" he recalled in a 2012 interview with Salt and Light Television. Keeping schools open was one of George's major objectives during his tenure in Chicago. And yet, due to economic constraints and demographic shifts, George had to make the difficult decision to close a number of schools and parishes during his tenure, even including the church where he was baptized. Arguing that it was more important to devote resources to forming people rather than repairing structures, George said in a 2014 interview with Chicago's Fox affiliate, "People last forever, buildings don't. Parishes come and go, dioceses come and go, even countries come and go." For George, the Church's true asset is God's people. "The Church has always been richer in people than in cash," he observed.[18] And he saw the future of the Church as one that needed to invest in this reality more than in the brick-and-mortar structures, which at times could even encumber the Church's mission in a radically changing society. Pointing out how the vast archdiocesan cemetery system was far more endowed than that of the Catholic schools, George commented, "I'm not sure what it means to say that we are better placed to take care of graves than we are of school children."

A great deal of George's efforts as archbishop were directed to advancing the mission of Catholic schools within the archdiocese, which were often a place of love, peace, and safety amid the urban strife within which their students resided. He enjoyed visiting schools and meeting students, whether in the course of a parish visit, during Catholic Schools Week, or on some other occasion. He was concerned about Catholic school funding and closures, especially what closures would mean for poor and minority children. Educational endowments for the schools of the Archdiocese of Chicago were a priority. He often said that when a school is closed, "you close a child's world." He called the Catholic schools, particularly those in poorer neighborhoods, "oases of safety and of love that create an environment where our kids can learn."[19] George believed wholeheartedly that a Catholic education offered students a "very, very good chance of being good members of this society and living with the Lord forever in heaven."

Many of the secondary schools in Chicago had historically been operated by religious orders. George saw to it, in many cases, that the archdiocese would find a way to help the schools survive, even as the orders began pulling out of such ministries. Yet he was not naïve or idealistic about the situation. Toward the end of his time as Chicago's archbishop, George expressed regret that he had opted to delay closing some schools instead of acting sooner — an unsuccessful gamble that ended up draining archdiocesan resources. Overall, he believed that the place for real investment was not in the structures and institutions on their own, but only inasmuch as they were useful to the Church's mission.

> In a period of institutional decline, one saves as much as possible the elements of institutional presence that are necessary for mission — parishes, schools, seminaries, etc. — but one pays particular attention to the formation of people. No matter how weak an institution might become, if enough people are well formed as disciples of Jesus Christ, the Church's mission is secure.[20]

George's support of Catholic education also extended to the Catholic universities in the archdiocese. He met regularly with their presidents to discuss topics of mutual concern. As a former professor, adept at thinking on his feet, he eagerly accepted invitations to visit college classrooms and Newman centers, where he fielded questions from students and challenged them with his own.

As a means to call attention to the plight of the poor and raise funds for their care, particularly through education, George floated publicly the idea of selling the historic archbishop's residence in Chicago. He shared his intent at the ordination of priests for the archdiocese in May 2002, just as the clergy sexual abuse crisis was ratcheting up in America. In George's own words from the homily that day: "I drew a contrast between how the priest, as an icon of the risen and glorious Christ, celebrates the liturgy in great splendor and beauty, and how the same priest, as a disciple of a Lord who embraced suffering and humiliation, lives personally in simplicity and lowliness."[21]

With the money that might result from the sale of his residence, George wanted to build the archdiocesan school fund, to prevent future school closures.

The residence, in George's description of the Queen Anne–style mansion on North Avenue, was "a red brick building with wood interiors, more curious than beautiful architecturally" (for example, it has seventeen chimneys). It had been built by Chicago's first archbishop, Patrick Feehan, in 1885 on property purchased by Chicago's first bishop, William Quarter, in the early 1840s. It sits on the edge of Chicago's Lincoln Park, now amid many tony high rises in the city's Gold Coast neighborhood. The mansion functioned as a combination archiepiscopal residence and chancery until 1915, when Cardinal George Mundelein, somewhat of a mythic figure known for massive institutional expansion in Chicago, moved the chancery offices downtown and used the house solely as his own residence. It played host, at different times, to future popes (Cardinal Eugenio Pacelli, later elected Pope Pius XII), sitting popes (Pope St. John Paul II), and a US president (Franklin D. Roosevelt).

As he was debating selling the residence, George wrote to his flock that while it "belongs to our history," it "also belongs to an image of office that is arguably no longer supportive of an archbishop's ministry. This is a town cynical about 'clout,' whether accurately or not, and the Church must be transparent. The Church points only to Christ, and anything that gets in the way of that proclamation weakens her mission."

And had he sold it, where would George have gone? He indicated his desire to "move to simpler quarters in greater proximity to the poor." But he never got that far. A great outcry among the clergy and faithful followed George's suggestion of selling the property, even as he and his councils and advisors were looking into the possibility. In the end, he never sold the residence, and he never left it, even in retirement. He would breathe his last in this historic manse.

George's sensitivity to those who suffered is highlighted by his 2001 decision to "right a historical wrong"[22] related to one of his predecessors who battled mental illness. Bishop James Duggan came to Chicago at the age of thirty-three and guided his flock through the highly stressful years of the Civil War. A decade into his tenure, he had been labeled "hopelessly insane" and shipped off to a St. Louis institution. At a time when, as a general rule, bishops did not resign, he maintained his office as bishop of Chicago for nearly another decade while another bishop served as coadjutor and administrator. Duggan even outlived his coadjutor before dying in a sanitarium in St. Louis in 1899. Originally buried in Calvary Cemetery in Evanston, just north of Chicago, Duggan's body was not moved to the archbishops' mausoleum when it was built in 1912, as was the case for the rest of Chicago's past bishops who had died in office. George oversaw the ceremonious transfer of Bishop Duggan's remains in 2001 to "make visible the silent suffering of mental illness and that we will never leave anyone behind as we left Bishop Duggan behind."[23] George observed:

> Bringing him to the mausoleum over one hundred years after his burial made it possible to talk about how we accept and relate to people who are mentally ill, people who are sometimes a cross both to themselves and to others. Mental illness can be a silent

suffering and, silently, those with it can be left behind by those impatient with them and even by society itself.

Nationally, George served as episcopal moderator of the National Catholic Office for Persons with Disabilities. For him, the life issues he was passionately outspoken about — fearlessly proclaiming the teachings of the Church and the consequences of an alternative approach — were also connected to the cause of the disabled. "If today it is terminally ill but competent people who are being killed, tomorrow it will be the mentally handicapped and the day after the physically disabled, disfigured, the unwanted."[24] Himself disabled since he was thirteen years old, George noted his solidarity with "my brothers and sisters with disabilities," saying that he "had to come to terms with limitations" and "experienced some of the frustrations" they suffer.

Shortly after arriving in Chicago, George attended an annual meeting of the National Catholic HIV/AIDS Ministry Conference. When asked why an archbishop would attend, George quipped, "Why not?" He continued: "This is a way of being present to people who are performing a very important ministry in the Church — accompanying suffering people — and that's where the Church belongs, so that's where the bishop should be."[25]

For many years on Christmas morning, George offered Mass for prisoners at the Cook County Jail and then visited patients and families at Ann & Robert H. Lurie Children's Hospital of Chicago. At the time of George's death, the hospital stated in a social media post that "his presence was the real present, his spirit, faith and hope, the real gifts that he shared with all. Whether holding a tiny hand, encircling a father's shoulder or blessing an infant waiting for a heart transplant, Cardinal George knew how to be with people in the moment and reside with them there."[26]

In one particularly moving account, Thomas F. Roeser, a conservative commentator, talk-radio host, and former vice-president of the Quaker Oats Company, recounted how he witnessed George's pastoral skills at the bedside of his dying priest-cousin Fr. George J. Helfrich in 2006.[27] His words were especially significant coming from a longtime critic of George. In 2010, he had described George as a "fashionable liberal old duffer" and "smallish balding ex-university professor" who "scaled the bishopric and whose hands are soft as a woman's. … Never having worked a day in the private sector and nurtured in the then hot-house seminaries sheltered from the world. … George and his vintage haven't a clue in the world." [28]

But the emotional events of that day prompted him to — at least that once — speak admiringly of George. "Lowering his head and speaking distinctly so as to be heard by Fr. Helfrich, the prelate spoke in calm, measured, and powerfully edifying tones," Roeser wrote. "'George, the Lord Jesus Christ loves you,'" Roeser recounted Chicago's cardinal saying to his cousin that day "in a voice that gave a kind of thrilling affirmation of the fact." The cardinal continued, in Roeser's account:

> Moreover, all the suffering you are enduring now and have endured is being put up for you as a treasure for your eternal reward. And let there be no mistake: All of us must, one day, face the same trial you do today — and God grant that we will do so with the courage you are exhibiting today, which is such an inspiration to us all. You are indeed a champion, and we are proud of you and love you.

Roeser argued that not only did he hear "exquisite words" that day, but, more significantly, "the tender solicitude of a loving father … the gentle stroking of the dying priest's brow, the brushing back of his unkempt, disheveled hair … the prelate's soft patting of the patient's sagging, stubble-filled cheeks with the skill of a medical nurse." For Roeser, George's care for his dying priest-cousin that day was done "with such care that the medical personnel, standing around, waiting to react in case of emergency, were stunned."

What Roeser saw that day was something many came to know about George in his years as a priest and bishop. "This was a cardinal who knew how to soothe, who could easily become, with the delicacy and grace he showed, an expert caregiver himself," he wrote. "The soft words, barely audible, reflected the cardinal's praise for the life of Fr. Helfrich that was so humble. Cardinal George stirred Fr. Helfrich, himself an intellectual, to see that the nature of the priest was to repudiate the egotistic pleasure employed since Adam to find fulfillment beyond and above himself. It was the cardinal's greatest sermon, delivered to an audience of one," Roeser concluded.

THE DEATH PENALTY

George used his position as archbishop to advocate against those laws and policies that he perceived as antithetical to what it means to be a Catholic. His mercy and concern for minorities and the poor laid the foundation for George's opposition to the use of the death penalty in modern-day American society. He argued that the application of the death penalty was immoral since Black persons and the poor have been targeted in the use of capital punishment in the United States.

In a column in 2001, George clarified that the use of the death penalty "is legal and is moral in itself, unless there is another way to defend ourselves without killing," but he cautioned that "we should, as in a just defense, exhaust non-violent ways first to defend ourselves."[29] This has also been the teaching of modern popes and resulted in a nuanced presentation of the issue in the *Catechism of the Catholic Church*.

George denounced the death penalty in a 2001 talk given to a group in the Diocese of Evansville, Indiana. "Capital punishment is inconsistent with the way and thinking of Jesus, who could have called the twelve legions of angels to his defense, but instead chose to die so that even his enemies might have life," he said.[30] George argued that people of faith "cannot accept Jesus as the lover of life and be for the death penalty."

His speech came just months before the scheduled execution of Timothy McVeigh, who was put to death in the federal prison in Terre Haute, Indiana, for the 1995 bombing of the federal building in Oklahoma City. In the wake of the execution of McVeigh — himself a Catholic who requested and received the Anointing of the Sick before his death — George encouraged Catholics to conduct prayer vigils and offer Masses for the repose of his soul. George advocated for forgiveness, using McVeigh's case as an example, "so that what he has done does not kill us morally."

In 2000, George wrote that the death penalty "should be abolished because, among other reasons, we cannot be absolutely certain that an innocent man or woman will not be executed."[31] This came on the heels of then-Illinois Gov. George H. Ryan's moratorium on the death penalty, following innocent verdicts for thirteen death-row inmates in new trials. In a 2001 column, George observed that "the State executes criminals in the name of each of us; many of us now ask that the State stop doing that because a permanently incarcerated criminal is no longer a threat."[32] Cutting to the heart of the matter for people of faith, George said, "Jesus loved his enemies, including all of us who are sinners. He went freely to his death for our salvation." He encouraged Catholics to "have his crucifix in hand as we think about the death penalty."

ENDING URBAN VIOLENCE

George was long involved in community movements for peace and anti-violence initiatives in Chicago. He hosted more than 150 members of the clergy, religious, and community leaders who mutually agreed to several action items presented in a document called "Covenant for Peace in Action." These items were all directed toward curbing urban violence, including making use of the pulpits and the streets to raise awareness against violence and offer assistance to the city's most at-risk young people.

For more than a decade, George joined or led marches throughout Chicago that followed violence and shootings, and he was quick to engage individually with youth in the communities affected by violence. In the basement of a private home on Chicago's southwest side, George once negotiated peace among gang rivals.

George's interest in helping effect urban transformation and renewal allowed him opportunities for ministry among some of the city's most vulnerable. He was intrigued by the work of Dr. Gary Slutkin, an epidemiologist who founded a violence interruption project that was called CeaseFire. Slutkin's approach, which George found creative, was to approach violence as if it were an epidemic. Slutkin saw George's keen interest and support for CeaseFire's work from their first meeting. Although it took him nearly two years to arrange a meeting with George through his advisors, Slutkin said that the meeting, which was slated to last twenty minutes, lasted nearly three hours, during which time George agreed to chair CeaseFire's board.

In a piece praising George's effort against violence at the time of George's death, Slutkin said George's level of involvement was impressive and surprising, and he remembered George "humbly sitting at the table like any other member, opening up the file and discussing the neighborhood situations and the data which was of great interest and importance to him."[33] Slutkin also recalled that one of his most significant memories of George was when he joined him on a visit with a quadriplegic former gang leader in a highly secured hospital ward. Slutkin said that he often got "a sense that Cardinal George never lost his heart for people," and that George told him that "his most joyous times came when he was out with the people [such as when he was] leading marches to highlight youth violence or talking with high-risk youth in Chicago." He added: "He had a heart and warmth for people which radiated from the depths of his soul. His faith was so certain, it moved me and continues to cause me endless hours of contemplation."

IMMIGRATION

George was also no stranger to debates about welcoming the stranger into our midst. At a rally that drew thousands to Chicago's Grant Park in 2006, George spoke powerfully about respect for all as children of God, which also "means that families, in which each of us first learned what it means to be a human being, should not be divided, that husbands should not be separated from wives, nor mothers from their children. Respect means that people who have been part of this country's social and economic fabric for years should not now be treated as if they do not count, as if their contribution can be simply dismissed and be sent away."

He maintained in a 2012 column that our country's "broken" immigration system even "seems schizophrenic" because "there is much hopeful rhetoric and even concrete gestures" but "the number of people deported is greater than ever."[34]

At a 2009 immigration reform rally, George called on the Obama White House to stop splitting up families. There he urged Christians to come to the defense of immigrants against unjust laws. "We are called as people of faith to reflect the purifying and healing light of our Savior Jesus Christ," George said. "There is a darkness cast upon many families living among us who have been caught between society's need for cheap labor on one hand and the badly broken immigration laws on the other. We, along with other leaders of our society and people of good will, and with our elected officials, are called to be light for those forced by broken laws into the shadows."

George did not advocate for immigrants to ignore the immigration laws. As he explained it, the government had already done that — as they had "often been unable or unwilling to stop the flow of workers," even "looking away, because, in fact, their labor supported our economy." But, while reiterating that no one has a right to enter a country illegally, he remained very disturbed by the country's deportation practices, which above all damaged families. "Our Church teaches that the family is sacred, it is the cradle of life, the core institution of our society. To separate families, wives from husbands, children from parents, is to diminish what God has joined," he said.

George brought forward and drew together common themes regarding where American law failed to protect the vulnerable and poor, and he likened our treatment of undocumented immigrants to our treatment of infants in the womb. "A family is destroyed by deportation. A family is destroyed by violence in the streets and in our schools. The family is destroyed by violence in a mother's womb," he said. "Unborn children are undocumented. They are not citizens, but they are part of a family. An unborn child is someone's son, someone's daughter, someone's brother, someone's sister. They, too, should be protected in law."

George recalled in a 2001 column that "the first Archbishop of Chicago, Patrick Feehan, established 140 parishes to accommodate Catholic immigrants to Chicago in a 20-year period from 1880 to 1900."[35] Given that today's practice in the United States "is to form multicultural and multilingual parishes," George lauded the "welcoming attitude" of Catholics, which "helps to ease the transition for immigrants as they learn how to live here as practicing Catholics."

In George's thinking, the Church's concern and advocacy for immigrants is a reflection of her own history as an "institutional immigrant," sent forth from Jerusalem to all nations by Christ two thousand years ago. "The Church is everywhere an immigrant, and no immigrant escapes her concern," he wrote. "By reason of our faith, we are, as the Epistle to the Hebrews (11:9) reminds us, 'strangers in a strange land,' even when we call that land our home."

RACISM

From the first moment George arrived in Chicago, he observed the racial tensions that plagued the archdiocese. On the very day of his announcement as archbishop, after the introductory press conference, George made his way to a variety of places, including Mundelein Seminary and the tombs of his predecessors at the archbishops' mausoleum at Mount Carmel Cemetery in Hillside. He also visited the hospital bedside of a Black teenager who was the victim of a severe beating that had left him in a coma. The thirteen-year-old boy had been riding his bike along the edge of an invisible white/Black boundary, and he paid the price for crossing it. As George was getting settled into his role, the first executive assistant he hired was Sr. Anita Baird, who helped establish Chicago's Office for Black Catholic Ministries.

A few years later, after collaboration with a committee on racial justice, George published a major pastoral letter on the sin of racism titled "Dwell in My Love." Released in 2001 on the anniversary of Martin Luther King Jr.'s death, George invited the archdiocese into an examination of conscience on racism and its pervasive, destructive effects. George recognized that much work and prayer was necessary to change minds and hearts on this issue, saying, "It's easier to write a letter than change attitudes."[36]

In his pastoral letter, George acknowledged how the racial structures that defined the communities of Chicago and the surrounding area had negative ramifications on ecclesial life. Keeping parishes ethnically monotonous was one problem, and he called the practice one that created "parish fortresses" intended to keep others away.[37] "We have a history of segregated neighborhoods," George said.[38] He recalled learning about racism as a young boy when, upon returning from a summer trip to Tennessee, he became aware that his neighborhood had no racial diversity. Upon further reflection, he identified how his parents and their peers had acquaintances from the Black community, but the relationship stopped there. "The teaching in my home and in my parish was good; the experience just didn't match the teaching," George noted.[39] "That gap is called 'sin,' sometimes personal and social, sometimes institutional and structural, and sometimes all of these." George understood that when racism clouds hearts and minds it becomes institutionalized, creating an obstacle to overcoming its broader negative effects, such as discriminatory housing practices or food deserts in impoverished areas. George advocated for diverse Catholic communities, emphasizing that homogeneous communities in an ethnically diverse Chicagoland would only exacerbate the problem.

Not only did George call the Church to overcome the sin of racism, but he also extended his challenge to the wider society in Chicago, that collection of neighborhoods. In the letter, George identified institutional racism as having "patterns of social and racial superiority [that] continue as long as no one asks why they should be taken for granted." Noting that others "assume, consciously or unconsciously, that white people are superior," he said that society has institutions that "privilege people like themselves and habitually ignore the contributions of other peoples and cultures."

With characteristic honesty and Gospel-centered conviction, George concluded, "This 'white privilege' often goes undetected because it has become internalized and integrated as part of one's outlook on the world by custom, habit and tradition. It can be seen in most of our institutions: judicial and political systems, social clubs, associations, hospitals, universities, labor unions, small and large businesses, major corporations, the professions, sports teams and in the arts."

George noted the Church's history of standing against racism, particularly in Chicago, and reiterated that it would continue to do so. "I'm building on what is a very difficult history, and what is at the same time a comforting history," George said.[40] Just after the release of the pastoral letter, a public scandal arose when certain Catholic schools in the Southside Catholic Conference would not admit the predominantly Black St. Sabina school into their sports league, citing fear for the safety of white children in a Black neighborhood. George wrote that such fear "goes both ways."[41]

"African Americans have more reason to fear being unwelcome in white neighborhoods than vice versa. Concern for safety and fear of violence are legitimate fears; but the words are, as we all know, often code words to mask racism," he wrote. "Whether 'fear' is being used to excuse racism in this incident is a judgment that should be made only when one knows the people involved. Racism, of course, prevents our being holy because it separates us from one another and therefore from God. Fear also prevents our progress in holiness, because it means we do not trust God's providence."

George wanted the pastors to oversee the discussions and bring healing to the situation, which he understood to be a primary duty of his role as bishop. "The goal is to have sporting leagues, especially any that bear the name 'Catholic,' open to all races so that friendships can be formed across racial and cultural lines." He added: "It is always the children who get chewed up in these disputes. In the meantime, it is helpful, even for the sake of our own advance in holiness, if we avoid calling one another names."

Most importantly, George reiterated that his role, along with other clergy, was "to bring people constantly back to the goal: the children should be able to play together. Playing together will strengthen the unity of the Church and help the children live in a world less divided than our own," he said.[42]

In his seventeen years leading the Archdiocese of Chicago, George epitomized what it meant to be a good neighbor. Through his defense of the poor and the marginalized, his advocacy and support for a more welcoming and generous society, his friendships with those from other Christian communities and other religions, and countless other ways, George responded to a community greatly in need. And he did so in a way that kept Christ at the center of it all. "Dialogue with others isn't possible without a strong sense of Catholic communion," he once wrote.[43] "Why should anyone talk unless he or she has something to say, to share? What we say as Catholics comes to [us] from the apostolic community that unites us to Christ and witnesses to him in Scripture and Tradition. Catholics who dialogue, like those who evangelize, need to know and appreciate their faith."

TWELVE
A Missionary to the Culture

*The culture in which we evangelize needs to be evangelized
because evangelizing means bringing people to faith in Jesus
Christ within his Body the Church, where they can get to know
him as he truly is and experience his action in the Word of God,
the sacraments, both of which are expressions of his love.*[1]

CARDINAL FRANCIS E. GEORGE, O.M.I.

Throughout his tenure as a bishop, Cardinal George was particularly
concerned about the Church's ability to fulfill the Lord's command
to spread the Good News. This mission was especially dear to his heart
as an Oblate missionary. His service in episcopal ministry was a living
embodiment of how he described the office at the 2001 Synod of Bishops
— wherein the bishop's ministry as "Servant of the Gospel of Jesus Christ

267

for the Hope of the World" was the topic. "In his care as pastor, in moving his people from comfort to conversion, the bishop unites divided minds and heals divided hearts. In teaching minds, the bishop doesn't just share words and ideas; he brings his people to put on the mind of Christ. ... The bishop brings to public teaching in the Church the charism of making the faith recognizable, of identifying it and proclaiming it courageously."[2]

The clergy sex abuse crisis, which engulfed much of his tenure in Chicago and even absorbed much of his attention nationally and internationally, was just one of myriad of challenges the Church faced in living out her mission. A unique ability to survey the landscape and discern the signs of the times undergirded George's missionary urgency. Making evangelization a top priority, he pressed on amid many competing voices to share the Gospel message with an American culture not very interested in hearing it and, as such, called the Church to more fully live out her mission.

In 2004, while joining the bishops from Illinois, Indiana, and Wisconsin at an audience with Pope John Paul II, George pointed out some of the threats to the Church's mission, stemming from both internal and external forces. "The freedom of the Church is now threatened by movements within the Church and by government and groups outside the Church," he said.[3] "The Church's ability to evangelize is diminished."

The internal threats to the Church's mission that George identified were derived from "divisions which paralyze her ability to act forcefully and decisively." He continued:

> On the left, the Church's teachings on sexual morality and the nature of ordained priesthood and of the Church herself are publicly opposed, as are the Bishops who preach and defend these teachings.
>
> On the right, the Church's teachings might be accepted, but Bishops who do not govern exactly and to the last detail in the way expected are publicly opposed.
>
> The Church is an arena of ideological warfare rather than a way of discipleship shepherded by Bishops.

Eight years later, in his 2012 quinquennial report to the Holy See, George reflected on similar points. "Ideological division paralyzes the Church," he said, and he reinforced how "a Church with a divided mind cannot fulfill the mission of Christ to teach all nations." He further expressed his frustrations at how the ideological divisions are festered by "a left that hates the Church's teaching and the bishops who uphold it and a right that hates bishops who don't immediately accede to their sectarian demands." As a bishop, George worked very hard to help foster the unity that Christ wills for his Church. For George, unity — *ad intra et ad extra* — was bound up with the Church's very mission. At one of his last gatherings with the priests of Chicago in 2014, he said, "My own purpose as a bishop, my own personal purpose, was to create unity around Christ, but around Christ as he reveals himself, not a made up Christ or a Christ in our imagination. To therefore be close to the sources, and to understand who Christ is ... I've always said to start with the relationships and the rest will fall into place. And the primary relationship is to Christ."[4]

With two doctorates and a lack of diocesan management experience, George was a rarity among American bishops. His missionary formation made him unique, even among the other American cardinals. Most American cardinals came up through the ranks of the hierarchy after serving in diocesan priesthood and administration — something George had no experience with before becoming a bishop himself. He had, however, overseen an international missionary congregation, and those assignments provided him with knowledge and perspective that proved invaluable to him as a bishop.

The Oblates were founded to be missionaries who "preach the Gospel to the poor." The experiences of the congregation's founder, St. Eugene de Mazenod, very much shaped the Oblates' missionary thrust and therefore George's focus. De Mazenod's charism is twofold: first, to bring the Gospel to the ends of the world, including to those on the peripheries; and second, to bring the light of faith to those who have abandoned its practice. These aims also characterized George's own efforts in evangelization.

ON A MISSION

George knew that if the Church were properly ordered, she could be effective in her mission to be a sign and sacrament of salvation and unity for all mankind. To do this, as George articulated it, the Church must adhere to Vatican II's teaching on the Church as a communion:

> I really believe that if we come to understand the Church as a communion rather than a corporation or a society or a club, we will live in trust. We will know that it's because the gifts are present to us that we can trust each other to share them, that we can desire to move out from the visible confines of the communion as presently constituted with a sense of mission to bring more and more people into that communion. We can trust that when the bishops reach out to try to make that communion visible, it is not because they are trying to control or to destroy anyone, it is simply because they must reach out as the sign of that communion, they must make those relationships visible. The relationships are what keep us one in Christ and are our lifeline to the heavenly Jerusalem.[5]

And that was his vocation. "The bishop is the center of unity, visible unity — the Holy Spirit is the center of invisible unity in the Church — so you try to keep people together for the sake of the mission," he said.[6] "Whatever is necessary for that purpose is what I've tried to do."

With this programmatic vision as the backdrop, George's approach to evangelization was a continuous "reaching out." Confident in himself and in the Church, he was engaged and informed on the issues, and he took great care not to conflate his voice with politics or ideology. Instead, he articulated specific issues and shied away from a focus on policy. Whenever George showed up to talk with his neighbors, Catholic or not, he was prepared to speak of and share the gifts of Christ.

As a bishop, George was known and is remembered for holding nothing more dear to his heart than renewal of faith and evangelization.

George's departing words for his flock in Yakima reflected this, when he wrote, "My prayer is that nothing will deter you from sharing the Good News of Jesus Christ in a society that so little understands who he is or what he has done."[7] Naturally, this was a primary characteristic of his ministry in Chicago as well. Archbishop José H. Gomez of Los Angeles — and one of George's successors as president of the United States Conference of Catholic Bishops — "admired him as an apostle of the new evangelization, and especially his commitment to bringing American culture to a new encounter with the beauty and truth of Catholic teaching."[8]

In 2001, concerned over why the number of practicing Catholics had dropped so much in recent decades, George mused on its connection to the challenges of evangelizing:

> I suppose the basic reason is because it's hard to be Catholic. So much of what the Church has received from the Lord and teaches about her own life, about probity and justice in public life, about sexuality and marriage in personal life, runs against conventional wisdom, as our culture and society have developed in the past 40 years. Usually, when there is a clash between cultural norms and faith, the culture wins hands down. Culture is a lot more pervasive around us and persuasive within us than the faith, especially for those who don't worship regularly. All the national statistics on the difference of attitudes between practicing and non-practicing Catholics on issues of social justice and human sexuality bear this out.[9]

George saw sexuality as the real place of difficulty for those breaking with the Church or having animosity toward it. "When personal freedom," he said in 2012, "is reduced to sexual freedom, the Church's moral teaching becomes an object of disdain and even, at times, of hatred. It is dismissed and then actively opposed," he said.[10]

George himself described the "core" of his ministry, in his 2012 quinquennial report to the Holy See, as "promoting and safeguarding the faith." In order to teach the Faith, he began a regular column in Chicago's archdiocesan newspaper, as had been his custom in Yakima and Portland. He wrote it "with instruction in mind. Sometimes it will reflect the Church's teaching and sometimes it will be just an expression of my personal opinion."[11] Ending with his signature sign-off, "Sincerely yours in Christ," the columns attracted an audience far beyond Chicago. In written word and public speech, George did not shy away from teaching the Faith, even on the most thorny and controversial topics. George knew such topics often came with a call to conversion as disciples, which is where, George taught, evangelization must begin. As disciples oriented to Christ, we receive the gifts he gives and are charged with sharing them with others. "Christ changes us by giving us his gifts: new life, the Gospel, the sacraments, apostolic governance," George said.[12] "These transform us personally and collectively, so that we live no longer for ourselves but in Christ and for him and his people. We are disciples."

He also wrote the first of his two pastoral letters in Chicago on the topic of evangelization, which he framed as a task of all the baptized, not just the ordained. "A disciple of Jesus Christ must share the gifts he or she has received," he said. "The Church is formed in sharing the gifts of Christ. Sharing the spiritual gifts is called evangelizing. Sharing the material gifts is called stewardship. Both are necessary to the life of the authentic disciple of Jesus Christ. God's grace in Jesus makes us DISCIPLES who are EVANGELISTS, sharing the Gospel, the sacraments and apostolic governance; and STEWARDS, sharing time, treasure and talents" (emphasis his).

George's engagement with culture included not only critiquing it but also appreciating what enabled it to draw people closer to the fullness of truth, goodness, and beauty found in God, especially through the arts. His boyhood familiarity with music and painting grew stronger and broader during his years in Rome and his worldwide travels. From his Chicago upbringing, George also inherited a deep appreciation of Chicago's artistic and cultural institutions, such as the Chicago Symphony Orchestra, the

Lyric Opera, and the Art Institute of Chicago. He was pleased to attend concerts, plays, and art exhibits when invited to do so, and the comments he offered on such occasions could be as incisive as those printed in guidebooks and programs. He was a strong supporter of the Illinois chapter of the Patrons of the Arts in the Vatican Museums, and he used his gathering with them to highlight how fine art and clear theology are complementary; both support a vibrant, evangelizing life of faith.

EVANGELIZING THE CULTURE

George received Pope John Paul II's call for a New Evangelization with the utmost seriousness. As George once described it during a talk at the University of Notre Dame in 1999, evangelization requires new efforts because we are mostly evangelizing a people who have heard the Good News yet do not find it compelling or have drifted away. To them, George said, "the Gospel is not news, and it's not good. We have to go in and find again a new form of expression."[13] During George's *ad limina* meeting with John Paul in 1998, he was prepared to discuss the reports he submitted about his ministry and the status of the archdiocese. The pope pushed the reports aside and asked instead, "What are you doing to change the culture?"[14] The question became a motivator for George.

Taking issue with the term "culture warrior," George explained that his method was about engagement, not war. "I've seen myself for a long time as engaging culture. Engagement is not warfare. I know that's less dramatic to say, and people like to have drama, but calling it 'war' deforms what I'm about. It really denigrates my motivation, and I resent that."[15] George often reiterated that his motivations were pastoral in scope: "I'm not trying to beat anybody up at all; I'm trying to proclaim the truth of the Gospel, which I have an obligation to do." While recognizing his limitations — "maybe there are times I could do it more skillfully, or in a way that seems less abrasive" — George lamented that there were "some people who think it's abrasive as soon as you say, 'I disagree with you.' There's not much I can do about that."

Like an Apostle, George wrote to his flock, instructing them on how the Gospel must illuminate every facet of life. He went wherever he was welcomed or invited and spoke the truth of Christ, be it halls of power in Springfield, Illinois, in Washington, DC, or abroad. He preached the Gospel in houses of worship and during gatherings of other faith traditions, on college and university campuses, at prayer vigils in front of abortion clinics, and at the threshold of family homes on Chicago's southside on an evangelization crusade. "As a Church, outreach has always been a part of what we do, but it's usually been through services like Catholic Charities, schools and hospitals. What we want to do is attach to that a clear invitation of evangelization," George said when he walked through snow-covered streets with parishioners of St. Sabina parish in 2000, to "make disciples of all nations."[16]

George made it a priority to attend as many World Youth Day events as possible to help evangelize young people and encourage them to be a leaven in the Church and in society. The first World Youth Day in which he participated took place in 1993 in Denver, Colorado, where as a young bishop he saw this event transform the group of pilgrims from Yakima, helping young men and women from a small rural diocese to understand that they were part of a universal Church.

"If the Church looks old and decrepit, it's because our sins continue to drag us down. Holiness is always contemporary and is constantly attractive, especially to young people," George once wrote.[17]

George was always a popular speaker at the various catechesis events for US and international pilgrims at World Youth Days. A participant at one of the events recalled George's particular interest in the youth at one lunch gathering after such an event. The American pilgrims were in a hot area, without chairs, while a tent with tables and air-conditioning was prepared for bishops. George opted to sit on a curb and share his lunch with some of the American teens.

The gatherings deepened George's understanding of his global ministry as a bishop and cardinal. After World Youth Day in Toronto in 2002, he said it gave him the sense that he was a "bishop for young people not only of my own diocese, but from all over the world."[18] At the same event,

George expressed to the youth the courage that is necessary to live the Faith. "Life is meant to make you heroes. It takes a certain kind of heroism and courage to live up to your Baptism," he told them.

At the 2005 World Youth Day in Cologne, George told participants that Jesus "wants a change in your life, and his path is not always easy. Don't shrink him down to size, but let him elevate you to his, for he will lead you to a truth beyond your imagining."[19] He reminded them that "it takes courage to meet him, to be willing to change, and then go out again into the world where we don't always fit. A scary thought, but we are never alone in our faith."

As George put it, evangelization is not "beating people over the head with a Bible or a Catechism or our own spiritual experience stridently repeated; but it does mean more than the quiet witness of Gospel living and Christian service."[20] Evangelization is sharing one's relationship with Jesus Christ, which begins in the evangelizer's own repentance and conversion.

> With great respect, the evangelizer will look for opportunities to tell others who Christ is, because it is impossible for us not to speak of someone we love. But we know the appropriate moment for speaking because we have discerning hearts. This Jesus we love wants us to introduce people to him so that the gifts he left his Church — the Gospel and divine revelation, the Sacraments and other means of sanctification, the pastoral governance which continues the ministry of the Apostles — can be shared universally. Sharing these gifts brings us into the mind and heart of Christ and makes us God's agents to change a divided and sinful world into something which resembles at least a little bit more the kingdom of God.

According to George, Catholics are not to impose their faith out of a sense that they are superior to others, but instead are "to consider carefully our own hearts and speak only from a sense of gratitude for the gifts of God, with humility and love." Catholics also should not let apprehensions about their inability to answer questions that might arise prevent them from evangelizing, he said, as Catholics should be "helping one another learn more about Christ and the Bible and the Church's teachings and history."

Once, George received a letter from a man in his archdiocese who, upset with Pope John Paul II's opposition to the Iraq War, had returned his baptismal certificate. George wrote him back, "No matter what you accept or don't accept of what I've written, I see by your baptismal certificate that you are sixty-five years old. In a very few years, you will appear before the Lord Jesus Christ. He's not going to ask for your US passport, but he will be interested in knowing that you were baptized."[21] He returned the baptism certificate too.

One model of evangelization to whom George turned in his pastoral letter on evangelization was St. Thérèse of Lisieux, the cloistered Carmelite whose "little way" of holiness "helps us to read the Gospel in a more profound way."[22] Since Saint Thérèse is the patroness of missionaries, George entrusted her with evangelization efforts in Chicago. He clearly admired how St. Thérèse possessed "the heart of a missionary" and "a great and consistent desire, even through her final illness, to go where Christ was not yet well known." He prayed that the faithful of his archdiocese would have the same resolve.

Perhaps, more than anything, Saint Thérèse shaped George's missionary outreach because of her articulation of love as its center, which defined her vocation "to be love in the Church." George explained, "She wrestled with the various callings that came to her from her study of God's will and came one day to an insight: 'I understood that love comprised all vocations, that love was everything, that it embraced all times and places … I cried out … my vocation, at last I have found it … my vocation is love. Yes, I have found my place in the Church.' Because she found her place, we can find ours — to be signs and agents of God's universal love."

George knew that in order to evangelize, love had to come first. "We love America and we love our culture, therefore we have the possibility of transforming it," George said.[23] And he knew and showed that the only truly effective way to love is "through the witness and practice of holiness."

LAW AS CULTURE

While engaging the culture through truth and charity was one of George's unique gifts as an evangelizer, he was also able to identify and articulate those external forces that threaten the Church's mission. In the same 2004 *ad limina* address given to Pope John Paul II, George identified the rise of "a more overt expression of the anti-Catholicism which has always marked American culture. In this context, courts and legislatures are more ready to restrict the freedom of the Church to act publicly and to interfere in the internal governance of the Church in ways that are new to American life. Our freedom to govern ourselves is diminished."[24]

"The Church's mission is further weakened," George added, "by her inability to shape a public conversation that would enable people to understand the Gospel and the demands of discipleship." He attributed this to public conversations in the United States being less concerned about the common good than individual rights. "Matters that should fall outside the purview of law in a constitutional democracy with a limited government — the nature of life, of marriage, even of faith itself — are now determined by courts designed only to protect individual rights."

He continued: "The increasingly oppressive legal system and the bureaucratic apparatus of the state are abetted by a media industry which selects for publication only facts which fit stories it wants to tell. The public conversation, like the political, legal, and economic systems, is based on the generation of conflict between individuals and groups."

The evangelization of this contemporary culture was George's goal, and Bishop Robert Barron, himself no stranger to the evangelization of culture, said it was the former's "missionary consciousness" that "informed [this] intellectual and pastoral project."[25]

In Barron's estimation, George was unique in his "clear grasp of the philosophical underpinnings of the Western and especially American cultural matrix — namely, he knew that the successful evangelist must love the culture he is endeavoring to address," Barron said. For George, this love was manifested in the conviction that "as grace builds upon nature, so faith builds upon culture, which is second nature. Culture is damaged by human sinfulness, but it is not hopelessly corrupt."[26] In the end, he argued, "a culture is a field which offers plants from native seeds for grafting onto the tree of faith."

George understood the pull of the culture, describing it as the "non-biological inheritance that creates our life," and, "like faith itself, shapes our very lives." This means that "both culture and faith tell us how to behave and what to believe," he said. "Both give us norms for acting and for thinking and for loving."

And this means that the process of evangelization can be easier or more difficult depending on the message the culture is sending. George's approach to evangelizing the culture was, in many ways, through a focus on law. "The law created us as a people. We take our identity as a people from our relationship to the Constitution, and one's identity before the law is a primary source of one's personal value and of one's relation to others," George said in 2010.[27] "The myths of the settling of the West are based upon the coming of the law to an uncivilized wilderness. Legal proceedings constitute much of our news. As diverse as we are in culture, in language, in religion, in economic class, what we all have in common is the law. We are a nation of law."

His focus on law was significant, for in response to John Paul II's question, George identified — in a 1998 Red Mass homily in Washington, DC — that "law is the primary carrier of culture. In a country continuously being knit together from so many diverse cultural, religious, and linguistic threads, legal language most often creates the terms of our public discourse as Americans."[28]

Reflecting further on John Paul II's question of what he was doing to evangelize the culture, George said, "But how can we speak of change in America today when the law itself blinds us to basic truths? One egregious blind spot is our very sense of liberation construed as personal autonomy." He continued: "The fault line that runs through our culture, and it is sometimes exacerbated rather than corrected by law, is the sacrificing of the full truth about the human person in the name of freedom construed as personal autonomy. ... Such a profound error makes our future uncertain. Will the United States be here when the human race celebrates the end of the third millennium? Not without a very changed, a very converted culture."

This cultural fault line that George identified — that in American culture it is personal freedom that reigns above all else — was the foundation for the laws and interpretation of laws that paved the way for abortion, euthanasia, same-sex marriage, and the death penalty, to name a few. At the 2004 *ad limina* audience with John Paul, George said:

> In this culture, the Gospel's call to receive freedom as a gift from God and to live its demands faithfully is regarded as oppressive, and the Church which voices those demands publicly is seen as an enemy of personal freedom and a cause of social violence. The public conversation in the United States is often an exercise in manipulation and always inadequate to the realities of both the Country and the world, let alone the mysteries of faith. It fundamentally distorts Catholicism and any other institution regarded as "foreign" to the secular individualist ethos. Our freedom to preach the Gospel is diminished.[29]

Despite the challenges, George preached boldly. He approached social issues head-on, believing that evangelizers needed to be a part of the public conversations in order to bring to them the perspective of reason and the Gospel. George articulated these challenges in his archdiocesan newspaper column each week, explaining the Church's teaching and prophetically tracing out the consequences for the nation and Catholics alike. Nearly two dozen of his columns touched on the abortion issue alone.

His articulation of the deficiencies in the American legal system led him to identify all the ways in which human life was cheapened and trivialized. He reminded the US bishops in 2010 to speak the voice of Christ in all things:

> The voice of Christ speaks always from a consistent concern for the gift of human life, a concern that judges the full continuum of technological manipulation of life, from the use of artificial contraception to the destruction of human embryos to the artificial conception of human beings in a Petri dish to genetic profiling to the killing of unwanted children through abortion. If the poor are allowed to be born, then the voice of Christ continues to speak to the homeless and the jobless, the hungry and the naked, the uneducated, the migrant, the imprisoned, the sick and the dying. Our ministry is consistent because the concerns of Jesus Christ are consistent. He is at the side of the poor. Each of us in his own way speaks with Christ's voice, and each of us governs a particular church that lives with the poor, who are the first citizens of the kingdom of God. Ours is a consistent ethic of Christ's concerns for all his people, especially the poor.[30]

ABORTION

George focused often on the plight of the unborn. In a 2009 talk, he highlighted the hypocrisy of the American constitutional order, which he observed "gets its legitimacy from its legal protection of everyone, citizen or not."[31] Even when it failed in practice, such as with Blacks and others, "in theory our legal system protected everyone, including the unborn. Until Roe versus Wade." In a 1999 address at The Catholic University of America, George was stark: "I believe that fifty years from now when the inner contradictions of our national policy governing life and death have been resolved in either a change in our laws or the destruction of our nation, people will look back and ask if anyone tried to stop the horror of abortion."[32]

George explained that the abortion issue cannot be dependent on either the changing of laws alone or simply the changing of hearts alone. In a 2002 address at Ave Maria Law School, George stated:

> When it comes to abortion and other sanctity of life issues, we should not suppose that our choice is between reforming the law and working to change the culture. We must do both. The work of legal reform is a necessary, though not sufficient, ingredient in the larger project of cultural transformation. Yes, we must change people's hearts. But, no, we must not wait for changes of heart before changing the laws. We must do both at the same time, recognizing that just laws help to form good hearts; and unjust laws impede every other effort in the cause of the Gospel of Life. Teaching and preaching that Gospel, reaching out in love and compassion to pregnant women in need, all of this "cultural" work is indispensable. Without it, we will never effect legal reform or, if we do, the laws will not bear the weight we will be assigning to them.[33]

Pro-life evangelization, George urged in his 1999 talk at Catholic University, must begin with listening. And when one does speak, it should be "in a tone and manner that is always compassionate and caring, judging the act, being very slow to judge a person" and "not in such a way that people avoid us in the supermarket and at Little League games."[34] And "because we know the Holy Spirit is always there ahead of us, at work in the world, and in the life of the person that the evangelizer is talking to," George said our listening is attentive to "the movement of the Spirit in a friend's heart." He added: "With great respect, then, we look for opportunities to proclaim the Gospel of life because it's impossible for us not to speak lovingly what we know is the truth. But we also have to look for the appropriate moment and the appropriate forum because, precisely, we have discerning and loving hearts."

Abortion, George believed, is just as damaging to America's values as slavery had been. "The law's refusal to interfere with the institution of slavery helped to establish and maintain a culture corrupted by an ideology of racial superiority and inferiority," he said.[35] "The law's refusal to protect the unborn similarly shapes and hardens a culture corroded by the treatment of unborn human beings as 'nonpersons,' lacking the right to life that for the rest of us is protected by law."

Actions spoke just as loudly as words about George's clear thought around the abortion issue. Rarely did he miss the Vigil Mass for Life and the March for Life in Washington, DC, each January, which marked the anniversary of the Supreme Court's *Roe v. Wade* decision. He also "walked the walk" by actions such as praying outside abortion clinics. In 1999, after one instance of leading a peaceful prayer service outside one such facility in Chicago, George reflected on the experience in a column.[36] Noting that "the Church always accompanies the dying with prayer," George was drawing attention to the reality that "people die in an abortion clinic, and it is good to pray for them and for the living they leave behind." He also expressed his hope that the abortion clinic might do something with its income to help alleviate the poverty in its surrounding neighborhood. "They are the problem of a culture that systematically replaces living people with dead things and calls that a solution."

"Why are you here?" George said he was asked many times. He wrote:

> I was there because it must be said again and again that our society cannot indefinitely sustain the playing off of a mother's freedom against the death of her child. The country itself will eventually come apart. And I was there because no mere argument, no matter how well crafted, will convince those who sincerely believe in a civil right to abort a baby. What is left, along with peaceful and respectful discussion in the public forum, is prayer, in season and out of season.

What was clear in George's mind is that abortion is the iconic issue of what he understood to have "cheapened human life and changed our way of life."[37] In 2009, he observed that "in every generation we have killed in order to be free."[38] He brought this up in 2003 as the United States government was preparing for war with Iraq. As he recalled a line from Mother Teresa in 1994 — "the greatest destroyer of peace today is abortion" — George argued that "few make the connection between the deliberate destruction of an unborn human being and the deliberate destruction of those already born; but only the means are different."[39]

"Even the means, now that both medical procedures and war are so transformed by technological advances, tend to look more and more similar," George observed in his analogy. "Certainly, the way we talk about both abortion and war and the reasons given for engaging in either practice tend to sound eerily alike: protecting freedom, using no more violence than necessary, reluctantly concluding that we have no choice, needing to maintain our way of life." As he noted also in 2009, the connection between war and abortion works in the reciprocal too:

"In every generation we have killed to be free and now we've come along with an abortion procedure that says you have to kill in order to be free. We say, well alright, we've done that all along. It's very hard culturally to fight that argument. But we're in deep trouble unless we continue to do so."[40] He explained, "So when we made those people outlaws, when we took the protection of law away from the unborn, we destroyed our constitutional order, and we've had nothing but violence ever since. Because if you can solve a personal problem by killing someone who's still unborn, you can solve a personal problem by killing someone who is born. And I think that, unless that's changed — it's an immoral law — we're going to dissolve. I really believe that."

Because of this, the abortion issue inherently must shape our politics, George argued:

> In our country, the basic human right to life is inadequately protected by our system of legal or civil rights. Jurists and legislators who support laws permitting abortion betray their own vocation. Sometimes a jurist or legislator will say that he or she

personally believes abortion to be wrong but that personal morality cannot be legislated in a pluralistic society. This is an intellectually dishonest argument, because the protection of basic human rights is the duty of government officials, lest they sin against the common good; and the common good is fractured in a legal system that permits abortion. ... In any society, the law is a public standard for all; it should be designed to stop killing, not protect it.[41]

At various times over his tenure in Chicago, George presided over the burial of aborted children at archdiocesan cemeteries. Once, Mary FioRito, George's executive assistant, asked him what was going through his mind as he was standing quietly next to the container filled with the remains of the aborted children. She said George quietly replied, "I asked them to pray for me."

SAME-SEX "MARRIAGE"

"What has happened to our vaunted American liberties?" George once asked.[42] "Except for property rights, they are all being traded off in favor of freedom of sexual expression. That 'freedom' has become the trump card in almost every social dispute."

It was this rabid desire for sexual freedom that George was convinced became the common foundation of the push to legalize both abortion and same-sex marriage, among other things. This mindset, George believed, had much to do with the prominence of Sigmund Freud, the standard-bearer of modern psychology, who, according to George, "trained several generations of intellectuals to believe that sex is at the center of human life and affects or even explains everything we do or stand for."[43]

"The American search for happiness seems now to have become less closely bound to the desire to love and be loved than to a sometimes relentless quest for genital sexual experiences," he wrote. "What is most popularly contested today, therefore, is not the Church's understanding of the Triune God but the Church's teaching on the use of God's gift of human sexuality."

George's time in Chicago coincided with the local and national move to legitimize and legalize same-sex marriage and gay rights. In approaching this sensitive topic, he was careful to be just as critical of groups in the Church that compromised her official teaching regarding human sexuality as he was supportive of defending the dignity of homosexual persons.

The first same-sex marriages in the United States legally occurred in San Francisco in 2004. At the time, George observed, "Attempts at 'gay marriage' are not new in human history. The Roman Emperor Nero, almost two thousand years ago, went through a public marriage ceremony with one of his male concubines and managed to shock even degenerate Roman pagan society."[44] George was concerned that the modern-day attempt "to cloak immorality in the language of 'civil rights' is destructive of both moral and civil orders." The occasion marked a new rise of "moral blindness" in America's civil order, he said, but familiar territory in the story of sin.

George observed that the fundamental question at hand was: "Are homosexual genital relationships immoral?" If they are not, they should be legalized, "not just as 'privacy' rights but as well-ordered manifestations of human sexuality." But if they are immoral, "there is no more civil right to enter into 'gay marriage' than there is a civil right to steal," he said. And though Scripture attests to the immorality of homosexual genital relationships, it is not solely a religious question. "In fact, the argument about the nature of marriage has little to do with religion of any sort. The nature of marriage is knowable by human reason and always has been," George said.

As for the legalization of same-sex marriage, George issued a letter, signed also by his auxiliary bishops, that straightforwardly argued that it would be "against the common good of society."[45] He observed that it "will have long-term consequences because laws teach; they tell us what is acceptable and what is not, and most people conform to the dictates of their respective society, at least in the short run." The legislation that was passed in his state of Illinois in 2013, George warned, would mean that those who "continue to distinguish between genuine marital union and same-sex arrangements will be regarded in law as discriminatory, the equivalent of bigots." George added in his column, published at the same time as the letter, "A proposal to change this truth about marriage in civil law is less a threat to religion than it is an affront to human reason and the common good of society. It means we are all to pretend to accept something we know is physically impossible. The Legislature might just as well repeal the law of gravity."[46]

Ignoring the natural law, the complementarity of male and female, meant, George said, that "the natural family is undermined."[47] For a man of George's vision, this phenomenon had far more wide-reaching effects, some of which could not be foreseen at the time; it opened up a Pandora's box of possibilities. "Our individual lives become artificial constructs protected by civil 'rights' that destroy natural rights," he wrote. "Human dignity and human rights are then reduced to the whims of political majorities. When the ways of nature and nature's God conflict with civil law, society is in danger."

George matter-of-factly addressed division within the Church around the issue, as there are Catholics who consider the acceptance of same-sex marriage "an exemplification of compassion, justice, and inclusion." [48] These same sentiments can further be used, he argued in his column, "to justify everything from eugenics to euthanasia."

"If religion is to be more than sentiment, the moral content of these words has to be filled in from the truths of what human reason understands and God has revealed," he said. "Same-sex unions are incompatible with the teaching that has kept the Church united to her Lord for two thousand years."

George observed in 2011: "Law can destroy rather than protect," and he was concerned about what that meant for Catholics in the future.[49] Prompted by a law in Illinois allowing civil unions and declaring it a right for homosexual couples to adopt children, he commented, "If today, our civil laws have been changed so that no one can be destroyed by immoral racial slavery, laws can nevertheless be used to destroy other freedoms, including the freedom of the Catholic Church to be herself, to teach freely and to control her own ministries and religious activities." In 2011, Catholic Charities and other religious organizations were forced to suspend adoption services for vulnerable children in order to avoid betraying their conscience. George stood against the state, which meant the possibility that the Church would be "punished because she teaches the truth about the nature of marriage and because her various educational and charitable ministries reflect this Gospel truth."

As for the pastoral care of homosexual persons, George reiterated Church teaching that has "consistently condemned violence or hatred of homosexually oriented men and women," adding that "good pastoral practice encourages families to accept their children, no matter their sexual orientation, and not break relationships."[50] In 2003, George dramatically took to the pulpit at Holy Name Cathedral to defend a "false accusation" leveled against Pope John Paul II by the *Chicago Sun-Times*, which claimed that the pope had launched a "global campaign against gays," an accusation prompted by the release of a document published by the Holy See's Congregation for the Doctrine of the Faith (CDF) that, among other things, called on lawmakers to oppose same-sex marriages for the harm such unions pose to society.[51] George reiterated, as did the CDF's text, that "marriage is the lifelong union of a man and a woman who enter into a total sharing of themselves for the sake of family." As marriage itself was decided by biology and predates the Church, George noted that neither the Church nor governments have any authority to change it. "Because of a concerted effort in TV shows in recent years to shape public imagination and opinion into accepting same-sex relations as normal and morally unexceptional, obvious truths now are considered evidence of homophobia," George said.[52] In addition, George made it clear that the pope's voice is no mere "opinion of the Vatican," as the newspaper stated, but the principle of unity in Catholic teaching, which "makes up nothing that he teaches ... because he is the primary witness to the faith that unites us in Christ." George wrote a letter of apology to the pope expressing how he was "ashamed that this false accusation against the pope was made in our city. At the very least it is unfair, and we pride ourselves on fairness." Such disdain for and hatred of the pope, George said, "are sure signs of anti-Catholicism." As "a bishop likes to presuppose good will," George observed "a line has been crossed, and Chicago Catholics cannot ignore what happened." The *Sun-Times* defended its story.

In late 2011, George made the news himself when he expressed his frustrations about the Chicago Gay Pride parade, which announced a route that would shut off vehicle traffic to a Catholic parish in the city on a Sunday morning. Made aware that Masses would necessarily be canceled that day because of the restrictions imposed by the parade route, George observed in an interview with Chicago's Fox affiliate, "You don't want the gay liberation movement to morph into something like the Ku Klux Klan, demonstrating in the streets against Catholicism." George did not want the gay rights movement to be hijacked for ulterior motives and become itself intolerant, in this case of Catholics. Admitting to his interviewer that the comparison was indeed strong, George nevertheless insisted on pointing out the similarities in rhetoric between the two instances. "The rhetoric of the Ku Klux Klan, the rhetoric of some of the gay liberation people. Who is the enemy? Who is the enemy? The Catholic Church," he said. A firestorm ensued, with many demanding an apology.

In a statement, George observed that the parade was held for many years without disrupting attendance at houses of worship in the city. He argued that since the parade organizers that year decided to proceed with a new route, even after being informed that it would disrupt worship in a Catholic parish, they "invited an obvious comparison to other groups who have historically attempted to stifle the religious freedom of the Catholic Church."[53] He added that in our nation's history, the Ku Klux Klan "paraded through American cities not only to interfere with Catholic worship but also to demonstrate that Catholics stand outside of the American consensus. It is not a precedent anyone should want to emulate."

Given the mischaracterizations, especially in light of the sound bite taken out of context, George reiterated that "it is terribly wrong and sinful that gays and lesbians have been harassed and subjected to psychological and even physical harm. These tragedies can be addressed, however, without disturbing the organized and orderly public worship of God in a country that claims to be free." In the end, the parade moved its start time to not conflict with the celebration of Sunday Mass.

Shortly thereafter, George further clarified his thoughts in a statement on the matter and did apologize "for the hurt that my remarks have brought to the hearts of gays and lesbians and their families," acknowledging some members of his own family who were homosexually oriented.[54] "I can only say that my remarks were motivated by fear for the Church's liberty," George wrote. "This is a larger topic that cannot be explored in this expression of personal sorrow and sympathy for those who were wounded by what I said."

In 2010, while serving as president of the United States Conference of Catholic Bishops, George raised serious questions about a group called New Ways Ministry. He noted that, since its founding in 1977, the group has not presented "an authentic interpretation of Catholic teaching" on sexuality and marriage. The group describes itself as "a gay-positive ministry of advocacy and justice for lesbian and gay Catholics and reconciliation within the larger Christian and civil communities." Because of the errors in their approach, the founders were barred by the Holy See's Congregation for the Doctrine of the Faith from any ministry in this particular area in 1999. George's 2010 declaration stated:

No one should be misled by the claim that New Ways Ministry provides an authentic interpretation of Catholic teaching and an authentic Catholic pastoral practice. Their claim to be Catholic only confuses the faithful regarding the authentic teaching and ministry of the Church with respect to persons with a homosexual inclination. Accordingly, I wish to make it clear that, like other groups that claim to be Catholic but deny central aspects of Church teaching, New Ways Ministry has no approval or recognition from the Catholic Church and that they cannot speak on behalf of the Catholic faithful in the United States.

Why was George so passionate about protecting the family and marriage, as it has been known for millennia, as only the union of a man and a woman? Because he understood that a society that redefined marriage — a society that was thoroughly secularized — is built around the individual. Such a system, in which "you purposely destroy families," George said in his 2012 interview with Salt and Light, "that's not civil society." And he argued, ominously yet prophetically, that with continued secularism and the inevitable dissolution of families that follows, "society is going to become a very ugly place." More to the point, he explained, "if the family is weakened, society is destroyed."[55]

SECULARISM

Papal biographer George Weigel argued often that it was Cardinal George who sounded warning bells on the threats to religious freedom facing the United States in the late twentieth century. "His calm insistence that there were and are deep cultural problems in American democracy was a needed wake-up call for many," Weigel said.[56]

George often expressed that one of his primary concerns regarding American culture was that "religious truth is no longer a public virtue," as he wrote in 1992.[57] "Transforming our national purpose in the light of God's plan for all peoples means listening to a source of truth not limited by American experience."[58] He argued that, while the Church can contribute to the conversation on common values such as justice and freedom, "the public authority, the government, while it must protect freedom and foster justice, cannot teach. But the Church can; and this claim to teach the truth is truly counter-cultural. ... Since the culture is too narrow for Gospel truth, Catholic evangelizers want to enlarge it."[59]

George was keen to note that the shift from a religiously dominated to a secularized culture made things much more difficult for people of faith. He ended an address to members of Congress at the Library of Congress in 2007 by recalling the centrality of religion in American democracy. "What kind of democracy leads to secularism?" he asked.[60] "Ours, if it reduces the realm of human freedom in the name of individual civil rights. What kind of democracy protects freedom? Ours, if it limits itself to its properly secular purposes." And he countered, "What kind of democracy promotes freedom? Ours, if it becomes totally free. What kind of democracy destroys freedom? Ours, if it becomes totally secularized."

A totally secularized society, George said, is one that does three things: first, makes "all truth relative and all religion a matter of personal opinion, not to be imposed on anyone else;" second, creates "a world so free of danger and threat that it becomes a prison for everyone;" and third, reduces "poverty by reducing the number of people, by killing those who are too weak to defend themselves."[61]

Toward the end of his tenure in Chicago, as George reflected on what all these societal changes meant for Catholics, he wrote about "a tale of two churches" in his regular newspaper column. The piece puts into context the situation in which American Catholics find themselves in the first part of the twenty-first century and illustrates his view of how a totally secularized democracy destroys freedom. He explained that not only is Judeo-Christian morality no longer upheld, but, worse, those opposing it call the Church's teaching intolerant and opposed to what civil law dictates and upholds. As George described it, the new dispensation of moral arbitrariness invades every aspect of culture and society, setting up a de facto religion itself, and making precarious the citizenship of those who do not subscribe to it. He worried what Catholics might suffer at the hands of the self-professed "'progressive' and 'enlightened.'"

George saw that this reality would bring a crisis of faith for many believers, one that would make them have to decide which "church" to believe in. He wrote:

Throughout history, when Catholics and other believers in revealed religion have been forced to choose between being taught by God or instructed by politicians, professors, editors of major newspapers and entertainers, many have opted to go along with the powers that be. This reduces a great tension in their lives, although it also brings with it the worship of a false god. It takes no moral courage to conform to government and social pressure. It takes a deep faith to "swim against the tide." ...

Swimming against the tide means limiting one's access to positions of prestige and power in society. It means that those who choose to live by the Catholic faith will not be welcomed as political candidates to national office, will not sit on editorial boards of major newspapers, will not be at home on most university faculties, will not have successful careers as actors and entertainers. Nor will their children, who will also be suspect. Since all public institutions, no matter who owns or operates them, will be agents of the government and conform their activities to the demands of the official religion, the practice of medicine and law will become more difficult for faithful Catholics. It already means in some States that those who run businesses must conform their activities to the official religion or be fined, as Christians and Jews are fined for their religion in countries governed by Sharia law.[62]

He lamented how in history many Catholics have chosen the path of least resistance, acquiescing to the societal powers to make their lives easier. But this, George said, means worshiping a strange god. Another result of all this, according to George, is the weakening and destruction of the family in American law. He concluded his argument on a note of hope, however: We have Christ's promise that the Church will last until the end of the world, but he made no such promise about any society or system of government.

A VISION FOR THE FUTURE

The Catholic vision of life and its approach to social issues offers a complete, consistent ethic, which is clearly a countercultural witness in America in our day. Conversely, today's culture "fosters the dissolution of human community" on account of the fact that it is incapable of "integrating, legitimizing, and evaluating human experience," George said in 2003.[63] "The

Church's primary concern, after all, is not to integrate a society, but to be faithful to Christ in every age and cultural situation." What this meant for American Catholics was uncertain, of course, but, as George wrote to a friend in 1985, "North Africa once had flourishing Catholic communities. Why should North America be an historical exception?"

He elaborated on this thinking some years later as archbishop of Chicago at a 2003 address at the University of Notre Dame Law School:

> What if we are destined, because of cultural flaws which are intrinsic to our system of government and life, to go the way of all empires? What if we are permitted by Almighty God to overreach so that the institutions that have shaped us, particularly the law, the Constitution, the legislatures, will dissolve in order that something truly new can be created for the sake of a more global common good? Americans have flourished with this nation-state. ... We'll defend it to the end. But what if the end desired not by us but by God, is a form of global society that means that (our law) disappears from history. I would, as Archbishop of Chicago, have a successor, but perhaps not in what we now call Chicago. Mine might be a title for an auxiliary bishop in Africa or South America or wherever the next development in human culture will be found.[64]

It was not uncommon for George to hypothesize about the future in this manner, and he often suggested that things would get worse before they got better. At a Louisiana priests' convocation in 2009, George offered what is perhaps one of his best-known quotes about what the complete secularization of American society might resemble. The quote was posted into the digital realm and went viral — but only in part. George, clarifying his comments in a column a few years later, stated:

> I am (correctly) quoted as saying that I expected to die in bed, my successor will die in prison, and his successor will die a martyr

in the public square. What is omitted from the reports is a final phrase I added about the bishop who follows a possibly martyred bishop: "His successor will pick up the shards of a ruined society and slowly help rebuild civilization, as the Church has done so often in human history." What I said is not "prophetic" but a way to force people to think outside of the usual categories that limit and sometimes poison both private and public discourse.[65]

He elaborated on the meaning of his analogy further, focusing on the source of the Church's hope as she faces life in a totally secularized society:

> Only one person has overcome and rescued history: Jesus Christ, Son of God and Son of the Virgin Mary, Savior of the world and Head of his Body, the Church. Those who gather at his cross and by his empty tomb, no matter their nationality, are on the right side of history. Those who lie about him and persecute or harass his followers in any age might imagine they are bringing something new to history, but they inevitably end up ringing the changes on the old human story of sin and oppression. There is nothing "progressive" about sin, even when it is promoted as "enlightened."

In 2004 remarks celebrating the 150th anniversary of the declaration of the dogma of the Immaculate Conception, George stated that society would "go far in creating a civilization of love" and building God's kingdom by adopting "our vision for social transformation."[66] He elaborated:

> Here on earth, we can imagine a society where every person, man, woman and child, born and unborn, is accorded the dignity which is theirs as a son or daughter of God. A world structured so that it will be more difficult for one person to use another, to reduce a human being to a consumer in a marketplace, a cog in an industrial machine, a functionary of a totalitarian state,

an object of empirical laboratory research, a sexual playmate to slake the biological drives of another, a mere instrument of another's designs or plots or whims.

But while "moral reform is necessary," he argued it is "not enough." He said, "Morality without charity, without the love of God, is not the Gospel of Jesus Christ. The kingdom truly exists where God's infinite love is like water that covers the sea; where his love is enough and more than enough, for it satiates our every desire, it fulfills our every yearning; it controls our every moment and fills the world with a joy so great that God is all in all. The kingdom is God's, not ours."

It is this reality that shaped George's own life and his response to bringing about the kingdom of God as a priest. Reflecting on his fifty years as a priest in 2013, George observed, "The idea it would be difficult to be a Catholic in the United States as it's becoming now was certainly not with us" when he was ordained.[67] "What I promised to uphold and believe fifty years ago I still believe, and I do. But the context of doing that is so much more difficult than it was then."

The archdiocese hosted a large, beautiful celebration to honor the occasion. It began with a Mass George celebrated at Holy Name Cathedral, attended by over one hundred bishops from across the country. George was uneasy with such gatherings, preferring to avoid being the center of attention. "When you're a bishop you belong to the people and the diocese you serve, and enough of them said we should mark this," he said. "As long as what they're marking is the impact of the priesthood on their lives, I'm very glad to do it."

In the end, George saw his task as bishop to be rather simple, as he encouraged the US bishops to proclaim in 2002, "Dear brothers and sisters, in this culture, God wants us all to be Catholic. Here's how you go about it. If you do so, God will set you free. God is doing wonderful things here. Why shouldn't he? He is God, and we are not."[68] After that, he said, bishops should "trust the laity to work it out in the world and, in the name of Christ and with his authority, hold them accountable in this world, as Christ will in the next."

A decade later, in what would be his final quinquennial report to the Holy See, George said that what the world and what the culture needed most were holy men and women. "What we need are saints … a Catherine of Siena or a Francis of Assisi," he said. "The major task of the bishop is to look for the saints and encourage them." Cardinal George attempted to follow this rubric, fostering holiness among his flock as he helped them navigate the murky waters of contemporary American society. He was, in short, living out his missionary vows: proclaiming Christ bravely and faithfully and speaking truth in charity.

THIRTEEN
An Instrument of the Lord

He was indefatigable. Such a person proceeds with a
good deal of mystery about them, but it's hard to find
anyone who supersedes them in terms of their gifts,
their abilities, or their accomplishments. He moved
through life a couple of inches above the earth.

Most Reverend Joseph N. Perry, auxiliary bishop of Chicago

Cardinal Francis George once mentioned in a column that, while he had felt drawn to St. Thomas Aquinas earlier in his life, his affinity was redirected over the years to St. Augustine, the theologian-monk who became a bishop and died in the year 430 at the age of seventy-five. It makes sense that George would relate to him so well, finding in Augustine a kindred intellectual and a source of inspiration and intercession for the times in which he lived. He described the fourth- and fifth-century pastor as having "watched the Roman Empire dissolve violently and tried to understand what God was telling us as the ancient world came to an end."[1] But, more importantly, he observed that "as society came apart around him, St. Augustine saw everything put together in the light of faith."

While things were not quite as drastic in George's day as they were in Augustine's, George had an abundance of opportunities to share Augustine-like commentary on the cultural situation in which he lived and the direction America was taking as it became so rapidly secularized. This commentary, in which he brought his philosophical and theological acumen to bear on issues of the day, propelled George, as archbishop of Chicago and then as a prince of the Church, to national and international renown. His rise within the Church was no less striking considering he might never have been ordained a priest in the first place.

Clergy and parishioners in Yakima and Portland were not surprised that George rose to the top of the American hierarchy. It was something of a fast ascendancy, with only seven-and-a-half years between his nomination as a bishop and his creation as a cardinal, with moves to two other dioceses in between. George's formal nomination to the College of Cardinals came two days after his sixty-first birthday, and he received the red biretta and cardinal's ring in February 1998. Upon returning home from the ceremonies in Rome, George celebrated his first Mass as Chicago's truly hometown cardinal, where he stated that he was not sure exactly what it would be like to be a cardinal but that he would learn as he went along. He further described the honorific in a 2007 address at Brigham Young University: "Cardinals, like all ministers of the Gospel, are merely instruments of the Lord who is the true Shepherd of the flock. Most important of all, I am a bishop, and therefore a pastor to the people Christ has given me to love and care for, even to the point of shedding my blood for their spiritual and physical wellbeing if that were ever to prove necessary."[2]

Many Catholics saw George as a warrior for truth and good. Others, himself included, believed he was often weaker than he should have been and lacked courage. A sense of George's character and pastoral sensibilities might best be summed up in descriptions offered by two bishop friends: Bishop J. Basil Meeking, who described George as having a "spine of steel," and Archbishop Charles J. Chaput, who said that George could sometimes promise to come to a fight with a warship but instead show up in a rowboat.

Despite his own reluctance to become a prominent Catholic voice, George found himself drawn into a variety of national and international issues that required a man of his talents and skill and greatly benefited from his authenticity and sense of mission. In some ways, given his position in one of the most prominent American sees, it was inescapable. But even more so, because of his brilliance and good sense, his charity and tenacity, his clarity and incisiveness, it was inevitable.

George asked physician Fr. Myles Sheehan, whom he had gotten to know well over the years, especially during his first serious battle with cancer in 2006, to be his doctor not long after the two shared a meal together with a mutual friend. On that day, Sheehan commented to George about how he had been teaching his medical students the principle of double effect in moral theology. George, as a former university professor who relished classroom repartee, drilled him on the subject. In recalling that incident, Sheehan observed that George's inquisitive nature could often be interpreted as pugnaciousness.

Sheehan believed this was somewhat true, noting that George "probably had to be combative to overcome the polio." But he also believed George's background in philosophy and theology meant he was always "pushing, pushing, pushing to get the right idea." As Sheehan put it, George "wasn't satisfied with pious phrases and sloppy thinking. He wanted precision and sharpness."

At the same time, Sheehan was quick to point out how warm George could be — a side of the cardinal that many experienced but that was not always readily apparent in media sound bites, which could be taken out of context. George was aware of his tendency to say "here is the general principle but here are the qualifications" and also aware that "all they catch is the first part." This, he said, is the way that "I habitually speak," adding that it "has to be looked into — just for the sake of accuracy." In some ways, his open and honest manner of speaking was an Achilles heel that worked against him, especially when it came to media coverage.

During George's time in the College of Cardinals, many of the important decisions and functions of the body of American bishops often bore his fingerprints. This is not to say that he dominated discussions or was always successful in his arguments; but it does mean that, time and again, the bishops sought out George for his ability to see issues clearly, to cut through any distractions, and to get to the heart of the matter. "He was a believer," as Archbishop Jerome E. Listecki of Milwaukee — ordained by George as an auxiliary bishop in Chicago in 2001 — described him. Countless bishops have recalled that when George rose to speak at meetings of the US bishops, all the bishops paid attention. George's tenacity and courage enabled him to stand up for what he regarded as principles that necessarily build up ecclesial communion. And he was rarely afraid to tell people exactly where he stood, as Cardinal George Pell recalled. He observed that George "was capable — this is not universal in any section, quite possibly not even in the hierarchy — he was capable of direct speech."

"Once in a blue moon, once in a while, he could be devastatingly blunt, and state the situation just the way it was," Pell said. "Now, he probably suffered as a result of that. But he was a man of faith and he was very well educated. A very clear thinker. He meant what he said, and he said what he meant." Bishop Thomas J. Paprocki of Springfield, another of George's former Chicago auxiliaries, remembered how others would ask him for copies of George's brilliant talks, which turned out more often than not to be chicken scratch on an index card. It was a surprise to learn that, considering how George would still speak with complete, full sentences, grammatically precise.

In 2012, Bishop Donald J. Hying of Madison, then an auxiliary of Milwaukee, attended a dinner with George, who had just turned seventy-five. Hying recalled him saying that "he had just started telling people exactly what was on his mind." Hying replied, "Your Eminence, has anybody noticed the difference?" Having long admired George's character and "his courage in speaking the truth in charity to our confused culture of today," Hying hoped George would be amused. "To my relief, he burst into a hearty laugh!" Hying remembered.

LITURGY

In 2008, when standing with Fr. Bartholomew Juncer after his ordination to the priesthood and waiting for a picture with the new priest's family, George leaned over and gently informed him that he had mispronounced the Latin verb *habēre* in the Eucharistic Prayer. Father Juncer nervously joked to George that in the seminary they had been taught that no priest ever says the perfect Mass. To which George quipped back, "Well, at least you could try!"

It was his straightforward approach to liturgy that earned George the pejorative nickname "Francis the Corrector." But it was for the same liturgical attentiveness that the bishops of the Church turned to him for leadership on this sensitive subject. In 1997, George was chosen as the delegate of the US bishops to the International Committee for English in the Liturgy (ICEL), which positioned him for several other liturgy-related appointments throughout the years. This liturgical and linguistic work was fitting for George, a polyglot who recognized the important role that unity in prayer and sacrament played in building up the unity of the whole Church and, thereby, strengthening her for mission. When the US Church implemented a new translation of the Mass in 2011 — a major moment in the life of the Church in English-speaking countries and perhaps the biggest change experienced since the liturgical reforms of the Second Vatican Council — it did so largely because of George's leadership.

A rushed, unsatisfactory translation of the Missal in the early 1970s, on the heels of various misinterpretations of Vatican II, slowly created divisions in ecclesial life. Some clergy began taking too many liturgical liberties, causing frustrations and confusion. This concerned George, who wrote in 2001, "Nothing is so destructive of the full participation desired by the Second Vatican Council than an individual, priest or reader or anyone else, making up changes to the texts as the liturgy is celebrated. Such changes draw attention to the individual and away from the rites which enable us to pray together. They weaken participation by leaving people unsure of what is going to come next."[3]

He added: "The Eucharistic liturgy is where the risen Christ is made visible in the sacrament of his Body and Blood; it is not a form of personal self-expression, except to the extent we are truly 'in Christ.' If we start with that basic conviction, linguistic problems have a chance of being worked out in such a way that our unity in worship is preserved. Any other agenda will divide us."

Preparing a more suitable English translation of the Roman Missal had been a drawn-out, highly contentious and complicated process, rife with theological and ideological bickering within the Church's leadership. George's main task — and a daunting one at that — was to provide unity. When he set out on this mission, the process of preparing a newly translated Missal had already been underway for nearly a quarter of a century. Adding to the significance of his voice, in 2001, George was elected chair of the US bishops' Committee on Liturgy. The drama over liturgy around the time, he wrote after the election, prompted him to stand for office, believing "we have to find some way to move beyond controversy to a less contentious way of producing liturgical texts in the English language."[4] There was no small amount of controversy surrounding the liturgy, even, and perhaps especially, among the bishops themselves. The internal discord that had come about from the enduring liturgy wars was counterintuitive to the Church's mission, George said, and it discouraged participation in ecclesial life. "Who wants to get into tugs-of-war, even around the Mass, which is supposed to be the source and sign of our unity?" George asked rhetorically. He observed "some delight in" such fights, but he argued that they end up making the Church's life "resemble ward politics more than the kingdom of God." Ultimately, he said, "they disturb our life with God and paralyze the Church's mission."

According to Abbot Jeremy Driscoll of Mount Angel Abbey, a renowned liturgy professor who collaborated with George in the translation work, George pushed authorities in Rome, particularly within the Congregation for Divine Worship and Discipline of the Sacraments, to act decisively, to "take hold of the translation question [and] to establish guidelines for how translations would be made." This was a key component of the process that had been found wanting. For George, it was vital that bishops have direct oversight over translations.

Driscoll observed that George "had the ecclesial clout to push the point, and he knew how to get the kind of the authority structures that exist in the Church motivated in the right direction to make decisions against cultural currents that were moving the translation in other directions." As George himself described it, the existing translation was "too close to a zeitgeist" and dependent on "the desires or proclivities of a particular group and is forgetful that popular culture itself changes very, very rapidly."[5]

George "understood what the text's theological importance was," Driscoll said. As far as how the Missal was revised in the English-speaking world, Driscoll said George "was one of the biggest players. He was the leader in the American Church, very definitely."

Great advancement toward the new translation of the Missal, particularly in English-speaking countries, was made in 2001 when the Congregation for Divine Worship promulgated *Liturgiam Authenticam.* This document provided instruction on how to implement the Second Vatican Council's Constitution on the Sacred Liturgy, *Sacrosanctum Concilium,* especially where the use of the vernacular is concerned. The following year, Pope John Paul II approved the third typical edition of the Roman Missal. From that edition stemmed its new translations into the vernacular. That same year, the Congregation for Divine Worship established the Vox Clara committee, made up of senior bishops from episcopal conferences throughout the English-speaking world, to advise the congregation on English-language liturgical texts and their translation. George was among its first members.

According to Driscoll, himself a consultant to the committee, George "recognized the importance of a full, accurate translation of the Latin text." Recalling one instance of a tense debate surrounding the translation, Driscoll added that George "could cut to the chase when there was nonsense going on." In one such episode, amid a serious dispute with a particular theological interlocutor, Driscoll recalled George replying, "No, that's a different religion."

A "good translation," George said in 2006, "is faithful not only to the meaning of the original language but also to the form."[6] Pointing out "different ways to instruct someone to turn on a light" — "I could say, 'Turn on the light,' or I could say, 'Would you turn on the light?'" — George noted that, although "the information is the same in both sentences ... the form is different." He continued: "*Liturgiam Authenticam* instructs the translator to pay attention to both the content and the form of the original language." In George's view, this meant that the new translation of the Missal would "consequently be somewhat more polite, more courteous in form than the texts we now use." He also said that it would "restore parts of prayers currently not translated and pay special attention to the biblical context of many of the prayers of the Roman rite."

In 2000, George established the Liturgical Institute at Mundelein Seminary in the Archdiocese of Chicago, through which he hoped to bring about a "new era in liturgical renewal," as he found that "the influence of sacramental theology wasn't as strong as it should be in liturgical studies."[7] His inspiration, according to the institute's former academic director Dr. Denis McNamara, originated because "he saw a problem, that people didn't understand how they should interpret liturgical decisions."[8] The institute was founded partly to attend to the issues of translations, McNamara said, after George's "particular insight that the knowledge of God and his self-revelation is the lens through which you see all things in the study of how God wants to be worshipped." The institute has produced liturgical theologians for leadership and service to dioceses and ecclesial institutions all around the country and the world.

As if liturgical infighting was not enough of a threat to accomplishing what the Church is meant to do in the liturgy, ecclesial unity was further disrupted and wounded by the clergy sexual abuse crisis — a still unfolding scourge on Christ's Body. It was during George's work on the liturgical translations, in addition to his other roles and responsibilities, that the clergy sexual abuse crisis began demanding much of his attention locally, nationally, and internationally.

CLERGY SEXUAL ABUSE CRISIS

In 2001, as a member of the synod for bishops, George said in his intervention, "When bishops and priests and those consecrated by vow to God fail in chastity, hope for others withers as well. This sin, as much as any today, destroys the Church's credibility and diminishes every bishop's effectiveness as pastor."[9] Just a few months later, the reality of his words were recognized on a global scale as the media, led by the *Boston Globe*, began to publish widespread reports of clergy sexual abuse and its episcopal cover-up. George recalled that when Pope John Paul II summoned the American cardinals in 2002 after the Boston scandal erupted, he told them that "at the end of the suffering, the Church will be purified and your love will be strong."[10] George came to realize, as he continued in a speech in the Canadian Diocese of Corner Brook in 2006, that the Church must "embrace this suffering because ... in order to heal the victims, we have to purify the priesthood and to purify the Church ... and it entails great suffering, but it is also only within the Eucharist and our love for one another [that] we touch the love of Christ."

Given his dozen years in Rome as Oblate vicar general and his close-up experiences interfacing with the Roman Curia, George's brother bishops often considered it beneficial to have him involved in discussions or negotiations with the Holy See. This was the case in the early days of the crisis, as bishops attempted to get a handle on the great earthquake that had shaken the Church to her core. George was an influential voice at the Dallas meeting of bishops in June 2002, particularly in the discussions related to the formulation of the *Charter for the Protection of Children and Young People*.

At once praising George as one who admitted "we are at a turning point" and that post-Dallas "this will not be the same Church," the *Chicago Tribune* also stated that his status as "a new and uncompromised cardinal" meant the pressure was on him to deliver a policy of reform and accountability. Though it was unfair to place the burden so squarely on George's shoulders, it is now clear that George was not simply, as they claimed, "in a listening mode," though that in itself is not a bad posture for those in leadership. In preparation for the June meeting in Dallas, George consulted far and wide. At his request, the Catholic Lawyers Guild of Chicago conducted a series of hearings to gather public reactions and solicit responses regarding the crisis. Presenting their findings in the document "Views of the Laity," the majority of the estimated ten thousand Chicago-area Catholics who participated overwhelmingly supported a "zero-tolerance" response to clergy abusers. The guild's work helped shape George's perspective on the issue.

As much as George was speaking to laity, professionals, bishops, and other cardinals privately, he was also vocal publicly. "There have to be sanctions for a bishop who has been negligent, the same as there are sanctions for a priest," he said, a piece of advice that turned out to be as prophetic as it was ignored.[11] It has been reported that Theodore McCarrick, a former cardinal who was dismissed from the clerical state in January 2019 for sexual misconduct involving minors and adults spanning decades, was one of the most vocal advocates both of leaving any abuse by bishops untouched by the Charter and of removing any procedure to discipline bishops who covered up abuse. George knew, as he told John Paul II in 2004, that the abuse crisis meant a new wave of anti-Catholicism. But more than that, given the tragic culture of episcopal cover-ups, he knew that it meant also that the "freedom to govern ourselves is diminished."[12]

During the height of the McCormack affair in 2006, George expressed at a meeting with Chicago priests that, while the crisis was deeply troubling, he trusted God would bring about good, and he hoped that the laity could help the clergy find a way forward. "The people are holy and they're going to sort it out in ways perhaps that I didn't think through," he said. "I'm not sure, other than the grace of God, why that might be.

They're going to sort it out because the priests can't sort it out."

George's involvement at Dallas was just the beginning of his advocacy for reforms in the wake of the clergy sex abuse crisis. The Charter created a variety of issues pertaining to the Church's canon law, which required the advocacy of the US bishops in Rome, where the idea of "zero tolerance" as a response to the clergy sexual abuse of minors initially was not well received. A "mixed commission," composed of four American bishops and four bishops working in the Holy See, was formed to work through these challenges. George was one of the Americans — in addition to then-Archbishop William Levada of San Francisco, then-Bishop William Lori of Bridgeport, and Bishop Thomas Doran of Rockford — and in that capacity pushed very hard to justify the zero-tolerance implementation. Careful negotiations ensued between this commission and four officials from the Holy See: Cardinal Darío Castrillón Hoyos, prefect of the Congregation for Clergy; then-Archbishop Julián Herranz, president of the Pontifical Council for Legislative Texts; then-Archbishop Tarcisio Bertone, secretary of the Congregation for the Doctrine of the Faith; and then-Archbishop Francesco Monterisi, secretary for the Congregation for Bishops.

The body of US bishops knew that keeping George's voice front-and-center was crucial as the Holy See took its time to approve the Essential Norms for Diocesan/Eparchial Policies Dealing with Allegations of Sexual Abuse of Minors by Priests or Deacons that would codify in canon law the promises the bishops made at Dallas in 2002. George was elected vice president of the bishops' conference in 2004, serving under the leadership of his own co-consecrator and predecessor in Yakima, Bishop William Skylstad of Spokane. Another important development in this regard was the 2005 appointment of then-Archbishop William Levada — a member himself of the mixed commission — as the prefect of the Holy See's Congregation for the Doctrine of the Faith, which was the dicastery charged with overseeing the trials of clergy abusers.

George's election as vice president of the United States Conference of Catholic Bishops came about in a third ballot, in which he defeated then-Bishop Donald Wuerl by just six votes. His election allowed him to be present for various annual meetings with heads of the Roman Curia. Years later, George's election can be regarded as even more providential, given what has emerged regarding Wuerl's knowledge — and repeated denials of what he knew — about the egregious misconduct by his predecessor in Washington, DC, former cardinal Theodore McCarrick.

George worked behind the scenes with integrity and tact, even in the halls of the Vatican, to advocate on behalf of survivors and for reform in the Church. George was impatient at times with the hesitancy of the Holy See to move forward more concretely in response to the crisis. Looking for more guidance and support from Rome, he told Pope Benedict XVI in a 2005 meeting that the US bishops "would be supportive of any effective initiative that would bring greater support to victims of child sexual abuse, protect children from such abuse and ensure that clerics known to have abused be removed from ministry."[13]

George often reiterated that the inability to govern was a serious concern related to the implementation of zero-tolerance. A 2005 meeting during visits with curial officials showed what the US bishops were up against in maintaining the penalty of zero tolerance and seeing to its harmonization in the Church's law for application in the United States. While the US bishops were being cajoled with promises from high-ranking curial officials that things would work out, hopes for the approval of the Essential Norms looked bleak at times. George clearly understood that the crisis confirmed an underlying attitude among some in the United States that the Catholic Church is corrupt and that it caused a deep wound. "He spoke very courageously to the congregations and leaders in Rome, helping them to see the pain of victims," recalled Bishop Gerald Kicanas, once an auxiliary bishop in Chicago and vice president to George after he assumed the role of USCCB president from 2007 to 2010.[14] "They didn't always have the occasion of meeting victims face to face," he said, indicating that George, however, did.

George reiterated to Roman Curia officials during those meetings that the US bishops made three promises to their people: First, to assist with the healing of victims of clergy sexual abuse of minors; second, to remove priests from ministry who have abused; and third, to protect children from future abuse. He insisted that legal norms approved by the Holy See had to keep those promises in place. "If we do not keep these promises, we're done for," he warned officials at the Secretariat of State. Then-Archbishop Leonardo Sandri, at the time the *sostituto* at the secretariat, countered, "We must be good to priests," to which George replied, "But not protect predators." In another curial office, George warned against giving the appearance that the Holy See was reneging on the good faith process overseen by the mixed commission, wondering what the point of it was if the Holy See was changing the results. "Without zero tolerance we cannot govern. Bishops will resign, because governance is impossible," George told Cardinal Giovanni Battista Re, then-prefect for the Congregation for Bishops.

One of the principal figures in Rome who signaled displeasure with codifying zero-tolerance in the law was Cardinal Darío Castrillón Hoyos, prefect for the Congregation for Clergy, who had long dismissed the seriousness of a crisis that was then regarded by some in the Curia as primarily an American problem. At the 2005 meeting, he challenged George on the approval of the norms. "Some of us have problems," he opined. "We wonder if the human rights and civil rights of clerics are being violated." George was unafraid to confront him. "We also have the human and civil rights of those who have been violated to look at here," he said.

George went on to state: "The credibility of Rome is at stake here, too." Castrillón responded, "We are not afraid of this in the Holy See. We have theological aspects to consider, as well as praxis over centuries." George, however, advised that the Holy See begin their considerations "with the crimes of priests and bishops which have been horrible," to which Castrillón responded, "Prove it." Castrillón was gone from his position a year later.

USCCB PRESIDENT

In 2007, George was elected president of the United States Conference of Catholic Bishops by an 85 percent majority for the standard three-year term. The election took place a year after George recovered from his initial bout with cancer and in the wake of the McCormack scandal in Chicago. The position took up a good deal of George's energy, especially as he strove to bring clarity to issues that equally divided the nation and the Church. It was a providential time for George to take on the role, for he, perhaps more than any other, could articulate with characteristic laser-like precision and foresight what the Church was up against at that time, the stakes involved, and how best to proceed.

Part of George's task was to help oversee a process of slimming down the bishops' conference apparatus to, as he explained in a 2014 EWTN interview, "make it a more responsive instrument."[15] George explained that this was necessary for two reasons, which were similar to those he had faced in Chicago: because they "couldn't afford" to maintain the "huge bureaucracy" that had in too many cases functioned in independent silos, and, more importantly, because "it wasn't serving the mission" defined and articulated by the bishops. "We had to start with the mission, always start with the mission: Why are we doing this?" George said. "We got it down to four or five mission goals. What do we need to reach those goals? It was out of control. Now it's in control. The bishops own the conference; it's their conference."

Even before he was president, George was often drawn from Chicago to attend various conference-related committee meetings, to give speeches or lectures, or to attend events and curial meetings at the Vatican. In his 2012 quinquennial report to the Holy See, George observed, "I believe that the post-Conciliar form of ecclesiastical governance, dependent on many meetings and much travel, has to be re-thought, to save money if for no other reason. Teleconferencing is possible and should be more frequently used."

In addition to the many meetings pertaining to ordinary conference business of the president, there was a daily phone call with the General Secretary of the US bishops' conference — then-Msgr. David Malloy, who was at the time a priest of Milwaukee. He was later named bishop of

Rockford, Illinois, and ordained by George in 2012. This call kept George abreast of the issues facing the conference and gave him the opportunity to provide input. It could be reasonably argued that George's tenure in that office was busier than most. It included the 2008 visit to the United States by Pope Benedict XVI and, following the election of Chicago's Barack Obama as president of the United States later that year, a fight for religious liberty that the bishops neither anticipated nor relished.

"Legal cultures also come and go," George said.[16] "The Church has lived through times of favor and times of disfavor, even persecution, here and in other parts of the world. In all those times, it remains incumbent upon the Catholic community to continue to make efforts to live up to their duties as believers and to contribute therefore to the building up of a sane and healthy society in our country."

George was demure about holding the presidency of the episcopal conference, explaining in a 2012 interview with Salt and Light Television, "Well, the president doesn't really preside over the American Church. The president is president of the American conference of bishops, which means when they get together you preside. ... But you don't have authority over anybody at all ... but you do have to see to it that the bishops stay together." And George was up to the task. The mail also greatly increased during George's time in office, and his replies to the complaints he received about various issues he typically had no control over usually included some kind of reminder that, as he put it in the 2012 Salt and Light interview, "Bishops don't run the country — you do. In a democratic country, you get the government you deserve. So, if you don't like the government, do something about it. But don't tell us to do something about it."

The method of engagement with the federal government at the time of George's leadership was to speak clearly about principles but to leave the policymaking to others. He explained in the 2012 Salt and Light interview, "Society is in the hands of lay people. It's governed by them, not by bishops. But we're to give them the spiritual gifts, if they're Catholic, to do it well, according to Catholic social teaching and moral teaching," he said. "And so we don't talk about everything, we talk about the moral issues. ... With the federal government, it is very important to say 'here are the principles and here's where you're transgressing them,' and then try to do our best to persuade them not to do that."

In the 2012 interview, two years removed from his time as USC-CB president, George acknowledged how "episcopal authority is much wounded" because of the clergy sexual abuse crisis. "But," he added, "just as you have to take responsibility in discipline, you have to take responsibility in doctrine. It's interesting that people who want you to take discipline of priests don't want you to correct their doctrinal errors. And sometimes vice versa. But you have to do both. And when you don't, we are truly remiss. But we have to stand before the Lord and before our people and give an account of our stewardship." That same year, in his quinquennial report, George informed the Holy See that "for a generation, bishops have presided over the dissolution of the Church. The USCCB has often taught well but has not been of much help in pastoral governance."

Such was George's task when, as president, he had to confront the Obama administration regarding health care reform. The bishops historically had been in favor of universal health care, because, George reiterated in the 2012 interview, "everyone should be taken care of." At the same time, he cautioned that "we also said nobody should be killed deliberately." He helped the US bishops articulate their desire for "a health care plan that did not use federal money for funding abortions."

Furthermore, George argued that the government's health care plan — the Patient Protection and Affordable Care Act, passed and signed into law in March 2010 — prohibited the Church from being herself. The law mandated that employers provide various kinds of contraception, including abortifacients, to employees free of charge, and it included a very narrow list of exemptions. Houses of worship, for example, were exempt. Other Catholic groups were not, such as the Little Sisters of the Poor, who eventually became the poster children for the fight against the contraceptive mandate. The crux of the problem, as George described it, was that the government for the "first time is telling us which of our institutions are religious enough to merit a religious exemption." In a 2012 video released by the Archdiocese of Chicago, George stated, "The Church is her ministries as well as her worship, and the government has told us, 'No, you're not. You're just your worship.'" During his years as president of the bishops' conference, George led the charge against that claim, both on the national level and in various presentations he made around his own archdiocese.

The Obama administration did not back down in its demand that health care must include abortions, sterilizations, abortifacients, and contraception. As a result, as George noted in the 2012 interview, a door was opened "to mainstreaming abortion, taking it out of clinics, putting it in the hospitals, [and] using new insurance schemes that will be funded federally that will open the way to greater involvement to the federal government in killing the unborn." This meant that, while they approved of many parts of the Affordable Care Act, the bishops could not throw their support behind the law. George worried that without the protection of conscience rights, the country was moving "from democracy to despotism."[17] He said, "No government should come between an individual person and God — that's what America is supposed to be about."

The revision of the nation's health care system became not only a politically divisive issue but divisive among Catholics. George acknowledged in the 2012 interview that "the bishops know that they don't speak for every one of the 61 million American Catholics in this country" but that they do "speak for the Catholic faith," adding that "those who share the faith will gather around."[18] The Catholic Health Association, in opposition to the US bishops, expressed its support for the Obama health care plan, stating that it was a "false claim" on the part of the bishops to state that the law as written opened the way for taxpayer-funded abortion. In response, George told his brother bishops at their spring meeting in 2010 that "the Catholic Health Association and other so-called Catholic groups provided cover for those on the fence to support Obama and the administration."[19]

George first reached out privately to the association's president, Sr. Carol Keehan, and then again with the help of three other bishops who formed the USCCB's ad hoc Health Care Concerns Committee: Bps. Kevin Rhoades of Fort Wayne-South Bend, Kevin Vann, then of Fort Worth, and Thomas Paprocki of Springfield in Illinois. These overtures all yielded "the same frustrating results," George said. He was disappointed and concerned about what these groups accomplished, and he observed, "In the end, they have weakened the moral voice of the bishops in the US." The actions of Keehan and others "resulted in confusion and a wound to Catholic unity," he said.

In his final address as president of the US bishops' conference, George reiterated that the bishops, in union with the pope, "speak for the Church in matters of faith and in moral issues and the laws surrounding them. All the rest is opinion, often well-considered and important opinion that deserves a careful and respectful hearing, but still opinion."[20] He said the health care debate made clear to him:

> That, at a certain point, there were those who started with the faith in its integrity and all its demands and fit their political choices into the context of the fullness of the Church's teaching, and there were those for whom a political choice, even a good choice, was basic and the Church was judged useful by whether or not she provided foot soldiers for their political commitment, whether of the left or the right.

While stating that "for too many, politics is the ultimate horizon of their thinking and acting," George reiterated that the Church calls Catholics to "orthodoxy in belief and obedience in practice." Citing a 1990 reference to St. John Henry Newman, made by then-Cardinal Joseph Ratzinger in comments to the US bishops, George recalled, "The whole duty and work of a Christian is made up of these two parts, faith and obedience; 'looking unto Jesus' (Heb 2:9) and acting according to his will." He continued:

> Orthodoxy is necessary but not enough; the devil is orthodox.
> He knows the catechism better than anybody in this room; but
> he will not serve, he will not obey. There can be mistakes in our
> thinking, but there can be no self-righteousness in our will, for
> this is the sin against the Holy Spirit. We should not fear political
> isolation; the Church has often been isolated in politics and in
> diplomacy. We need to be deeply concerned, however, about the
> wound to the Church's unity that has been inflicted in this de-
> bate and I hope, trusting in the good will of all concerned, that
> means can be found to restore the seamless garment of ecclesial
> communion.

In George's conversations with Obama — according to private comments
he made in 2009 to a group of Louisiana priests that he thought were off
the record — George found a "very gracious and obviously a smart man,"
but one who was hard to disagree with "because he'll always tell you he
agrees with you."[21] George maintained that he always had to reiterate
they did not agree on everything, especially abortion. "But we can agree
on a lot, and we do, and that's why there is so much hope," George said.
"I think we have to pray for him every day." He also stated many times
how heartened he was that Obama made history when he was elected
the first Black president and that he wanted him to succeed in his efforts
to straighten out the economy, advocate for peace globally, and assist the
poor. On the abortion issue, however, George said he believed Obama
"was on the wrong side of history." In George's estimation — referring to
the famous 1858 debates for a US senate seat between Illinois' anti-slav-
ery Abraham Lincoln and pro-slavery Stephen Douglas — abortion is "a
society-dividing issue," in which "we're with Abraham Lincoln and he's
with Stephen Douglas, and he doesn't like to hear that, but that's where
he is." He added: "For eighty years we were a slave republic, and it took
a terrible war to end that. And now for forty years we're in an abortion

regime, and I'm not sure how that's going to end."

The comments that George made in Louisiana, which he regarded as taken out of context, apparently made their way to Obama. Correspondence shows that then-cardinal Theodore McCarrick, then in direct communication with Obama and trying to serve as a conduit between his administration and the US bishops, informed George that Obama felt personally attacked. Reiterating his respect for Obama's office and his insistence on praying daily for him, George stated, in a drafted reply, that "there is a disagreement in principle around the protection of unborn human life, but a disagreement in principle should not be considered a personal attack, lest public discussion of controversial issues be rendered impossible." [22]

George's comments coincided with Obama's 2009 invitation to speak at the May commencement ceremony for the University of Notre Dame. At this event, the university also planned to confer upon Obama an honorary degree, which resulted in great outcry from sizable numbers of Catholics around the country and the world. In George's view, not only did Notre Dame offend the bishops by awarding him such an honor, but the university also put them in a very uncomfortable position, since Obama and his administration had given every indication that abortion would be enshrined as a permanent civil rights law. Mary Ann Glendon, a former United States ambassador to the Holy See and recipient that year of the university's prestigious Laetare Medal, refused to accept the award or attend the ceremony. The local bishop, John D'Arcy, did likewise.

George's primary concern about Notre Dame's invitation to Obama was the damage it did to Catholic communion. As he argued, "No institution that calls itself Catholic can be unilateral." [23] Speaking at a pro-life gathering in March 2009, George said, "When you're Catholic, everything you do changes the life of everybody else who calls himself or herself Catholic," explaining, "it's a network of relationships." [24] In this case, George said, the problem is that "the flagship Catholic university" in the United States "brought extreme embarrassment to many, many people who are Catholic." He concluded that "whatever else is clear, it is clear that Notre Dame didn't understand what it means to be Catholic when they issued this invitation."

George admitted that he had no control over the university, nor did any bishops, but he encouraged the faithful to express their concerns to Notre Dame, and he did the same. "Being in Catholic communion — especially in the case of a renowned Catholic university — means that every major decision affects other Catholics; and many Catholics were deeply troubled by Notre Dame's decision," George wrote to Notre Dame's president Holy Cross Fr. John Jenkins on May 12.[25] "A decision made to foster dialogue should have been discussed with those affected by it before it was made final. Now, we all live with its consequences."

The university was flooded with calls and letters. Busloads of protesters descended on Notre Dame's campus for graduation weekend. Bishop D'Arcy, then of Fort Wayne-South Bend, participated in a holy hour of reparation. But the university did not disinvite Obama, nor, out of respect for the office of the presidency, did George advocate its doing so.

Although tensions existed between American Catholics and the Obama administration, George was grateful in 2010, the last year of his presidency of the episcopal conference, for Obama's executive order that put in place "some administrative protections" for the contraceptive mandate in the Affordable Care Act.[26] "But," he added, "an administrative order doesn't substitute for a statute." In George's mind, this was all emblematic of the next wave of growing secularism in America.

As he was accustomed to doing in Chicago, where he developed great relationships and even traveled with leaders of other faith traditions, George was also called into dialogue with other religious groups in his capacity as president of the US bishops' conference. An invitation to Salt Lake City brought George into conversation with the Church of Jesus Christ of Latter-day Saints, during which he offered a presentation that described Mormons as partners in defending religious freedom in America. He called on Mormons to stand together with Catholics as a "vital bulwark" in an increasingly secularized society that wants to "reduce religions to a purely private reality."[27] George was grateful for the opportunity to stand together with Mormons in fighting against the eradication of conscience rights, refusing to compromise on participation in abortion and euthanasia, and defending the definition of marriage according to natural law.

George had traveled to Salt Lake City with his parents as a young boy because his mother had wanted to hear the Mormon Tabernacle Choir in concert. That same group gave a performance near Chicago a few months before George was elected president of the bishops' conference, and he was invited to try his hand wielding the conductor's baton. "All of a sudden, that vacuum of expectant silence was filled with this magnificent, overpowering sound, all in unison, all in harmony," George recalled of his experience after giving the downbeat. Then he quipped, "I thought to myself, 'I'm doing better with the Mormons than I am with the Catholics!' I have a lot harder time getting them to sing together!"

Such difficulties only multiplied in his years as bishops' conference president. Another thorny issue that resulted in much disunity among US Catholics was that of pro-abortion politicians receiving Holy Communion. This issue was exacerbated by the Democratic presidential nomination of John Kerry in 2004 and the vice presidency of Joseph Biden, which began in 2009. George observed that many Catholics were angry with the Catholic politicians who claim to be personally opposed to abortion but support and protect it as a legal right.

Far-right critics were often disappointed with George's stance regarding similar cases in Chicago and Illinois, particularly that of Illinois' Catholic US Senator Richard Durbin and swaths of local Catholic politicians. He addressed the issue in a column in the archdiocesan paper:

> Do all Catholic politicians understand their obligations in conscience? Apparently not, which means that their pastors have to take the time to speak with them personally. A pastoral conversation about the formation of conscience is not an interference

in the political process. It is an exercise in pastoral charity, motivated by a desire for a politician's salvation. The politician will someday be asked by the Lord: "What did you do to the least of my brothers and sisters?" And the pastor will be asked by the same Lord: "What did you do to warn them? How did you help them form their conscience?" [28]

George recognized that addressing the problems posed by Catholic "pro-choice" politicians and their reception of Holy Communion demands nuance and taking the question into consideration of the whole.

> Should Catholic "pro-choice" politicians receive Holy Communion? Objectively, no; but subjectively a politician may have convinced himself he is in good conscience. ...
>
> Should a minister of Holy Communion give a "pro-choice" politician the Body of the Lord? If a voting record is evidence of "manifest and obstinate" sin, no. The objection is raised that voting for abortion isn't the only political sin, even though abortion and euthanasia are the moral bottom line. Nevertheless, a firm case can be made that refusing Communion, after pastoral counseling and discussion, is a necessary response to the present scandal. Some bishops have made that case. If I haven't made it in this Archdiocese, it's primarily because I believe it would turn the reception of Holy Communion into a circus here. Who should be excluded?

George's name surfaced in the so-called Vatileaks scandal on a related topic. Among the documents leaked from Pope Benedict XVI's private papers was a message from the apostolic nunciature of the US to the Holy See's Secretariat of State, which conveyed a request from George that the Community of Sant'Egidio withdraw an award it had conferred upon then-Illinois governor Patrick Quinn. Although the award was intended to honor Quinn for his suppression of the state's death penalty,

George objected to the honor on account of Quinn's support for abortion and same-sex marriage.

OTHER ROMAN CONTRIBUTIONS

George was well respected among his brother bishops in America and abroad. He was appointed or elected to participate in many synods of bishops in Rome over the years, including in 1994, 1997, 2001, and 2008. George was due to attend the synod in 2012 but was unable to make the trip for health reasons.

At the 1997 Synod for America, George's own intervention described the cultural milieu of Catholicism in the United States, particularly in the context of immigration and the culturally Protestant flavor of American society that even defines Catholics. He said this foundation gives the "disadvantage of filtering the Catholic faith through a lens that rejects the Catholic understanding of Church in theory and that often in practice fears and resents the Catholic Church as a source of spiritual and psychological oppression."[29] He proposed that the New Evangelization must include "a new apologetics, a loving and non-defensive but clear response to the arguments raised against the Catholic faith." He added that the Catholic Church can contribute to the culture if she is true to Christ and "can be a principal agent in creating a culture for the new millennium: global, truly communitarian and able to sustain human development." George was named a cardinal just months after the synod and became a key figure in helping to implement this vision in America throughout the next two decades.

During Lent of 2001, Pope John Paul II chose George to preach the annual retreat for the Roman Curia — only the second US prelate ever to be so designated. His talks were centered on the theme "A Faith for All Peoples: Conversion, Freedom, and Communion in Christ," in which he drew from his own experiences in dialogue with people around the globe. In his talks, he examined "how the faith crosses cultures, how the faith enables us to dialogue with the whole world."[30] Ultimately, George spoke of our identity in God as being what unites us: "The secret of my true identity is hidden in the love and mercy of God. I cannot hope to find myself in any other place except in God." He was back in Rome that fall to prepare for the upcoming synod when the September 11 terrorist attacks occurred. George wrote privately of how difficult it was to be away from his flock at that time, and he clearly wrestled with his need to remain in Rome amid his duties. At that time, it was rumored in some Church circles that George was offered the position of Prefect for the Congregation for the Evangelization of Peoples, while some in the Chicago media were hearing that he was set for the Congregation for Divine Worship and Discipline of the Sacraments or the Congregation for Doctrine of the Faith.[31]

At the 2008 Synod on the Word of God, George's intervention highlighted his regret of a lack of biblical language and imagery in contemporary popular culture. He cited how Western culture had been shaped over time by the Bible, with references like "prodigal son," "the good Samaritan," or "Sodom and Gomorrah."[32] In his mind, the decline of such terminology in modern vocabulary illustrated "the loss of a sense and an image of God as an actor in human history." And so George argued for a "pastoral attentiveness to the need for conversion of imagination, of mind and will," which will allow Catholics to "not fear confusion when they read the Bible." He argued, "It will not be for them a grand puzzle but a path to the freedom that comes from personal surrender to God's word, God's mind, God's will. If the power of God's word in Holy Scripture is to be felt in the life and mission of the Church, pastors must attend to personal context as well as to inspired text." He added to this theme in the 2012 Salt and Light interview, saying, "Without imagination and stories in our literature it's very hard to preach the Gospel. What I am very concerned about is that the Catholic Church is not the bulwark against secularization that it once was."

George was expected to participate in the 2012 synod on the New Evangelization but had to bow out when he was again diagnosed with cancer. The 2014 Synod on the Family caused a bit of controversy: Pope Francis conducted it according to a different process than other synods after Vatican II. George, offering his observations as a longtime synod participant, said the widespread confusion among bishops was understandable given that the established rules of procedure had not been followed. George noted in the 2014 EWTN interview that the synod's midterm report apparently "did not reflect what was being said" during the synod's sessions, and he believed "that's a question that should be pursued." In light of the concern about the report, he believed it was important to reiterate that "it isn't that the Church is up for grabs, it's that this synod's method didn't follow the book," which meant that "people didn't know what to expect next."

CONCLAVES

Being a cardinal required George to give voice to the pope's teachings in Chicago and in the United States. Practically, it meant he was a member of the clergy of Rome and that he had a church in the Eternal City, St. Bartholomew on the Tiber Island. For all intents and purposes this "titular church" is ceremonial, but George took his relationship to it seriously nonetheless. He celebrated Mass there during various trips to Rome and had a good relationship with the Community of Sant'Egidio there, a lay ecclesial movement with which he had grown well acquainted during his years living in Rome. Additionally, George was called to advise the pope and help oversee the governance of the universal Church. That meant he, like all cardinals, was appointed by the pope to various dicasteries of the Holy See, including the Congregations for Evangelization of Peoples, Divine Worship and Discipline of the Sacraments, Institutes of Consecrated Life and Societies of Apostolic Life, and the Pontifical Councils *Cor Unum* and for Culture. In 2010, he was selected as one of more than a dozen cardinals to serve on the Pontifical Council for the Study of the Organizational and Economic Problems of the Holy See, which helped to oversee Vatican finances. In 2014, George commented that it was very hard to get a handle on Vatican finances because "the arithmetic was right but you couldn't understand what the numbers stood for." Cardinal George Pell, who served on that council with George and was tapped in 2014 by Pope

Francis to begin internal reform of Vatican finances, recalled that George was sounding alarm bells more than a decade ahead of anyone else regarding what Pell described as "very, very real pressures on the Vatican pension fund." This fund, Pell described in late 2021, had begun to face a deficit of hundreds of millions of dollars in about a decade's time.

And topping the list of a cardinal's duties, of course, is his participation in the election of the next pope. George was summoned to Rome for that purpose in 2005 after the death of Pope John Paul II. The loss of his mentor and friend was very difficult for George. American Cardinal James Harvey, who served as prefect of the Papal Household for the last six years of John Paul II's pontificate and as an official in the Holy See's Secretariat for more than a decade and a half before that, had an upfront perspective during John Paul II's pontificate. He described George as having developed "a spiritual kinship with John Paul," whom he described as having "taught Cardinal George how to be a philosopher-pastor." In Harvey's assessment, George was able to understand and interpret John Paul's thought and pick up on what he was saying "in a depth that other people would not, maybe, be able to grasp immediately." In the third volume of his "Prison Journal," Cardinal George Pell described George as "an outstanding John Paul the Great archbishop."[33] He elaborated on what he meant by that in 2021:

> He put Christ at the center of things. He believed in the priesthood. He believed in the Ten Commandments. He didn't believe in using the concept of conscience to subvert The Ten Commandments. He was very clear that we stand under the rule of Faith, under the Apostolic tradition, that we have no capacity to change or improve the Apostolic tradition, or to improve Jesus' teachings. We're followers of Christ, we certainly believe in reason and theology, but Jesus' Revelation has the last word.

An interview for a CNN documentary produced about the final days and funeral of John Paul — *The Last Days of Pope John Paul II: The Untold*

Stories — captured a rare display of George's emotional side, expressive of the depth of admiration and unity of faith and thought that existed between George and John Paul. In the interview, George broke down and wept while he recalled how the cardinals attending the pope's funeral stood afterward in two lines inside St. Peter's Basilica. As John Paul's casket passed by them one last time, George recalled how they each removed their zucchettos, as is the custom when greeting the pope. "He was a great man," George said of the now-canonized pontiff, fighting back his tears before the camera cut away.[34]

Writing after the 2005 experience, George observed, "The time between the death of one pope and the election of another was tense and all engrossing. It reawakened in me and in many others a sense of what apostolic governance in the Church really means. From a sense of loss to a feeling of relief and conviction that the College of Cardinals had done their very best to fulfill God's will for his people, the emotional journey of the last month has been intense and joyful."[35]

George was even rumored to have been *papabile* in 2005. In a speech not long after the 2005 conclave, George joked about the voting, "I figured that being from Chicago ... I might vote [for] all my dead predecessors ... but evidently our natural proclivities in Chicago aren't as unique, so they've got the rule that you must count all the ballots one by one."[36] He also remarked that he believed he was the first native-born Chicagoan to cast a vote in a papal conclave, which must have meant that in the voting line he was ahead of Chicago-born Cardinal Edward M. Egan of New York.

George recalled the solemnity of the moment when, gathered for the conclave in the Sistine Chapel under the Last Judgment fresco by Michelangelo, each cardinal, ballot in hand, swore the following oath: "In the presence of Jesus Christ who will be my judge, I swear that I am voting for the one whom I judge to be best suited for the office." It was, George said, "a very serious enterprise" since, in voting for the one judged to be best suited to be the new pope, "you put your salvation on the line."

George recalled after the 2005 conclave that the newly elected Pope

Benedict XVI "certainly didn't seek" the office.[37] "Who would, in his right mind?" George rhetorically asked with his trademark laugh. But George was just as surprised as anyone else at the time of Pope Benedict's historic resignation from the Petrine ministry in early 2013. He noted in an interview with the *National Catholic Reporter* just before the conclave that year that he thought a papal resignation can be something that "leaves the Church stronger."[38] George believed Benedict "made his decision to resign the papacy out of love for the Church, after coming to the conclusion that he no longer had the physical strength to fulfill all the tasks of his office."[39]

"Benedict XVI is as good as he is smart," George observed, remarking that he was grateful for many aspects of Benedict's service to the Church as pope, especially his concern for right worship, his teaching of the Faith, and his pastoral heart. He deeply appreciated Benedict's writings too. He highlighted Benedict's reflections "on Christ and on the self-sacrificing love Christ brought back to a world that was created good and delightful before the fall," which George called "a symphonic masterpiece that will inspire the faithful for generations to come."

George's reluctance to engage in ecclesiastical gossip was evidenced by how seriously he took the oath to secrecy at the conclaves. Nonetheless, before and after the conclaves, George was popular with the media on account of his honesty, precision, and candor, and he made himself generously available to them. This was especially true before the conclave of 2013, when he managed to be quite open while still adhering to confidentiality. He spoke somewhat freely about the process, not about particulars, but principles — how cardinals interacted and solicited information from each other and what was looked for in the ideal candidate. At least one elector shared that George was a cardinal whose opinion was regularly solicited as cardinals discussed candidates and that his opinions and assessments were clearly well regarded.

It was alleged that Cardinal Angelo Sodano — the dean of the College of Cardinals and presider over the 2013 conclave — eventually asked George not to attend the daily media briefings the American cardinals were holding at the North American College auditorium. Theodore Mc-

Carrick was to take his place as a non-voting member of the conclave who was participating in the general congregations or meetings that led up to it. Instead, Sodano put an end to the press conferences altogether. Before the cardinals were silenced from formally speaking to the press, though, George told the *Chicago Tribune*, "Ties to anyone guilty of sexual misconduct — whether intended or unintended — could put a man's candidacy in question if it could distract from his spiritual mission." He added, perhaps more revelatory about himself than others, "Given the troubling circumstances surrounding the issue of priest sex abuse, cardinals aren't just asking about leadership and communication style. They are asking about each man's moral character," adding, "Does he have a past?"

Going into the conclave, George identified the ideal Holy Father as one who possessed "personal stability" and "the depth of character founded upon his conversations with Jesus," adding, "there's got to be an identification with Jesus as shepherd of his Church."[40] But he also noted that the next pope must "have a heart for the poor around the world." A piece in the Italian media stated that George was against the idea of electing Cardinal Leonardo Sandri, who in George's opinion was not worthy of consideration given his ties to the disgraced sexual predator Marcial Maciel Degollado, founder of the Legionaries of Christ.

In non-conclave discussions that surrounded the elections of each pope, George had expressed to some friends that Cardinal Jorge Bergoglio was an intriguing candidate in the 2005 conclave and was regarded as someone who had a reputation as a reformer. This narrative had resurfaced in the 2013 conclave. Others in that conclave said George was part of a coalition of cardinals who had coalesced around a desire for reform in the Roman Curia, which, according to one member of the conclave, was never fully defined and consisted of two very different ideas of what was meant by the word. George, after hearing Bergoglio's intervention in pre-conclave gatherings on March 7, reportedly told Cardinal Cormac Murphy-O'Connor — a vocal supporter of and surrogate for Bergoglio — that "he understood what they had meant about him."[41] Despite the restrictions placed on cardinals, George eventually broke his silence once the cardinals had set a date for the start of the conclave. Upon leaving the synod hall on March 7, after pre-conclave discussions wrapped up, he reportedly announced, "We're ready!"

On the eve of the 2013 conclave, George expressed to a friend on March 10 that he had misgivings about Bergoglio, whose name had surfaced to the top of the field of candidates in the pre-conclave discussions. He had difficulties accepting him on account of his Jesuit formation background, as George had long regarded that order's spirituality as too subjective. George — reportedly seeing his top candidates as Cardinals Angelo Scola and Marc Ouellet — was concerned about Bergoglio's age, asking a group who discussed his name, "Does he still have vigor?"[42] After Francis's election, George went up to the new pope and said in Spanish, "My name is also Francis, Holy Father." For a year and a half, Chicagoans would have two Francises named in the Eucharistic Prayer, until it was time for the first to name the second's replacement.

In 2014, George indicated that Pope Francis had been chosen because of the experience he had in governing, which was necessary because the Roman Curia was in need of reform. George believed this expectation was undoubtedly being met, particularly in the arena of Vatican finances, in light of the appointment of his friend Cardinal George Pell as Prefect of the Secretariat for the Economy. George was pleased by Francis's promotion of a "culture of encounter," since when you encounter Christ you encounter those whom he loves.[43] He was likewise pleased by Francis's closeness to the poor, as he stated many times, as well as with his "very different" and "informal" ways of speaking. But George also had his concerns, especially with Francis's "populist style of ministry" — one in which he would go "over the heads of the curia and others in order to reach directly to people in a way that we weren't accustomed to, and didn't expect because that isn't the way he operated in Buenos Aires. Even the people from Argentina say we don't recognize this populist style," George said in the 2014 EWTN interview. He added: "If you're going to make some changes that necessarily generate some opposition, because people are losing their jobs, it's pretty smart to build a base. He's got that.

What he's going to do with that, I don't know."

Francis's style of governance quickly appealed to the press and others even in the Church. But George likened Francis to a Rorschach test. "Everybody reads into him what they want to read into him," he said. "People who want to see the pope as someone who's going to change the fundamental teachings of the Church — which I don't believe he will do because he can't do it — they will try to create the old scenario of this wonderful reformer which means to conform the Church to modern times, as opposed to the stodgy old people who can't see whatever is in their clothes closet."

Francis's unorthodox leadership approach also appears to have directly affected the choice of George's successor in Chicago. George had noted from his earliest days in the Windy City that he hoped to be the first archbishop to retire there. In the spring of 2014, he informed the apostolic nuncio that he believed it was time to begin the process of identifying his successor. Rumors have long swirled about that particular appointment process, and claims have even been made that George's eventual successor was not named on the typical terna of candidates presented to the pope. George confirmed in a 2014 interview with EWTN that the plenary session of the Congregation for Bishops had not met to discuss the appointment. "I think that it was supposed to happen a little later, and they would've had a chance to meet, but because my own health is so uncertain, I think they moved the whole thing up a bit. And so, they created a process where the pope I think was — perhaps, but I'm not sure — more directly involved in consulting outside of the circles of consultation. But I don't know that for sure. I suspect that's probably true." Most notable of all, though, was that George said, "I don't know who he consulted," indicating he was left out of the process. Riddled with cancer, for which he was engaged in experimental medical treatments and was admittedly unable to adequately fulfill the duties of his office, George said he left the archdiocese in hands better than his own.

Anticipating his own retirement at the end of 2013, George recalled that when he came to Chicago he had wondered what Cardinal Bernardin had and hadn't known. "If he had been around, it would have been a big help for me," he said. "If that's possible, I'd like to provide that service to my successor, whoever that might be."[44]

In his final year in office, George had wanted to see Pope Francis for a private discussion about the impression the pontiff at times could give that Church doctrine was "up for grabs," according to George in the 2014 EWTN interview. As the members of the College of Cardinals are the closest advisors to the pope, George had been known to speak freely and candidly to popes from time to time over the years. Not long before Benedict XVI's resignation, in the wake of the "Vatileaks" scandal, a source from the Papal Household reported that George requested an audience with the Holy Father to express his concerns that the pope was not well-served by many within his inner circle — a conversation George would have seen as a cardinalatial duty in service to the papacy. "Obviously something's not working if the personal papers of the pope can be purloined from his desk and be printed in the media, including papers we've sent," George said about the matter in an interview with the *National Catholic Reporter* just before the 2013 conclave.[45] It seems that George identified his concerns early on in Francis's pontificate and was the first notable American bishop to speak about them (at least publicly).

One example related to Pope Francis's statement, "Who am I to judge?" George wanted to know if Francis thoroughly understood "what has happened just by that phrase."[46] This sound bite heard around the world, George said, "has been very misused … because he was talking about someone who has already asked for mercy and been given absolution, whom he knows well." He added: "That's entirely different than talking to somebody who demands acceptance rather than asking for forgiveness." The pope's original remark concerned a Vatican staffer, Msgr. Battista Ricca, who oversees the Vatican's Casa Santa Marta, where Pope Francis took up residency upon his election. Ricca had been long rumored to engage in homosexual misconduct, which was noted in the press shortly after Francis appointed him in 2013 as prelate of the Vatican Bank.

"Does he not realize the repercussions? Perhaps he doesn't," George asked about Francis's sound bite. "I don't know whether he's conscious of all the consequences of some of the things he's said and done that raise doubts in people's minds." And George said, "The question is why doesn't he clarify" such statements that can be so easily taken out of context. "Why is it necessary that apologists have to bear the burden of trying to put the best possible face on it?"

George warned that the impressions Francis was giving could also harm the pope's own ability to govern. "At a certain moment, people who have painted him as a player in their own scenarios about changes in the Church will discover that's not who he is," George said. And then, George anticipated that the pope would "get not only disillusionment, but opposition, which could be harmful to his effectiveness."

Another "big question" George had for Francis was related to who advises him. "Obviously he's getting input from somewhere," George said. "Much of it he collects himself, but I'd love to know who's truly shaping his thinking."

Francis's regular emphasis on Satan and the end of the world also intrigued George, and he wanted to know exactly how it was shaping his agenda. If the pope really thought that the Lord's return was imminent, George observed, maybe that is why he "seems to be in a hurry."

"I hope, before I die, I'll have the chance to ask him how you want us to understand what you're doing, when you put [the end-times] before us as a key to it all," he said. "I didn't know him well before he was elected, and since then I haven't had a chance to go over for any meetings because I've been in treatment." For George, the questions he wanted to put to Francis were more about being faithful to his role as a bishop and cardinal, not satisfying his own personal curiosity. "You're supposed to govern in communion with the successor of Peter, so it's important to have some meeting of minds," he said. "I certainly respect him as pope, but I don't yet really have an understanding of, 'What are we doing here?'" George was never able to travel to Rome, prevented by the deterioration of his own health. There was a report that George sent a letter to Francis containing many of these ideas and questions, but it has not been made public.

FOURTEEN
Simply Catholic

[The bishop's] work for his people draws him into the self-sacrifice which conforms him spiritually to Christ. Because his vocation and mission in the Church are Trinitarian, so must be his personal spiritual life. But in his life with God, the bishop never lives alone. Because "the bishop is in the Church and the Church is in the bishop" (St. Irenaeus), the bishop becomes holy only with and through his people.[1]

CARDINAL FRANCIS E. GEORGE, O.M.I.

The history of the Church is riddled with the agendas of individuals who seek to satisfy their own desires instead of those of Christ. This is the original sin of mankind — the seeking of our own will above that of God. But it is similarly filled with the stories of those men and women who opted for the narrow way, who sought to be followers, not leaders, in the best sense of what it means to be a disciple of the Lord.

Throughout more than five decades of ordained ministry to the Church — indeed in his seventy-eight years of life — Francis George's agenda was simply that of Christ. George's concerns were, in his mind, those that should belong to any other bishop. Focused on the flock entrusted to his care and attentive to the common good and the welfare of society, George offered his life as an oblation in service to the good of the Church, his bride. His episcopal motto, "To Christ be Glory in the Church," reminded others of what should arbitrate their lives. "Despite my own faults and failings and those of many others as well, that conviction remains the bedrock of my ministry. In faith, I believe it; in practice, I experience it here, and I am grateful," George wrote in 2002.[2]

George's ministry as a bishop during the first half-century after the Second Vatican Council was marked by the paralyzing effects of polarization in the Church, which he detested and saw as prohibitive to the Church's fulfillment of her mission. This lack of true unity in the Church was one of George's great laments. He understood that his vocation as a shepherd at this time in history meant he must help guide the Church through this turbulence and toward stabilization in the unity of Christ.

George devoted his entire ministry as a priest and bishop to implementing the reforms of the Second Vatican Council. He perceived clearly the way that misunderstandings of and hesitations about the council had contributed to the divisions in the Church. As George described it:

> For some, the Council itself was the work of the Spirit, but its implementation has been hijacked by left-wing or right-wing ideologues, depending upon one's choice of enemies. For others, the Council itself was flawed because its documents are ambiguous or even inconsistent with apostolic tradition. The extremists in this line made tradition another word for museum and lost the sense of a living Body of Christ.[3]

The themes of Vatican II became the themes of George's episcopacy, built on the foundation of the Church's self-understanding as a communion. "The Council's emphasis on ecclesial communion means that everything and everyone in the Church is related. Nothing can be understood apart from our relationships among ourselves and with all those who have gone before us in faith. This communion or network of relationships across space and time is made vital through the action of the Holy Spirit."

Knowing that the implementation of the council was a mixed bag, George observed that while "much that is positive and helpful in the Church today comes from the instructions of the Council," at the same time, "much that is negative and destructive in the Church today comes, it seems to me, from fratricidal arguments about elements of the Church's life and teachings, conflicts that distract Catholics from attending to the reason the Council was called: the conversion of the world."

George labored throughout his ministry to help the Church move beyond internal disputes that were often caught up in the liberal/conservative cliché and instead reorient her toward the mission with which she had been entrusted by Christ. This meant seeing the Church for what she is and for what she isn't — and one of the things it most certainly is not is a country defined by politics. "Jesus doesn't talk about being conservative or being liberal. He talks about knowing the truth or living in darkness. It is true and false that define our internal dynamics and not politics or law directly," George said.[4] Nor is the Church a spiritual club. "Find the church that conforms to your belief, we're advised, and then join it. That means that you're the one who determines what God has revealed or who is your god; but the Church is not a club and therefore we can't just change the rules because we want to change them." Indeed, all are welcome in the Church. As George once put it in a talk at Mundelein Seminary in 2014, "Everybody is in [the Church] on the same terms, and they're Christ's not ours."[5]

For George — as is true for the Church's own self-understanding articulated at the Second Vatican Council — "the Church is Christ, head and members, and we are in the Church to the extent that we are in and of Christ. We're members of his Body, alive in ecclesial communion. This recognition is hindered by controlling models that, if people don't critically examine their thinking, will give them a false understanding of Church."[6]

George saw "liberal Catholicism" as an example of this. This critique was a recurring theme for him: He drew attention to it on the eve of his nomination as a cardinal in 1998, when he first publicly stated, "We are at a turning point in the life of the Church in this country. Liberal Catholicism is an exhausted project. Essentially a critique, even a necessary critique at one point in our history, it is now parasitical on a substance that no longer exists. It has shown itself unable to pass on the faith in its integrity and inadequate, therefore, in fostering the joyful self-surrender called for in Christian marriage, in consecrated life, in ordained priesthood. It no longer gives life."[7]

He elaborated on this at another time:

> I don't believe that liberalism has failed the Church, I believe it's a victim of its own success and is therefore an exhausted project. An exhausted project is not a failure. We're simply at another moment. The split between liberals and conservatives, however, is a division that has to be healed within the Church by a non-defensive apologetics, a conversation, precisely without our own unity being much stronger than it is now, the world will not listen to us and the mission will be paralyzed. That was Jesus' prayer at the Last Supper, wasn't it: "May they be one as you and I are one, Father, so that the world may believe."[8]

A man of vision, judiciousness, and wisdom, George also knew that "the answer is not to be found in a type of conservative Catholicism obsessed with particular practices and so sectarian in its outlook that it cannot serve as a sign of unity of all peoples in Christ."[9]

Rather, he proposed "simply Catholicism," which he described as [the Catholic faith] … in all its fullness and depth, a faith able to distinguish itself from any cultures and yet able to engage and transform them all, a faith joyful in all the gifts Christ wants to give us and open to the whole world he died to save. The Catholic faith shapes a church with a lot of room for differences in pastoral approach, for discussion and debate, for initiatives as various as the peoples whom God loves. But, more profoundly, the faith shapes a church which knows her Lord and knows her own identity, a church able to distinguish between what fits into the tradition that unites her to Christ and what is a false start or a distorting thesis, a church united here and now because she is always one with the church throughout the ages and with the saints in heaven.

George's elaboration on this came in an essay he penned for *Commonweal* magazine after critics took exception to his original thesis. The key to the proper understanding of the Church for George was for the Church to recognize her identity through her relationship to Christ:

The Church is aware of herself as vital, and so calls herself a body. The Church is aware of herself as personal, and so calls herself a bride who surrenders to Christ. The Church is aware of herself as a subject, as an active, abiding presence that mediates a believer's experience, and so calls herself mother. The Church is aware of herself as integrated, and so describes herself as a temple of the Holy Spirit.

In his analysis of "simply Catholicism," Bishop Robert Barron expanded on this relationality of the Catholic Faith. "Notice please the words being used here: vital, personal, present, surrendering, mother, integrated. They all speak of participation, interconnection, relationship, what Cardinal George calls '*esse per*' (being through). This is the living organism of the Church which relates in a complex way to the culture, assimilating and elevating what it can and resisting what it must. This is simply Catholicism."[10]

This was not some mere idea for Cardinal George, but a lived existence. In the 2012 Salt and Light interview, George was asked, "What is it that keeps you going?" George's response was simple but profound: "Well, Jesus Christ, of course." He added: "I think if one falls in love with the Lord, and permits himself to be embraced by the Lord, so that your whole life is a series of transformations, of conversions big and little, then there's this certain security that enables you to continue when things aren't so good, remembering the good times and the bad times."

In his last Christmas homily as archbishop of Chicago, Cardinal George uniquely laid out the vision of what it means to be united to Christ and how "he bids us to go to others in his name, sharing the joy of the Gospel."[11] To prepare us for mission, George notes that "Jesus asks us three questions to deepen our encounter, our relationship, our friendship with him: First, what lasts beyond lifetimes, even forever? If I must die, then how should I live? Second, where do you find hope, day after day, in a world closed hopelessly in on itself, like a huge prison? And third, where do you find yourself truly free?"

George said Jesus has us ask ourselves these questions "because Jesus answers them." He continued: "Often it takes a long time to recognize the truth, to follow the way; but when we do, we receive our life as the gift it is from a God who is infinite love, forever and ever."

FAITHFUL AND PERSEVERING

When bishops are nominated, one of the many details of preparation for ordination that needs attention is the design of a coat of arms. Personal elements of the bearer's life are chosen, often depicted by symbols representative of their particular devotions or patron saints, life events, or genealogy. Additionally, below the shield is the motto chosen by the bearer, which typically originates from Scripture.

George's coat of arms was designed in 1990 after his appointment as bishop of Yakima. As one might expect, it does not contain much reference to personal traits aside from his own vocation, both as an Oblate of Mary Immaculate and as a bishop. If a bishop's personal coat of arms is to be taken as a sign of the roots and aspirations of his life and ministry, George's is a microcosm of his own spiritual life and character, pointing to some main themes that synthesize his life and mission. George's coat of arms features two main colors, silver and blue, which represent the Faith and the Blessed Virgin Mary, respectively. The blue also "speaks of truth, perseverance, and all the virtues so important in our spiritual pilgrimage."[12]

Two of the three primary symbols on George's coat of arms are evocative of his life as an Oblate of Mary Immaculate. Each is blue with a silver background. One is a six-pointed star from Eugene de Mazenod's own episcopal coat of arms, which is pierced so as to allow the silver representing the Faith to shine through, showing his missionary "commitment to witness faithfully to the Gospel." The second is a crescent, a symbol traditionally associated with Our Lady's Immaculate Conception.

The significance of George's life as an Oblate cannot be understated. In his vocation to religious life, in taking the vows of poverty, chastity, obedience — and, as an Oblate, perseverance — George committed himself to the pursuit of holiness. In a September 8, 2004, letter to Oblate Fr. Wilhelm Steckling, then–Superior General of the Congregation, George expressed his gratitude for his life with the Oblates. "I thank God for my vocation as an Oblate, because the Congregation taught me how to pray, how to live as a disciple of Jesus Christ and how to understand the universal mission of the Church, with the poor as both objects and subjects of that mission," he wrote.

As an Oblate, George continuously worked to give himself completely to the Lord in the manner of Mary. Her Immaculate Conception, George said in 2004, informs us that "her life is all gift, and she knew it."[13] Mary informs the mission of the Church and teaches us to use the gifts we are given by returning them to the Lord as an oblation. He said, "She who said in Nazareth: 'Let it be done unto me according to thy will,' spoke to others at Cana of Galilee: 'Do whatever he tells you.'" Like Mary,

George's life and work always beckoned others: "Do whatever he tells you." In this way, George's life embodies the perseverance that he vowed as an Oblate, which is summarized in the Oblate constitutions as "the unreserved gift we make of ourselves in our oblation, an offering constantly renewed by the challenges of our mission."[14]

Despite tremendous challenges, much pain, and great suffering, George persevered in the disciple's call to holiness. And he committed himself to building up the Church toward that same end. George reiterated time and again the simple belief that "the Church's ministry forms saints." He knew that to be what the Christian life is all about.

At a 2009 event related to the release of his book *The Difference God Makes*, George observed that "holy people might not reflect on sanctity as such. They don't always make the headlines. But they are everywhere; they're the leaven of society, the tissue that keeps us together. Fathers and mothers of families — people dedicated not only to their faith but also to their work in society and helping others. The difference God makes is holiness in his Son Jesus Christ using his Body the Church."

Responding to this call to holiness was the driving force of George's own life and ministry, and it was obvious to everyone around him. Just before Fr. Joshua Caswell was ordained to the priesthood by Cardinal George for the Canons Regular of St. John Cantius — the last priest upon whom George would lay hands at an ordination — he asked the cardinal what his secret was for accomplishing all that he did. He specifically wanted to understand how George remained tethered to Christ and his Church so effectively in spite of many difficulties. George thought for a while and then answered that it was simply "habit" — a practice of living the Faith, day in and day out.

George often regretted the loss of common habits and the dissolution of a distinct culture that had defined Catholics for generations. And he believed that a "great deal" of the responsibility for this loss rested in the hands of the bishops. He told the US bishops in a 2003 address:

We have to develop people who have a distinctive way of life. ...

There is a way of life that is bound up with being a disciple of Christ in his Church, a common way of life not constructed by individual choice. It has a common calendar. It has penitential practices. It has common prayer. It has common devotion. It has a common vocabulary. It is a way of life which tells me every moment of my life that the Church can make demands upon me and must make demands because she is the Body of Jesus Christ, to whom all authority has been given in heaven and on earth.[15]

He elaborated on this point in 2004, again in addressing the US bishops, connecting it to what many have called a crisis of vocations in our time: "To rebuild a sense of vocation, to strengthen marriage and family life, priesthood and consecrated life, we have to re-introduce customs that habituate our people to self-sacrifice for the sake of the Gospel."[16]

And George expounded again on this theme at the 2009 book launch address, saying, "Religion is not so much a matter of choice as it is a matter of habit."[17] He continued:

When people build their lives, they make choices at times, but much of it is simply habitual. If you have good habits, you'll be saved from your own individual, evil inclinations at times. If you don't have those good habits, [if] each time [you are] faced with good and evil, you have to make a choice, too often you won't choose what is truly good. People live their lives, they live their faith, they go to Mass regularly, they do their best to build up their family and contribute to society. Catholicism is a way of life, a way of thinking, and a way of loving that incarnates a vision uneasy with itself if it is not finally, truly global.

Toward the end of his life, George was considering a pastoral letter on Catholic habits and customs. He never had the chance to finish it but had hoped it might "remind people that there are customs that identify a Catholic way of life and that, if we've lost them, the Church becomes a debating society instead of a Church."[18] He often shared his disappoint-ment that universal abstinence from meat on Fridays was altered in the United States, because it gave American Catholics an identity. Losing such simple habits, in his mind, contributed to the rancor and divisions in the Church. "It was part of the Catholic way of life, a marker, and kept people together sometimes even when they disagreed on other things. Going to Mass every Sunday was very much part of a Catholic way of life, and devotion to the saints and a lot of devotional practices that kept you involved with the family of God. Those things have been much weak-ened or disappeared." He wanted his flock to know, as his ministry so often related, that "the Church is a way of life; faith creates a way of life protected by the Church. It is that way of life and the habitual customs that mark it that have been much weakened." He expressed regretfully, "We're not as cohesive a group as we should be."

BRILLIANT, YET SIMPLE

The third symbol on George's coat of arms depicts a prominent ship's anchor, described as "an ancient Christian symbol of hope, confidence, and stability in a sea of temptations and difficulties."[19] Attached to it is a red rope symbolizing Christ's Precious Blood, "by which we take hold of hope in the Church." The bishop makes visible this hope in his diocese. It was no secret to anyone that George had a brilliant mind. And he com-bined his intellectual gifts with a pastor's heart and deep desire to give his people hope.

Papal biographer George Weigel reported that an auxiliary bishop of "a venerable archdiocese" once remarked on George's appointment to Chicago in a statement that perhaps revealed more about himself and others than it did George: "Oh, no, he's the one who gets up at meetings and uses all those words the bishops can't understand."[20]

In reality, George spoke with clarity and eloquence, drawing forth his words from a deep well of knowledge and wisdom. This is why he became a voice of authority. In an interview at the time of George's death, Msgr. Patrick Brennan of Portland, president-rector of Mount Angel Seminary during the time of George's brief tenure in the Oregon archdiocese, re-called, "He would speak at the drop of a hat on anything and it was like an encyclopedia, so logical, so clear. If you had a question, he would serve you by assisting you in that way."[21]

On a personal level, the people around him turned to George time and again precisely because of this brilliance and authenticity. Although often described as the smartest person in the room, he was not a man of guile, nor did it seem he made a practice of holding grudges. Just as George's brother Oblates turned to him when he was still a young yet authentic priest to lead them through troubling times for the order, his brother bishops turned to him for leadership amid great challenges within the Church. His logical, seasoned, and most of all faithful voice was the one they sensed they needed for guidance. Archbishop Alexander Sample of Portland recalled an episode at an airport when waiting for a delayed flight. A group of younger bishops who revered George as a father figure huddled around him, soaking up his answers to their questions. "He was a deep, deep thinker. You could see that he really thought and prayed about things. He had some incredible insights, ready to share them with his humor and a bit of sarcasm."

And yet, even with his great gift of intellect, George could be so utterly simple. He tried not to take himself too seriously. In his homily addressed to Chicago priests on the eve of his 1997 installation, he quipped, "If we can't occasionally make fun of ourselves, we're all in dire straits." And he didn't gravitate naturally to the center of attention. At another priests' gathering a decade later, this prince of the Church stated, "I don't like to be noticed too much. I don't like to be at the center of things publicly. It takes a little bit of effort for me to do that."

George's staff often joked, regarding the simplicity of his personal life, that while he was the member of the staff who took the vow of poverty, they all had to live it with him. "He was very serious about that vow, and I think it pained him to reside in a house where many assumed he lived a life of luxury. The opposite was true. He lived as simply as possible," Mary FioRito recalled. At home, George lived simply. His quarters were modest. If he had to be on the road all day for meetings or events, he often took a simple brown bag lunch with him from home. In a 2008 piece on a day in the life of Cardinal George, the *Chicago Tribune* shared how George was given a peanut butter sandwich on one such day by one of the Albertine nuns at his residence, with no jelly. "Just as he likes it, one of the sisters told him," the *Tribune* reports, only to quote George saying, "But I like jelly."[22] It turned out that George had once made an offhand comment about jelly being messy, and in their attentiveness and care, the sisters eliminated it from his sandwiches. George did not complain. Sometimes at night, if he had some down time, George liked to watch television in the kitchen at his residence and have a bowl of ice cream, or a PB&J he made for himself.

George lived a life of concern for others, quietly and gently reaching out in unassuming ways that didn't attract attention. He consistently and continually said "yes" to the Lord, approaching each day first as a disciple of Jesus Christ, wanting only to serve Christ and the Church in the role to which he was called, doing his best to be a saint. As George Weigel succinctly put it:

> For beneath the scintillating brilliance and the sparkling skill in argument is a man of holiness and courage: a polio survivor who has lived with chronic pain since he was a teenager, who has faced down cancer on several occasions, and who has borne suffering of body and spirit with the grace and fortitude that come from a lifetime of meditation on the mystery of the Cross. The episcopal example he leaves behind is not to be measured, in the final analysis, by his articles and books but by his fidelity to Christ the Lord, to whose love he responded by pouring out his own life, just as the Master had done.[23]

George's gifts — even if, as a trained philosopher and theologian, he sometimes might have been expressing simple concepts with technical language — were inspired and unique, warmly received across the various constituencies that he served locally, nationally, and internationally. Yet his simplicity could at times be misconstrued as idealism or naïveté. Consider his self-described disdain for conflict or his penchant for being too frank in front of reporters. Or his near prophetic ability to speak with clarity, precision, and vision. These characteristics were often on display together, as when on his first day in Chicago in 1997 he was asked what the biggest issue facing him was as a bishop. He immediately replied: the threats posed by "the epistemological dissonance of American society."[24] Notwithstanding the statement's prophetic clarity, it most certainly informed the Chicago press corps that a very different way of doing things in Chicago was beginning.

George's authenticity and simplicity were often easily perceptible to those who met him, even non-Catholic journalists. Longtime *Chicago Sun-Times* religion reporter Cathleen Falsani once described George sitting unfazed, reading the newspaper amid heavy turbulence on a plane bound for Rome. "That is a man secure in his mortality, I thought as I craned my neck to look for the flight attendant refilling wine glasses," Falsani wrote after George's death.[25] She could see the difference God made in his life in that moment, or any moment. "Cardinal George had an abiding faith," she wrote, "not the kind of faith that might be a point of pride, but the down-deep-in-his-bones kind of faith that is a gift, a gift about which he was ever cognizant and grateful."

George once told Falsani, "My introduction to Jesus was as a loving savior whose own suffering rescues me from my sinfulness and therefore enables me to live with him and the Father and the Spirit forever, and all of his friends." Although they disagreed often, she recalled "the man in the red dress" for his humanity and kindness, "his huge, easy smile and infectious laugh ... practically guileless, like that of a happy kid."

Falsani described her "unlikely friendship" with the man she and some others in the Chicago press affectionately called "Frannie G." with another memorable vignette that speaks to his care and concern for others. Once when in Rome, George caught word that Falsani had been robbed. When he saw her outside the Vatican press office, he called out to her, "Cathleen, are you all right? I heard you were robbed. Do you need some money?"

Many have called George "the genuine article" or "the real deal." His authenticity and honesty — sometimes visible to a fault — were attractive and appreciated by a multitude of individuals. Archbishop Alexander Sample noted there was "no duplicity in him" and admired "there wasn't an ambitious bone in his body." Many saw holiness in George, as Abbot Jeremy Driscoll noted simply through "the things he said at meetings" and how "he was into it with his whole being." He appreciated one thing George "often said about dumb theological ideas: 'I wouldn't die for that' — of course, implying he would die for other things." George's characteristic genuineness, as a "human being fully alive," was fueled by a deep faith and sustained by prayer. His spirituality was straightforward and pure.

After observing George up close amid the difficulties and suffering resulting from his first major battle with cancer in 2006, his physician, Fr. Myles Sheehan, observed that George "handled his illness in a way that was virtuous and heroic and had the things you would expect to see in a saint."

"He certainly was holy," Sheehan said. "He was charitable about people who were a pain in the neck. Although he'd feel criticism, he'd shrug his shoulders. He was aware of his faults, self-aware. He really had a heroic virtue that he faced and kept on going." Sheehan saw George particularly as a man of perseverance and humility, observing that "he was not particularly impressed that he was a cardinal."

The Albertine Sisters, whom George invited in 2002 to operate the archbishop's residence, cared lovingly for him and also maintained an atmosphere of warm hospitality and a rhythm of prayer within his house. George depended on the sisters to take his needs and concerns to prayer. In the chapel in his residence, where the sisters joined him for Mass and other opportunities for prayer, George kept a basket with prayer intentions from the people of the archdiocese. Their concerns were his own, and he read through several of them each day. "The bishop's prayer for his people enables him to bring their deepest concerns into the heart of God's love," he once wrote.[26]

The sisters recalled the late hours that George could be found on the kneeler in the center of the chapel, engaged in silent prayer before the Blessed Sacrament. "It was his strength," one observed, admiring his ability to kneel for long periods despite the discomfort to his braced leg. Praying before the Blessed Sacrament was clearly essential to his own spirituality as an Oblate, and it certainly must have been what grounded him and gave him strength to not only carry on but to give more of himself while doing so.

At times George would remark that he felt his prayer was insufficient. As one who loved the Lord, he desired to give more of himself in prayer while balancing out his call to serve his people as their archbishop. He wrote in a 2001 column, "In my celebration of the Eucharistic Liturgy and the Liturgy of the Hours each day, I speak to God about you and for you," imploring his flock, "please do the same for me."[27]

The Mass was the anchor and the breviary was the key to George's prayer life. As Bishop Robert Barron said, George "was a man of the Mass, that was like a nonnegotiable."[28] But it was a "simply pious celebration of the Mass" with "nothing flashy about it, nothing kind of grand or show-offy." George had a devotion to the Liturgy of the Hours, composed mostly of the Psalms, and he also loved praying the Rosary, which he said assists us to "identify our lives with those of the Lord and his Blessed Mother" and during which "we insert what happens to us into what happened to them."[29]

As George often said, his prayer life was very much shaped by his formation and life as an Oblate of Mary Immaculate. Marian devotion was central to his spirituality. Once asked about his favorite prayers, in addition to the Mass, George said he liked the *Memorare* and the Lord's Prayer. He also drew attention to a lesser-known prayer from seventeenth-century French spirituality, part of the Oblates' own tradition, "Jesus Living in Mary," which he recited every morning. He said, "It's a classical prayer, a short one, but I say it every morning at the end of meditation because it expresses who we are, united to Christ in Mary, and how we are expected to transform our lives day by day."

> O Jesus, living in Mary,
> come and live in your servants:
> in the spirit of your holiness,
> in the fullness of your power,
> in the reality of your virtues,
> in the perfection of your ways,
> in the communion of your mysteries;
> have dominion over every adverse power,
> in your own Spirit,
> to the glory of God the Father.
> Amen.[30]

George's prayer life fueled a vibrant life of service to Christ and the Church. Bishop David Malloy of Rockford, who worked closely with George during his years of leadership at the USCCB, observed, "Cardinal George combined greatness with simplicity in all he did."

Cardinal Timothy Dolan of New York reiterated this palpable sense of George's simplicity. "For the complexity of his thinking, and for the eloquence of his expression, for the breadth of his reading and study, he was a very simple man."[31] Dolan recalled the time when George's legendary green laundry bag went missing. George had received it as a young Oblate and traveled the world with it, and when he could not find it after returning home from a trip to Rome, he called up Dolan, then rector of the Pontifical North American College, and asked for his help. Dolan recalled George was so concerned about the bag that he called in a panic hoping Dolan could locate it, which he did. Dolan said that incident illustrated that George was a "salt of the earth kind of guy."

Former longtime Chicago-area congressman Daniel Lipinski recalled George, at the time of his death, as "an intellectual powerhouse who has a special ability to communicate great truths in a simple manner. Every time I hear him speak, I hear something that enriches both my mind and my faith. But his intellect is not a distant intellect of a philosopher in an abstract world, but is well-grounded in understanding the everyday lives of people. And as someone who appreciates straightforwardness, I have always liked his directness. Maybe that's because Cardinal George and I both come from Chicago."[32] Among the other tributes and remembrances that came pouring in after George's death — from ordinary parishioners to a host of dignitaries and Church leaders — one of the simplest yet most profound came from his longtime barber, Alfredo Fricano: "To me, he was one of the nicest men I've ever met."[33]

George's directness and ability to illustrate the truths of the Faith simply and comprehensibly was the fruit of a lifelong study of philosophy and theology. In a 2013 interview, George pointed to Popes John Paul II and Benedict XVI as influences on his thinking, as well as St. Thomas Aquinas and Oblate founder St. Eugene de Mazenod. Regarding the latter, George observed, "You have to assimilate what you've learned. You can't just repeat it like a parrot does; otherwise people know that you are somehow saying something that isn't your own."[34]

George admitted that his path as an academic, as a congregational leader, and as a bishop consisted of assignments he took on out of obedience. "I've always done what I was told to do, basically. My life isn't self-constructed. That's an odd thing to say. Studying philosophy is something I was told to do. I don't know that I would have done that if I had my own choices. I've done what I was told to do, and I've tried to do it as well as I could." He added: "The fundamental evangelical virtue is the obedience of faith in charity. Christ was obedient unto death. We don't talk about obedience, but in fact we are all obedient to God or else we're on our own, which is a way of saying we are sinners. If you're in touch with God, you're obedient to God. I've tried to be obedient to the Lord's will as expressed by the Church."

George also displayed heroic obedience in his endurance of chronic physical suffering. In 2010, he wrote privately that "physical disability is constant. I can't walk — I can't travel alone now nor carry things and keep my balance. This aggravates me endlessly."[35] But he seemed to view these trials as having a purpose, too, as "part of preparing for death" and the "immobility of [the] grave."

In January 2012, George submitted to Pope Benedict XVI his resignation as archbishop of Chicago, required by the Church's canon law for bishops who reached their seventy-fifth birthday. Even from his earliest days there, he had made it no secret he hoped to be the first archbishop of Chicago to retire. One of the reasons for this was that, upon his arrival in the city at the end of a six-month gap in leadership following Cardinal Bernardin's death, he had observed the negative consequences of a vacuum of governance. Midway through in 2012, doctors found malignancy in one of his kidneys and removed a nodule from his liver. George's cancer was back. He was, however, well enough to travel to Rome in 2013 to participate in the conclave that elected Pope Francis.

In 2012, after learning his cancer was no longer in remission, George was able to respond with the perspective gained from a life of suffering. "The world has no meaning beyond the point where I can feel I am in control," he noted. "But we are never in control. That is a Promethean dream that ends in meaningless tragedy."[36]

"YOU ARE MY LEGACY"

In early 2014, the cancer in George's right kidney required chemotherapy, and he recommended that the apostolic nuncio initiate the appointment of a successor. When he celebrated Mass at Holy Name Cathedral that Easter, he announced it would likely be his last celebrated there as archbishop. His retirement was accepted later that year, and Bishop Blase Cupich of Spokane was named to succeed him on September 20. George remained in office until Cupich's installation on November 18. Among his final archdiocesan actions were to announce a last round of school closures and release a dossier of priest files related to the clergy sexual abuse scandal. "Cleaning up things as best I can," he said "so that [Cupich] has a clean slate, and doesn't have to make major decisions that might bring criticism, in the first several months anyway."[37]

In the manner of a poetic bookend, Chicago's first homegrown arch-bishop left the sanctuary on crutches after his last public Mass in office in 2014, just like the same city's young Frannie, polio-ridden and reject-ed, left his home archdiocese on crutches in pursuit of his vocation. He was unable even to carry his crozier — the visible sign of the shepherd of souls that he was. About a year before, when George was asked in an interview about his legacy, he recalled his father's directive: "If you're go-ing to be a priest, be a good one." In light of that, he continued, "I would hope that people would remember that I tried to be a good priest and a good bishop, and that's enough."[38] He wrote years earlier, "And no matter when or where he governs, a bishop, even a Cardinal, does so aware that Christ will ask him at his death whether or not he loved the people given him to pastor."[39]

George's clearest and fullest answer to the common questions he of-ten fielded about his legacy, however, came in his final homily at that final public Mass as archbishop of Chicago. His answer might not have been the answer the media was searching for, but it was an authentic and honest appraisal from the man who also said, "I am a bishop; all the rest is someone else's fantasy."[40] Knowing that in Catholic communion everything is interrelated and that we are, in many ways, defined by our relationships, George's legacy was not about what he did but rather what the Lord did through him. George sometimes bristled at the idea of being asked about his legacy, since he found the question was "trying to make sense of my years here by fitting them into a narrative, a story line." But as a bishop, as with any Christian, his identity "is defined by Christ on one side and the people on the other." George continued: "Life is not a self-directed project but a consistent response to what is asked by those you love."

In his final public homily, George reflected on his legacy and what he imagined God might consider that same legacy to be:

The question often put to me by the media and by others is, "What do you see as your legacy?" … Different people, of course, will have different takes on my years here as archbishop. Some of them I might appreciate and some not, but that's the fate of anyone in a public post, a position of public trust. The question I have to ask myself is, "With what have I been entrusted?" and "What have I done with this gift?" ... At some point, Christ will question me: "What have you done with my people? Are they holier because of your ministry? Are they more generous? More loving toward others?" In short, you are my legacy.

The people of the archdiocese are what I will point to when the Lord asks me "What have you done with my gift to you?" The people of the archdiocese are what I point to when the media and others ask "What is your legacy?" Have I been at times too fearful to speak, to act, to love generously? Sometimes certainly. But others can note that, even when I don't. But have I invested myself in the people so they are better able to know and live their faith, able to worship God in spirit and in truth, able to give themselves for the salvation of others. Yes. ... Sacraments are celebrated, the Gospel is preached, people are gathered in communities of love so they can transform the world by God's love.[41]

About a month later, when asked, in a 2014 interview with Rich Daniels of the City Lights Orchestra, what he would want people to remember about him in fifty years, George said, "I would want them to remember that I tried very hard to love them. That's what a bishop is supposed to do, that's what a parish priest is supposed to do — love the people whom God has given you to pastor, to care for. ... I'm sorry for the times when my love was less than complete, that's for sure, or when in fact I didn't live up to the responsibilities that are mine."

As archbishop of Chicago, George faced much hidden suffering, and the difficulties of his office weighed on his heart. But he gave of himself without counting the cost, even as he wrestled with daily physical pain. He had bad days; he could be impatient; he could raise his voice or be cantankerous. But his comments were not borne of personal animosity.

He did not hold grudges. And he apologized when he knew he might have hurt someone, regardless of what might have caused it.

FACING DEATH

George had no developed plans for his retirement. As an active bishop, he had published two books. *The Difference God Makes: A Catholic Vision of Faith, Communion, and Culture*, published in 2009, offers a wide array of essays that examine man's communion with God and the implications of how that communion must transform the culture. His second book, published in 2011, *God in Action: How Faith in God Can Address the Challenges of the World*, reflects on the role of faith in the public square and examines religion's singular impact on the common good. In the months before his death, George was finishing up a third book, *A Godly Humanism: Clarifying the Hope that Lies Within*, posthumously published in 2015.

George had hoped to have time to write and speak as well as to more frequently hear confessions, and he expressed his desire to cross the Atlantic Ocean on a ship. After having flown across it so often for decades, he wanted to experience how it would feel to be in the middle of an expanse of water with nothing else around, "a little speck, in the ecosystem of our planet, let alone all the other planets," he said in a 2014 interview with Chicago's Fox affiliate. He added: "But I'm not sure that I'll do that, and if I don't, that's OK, too." He never did.

George Weigel's assessment of George at his death is shared by many. "He was a man of manifest faith and marked ability who struck a chord of personal integrity with just about everyone," he said. "Those qualities don't always make for a smooth passage through the rocks and shoals of ecclesiastical life, but I can think of very few people who didn't respect Francis George."[42] That respect was held by a diverse group of individuals, too, including Fr. Michael Pfleger. About a year before his death, George saw Pfleger in the vestibule of Holy Name Cathedral following an ordination and said that they should find some time to talk. Pfleger remembers it as a very cordial meeting in which George expressed both his respect for Pfleger's passion for ministry and his frustration over their struggles through the years. It seemed that as George faced the end of his life, he may have been attempting to reconcile a strained relationship. At that meeting, Pfleger recalled, George told Pfleger he forgave him for the times he made his life difficult and crossed various lines with his approach and outspokenness. Pfleger asked George to pray over him before the end of their meeting, and George acquiesced. Pfleger laughed when he recalled how George concluded his blessing with a gentle strike across the cheek, what he likened to "an old school confirmation slap." George asked Pfleger to offer his blessing in return — which he did, without returning the slap. It seems to be a testament to George's own magnanimity that, after all the struggles between them, George could seek out reconciliation with Pfleger and not be controlled by any resentments.

Despite his clashes with city leaders over the years, George was honored by the Chicago City Council with a rare accolade not long before he died. An alderman representing Chicago's neighborhoods thanked George, their neighbor, for his leadership and service. At the conclusion of the event, Mayor Rahm Emanuel awarded George the city's highest honor, the Medal of Merit — the first time it had been given out in fifteen years. "On behalf of the city of Chicago I want to say you will always be Francis our neighbor," Emanuel said.[43] "Thank you on behalf of a grateful city." George was quite moved by the assembly and the honor. "They spoke not only for themselves but also for people that they know and they serve in their wards," George said. "It means a lot more than simply an act of city council so I am very grateful, extremely grateful."

In speaking to the city council on this occasion, George likened his former position as archbishop to something like the work of the aldermen and mayor, even down to the types of mail they might receive. "In your office and mine, many of the letters that you receive are letters of complaint or discontent for something you've done or someone else has done that they don't like," George said.[44] With his retirement, though, he said he no longer dreaded opening the mail — and, in fact, doing so helped him to understand how he affected the lives of his people. "What I'm getting now — and what has truly transformed my own judgment on my time here — is letters from people who say, 'You don't know me, but you helped me.' … You say something occasionally. You reach out in some gesture of kindness. You do something that you're not even aware of … and you transform someone's life. That is what is eternal."

In the 1997 homily on the eve of his installation in Chicago, George recalled a 1971 scene at Chicago's Logan Square, at a time when "the nature of my vocation as a priest and religious was being questioned by others and by myself," he said.[45] In a conversation with a painter that day, George was asked if he had a family. "I stammered a bit about being 'single,' and then I said I was a Catholic priest. Without missing a beat, he said, 'Oh, everybody's your family!'" As George put it, "It was James Joyce's 'here comes everybody' with a Chicago accent."

Cardinal George was truly a man for all. A friendly voice on the phone for a deacon diagnosed with cancer. A shepherd for a priest troubled by a personal crisis. A voice for the victims of clergy sexual abuse, even in the halls of the Vatican. A prophet who could read the signs of the times and call the people to conversion. A friend who gave a troubled parishioner his private phone number when she needed a friend. A neighbor who could talk to you as if you were the only person who mattered. A cardinal who could provide the leadership his brother bishops needed. A man of suffering who nonetheless daily offered himself to Christ for the good of others.

AT THE END

Near the end of his life, in a 2014 interview with the Chicago Fox affiliate, George accused himself of being "desultory," "slow to make a judgment, too slow sometimes," and worried he might not have had the "courage" at times to act more quickly. He wished he had moved more rapidly, and he stated that his slowness might have contributed to the financial bind facing the archdiocese as he left the helm. He said he wished he had seen things more clearly but, as he often said, "History is what God remembers, and we don't know it entirely. We won't until he reveals it to us at the end of time."

He commented at the event launching *The Difference God Makes* in 2009, "In the end, 'all will be well,' as Julian of Norwich wrote. Where, in the end, God will show us how history is woven in such a way that he has continuously brought good out of evil. Evil is real, but in the end, God is able to bring good out of it. If we don't live in faith, at least, but also in some rational conviction, that there is that level of that reality, then we inevitably lead ourselves into a kind of cynicism that destroys relationships."

During an interview with the *New York Times* at the time of his retirement, a priest passing by told him to enjoy the years ahead. George replied with his characteristic sense of humor: "Or months or days."[46] George spent his last year in clinical trials for his cancer, which, as he said, ultimately showed that the doctors had "run out of tricks in the bag."[47] He had been in and out of the hospital, afflicted with cellulitis in his right leg, requiring crutches, or suffering from dehydration and recurring infections. It was a difficult time of new pains and new sensations that he had not experienced before, although he had become acquainted with similar situations since he was a boy with polio. His pain was managed well, and he admitted he did not want to die in pain. But he had not expressed any fear of dying. He was more curious about what it would be like to experience, if possible, the dissolution of the body, and about what he would know and see.

As he faced his own death, George exhibited a kind of wonderment, admitting in the 2014 Fox interview that he had "a certain intellectual curiosity" about "what's coming next." Recalling the days after his mother's death some forty years previously, he remembered that in discussions his father would often ask questions like, "What do you think she can know? Does she know we're praying for her?" George could only reply, "Dad, she knows what God wants her to know." And that, George said in the interview,s "is all any of us can say. But I don't know what that is."

In an interview with EWTN in late 2014, just six months before his death, he reflected:

I think the Lord, in his goodness, prepares us to meet him face to face, by stripping away a lot of the accoutrements of life, desires, even good desires, so that in the end there is one thing necessary, that is the love of God. You know, I kind of sense that I am being helped in that way. That the Lord is preparing me, despite my unworthiness, to meet him. Because, when you stop to think about it, you know, what does that mean? To see God, we say. We can't see without eyes. So, what are we talking about? It's a true vision? How does the spirit see, because we're part spirit and that's the part that survives death until the resurrection? So, there are all kinds of questions I can't answer … St. Thomas couldn't exactly. So, there are all that to be considered as you say, "what must I do to prepare for death?" The importance of your life is that it prepares you to live forever with God. And so it's very important that at the end of your life you sum it up and hand it over to him, and say, "here it is Lord, you know, purify me, and help me." So maybe that's going on.

George also turned to classic meditations from the Catholic tradition, such as the "*ars moriendi*" texts composed by spiritual greats like St. Alphonsus Liguori. He said he was intent on putting his focus on spending his last days figuring out "how do the saints die?" And he laughed at the suggestion of a "bucket list," saying, instead, that "what's necessary now is to prepare my soul to meet the Lord, so I want to spend more time in prayer."

Sr. Anne Joan Flanagan — a Daughters of St. Paul sister who served on the Chicago archdiocesan pastoral council for a time during George's tenure — recalled a conversation with George about the sisters' Michigan Avenue store in Chicago. George told her, "What I'd like to do when I retire is go down to the bookstore a couple of times a week and just sit there and be available for people's questions." Flanagan promised to hold him to that. It would have been a welcomed gift, no doubt, since her experience was that of so many: "I always left the Cardinal feeling challenged to think more broadly and more deeply, and to bring my perspective more and more in line with the Gospel."

Books were so much a part of George's life, both as a voracious reader and an accomplished author. A great deal of George's last days were spent finalizing his last book, which was something of a final testament regarding his hopes and vision for the Church — a song of praise for the intellectual life in the Church's tradition and a *vademecum* of sorts for brother bishops and all those who, like George, strive "to integrate wisdom and discipleship." At the end of its preface he wrote, "just as we pray to see God face to face, so God wants to see us face to face. We give him our time, which is all that we have, and he takes the gift and calls us when he is ready to do so. In the end, that is all that there is, and everything is summed up and integrated in that vision and desire." As evidenced by the outpouring of sadness at his passing, George gave God all his time — spent at the service of God's people — offering everything in an oblation of worship and love.

Death came for Francis Eugene George on the morning of April 17, 2015, at the historic archbishop's residence in his room overlooking the edge of Lincoln Park — the same one little Frannie had walked past on his way to see the famous gorilla at Lincoln Park Zoo. Wanting to die at home, not at the hospital, George had entered hospice care. He was seventy-eight years old, his body overcome by the third bout of cancer that had finally claimed his life.

George wanted to die like St. Eugene de Mazenod, founder of his Oblate religious congregation and also a victim of cancer, and have the *Salve Regina* chanted at the time of his death. And so it was by those who lived with him, including his faithful priest-secretary Father Flens, the Albertine Sisters who oversaw his household, and retired Chicago auxiliary Bishop Raymond Goedert, who lived at the archbishop's residence. Goedert commented that George's "was a beautiful death," and that at the end, "he just slipped away."[48] He also commented that George "was a saint," as have many others who both knew him best and watched him from afar.[49] George lived in such a way that he reflected the truth of his own wise words: "People who are holy, whether or not publicly recognized by the Church as saints, keep the world from turning into hell. They are the greatest gift to the human race in every age."[50]

George's body was brought to the Gibbons Family Funeral Home in the old Portage Park neighborhood where he grew up — the same funeral home that had helped bury his parents. As he had done so many times before during his many years of faithful and devoted service to George, Father Flens helped vest his bishop's body, now for the last time. On George's leg remained the brace he had worn for so many decades, a physical reminder of the suffering that had, in so many ways, shaped his life and united him to the cross.

On April 21, George's body was brought to Holy Name Cathedral, accompanied by the last class of priests he ordained for the archdiocese. Several days of ceremonies and liturgies afforded the opportunity for streams of mourners to pay respect to and pray for a man they had loved and cherished. They touched his hands in reverence, and many even touched religious articles to him, as if pilgrims at the threshold of saintly relics. It was clear that his life, which he gave away freely for others, would live on in the hearts and minds of the long lines of people who came to honor him.

At a gathering for priests and seminarians on the night after George's body was received into the cathedral, Archbishop Blase Cupich recalled how his predecessor "was unfailingly supportive to me," telling the crowd of gathered clerics and aspirants "how he must have been the same for you over these past seventeen years."

Three days of rites marked the funerary celebrations as Chicago said farewell to George. There was a gathering of priests and seminarians, another for men and women religious and permanent deacons and wives, and an ecumenical and interreligious observance. There were long hours of visitation and an all-night vigil led by lay ecclesial movements in anticipation of his funeral Mass.

George's funeral Mass was celebrated on April 23 — the optional memorial of Saint George the martyr — at Holy Name Cathedral. Illinois

Governor Bruce Rauner declared the day to be "Francis Cardinal George Day" statewide.

Before the Mass began, George's family said goodbye, and the archdiocese's auxiliary bishops gathered around his casket before it was closed. Archbishop J. Peter Sartain of Seattle, a friend and former neighboring bishop during his time in Joliet, Illinois, gave the homily from a sanctuary filled with several dozens of cardinals, archbishops, and bishops. In a beautiful narrative of George's own goodness, virtue, and holiness, Sartain wove together the various themes of George's life. Rather than reflecting on the great accomplishments of the late cardinal-archbishop of Chicago, Sartain instead articulated clearly how George was the epitome of a disciple of Jesus Christ. In perhaps the most memorable line from the homily, Sartain recalled a line George had shared years earlier after a Mass they concelebrated at the Chicago cathedral. The line captured the essence of who George was — as well as the essence of any disciple: "The only thing we take with us when we die is what we have given away."

This seems to be what remained most in the minds of mourners as they filed past his casket or as they lined the Kennedy Expressway for the funeral cortege, a rare privilege usually reserved for the motorcade of visiting American presidents. George gave himself away for the Church and the world, and those he touched kept a bit of him in their hearts.

George's lifelong friend Archbishop Roger Schwietz, O.M.I., presided over the final commendation at the conclusion of the funeral Mass. He bid farewell to George in the name of the Church and commended him to the mercy of God. He noted that it was "one of the greatest honors of my life" to say farewell to such "a humble man with a great heart."

As George's body was carried from Chicago's cathedral for the last time, the choral antiphon *Ecce Sacerdos Magnus*, or "Behold, the Great Priest," was sung by the choir. The piece is often sung as a bishop enters a church, usually on solemn occasions. But this time, it was sung as the eighth archbishop of Chicago left the cathedral for the last time.

"Behold a great priest who in his days pleased God: Therefore by an oath the Lord made him to increase among his people. To him He gave the blessing of all nations, and confirmed His covenant upon his head. Therefore by an oath the Lord made him to increase among his people," the choir sang in Latin. Not long before he died, though, George had joked to a friend that he should be carried out of the cathedral to French singer and actress Edith Piaf's *"Non, Je Ne Regrette Rien,"* or "No, I Will Have No Regrets," in English.

Every archbishop of Chicago save two others is buried in the bishops' mausoleum at Mount Carmel Cemetery in suburban Hillside, just on the western edge of the city.[51] An impressive structure, it is typically locked to the general public. But George chose to be buried farther north in his family's plot at All Saints Cemetery in Des Plaines, next to his parents and maternal grandmother, the first archbishop to be buried among the people of his archdiocese. As the funeral procession made its way to the cemetery, it drove down neighborhood streets lined with mourners and paused in front of St. Pascal Church, George's home parish and school, where he had attended and served Mass as a grade school student, where he had received his first Holy Communion and heard the call to priesthood, and where he was later ordained a priest.

Upon his grave sits an impressive ledger stone prominently featuring his coat of arms in mosaic form, beckoning the Church to take up his mission — the mission of the Church and the mission of Christ. George knew his grave was not the end. As he said in his 2012 Easter homily, "If the earth is our mother, then the grave is our home and the world is a closed system turned in on itself. If Christ is risen from the grave and the Church is our mother, then our destiny reaches beyond space and time, beyond what can be measured and controlled. And therein lies our hope."[52]

At the celebration of his tenth anniversary as archbishop of Chicago eight years before his death, George had noted, "My life is a network, a tissue of relationships that would never have been mine, and I would not have been privileged to be part of had I not been called to be the archbishop of Chicago. ... What we take with us from this life into the next are simply the relationships — everything else disappears, but they are eternal." George's choice of a resting place as he awaits the Lord's return reflects that principle. Close to his family, close to his people, desiring their prayers — which they regularly come to offer even as they ask for his, sometimes leaving candles, notes, photos, or religious articles on his grave.

After having been rejected there, the first native archbishop of Chicago returned home as a shepherd. In that city of neighborhoods, Francis, their neighbor, offered himself in the service of his people. He now lies among them. Even in death, the pastor remains accessible to his flock, even defined by them. He lies in death as he lived.

Afterword

Charles Gounod's "O Divine Redeemer!" gathers together a summation of Christian hope at death. It is an ode to hope as one leaves behind earthly life and meets Christ awaiting eternity.

Cardinal George's ministry could be defined as consistently and constantly teaching who Christ is, and he did not miss the opportunity for continuing that mission — even in death — by choosing this piece for his funeral Mass. Its words offered a thoughtful, prayerful meditation for those present in consideration of our own meeting with Christ one day. In the recognition that we are sinners, we cast ourselves at the feet of Christ the Lord, to beg his mercy, forgiveness, and pardon. In the end, our existence depends on him alone. In the end, glorifying Christ is all that matters.

> Ah! Turn me not away,
> Receive me tho' unworthy;
> Hear Thou my cry,
> Behold, Lord, my distress!

Answer me from thy throne
Haste Thee, Lord to mine aid,
Thy pity shew in my deep anguish!
Let not the sword of vengeance smite me,
Though righteous thine anger,
O Lord! Shield me in danger, O regard me!
On Thee, Lord, alone will I call.
O Divine Redeemer!
I pray Thee, grant me pardon,
And remember not, remember not my sins!
Forgive me, O Divine Redeemer!
Night gathers round my soul;
Fearful, I cry to Thee;
Come to mine aid, O Lord!
Haste Thee, Lord, haste to help me!
Hear my cry! Save me Lord in Thy mercy;
Come and save me O Lord
Save, in the day of retribution,
From Death shield Thou me, O my God!
O Divine Redeemer, have mercy!
Help me, my Saviour!

This dependence on Christ, by which one defines himself on Christ's terms above all else, was manifested in George's own life. It is said that the same day the holy bishop Thomas Becket was martyred in Canterbury's cathedral, miracles began occurring, attributed to his intercession. People were inspired by his holy life and moved by how he embraced his gruesome death. In the mix of virtue and holiness that they found in Becket, they were moved, as soon as his soul left the body, to begin praying to him. And, by the saint's help, God responded to their prayer.

The stories of the saints often unfold this way, with people turning to those renowned for their goodness and faith to help them with their difficulties. This phenomenon is not absent from the story of Cardinal

George. Countless bishops, religious, and members of the lay faithful throughout the country have remarked to this author that they pray to him daily, and they have reported that he intercedes for them. His grave is frequented regularly, with visitors leaving tokens of their gratitude for his life, hoping he can hear them and plead to God for them. Flowers, notes, and photos of sick relatives have been documented at the grave of Francis George, as he lies in joyful expectation of the new heavens and the new earth. George's love for his people, and theirs for him, continues to grow. Many individuals have spoken in public and private about the favors they attribute to his intercession after offering prayers to him. People still turn to his pastoral solicitude, albeit in a new way. George has even appeared in dreams and helped individuals find clarity amid life's troubles. He has been credited with intervening for safe birth amid difficulties in utero and the disappearance of cancer in certain individuals.

Even after his death, Cardinal George's life of suffering has continued to speak to the hearts of the faithful. Among these is Megan Rogers of Memphis, Tennessee. Rogers, who was born with cerebral palsy, first learned about George as an eighteen-year-old while watching his funeral Mass on EWTN. George's life of suffering resonated with her, a significant step in her conversion to Catholicism. "Francis George's life was truly an oblation, a sacrifice, to God, and he was keenly aware that his sufferings were united to the cross of Christ," Rogers wrote in a reflection. "I know this to be true of my own life: it is in suffering that God gives insight into the cross no one would ever ask for willingly, but it is the sweetest gift. It is only in being Catholic that that will ever make true sense."

Although his suffering resonated with her, there was a primary difference between George and herself, Rogers mused. She had been born with her affliction, while Francis George had contracted polio when he was thirteen. He had been able to remember his life free of physical pain, resulting in a sacrifice that she could not understand.

And that, too, was an inspiration. "Our crosses are fashioned for each one of us," she concluded. "He carried his well. I can only hope to do the same."

As Christians, we take up our crosses and follow Christ daily. Cardinal George's life and witness give us an example of how to do so as a means of glorifying Christ in the Church.

Acknowledgments

Cardinal George commented on various occasions during his years as a bishop that he wanted his tombstone to read simply, "Thanks." While that did not end up engraved on the impressive ledger stone above his grave, it was clear that he lived his life with that basic Christian virtue in the forefront of his mind. He knew his life was a gift, and he lived accordingly. He made a true oblation of himself in thanksgiving to the Divine Giver.

This work is the cause for much gratitude.

Thanks, first, to Cardinal George. One really comes to know his subject intimately during the research and composition of a biography. I have felt his presence accompanying me as I progressed throughout this work. His model for discipleship is a rock to which I cling amid the storms of life and of our times, particularly his pursuit of the truth in charity, his strength in suffering and his inability to keep the Lord's friendship to himself. Words cannot adequately describe what a joy and privilege it is to help tell his story. I hope and pray that his life will continue to inspire disciples to grow closer to Christ and give him glory in the Church.

Thanks, too, to my family. Thanks to my parents, Robert and Debra, and my grandparents — especially my dear grandma Betty, whose suffering and death from Alzheimer's disease coincided with the finalization of this manuscript. I have a heart filled with gratitude for my family's love and inspiration, especially for the many sacrifices they made which enabled me to attempt this work.

The generosity and kindness of my wife, Gretchen, have been beyond compare throughout my work on this book. She has believed in and supported me from the first time I had the idea to embark on this project and has been an invaluable counselor throughout, while lending her incredible talents as an editor in the finalization of the manuscript. To her, my best friend and greatest encourager, I dedicate this work.

I have been working on this book since before all three of my children were born, so this project is almost like their sibling. Their sweet and kind encouragement has often spurred me on amid challenges and road blocks. I am also grateful to my parents-in-law for their availability and dedication in caring for our children so many times while I traveled for research or was sequestered for writing.

Thanks to my bishop, Most Reverend Kevin C. Rhoades, for his support and encouragement of this project, especially in its earliest stages. And to many other bishops and clergy who have been quite helpful in their eagerness to see this book come to fruition.

Thanks to Fr. Daniel Flens, Cardinal George's longtime, dedicated priest secretary. I heard over and over again from people close to the cardinal that one could not find more loving care than that showed to him by Fr. Flens. His constant, devoted, and multi-faceted assistance throughout this project have been utterly invaluable to me, and it is a blessing to have come to count him as a friend.

Thanks to the Oblates of Mary Immaculate, who formed Cardinal George and counted him as a brother, for welcoming me so often as a brother in Christ and for permitting me to consult their archives.

Thanks to the various officials at the Diocese of Yakima, Archdiocese of Portland-in-Oregon, and the Archdiocese of Chicago who have been willing and able to collaborate with me in telling this story well.

Thanks to all those who spoke to me and allowed me to interview them during the research phase of this book. Their contributions have helped Cardinal George's story come to life in these pages. I am especially grateful to Cardinal George's sister, Margaret, who welcomed me into her home as I was first starting out on this project and gave me her blessing to proceed. I'm also grateful to Cardinal George's longtime friend and confrere Most Reverend Roger L. Schwietz, O.M.I., archbishop emeritus of Anchorage, for his willingness to support my efforts from the beginning, all through the editing process, and beyond.

The photograph signature of this book is robust thanks to the generosity in licensing provided by Margaret Cain, the *Chicago Sun-Times*, the Ravinia Music Festival, and Catholic News Service. I'm particularly grateful to Daniel Mitsui for providing a rendering of Cardinal George's personal coat of arms and for allowing use of his drawing "Resurrection, Christo Gloria in Ecclesia." And I'm indebted to Jeff Ebert of Ebert Studio in Oak Park, Illinois for his gracious permission to use his portraiture of Cardinal George on the cover and in the photograph signature.

Thanks to friends Fr. Andrew Clyne, Fr. John Hogan, Fr. Harrison Ayre, Shannon Last, and Mary Hallan FioRito for their dedication and assistance while editing this manuscript.

Thanks to publisher Scott Richert and editor Mary Beth Giltner for their dedication to this book, and belief in its need to be published.

Thanks to the Our Sunday Visitor Institute, whose assistance enabled me to conduct research in Italy and in the Pacific Northwest.

Thanks to all those special friends on earth and in heaven who have prayed for the success of this work and have interceded for me at pivotal and challenging moments along the way. I am particularly grateful for the prayerful support of so many of the Daughters of Saint Paul, the Canons Regular of Saint John Cantius in Chicago, the Discalced Carmelite Monastery in Des Plaines, Illinois, and the Poor Clare Monastery of the Immaculate Conception in Palos Park, Illinois.

And most of all thanks to Jesus Christ by whose cross we have been freed from sin and death and by whose Resurrection we have life. To him be glory in the Church!

APPENDIX

Homily for the Funeral Mass of Cardinal Francis George, O.M.I.

Three days of memorials for Francis Cardinal George concluded
with a funeral Mass at Holy Name Cathedral in Chicago on
April 23, 2015. At the request of Cardinal George, Archbishop J.
Peter Sartain of the Archdiocese of Seattle delivered the homily
at the funeral Mass. It is reprinted here with his permission.

As a pastor in Memphis twenty-something years ago, one day I picked up a national Catholic publication and read a talk by the bishop of Yakima, Francis George. I cannot recall the topic, but I do recall my reaction. Here was a clear voice, a voice I wanted to listen to, a pastor who helped me understand the faith and taught me how to teach it. From that point on, whenever I noticed Bishop George's name associated with a talk or an article, I read it. I was never disappointed.

Years later, a bishop myself, I heard the voice speak in person, and I found the same clarity, the same creativity, the same natural interplay of faith and reason, the same challenge to discipleship I had perceived in his written word. And I noticed something else: Cardinal George spoke not only from prepared texts but also frequently off the cuff, spontaneously from the heart, in an understated, almost under-his-breath, manner. And I learned that such "after-thoughts" were just as insightful as his written texts. They welled up from within, unrehearsed, and gave a glimpse of the fullness that was his interior life. In a certain sense, he couldn't not put these afterthoughts to words (although perhaps he wished, from time to time, that he hadn't!), because they were so much a part of him, from the tips of his toes to the top of his head. They literally rolled off his lips, because as the Lord had said, "From the fullness of the heart, the mouth speaks" (Mt 12:34; Lk 6:45). I always listened to his afterthoughts, and a personally memorable case in point was spoken here, at this pulpit, seven or eight years ago.

I had concelebrated Mass with him for the young adults of our two dioceses, during which I preached a quite forgettable homily. After Holy Communion, the Cardinal walked to the pulpit and offered some unforgettable, off-the-cuff, closing remarks. One echoes within me to this day: "The only thing we take with us when we die is what we have given away."

I pondered those words for a long time, and over the past few weeks, as he neared death, I became aware of similar remarks he put to paper through the years. He was fond of reminding us that our relationships with the Lord and with each other are all that endure — all else goes to the grave. He concludes the foreword of his forthcoming book, *A Godly Humanism: Clarifying the Hope that Lies Within*, with familiar thoughts:

> Pope Francis often contrasts our planning with God's providence. God is a God of surprises, Pope Francis explains, and the final horizon is God's infinite love. It can never be completely

responded to; but as the years here go shorter, it fills in with the realization that, just as we pray to see God face to face, so God wants to see us face to face. We give him our time, which is all that we have, and he takes the gift and calls us when he is ready to do so.

"The only thing we take with us when we die is what we have given away … the only things that endure are our relationships with God and with others … we give him all that we have, and he takes the gift and calls us when he is ready to do so …" Spontaneously, from the fullness of his heart, Cardinal George gave to the Lord and to us, and both his written words and his unedited afterthoughts brought to light a profound interior life motivated by hope, hope in the Lord.

Doesn't it make sense that an Oblate of Mary Immaculate would ever strive to make an oblation — an offering — a sacrifice — a gift — of his life? And that his oblation would be grounded deeply within, grounded in hope in the one by whose sacrifice alone we are saved?

Yes, perfect sense. But what did Francis George offer to God, and through God, to us? What did he give away?

He offered a life joined to the cross of Christ. When the polio virus attacked him at age thirteen, he learned early and quickly that suffering is not hypothetical but real, that pain is palpable and can have lasting implications. Only the Lord knows the stuff of their many conversations about that dreaded disease and another that would eventually take his life, but there is no doubt that they were spirited conversations — for the crosses of Francis George transformed him both exteriorly and interiorly into a man of compassion for all who suffered, no matter the cause. It was with the Lord's own love, poured out on the cross, that he loved us.

The book of Genesis recounts the night Jacob wrestled with the angel of God until dawn, when the match left him limping after the angel struck and dislocated his hip. Jacob realized something divine had taken place, and he said, "I have seen God face to face." Francis George's own lifelong wrestling in a body struck by polio gave him lasting insight into the mystery of the cross, through a wound that was somehow not just his but also Christ's.

He offered a life of faith, conviction, and courage. In the end, all of us need a rock foundation. Otherwise, as the Lord said, when the rains and winds come and buffet our house, we cannot stand. With heart and soul and both legs firmly planted in the Lord, Francis George lived a faith-filled life grounded in the conviction that, quite simply, God is everything. When one is convinced — deeply committed to a truth — then that truth becomes the guide and arbiter of every aspect of his life. The Cardinal's faith was simple, direct, without pretense or embarrassment, spontaneous, bold, profound, and even childlike. He was so utterly a Christian, so utterly a priest, that no circumstance or setting would have seemed to him inappropriate to give witness to Christ. He was convinced, as St. Paul was, that God is for us in a complete and uncompromising way, and that nothing — nothing at all — will be able to separate us from the love of God in Christ Jesus our Lord. Thus convinced, how could he not give witness to Christ everywhere, from the pulpit to the public square?

He offered a soul devoted to prayer. If God is everything, then prayer becomes one's lifeline. Prayer in solitude, unseen, at odd hours and at all hours. Prayer in common, with brother bishops and priests and deacons and religious and all the faithful of the Archdiocese. Prayer with those who have been harmed by the Church. Christ's own prayer in the sacraments, especially the Holy Eucharist and the Sacrament of Penance. For Cardinal George, prayer was the integrating factor of the Christian life, through which his relationship with God was nourished, sustained, and bore fruit both in love and in intellectual pursuit of the truth. Make no mistake, the homilies he preached, the classes he taught, and the pastoral care he gave flowed gently and compellingly from a life devoted to prayer. That is to say: All these things flowed from God through the friend and minister of God, Francis George, to us.

He offered a brilliant mind in love with God. No one could ever dispute the extraordinary intellectual gifts God gave Francis George, nor could one ever dispute the enthusiasm with which he put those gifts to work for the good of the Church and the world. I often consoled myself with the thought that though I could never have written the books he wrote, or prepared the talks he gave, I could understand them — but even that understanding came from his keen ability to communicate clearly what he believed. When a mind is in love with God, the pursuit of truth flows effortlessly along the vital relationship between faith and reason. When the pursuit of truth is fueled by a life of prayer, it is undertaken in communion with Christ, the Wisdom of God. And when one is joined to Christ, the Savior of the world, then the beauty and mystery of the world become the object of one's love. For whom and what Christ loves, the mind given to Christ loves.

He offered a vision of the New Jerusalem. As an Oblate, Francis George yearned for a life of mission, yearned to be sent wherever and to whomever the Lord would have him go. With an acute sense of God's infinite love for the human person and humanity as a whole, he saw in human culture the traces of God's handiwork and thus a doorway to God himself. The connection between faith and culture would fascinate him his entire life. Enlightened by prayer and love, impelled by the Christian vocation to evangelize, made bold and strong by the fire of the Holy Spirit, it took him literally around the world. In the vision of a New Jerusalem where God is all in all, Francis George saw the Church as a living witness in every human circumstance, whether frustratingly mundane or bewilderingly tragic. For where human life is found, there Christ desires to dwell in his Church, loving, healing, teaching, listening, feeding, leading, accompanying, giving to drink from a well that will never go dry. Since the earth is also God's creation, and since we humans, the crown of that creation, cannot save ourselves, Christ makes all things new through the Church, the New Jerusalem.

As Cardinal George preached one Easter Sunday:

We see only the results of faith and hope and love, but we live in our deepest reality when we are in their grasp. Sts. Mary Magdalene, Peter and John, when they were coming to believe but still not fully understanding, ran to the place where they learned to believe, to the person in whom they placed their hope, to the beloved Lord who shows us that revealed truth and self-sacrificing love are more real, more trustworthy, than anything else. If the earth is our mother, then the grave is our home and the world is a closed system turned in on itself. [But] if Christ is risen from the grave and the Church is our mother, then our destiny reaches beyond space and time, beyond what can be measured and controlled. And therein lies our hope.

From his heart's abundance flowed not only his words, but also his very life's oblation. What did Cardinal George offer to the Lord, what did he give away? He offered a life joined to the cross of Christ; a life of faith, hope, conviction, and courage; a soul devoted to prayer; a brilliant mind in love with God; a vision of the New Jerusalem. Because he gave these things and more away, he took them with him to meet the Lord.

He was uncomfortable with questions about his legacy because they were questions about himself. He responded to them by suggesting that you and I are his legacy, because everything he gave us was not his at all, but the living truth of Christ, the way, the truth, the life. St. Augustine once preached, in sober prose reminiscent of Cardinal George's own style, "Such is the topic, as I have presented it, for our inquiry and discussion. ... If I lack either the time or the ability to study the implications of so profound a mystery, he who speaks within you even when I am not here will teach you better; it is he whom you contemplate with devotion, whom you have welcomed into your hearts, whose temples you have become" (*Sermo* 293).

What Francis George received, he handed on to us. So has it ever been in the Church, and so shall it ever be, now through you and me.

His Eminence Francis Eugene Cardinal George, Oblate of Mary Immaculate, Eighth Archbishop of Chicago. Photo courtesy of Jeff Ebert, Ebert Studio, Oak Park, Illinois

Top: Francis George as a baby, age nine months. Bottom: St. Pascal altar boy, age thirteen. Right: First Holy Communion, May 6, 1945 — when he first heard the call to priesthood. Photos courtesy of Margaret Cain

The Holy Family of Nazareth as painted by a teenage Francis George as a wedding present for his sister, Margaret, and her husband, Jim, in 1952. Photo by Michael R. Heinlein

Top left: Francis George's 8th grade graduation, 1951; top right: Father George with Bishop Raymond Hillinger after his ordination to the priesthood, December 21, 1963. Bottom: Father George with Father Fernand Jetté, O.M.I. (left) following the 1974 General Chapter. Photos courtesy of Margaret Cain

Top: A visual elaboration of Cardinal George's episcopal motto by Daniel Mitsui, 2013. Courtesy of Daniel Mitsui. Used with permission. | Bottom left: Fifth Bishop of Yakima, 1990. Photo courtesy of Margaret Cain | Bottom right: Francis George greeting his sister, Margaret, at his installation as eighth Archbishop of Chicago. Photo courtesy of Karen Callaway/CNS

Pope John Paul II creates Francis Eugene George, O.M.I., a Cardinal Priest of the Holy Roman Church at the consistory in St. Peter's Square on February 21, 1998. Photo courtesy of Vatican Media

Top: Young people gather in Rome to hear a catechesis from Cardinal George at World Youth Day in 2000. Photo courtesy of Nancy Wiechec/CNS. | Bottom: Cardinal George, while bishops' conference president, greets Pope Benedict XVI in October 2008. Photo courtesy of Vatican Media

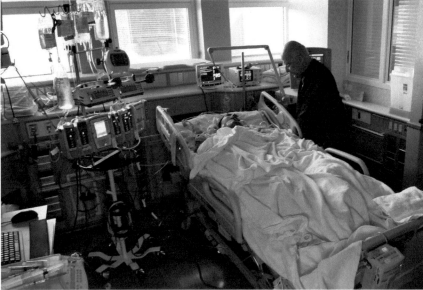

Top: Cardinal George celebrates Christmas Mass with the inmates at Cook County Jail, 2006. Photo courtesy of Brian Jackson/*Chicago Sun-Times* | Bottom: Cardinal George visits the pediatric intensive care unit of Children's Memorial Hospital, Chicago, Christmas 2011. Photo courtesy of *Chicago Sun-Times*

Top: Cardinal George reverences his episcopal pectoral cross at the end of a long day in 2008. Photo courtesy of *Chicago Tribune*/TCA | Bottom: Cardinal George kneels in prayer as the College of Cardinals waits for a Eucharistic prayer service to begin, just ahead of the 2013 conclave. Photo courtesy of Paul Haring/CNS

Cardinal George, president of the United States Conference of Catholic Bishops from 2007 to 2010, celebrates Mass on the opening day of the bishops' 2009 annual fall meeting in Baltimore. Photo courtesy of Bob Roller/CNS

Top: Cardinal George delivers an address on democracy and secularism at the Library of Congress in 2007. Photo courtesy of Nancy Wiechec/CNS | Bottom: Cardinal George places a flower atop a box containing the remains of unborn children after presiding over a proper burial in 2012. Photo courtesy of *Chicago Sun-Times*

Ever ready to evangelize the culture, Cardinal George attends a baseball game at Chicago's Wrigley Field in 2003. Photo by Richard A. Chapman/*Chicago Sun-Times*

Top: Cardinal George was a surprise guest conductor for the Mormon Tabernacle Choir at the Ravinia Music Festival in 2007. Photo courtesy of Jim Steere/Ravinia Festival | Bottom: Cardinal George greets Pope Francis after participating in the 2013 papal conclave. Photo courtesy of Vatican Media

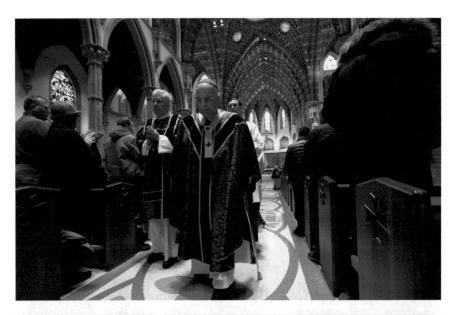

Top: George leaves his final public Mass as Archbishop of Chicago on crutches —
reminiscent of his departure from Chicago in 1951 Photo courtesy of *Chicago Tribune*/TCA
| Bottom: The faithful frequently venerated Cardinal George's remains as they laid
in repose for several days ahead of his 2015 funeral. Photo courtesy of Chris Walker/*Chicago
Tribune* via AP, Pool

Archbishop Roger L. Schwietz, O.M.I., bids farewell to his longtime friend in the name of the Church on April 23, 2015. Photo courtesy of John Smierciak

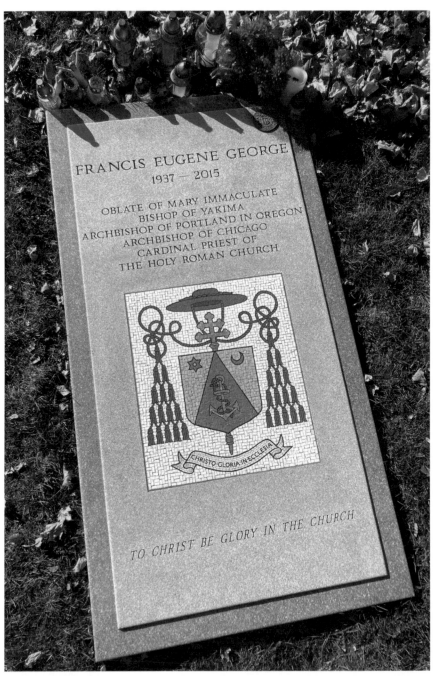

FRANCIS EUGENE GEORGE
1937 — 2015

OBLATE OF MARY IMMACULATE
BISHOP OF YAKIMA
ARCHBISHOP OF PORTLAND IN OREGON
ARCHBISHOP OF CHICAGO
CARDINAL PRIEST OF
THE HOLY ROMAN CHURCH

CHRISTO GLORIA IN ECCLESIA

TO CHRIST BE GLORY IN THE CHURCH

Ledger stone atop Cardinal George's grave, in his family plot, at All Saints Cemetery in Des Plaines, Illinois. Photo courtesy of Joseph G. Heinlein

Notes

ONE: From the Beginning

1. From "Little Gidding," from *Four Quartets* by T. S. Eliot. Copyright© 1936 by Houghton Mifflin Harcourt Publishing Company, renewed 1964 by T. S. Eliot. Copyright© 1940, 1941, 1942 by T.S. Eliot, renewed 1968, 1969, 1970 by Esme Valerie Eliot. Used by permission of HarperCollins Publishers.

2. Tim Unsworth, "Portland's George Goes Back to Chicago," *National Catholic Reporter*, April 18, 1997.

3. "New Chicago Archbishop Recalls Roots in Windy City," Catholic News Service, April 9, 1997.

4. E. L. Kummerer, Jr., *From Prairie to Parish: The First 100 Years of Saint Pascal Church*, rev. ed. (Chicago: self-pub., 2014), 122.

5. George's immediate ancestors on his maternal side of the family lived in the area surrounding Lexington, Kentucky, specifically to the city's northeast: predominately in Bourbon, Harrison, and Nicholas counties.

6. "Manners & Morals: The Jovial Gorilla," *Time*, June 26, 1950.

7. Kummerer, *From Prairie to Parish*, 111.

8. This and the following three quotations are from Francis E. George, "Address at St. Joseph Seminary and Newman Theological College in Edmonton, Canada" (unpublished manuscript, September 22, 2009), provided to the Author by Rev. Daniel A. Flens when he was trustee of the Francis E. George 2006 Living Trust. Hereinafter, all citations from materials provided to the author by the Trust will be cited as "Private Collection."

9. "New Chicago Archbishop Recalls Roots in Windy City," Catholic News Service, April 9, 1997.

10. Kummerer, *From Prairie to Parish*, 212.

11. "A Portrait of Chicago's New Archbishop as a Young Man," *The New World*, May 2, 1997, 5.

12. Kummerer, *From Prairie to Parish*, 112.

13. Francis E. George, "Our Sunday Visitor Centennial Symposium" (unpublished manuscript, September 28, 2012), Private Collection.

14. Kummerer, *From Prairie to Parish*, 111.

15. This and the following two quotations are from "They Knew Him Back When," *Catholic New World*, April 29–May 12, 2007, 21b.

16. "New Chicago Archbishop Recalls Roots in Windy City," Catholic News Service, April 9, 1997.

17. This and the following three quotations are from "A Friend for Life: Archbishop Has Kept Up Relationships with Friends, Teachers from St. Pascal," *The New World*, May 2, 1997, 9.

18. Kummerer, *From Prairie to Parish*, 213.

19. Louise Kiernan, "From 1st Grade, a Man Made for the Cloth," *Chicago Tribune*, April 9, 1997.

20. Francis E. George, *Guard and Tackle*, November 6, 1951.

21. "A Portrait of Chicago's New Archbishop as a Young Man," *The New World*, May 2, 1997, 5.

22. Francis E. George, "Address at National Catholic Bioethics Center Workshop for Bishops in Dallas, Texas" (unpublished manuscript, February 4, 2003), Private Collection.

23. This and the following quotation are from Kummerer, *From Prairie to Parish*, 121.

24. Francis E. George, "Address at National Conference of Diocesan Vocation Directors" (unpublished manuscript, September 6, 2010), Private Collection.

25. Francis E. George, "Through Christ's cross, suffering can bring spiritual growth," *Catholic Sentinel*, February 14, 1997.

26. "The Story of St. James' Stations of the Cross," on official website of St. James the Greater Parish, Sauk Village, IL, https://www.saintjamesthegreater.org/stations.html.

27. "In Catechesis Session, Cardinal George Urges Youth to Stay Faithful," Catholic News Service, August 17, 2005.

28. Kummerer, *From Prairie to Parish*, 121.

29. The letters are retained by the Joseph Cardinal Bernardin Archives and Records Center of the Archdiocese of Chicago.

30. George's own copies of the St. Pascal school newspaper are retained by the Joseph Cardinal Bernardin Archives and Records Center of the Archdiocese of Chicago.

31. This letter is retained by the Joseph Cardinal Bernardin Archives and Records Center of the Archdiocese of Chicago.

32. Kiernan, "From 1ˢᵗ Grade, a Man Made for The Cloth," *Chicago Tribune*, April 9, 1997.

TWO: Formation for Priesthood

1. Francis E. George, interview by Office of Radio and Television of the Archdiocese of Chicago, December 19, 2013, https://www.youtube.com/watch?v=ucYvN4jbTBk.

2. This document is located at the Joseph Cardinal Bernardin Archives and Records Center of the Archdiocese of Chicago.

3. Pichotta had been, in the view of many, abruptly and controversially dismissed from St. Henry's in 1968. George came to his defense in an April 22, 1968, letter to his provincial Fr. Leo Figge: "I just don't see how we can simply dismiss a man who has helped us run St. Henry's for eighteen years, whose chances of getting another job are minimal at his age, whose pension amounts only to 17 dollars a month. ... This is a public decision. As such it's open to

public review, and it's infantile to think it can be just swept under the rug with a curt letter of dismissal."

4. Francis E. George, *A Godly Humanism: Clarifying the Hope that Lies Within* (Washington, DC: The Catholic University of America Press, 2015), x.

5. George, *A Godly Humanism*, 20–21.

6. Copies of the journal are retained by the Archives of the United States Province of the Missionary Oblates of Mary Immaculate.

7. Francis E. George, "Kenrick Lecture at Kenrick-Glennon Seminary in St. Louis" (unpublished manuscript, March 22, 2000), Private Collection.

8. George's formation applications, records and evaluations are retained by the Archives of the United States Province of the Missionary Oblates of Mary Immaculate.

9. This quotation was attributed to George by Archbishop J. Peter Sartain in his homily at George's funeral Mass at Holy Name Cathedral, Chicago on April 23, 2015.

10. Orlando Quevedo, "Comments on Cardinal George's Death," April 27, 2015.

THREE: A Priest of Jesus Christ

1. Yvon Beaudoin, *Fernand Jetté, O.M.I.: A Wise Leader at a Critical Time* (Rome: 2012), 42.

2. Kiernan, "From 1st Grade, a Man Made for The Cloth," *Chicago Tribune*, April 9, 1997.

3. Steve Mills and Louise Kiernan, "The Reluctant Archbishop: George's Beliefs Take a Right Turn in Rome," *Chicago Tribune*, May 8, 1997.

4. This and the following five quotations are from Francis E. George's remarks at the University of Ottawa on September 19, 2008, Private Collection.

5. When he finished his thesis in 1970, George submitted it to the faculty of the University of Ottawa, where he had been a student during his residency in Ottawa. He consistently referred to that institution as his alma mater, since that is where he attended and studied. However, the ecclesiastical faculty was by then separate and distinct from the University of Ottawa, and known as St. Paul University. This split led to hard feelings among some Oblates at relinquishing

the University of Ottawa and creating St. Paul's.

6. Francis E. George, "On Mother's Day," The Cardinal's Column, *Catholic New World*, May 12, 2002.

7. Francine Knowles, "Cardinal George Reflects on 50 Years as Priest," *Chicago Sun-Times*, December 19, 2013.

8. Bishop Hillinger was a vocal advocate for racial justice in his time, and even declared that anyone who opposed the Church's teaching on this issue is "simply not Catholic." (See "Religion: Catholics & Negroes," *Time*, September 15, 1958.)

9. Knowles, "Cardinal George Reflects on 50 Years as Priest," *Chicago Sun-Times*, December 19, 2013.

10. Francis E. George, "Homily at the First Mass of Father Roger Schwietz, O.M.I." (unpublished manuscript, 1968), provided to the author by Archbishop Roger L. Schwietz, O.M.I.

11. Mills and Kiernan, "The Reluctant Archbishop," *Chicago Tribune*, May 8, 1997.

FOUR: Priest, Philosopher, and Professor

1. Francis E. George, "Civic Responsibility for a New Millennium," The Cardinal's Column, *Catholic New World*, November 7, 1999.

2. Francis E. George, address to Chicago priests, May 15, 2007, Private Collection.

3. This and the following two quotations are from Francis E. George, "Address at Purdue University: The Mission of a Catholic Scholar at a Secular Campus," October 21, 2005, Private Collection.

4. Francis E. George, address to Chicago priests, May 15, 2007, Private Collection.

5. This extended quotation and the following quotation are from Francis E. George, address to Chicago priests, May 15, 2007, Private Collection.

6. A copy of the manuscript is retained by the Archives of the United States Province of the Missionary Oblates of Mary Immaculate.

7. "Tulane Graduate Named Archbishop of Chicago," *Tulane Hullabaloo*, April 18, 1997.

8. "Man Of Faith," *Tulanian*, Summer 1999.

9. Francis E. George, "Society and Experience: A Critical Examination of the Social Philosophies of Royce, Mead and Sellars," abstract (PhD diss., Tulane University, 1969).

10. Mills and Kiernan, "The Reluctant Archbishop," *Chicago Tribune*, May 8, 1997.

11. This and the following two quotations are from "Conciliator Takes Main Stage in Chicago," *National Catholic Reporter*, April 25, 1997.

12. Mills and Kiernan, "The Reluctant Archbishop," *Chicago Tribune*, May 8, 1997.

13. The undated original is retained by the Archives of the United States Province of the Missionary Oblates of Mary Immaculate.

14. A copy of this document is retained by the Archives of the United States Province of the Missionary Oblates of Mary Immaculate.

15. "'Verbal abuse, ostracism' Prompted Fr. Linn's Letter," *The Creightonian*, October 10, 1969.

16. This and the following two quotations are from "Racism, Communication Theme of Convocation," *The Creightonian*, October 10, 1969.

17. Francis E. George, "Seminar on Black Student Results in Soul-Searching," *The Creightonian,* February 6, 1970.

18. The letter is retained by the Joseph Cardinal Bernardin Archives and Records Center of the Archdiocese of Chicago.

19. An original copy of this text is retained by the Joseph Cardinal Bernardin Archives and Records Center of the Archdiocese of Chicago.

FIVE: Oblate Leadership

1. This and the following two quotations are from General Administration of the Missionary Oblates of Mary Immaculate, *OMI Information* No. 75, June 2, 1972.

2. This and other quotations from George during the proceedings of the 1972 General Chapter of the Missionary Oblates of Mary Immaculate, unless otherwise noted, are retained in the congregation's General Archives.

3. George's private comments during the 1972 General Chapter, which are

herein quoted, are contained in his calendar, which includes daily notes. It is retained by the Joseph Cardinal Bernardin Archives and Records Center of the Archdiocese of Chicago.

4. Notes in the margin of a calendar Cardinal George kept during the 1972 Chapter, which is retained at the Joseph Cardinal Bernardin Archives and Records Center of the Archdiocese of Chicago.

5. More information on the difficulties at the end of Hanley's tenure as superior general may be found in Yvon Beaudoin, *Fernand Jetté, O.M.I.: A Wise Leader at a Critical Time* (Rome: 2012), 71–73.

6. Newsletters of the suppressed Central Province of the Missionary Oblates of Mary Immaculate are retained by the Archives of the United States Province of the congregation.

7. "No. 2 Oblate Official Wants Order's Spirit of Poverty Renewed," *Minneapolis Star*, January 18, 1975.

8. Cardinal Francis George, remarks at September 10, 2013, O.M.I. Jubilee celebration, Private Collection.

9. Father Jetté is quoted in the "Letter from the 1974 Capitulars to All Their Brother-Oblates" sent out at the conclusion of the 1974 General Chapter of the Missionary Oblates of Mary Immaculate.

10. Father Jetté's opening address and other comments during the proceedings of the 1974 General Chapter of the Missionary Oblates of Mary Immaculate, unless otherwise noted, are retained in the congregation's General Archives.

11. George's public comments during the proceedings of the 1974 General Chapter of the Missionary Oblates of Mary Immaculate, unless otherwise noted, are retained in the congregation's General Archives.

12. Fernand Jetté, Diary 1973–1974 (Archives Deschâtelets, Ottawa), 307, quoted in Yvon Beaudoin, *Fernand Jetté, O.M.I.: A Wise Leader at a Critical Time* (Rome: 2012), 81.

13. "No. 2 Oblate Official Wants Order's Spirit of Poverty Renewed," *Minneapolis Star*, January 18, 1975.

SIX: Oblate Vicar General

1. Francis E. George, "On Death and Other Limitations," The Cardinal's Col-

umn, *Catholic New World*, August 26, 2012.

2. These and the following four quotations are from Francis E. George, re-marks at September 10, 2013, O.M.I. Jubilee celebration, Private Collection.

3. This text is retained by the Joseph Cardinal Bernardin Archives and Re-cords Center of the Archdiocese of Chicago.

4. Francis E. George, remarks at September 10, 2013, O.M.I. Jubilee celebra-tion, Private Collection.

5. Paul VI, *Perfectae Caritatis*, 2, October 28, 1965, vatican.va.

6. Francis E. George, "Founding Founderology," *Review for Religious* 36, no. 1, January 1977, 40–48.

7. This and the following two quotations are from General Administration of the Missionary Oblates of Mary Immaculate, *OMI Documentation* no. 62, De-cember 15, 1975.

8. *OMI Documentation* no. 104, October 1981.

9. This and the following six quotations are from Francis E. George, "Oblate Spirituality and Oblate Prayer," *OMI Documentation* no. 164, April 1989.

10. *OMI Documentation* no. 130, December 1984.

11. *OMI Documentation* no. 79, February 1, 1978.

12. This and the following five quotations from Cardinal Francis George, homily at the May 23, 2009, ordination of Chicago priests, Private Collection.

13. Several such items of correspondence were located by the author among Francis E. George's personal items at the Joseph Cardinal Bernardin Archives and Records Center of the Archdiocese of Chicago in October 2018, including the following five quotations.

14. Francis E. George, "The Eucharist in the Church and the World" (Rome: International Eucharistic Congress, June 20, 2000).

15. "Bishop Gives Away a Wish," First Person, *Yakima Herald Republic*, April 12, 1992.

16. This and the following quote from Francis E. George, "On Death and Other Limitations," The Cardinal's Column, *Catholic New World*, August 26, 2012.

17. Francis E. George, Homily 1980 General Chapter of the Missionary Oblates of Mary Immaculate (unpublished manuscript, 1980), retained by the

Joseph Cardinal Bernardin Archives and Records Center of the Archdiocese of Chicago.

SEVEN: Returning to America

1. Francis E. George, "Evangelizing Our Culture," in *The New Evangelization*, ed. Steven Boguslawski and Ralph Martin (New York: Paulist Press, 2008), 44.

2. Mills and Kiernan, "The Reluctant Archbishop," *Chicago Tribune*, May 8, 1997.

3. Francis E. George, *Inculturation and Ecclesial Communion: Culture and Church in the Teaching of Pope John Paul II* (Rome: Urbaniana University Press, 1990).

4. Mills and Kiernan, "The Reluctant Archbishop," *Chicago Tribune*, May 8, 1997.

5. Francis E. George, "Self Gift in Generative Love: Priests Continue Jesus' Mission to Reveal the Father," (unpublished manuscript: Institute for Priestly Formation Symposium, Mount Saint Mary's Seminary, March 14, 2003), Private Collection.

6. Roger J. Landry, "The Difference God Made Through Francis Cardinal George," *Boston Pilot*, April 21, 2015.

7. "The Good Bishop," *Yakima Herald-Republic*, May 26, 1996.

8. "Bishop Gives Away a Wish," First Person, *Yakima Herald-Republic*, April 12, 1992.

EIGHT: A Missionary Bishop

1. "Cardinal George Talks About His Ministry, Life and Facing Death," *Catholic New World*, November 16–29, 2014.

2. Letter retained by the Archives of the Diocese of Yakima.

3. Francis E. George, "Address: Central Washington Catholic Foundation" (unpublished manuscript, September 19, 2009), Private Collection.

4. "Bishop of Yakima Ordained," *The Progress*, September 27, 1990.

5. Francis E. George, "Address to Bridges to the Future Conference at University of Denver" (unpublished manuscript, March 31, 2003), Private Collection.

6. "Bishop Gives Away a Wish," First Person, *Yakima Herald-Republic*, April

12, 1992.

7. Francis E. George, "State's Gay Rights Proposal Bad Law With Good Intent," *Seattle Post-Intelligencer*, March 16, 1994.

8. Francis E. George, "Coverage of Yakima Bishop's Address 'Misleading,'" Letters, *Catholic Northwest Progress*, November 17, 1994.

9. Francis E. George, "Oblate Interest," *Mission/Unity* no. 30, October 1994.

10. Francis E. George, "On Catholicism," Letters to the Editor, *Yakima Herald-Republic*, n.d.

11. "Hispanics in the Valley: Yakima Bishop Calls for Hospitality, Not Hostility," *Yakima Herald-Republic,* March 25, 1994.

12. Francis E. George, "Address at Cor Unum Conference on Charity" (unpublished manuscript, January 24, 2006), Private Collection.

13. Francis E. George, "Labor Day 2013: We Have a Dream," The Cardinal's Column, *Catholic New World*, September 1–14, 2013.

14. George, "Address at Cor Unum Conference on Charity, Rome," 2006, Private Collection.

15. Francis E. George, "Labor Day 2013: We Have a Dream," 2013.

16. Mark O'Keefe , "Portland Gains an Archbishop," *Oregonian*, May 1, 1996.

17. "Bishop George is a Tough Act to Follow," Editorial, *Yakima Herald-Republic*, May 2, 1996.

18. Francis E. George, "From the Bishop," *Central Washington Catholic*, May-June 1996.

19. Sister Maria Ybarra, "The Gentleman from the East," *Central Washington Catholic*, May-June 1996.

20. This and the next four quotations are from O'Keefe, "Portland Gains an Archbishop," *Oregonian*, May 1, 1996.

21. Francis E. George, "Through Christ's Cross, Suffering Can Bring Spiritual Growth," *Catholic Sentinel*, February 13, 1997.

22. Ed Langlois, "In Oregon, Archbishop Hoped to Transform Culture," *Catholic Sentinel*, April 10, 1997.

23. Ed Langlois, "New Archbishop Pledges to Work for Disabled, Excluded," *Catholic Sentinel*, May 30, 1996.

24. This and the following five quotations are from Langlois, "New Arch-

bishop Pledges to Work for Disabled, Excluded," 1996.

25. Francis E. George, "Archbishop Looks Forward to Meeting, Travel to Rome, Lourdes," *Catholic Sentinel*, June 21, 1996.

26. Francis E. George, "Pope, Patriarch's Representative Pray for Christian Unity," *Catholic Sentinel*, July 12, 1996.

27. A full account of this tragic episode can be found in Timothy J. Mockaitis, *The Seal: A Priest's Story* (self pub., 2008).

28. Francis E. George, "State Has No Right to Invade Sacrament," *Catholic Sentinel*, August 23, 1996.

29. This and the following quotation are from "State Has No Right to Invade Sacrament," 1996.

30. Mockaitis, *The Seal: A Priest's Story*, 100.

31. Francis E. George, "Death With Faith Makes Death a Friend," *Catholic Sentinel*, November 29, 1996.

32. "Possible Successors to Cardinal Bernardin," *Chicago Tribune*, November 15, 1996.

33. Steve Kloehn, "Choice of Successor to Affect Church in U.S.," *Chicago Tribune*, November 15, 1996.

34. This and the following quotation are from Secretariat of State of the Holy See, "Report on the Holy See's Institutional Knowledge and Decision-Making Related to Former Cardinal Theodore Edgar McCarrick," November 10, 2020, 127.

35. Ibid., 128.

36. Mark O'Keefe, "Portland Archbishop Will Lead Chicago Archdiocese," *Oregonian*, April 9, 1997.

37. Neil Steinberg, "Portland's Francis George is Bernardin's Successor," *Chicago Sun-Times*, April 8, 1997.

38. "Archbishop Says He'll Leave Portland With Heavy Heart," Catholic News Service, April 16, 1997.

39. Hazel Whitman, "Portland Archdiocese Bids Farewell to Archbishop George," *Catholic Sentinel*, April 25, 1997.

40. "Archbishop Says He'll Leave Portland With Heavy Heart," Catholic News Service, April 16, 1997.

41. "Cardinal's Impact Will Be Felt for Years to Come, Says Portland Priest," Catholic News Service, April 21, 2015.

NINE: Getting to Know the Place

1. Francis E. George, "The Bishop's Sacramentality," Origins, Catholic News Service, November 8, 2001.

2. This and the following three quotations are from "Overflow Crowd Greets Archbishop George at His Boyhood Parish," Catholic News Service, July 2, 1997.

3. "Archbishop Says He'll Leave Portland With Heavy Heart," Catholic News Service, April 16, 1997.

4. Gustav Niebuhr, "Conservative Intellectual Picked as New Archbishop of Chicago," *New York Times*, April 9, 1997.

5. Russell Shaw, "With a New Archbishop, What's Next in Chicago?," *Our Sunday Visitor*, April 27, 1997.

6. This and the following two quotations are from "Archbishop Addresses Moral Issues, Stresses Church Open to All," Catholic News Service, September 30, 1997.

7. This and the following three quotations are from "Conservative Intellectual Picked as New Archbishop of Chicago," 1997.

8. This and the following two quotations are from "Archbishop George Brings Mind and Heart," *National Catholic Register*, April 27–May 3, 1997.

9. This and the following quotation are from Paul Likoudis, "A Priest-Scholar Takes the Helm," *The Wanderer*, April 17, 1997.

10. "'I'll Work to become Your Brother,' New Leader Says," *Chicago Sun-Times*, May 7, 1997.

11. "Schönborn, Ratzinger, and Groër," *Leon J. Podles' Dialogue*, March 28, 2010, http://www.podles.org/dialogue/schonborn-ratzinger-and-groer-309.htm.

12. David Gibson, "Pope Francis Has a Long To-Do List, and It Starts With the Curia," Religion News Service, March 14, 2013.

13. Francis E. George, Homily at Mass of Installation as Eighth Archbishop of Chicago, May 7, 1997, O.M.I. General Archives.

14. Francis E. George, "The Cathedral as the Seat of Episcopal Ministry," Cathedral of St. James, Brooklyn (unpublished manuscript, June 4, 1999), Private

Collection.

15. Francis E. George, "To Christ be Glory in the Church," The Cardinal's Column, *Catholic New World*, April 27, 2007.

16. Francis E. George, address to Chicago priests, April 11, 2006, Private Collection.

17. Francis E. George, "Knowing the Place for the First Time," The Cardinal's Column, *Catholic New World*, April 28, 2002.

18. This and the next quotation are from Francis E. George, "Is Corruption a Sin?," The Cardinal's Column, *Catholic New World*, March 29, 2009.

19. This and the next quotation are from Francis E. George, "Penance, Mission, Mary: The Jubilee for Bishops," The Cardinal's Column, *Catholic New World*, October 15, 2000.

20. Francis E. George, "Mission and Money," The Cardinal's Column, *Catholic New World*, November 6, 2005.

21. This and the following quotation are from Francis E. George, Address to Priests' Convocation on June 19, 2014, Private Collection.

22. Francis E. George, "To Christ be Glory in the Church," The Cardinal's Column, *Catholic New World*, August 6, 2006.

23. This and the next two quotations are from Francis E. George, "To Christ be Glory in the Church," The Cardinal's Column, *Catholic New World*, August 6, 2006.

24. Handwritten Notes, 1999–August 2013, in a spiral notebook found in Cardinal George's personal materials in October 2018, retained by the Archdiocese of Chicago's Joseph Cardinal Bernardin Archives and Records Center of the Archdiocese of Chicago. Henceforth referred to as "Handwritten Notes."

25. This and the following quotation are from "With a New Archbishop, What's Next in Chicago?," *Our Sunday Visitor*, April 27, 1997.

26. This and the following quotation are from "Chicago Archbishop Addresses Priests at Prayer Service," Catholic News Service, May 8, 1997.

27. Gustav Niebuhr, "Conservative Intellectual Picked as New Archbishop of Chicago," *New York Times*, April 9, 1997.

28. This and the following quotation are from Andrew M. Greeley, *Furthermore! Memories of a Parish Priest* (New York: Tom Doherty and Associates,

1999), 298–299.

29. This and the following two quotations are from John L. Allen, Jr., "Still Telling Stories of Sin, Sex and Redemption," *National Catholic Reporter*, March 19, 1999.

30. "Chicago Archbishop Addresses Priests at Prayer Service," Catholic News Service, May 8, 1997.

31. "Archbishop George Welcomes Priests to His New Home," Catholic News Service, April 25, 1997.

32. This and the following five quotations are from Greeley, *Furthermore! Memories of a Parish Priest,* 1999, 80.

33. This and the following quotation are from "Archbishop George Welcomes Priests to His New Home," 1997.

34. This and the following quotation are from Greeley, *Furthermore! Memories of a Parish Priest,* 1999, 80.

35. Pam Belluck, "Priests' Missive Reveal Tensions in Chicago Archdiocese," *New York Times*, November 14, 1997.

36. Francis E. George, "Liturgy and Unity," The Cardinal's Column, *Catholic New World*, May 9, 2004.

37. "A Conversation with Roman Catholic Archbishop Francis George," Religion News Service, May 1997.

38. Francis E. George, "How Liberalism Fails the Church," *Commonweal*, June 17, 2004.

39. This and the following three quotations are from "Special Edition: Canons Regular Salute Francis Cardinal George, O.M.I.," *Via Sacra: Official Newsletter for the Canons Regular of Saint John Cantius* vol. XVI, May 2015.

40. This and the following quotation are from Francis E. George, "The Universal Call to Holiness: Jubilee and Eucharist," The Cardinal's Column, *Catholic New World*, December 12, 1999.

41. This and the next eleven quotations are from "Cardinal numbers," *Chicago Sun-Times*, March 10, 2002.

42. This and the next two quotations are from Pam Belluck, "Priests' Missive Reveal Tensions in Chicago Archdiocese," 1997.

43. This and the next four quotations are from Andrew M. Greeley, "In Sell-

ers' Market, Chicago's Priests are Emboldened," Religion News Service, 1997.

44. This and the next three quotations are from Pam Belluck, "Priests' Missive Reveal Tensions in Chicago Archdiocese," 1997.

45. This and the following quotation are from "Archbishop George Tells Priests: 'I Am Your Bishop,'" *The Wanderer*, May 15, 1997.

46. Francis E. George, "Pilgrimage of Love: Ministry of the Bishop and his Life with God," The Cardinal's Column, *Catholic New World*, February 14, 1999.

47. This and the following quotation are from Schaeffer, "Conciliator Takes Main Stage in Chicago," *National Catholic Reporter*, April 25, 1997.

TEN: Governing and Suffering in Crisis

1. Francis E. George, *The Difference God Makes: A Catholic Vision of Faith, Communion and Culture* (New York: Crossroad Publishing, 2009), 204–205.

2. Francis E. George, "The Body of Christ and the Spring Meeting of the U.S. Catholic Bishops," The Cardinal's Column, *Catholic New World*, June 9, 2002.

3. Francis E. George, Memo to All Archdiocesan Staff, February 2006, provided to the author by Reverend Daniel A. Flens.

4. This and the following quotations referenced to the 2006 gathering with Chicago priests is from Francis E. George, address to Chicago priests, April 11, 2006, Private Collection.

5. Francis E. George, address to Chicago priests, April 11, 2006, Private Collection.

6. "A Challenge to Cardinal George," Editorial, *Chicago Tribune*, June 2, 2002.

7. This and the following quote are from Francis E. George, "The Body of Christ and the Spring Meeting of the U.S. Catholic Bishops," 2002.

8. Francis E. George, "The Body of Christ and the spring meeting of the U.S. Catholic bishops," The Cardinal's Column, *Catholic New World*, June 9, 2002.

9. This and the following three quotations are from Francis E. George, "On Mother's Day," The Cardinal's Column, *Catholic New World*, May 12, 2002.

10. Francis E. George, "Self Gift in Generative Love: Priests Continue Jesus' Mission to Reveal the Father," (unpublished manuscript: Institute for Priestly Formation Symposium, Mount Saint Mary's Seminary, March 14, 2003), Private Collection.

11. Francis E. George, "Developing Lay Ecclesial Ministry," in *In the Name of the Church: Vocation and Authorization of Lay Ecclesial Ministry*, ed. William J. Cahoy (Collegeville: Liturgical Press), 142.

12. This and the following quotation are from Francis E. George, *The Difference God Makes: A Catholic Vision of Faith, Communion and Culture* (New York: Crossroad Publishing, 2009), 191.

13. This and the following eight quotations are from Handwritten Notes.

14. This and the following twelve quotations are from Handwritten Notes.

15. This and the following two quotations are from Joyce Duriga, "Cardinal George talks about 50 years as a priest," *Catholic New World*, December 22, 2013.

16. Handwritten Notes.

17. This and the following quotation are from Francis E. George, address to Chicago priests, April 11, 2006, Private Collection.

18. Francis E. George, address to Chicago priests, September 10, 2012, Private Collection.

19. Handwritten Notes.

20. This and the next four quotations are from Susan Hogan, "Bishop: I Was More Worried about Priest's Drinking," *Chicago Sun-Times*, November 14, 2007.

21. This and next two quotations from Tim Drake, "Bishop Kicanas Responds," *National Catholic Register*, November 12, 2010.

22. Defenbaugh and Associates' Report for Archdiocese of Chicago, March 20, 2006.

23. Discovery Deposition of Francis Cardinal George (reported by Lisa Marie Regan, January 30, 2008), 81.

24. This and the following quote from "George Takes the Main Stage," *Chicago Tribune*, November 17, 2002.

25. Manya A. Brachear, "Cardinal Lifts the Veil on Abuses," *Chicago Tribune*, August 13, 2008.

26. This and the following two quotations are from Francis E. George, "Finding the Face of Christ: What Kind of Year Will 2006 Be?," The Cardinal's Column, *Catholic New World*, February 19, 2006.

27. This and the following quotations are from Francis E. George, Memo to Priests of the Archdiocese of Chicago, February 2006, provided to the author by

Reverend Daniel A. Flens.

28. Francis E. George, address to Chicago priests, September 10, 2012, Private Collection.

29. This and the following quotation are from Discovery Deposition of Francis Cardinal George (reported by Lisa Marie Regan, January 30, 2008), 136.

30. Francis E. George, "Accountability and Transparency," The Cardinal's Column, *Catholic New World*, January 12, 2014.

31. This and the following three quotations are from Letter from Fr. Andrew Greeley to Cardinal George, February 20, 2006, retained by the Joseph Cardinal Bernardin Archives and Records Center of the Archdiocese of Chicago.

32. This and the following two quotations are from Francis E. George, "Finding the Face of Christ: What Kind of Year Will 2006 Be?," The Cardinal's Column, *Catholic New World*, February 19, 2006.

33. Handwritten Notes.

34. Francis E. George, "Atonement, Reconciliation and Reparation," The Cardinal's Column, *Catholic New World*, October 13–26, 2013.

35. Ibid.

36. George, "Finding the Face of Christ: What Kind of Year Will 2006 Be?," 2006.

37. John Paul II, *Salvifici Doloris*, February 11, 1984, par. 12.

38. Francis E. George, address to Chicago priests, April 11, 2006, Private Collection.

39. Francis E. George, "Participation in the Church and Participation in Political Life: A Matter of Conscience," The Cardinal's Column, *Catholic New World*, September 26, 2004.

40. Handwritten Notes.

41. Francis E. George, "God and Human Suffering," The Cardinal's Column, *Catholic New World*, March 2, 2008.

42. John Paul II, Homily for the Solemnity of Saints Peter and Paul, June 29, 1997.

43. "Pope Gives Pallium to 28, Including Archbishops George, Chaput," Catholic News Service, June 30, 1997.

44. Francis E. George, "The Primacy of Grace: to August 15 from December

8," The Cardinal's Column, *Catholic New World*, August 15, 2004.

45. This and the following quotation are from Francis E. George, "Self-Sacrifice: Lent, Lourdes and Marriage," The Cardinal's Column, *Catholic New World*, February 3, 2008.

46. Francis E. George, "To Christ be Glory in the Church," The Cardinal's Column, *Catholic New World*, April 29, 2007.

47. This and the next quotation are from "First Chicago Mass as Cardinal Caps Busy Week for Archbishop," Catholic News Service, March 9, 1998.

48. Hans Urs Von Balthasar, *Bernanos: An Ecclesial Existence* (San Francisco: Ignatius Press, 1996), 279.

49. "Catholicism Combats Destructive Individualism, Cardinal Says," Catholic News Service, October 8, 2009.

50. "Universities Must Teach Church's Intellectual Tradition," Catholic News Service, January 19, 2012.

51. Duriga, "Cardinal George Talks About 50 Years as A Priest," December 22, 2013.

52. "Cardinal Denies He's Leaving Chicago," *Chicago Tribune*, November 2, 2001.

53. This and the following two quotations are from Handwritten Notes.

54. "Cardinal Francis E. George, "Who Urged 'Zero Tolerance' in Abuse Scandal, Dies at 78," *New York Times*, April 18, 2015.

55. This and the following eight quotations are from Francis E. George, "Address to Priests of the Diocese of Corner Brook: Called to the Cross" (unpublished manuscript, June 29, 2006), Private Collection.

56. Handwritten Notes.

ELEVEN: A Good Neighbor

1. Francis E. George, "Kenrick Lecture at Kenrick-Glennon Seminary in St. Louis" (unpublished manuscript, March 22, 2000), Private Collection.

2. This and the following five quotations are from Francis E. George, Homily at Mass of Installation as Eighth Archbishop of Chicago, May 7, 1997, O.M.I. General Archives.

3. Francis E. George, Homily at Mass of Installation as Eighth Archbishop of

Chicago, May 7, 1997, O.M.I. General Archives.

4. Francis E. George, "Conversations in Spirituality: Religious Dialogue," The Cardinal's Column, *Catholic New World*, February 4, 2007.

5. Cf. Second Vatican Council, Dogmatic Constitution on the Church *Lumen Gentium*, par. 1.

6. These and the next two quotations are from Francis E. George, "The Ecclesiology of Communion: From Jurisdiction to Relationship," in *The New Evangelization: Faith, People, Context and Practice*, ed. Paul Grogan and Kirsteen Kim, (London: Bloomsbury T&T Clark, 2015), 83.

7. Schaeffer, "Conciliator Takes Main Stage in Chicago," *National Catholic Reporter*, April 25, 1997.

8. Francis E. George, "Kenrick Lecture" (2000), Private Collection.

9. This and the following two quotations are from Francis E. George, "Catholic Responsibility and the Unity of All Christians," The Cardinal's Column, *Catholic New World*, January 20, 2002.

10. This and the following quotation are from Francis E. George, "Full Communion: The Week of Prayer for Christian Unity," *Catholic New World*, January 24, 1999.

11. This and the next four quotations are from "Cardinal George on Why Churches Deserve Free Water," Change of Subject blog by *Chicago Tribune*, May 1, 2013, https://blogs.chicagotribune.com/news_columnists_ezorn/2013/05/cardinal-george-on-why-churches-deserve-free-water.html.

12. This and the next three quotations are from Duriga, "Cardinal George Talks About 50 Years as A Priest," Decemeber 22, 2013.

13. Francis E. George, "Presidential Address at the Fall Plenary Assembly of the United States Conference of Catholic Bishops," November 10, 2008.

14. "Cardinal Urges Pro-Life Activists to Speak Out in Love," Catholic News Service, January 21, 2000.

15. Francis E. George, "The Role of the Laity and the Contemporary Cultural Milieu: Address at the Spring Assembly of the United States Conference of Catholic Bishops," June 20, 2003.

16. Laurie Goodstein, "Cardinal Francis E. George, Who Urged 'Zero Tolerance' in Abuse Scandal, Dies at 78," *New York Times*, April 18, 2015.

17. James P. Moroney, "We Lost a Good Priest Today …" Monsignor Moroney's Blog, April 17, 2015, http://msgrmoroney.blogspot.com/2015/04/we-lost -good-priest-today.html.

18. This and the following quotation are from Francis E. George, "On Being 'Fully Funded … in Christ," The Cardinal's Column, *Catholic New World*, January 28, 2001.

19. This and the following quotation are from National Catholic Education Association's Tribute Video honoring George as 2011 Seton Award winner, November 16, 2011, https://www.youtube.com/watch?v=qmCdJED2Rhc.

20. Francis E. George, "Lent: Taking Stock of Our Lives," The Cardinal's Column, *Catholic New World*, March 9–22, 2014.

21. This and the next eight quotations are from Francis E. George, "Pentecost: The Ordination of Priests and the Ministry of Lay People," *Catholic New World*, May 26, 2002.

22. Julia Lieblich, "Slighted Bishop Now With His Brethren," *Chicago Tribune*, March 30, 2001.

23. This and the following quotation are from Julia Lieblich, "Slighted Bishop Now With His Brethren," *Chicago Tribune*, March 30, 2001.

24. "Welcoming 'One of Us,'" *Catholic New World*, May 2, 1997.

25. "Catholics Must Be Present in AIDS Ministry, Archbishop Says," Catholic News Service, July 23, 1997.

26. Facebook account of Ann & Robert H. Lurie Children's Hospital of Chicago, April 23, 2015, https://www.facebook.com/luriechildrens/photos /a.357468387606833.81316.167818016571872/924025074284492/.

27. The entire account of Roeser's interaction with George, except where indicated, quotes from "Chicago's Cardinal Delivers His Greatest Sermon," *The Wanderer*, June 8, 2006.

28. Michael Miner, "Cardinal George and the Dragon," *The Chicago Reader*, April 15, 2010, https://www.chicagoreader.com/chicago/cardinal-frances-george -tom-roeser-catholic-citizens-of-illinois/.

29. Francis E. George, "Respecting Life While Responding to Deadly Attack," The Cardinal's Column, *Catholic New World*, September 30, 2001.

30. This and the following two quotations are from "Cardinal George Criti-

cizes Effectiveness of Death Penalty," Catholic News Service, February 28, 2001.

31. Francis E. George, "The Face of Evil: Demons and Death," The Cardinal's Column, *Catholic New World*, October 1, 2000.

32. This and the following two quotations are from Francis E. George, "He Was Crucified for Our Salvation …," The Cardinal's Column, *Catholic New World*, March 11, 2001.

33. This and the following three quotations are from "Mourning the Loss of Cardinal George," Cure Violence website, April 21, 2015.

34. Francis E. George, "Deporting Illegal Immigrants," The Cardinal's Column, *Catholic New World*, August 12, 2006.

35. This and the following six quotations are from Francis E. George, "Immigrants and the Catholic Church," The Cardinal's Column, *Catholic New World*, August 19, 2001.

36. "Dwell in My Love," *Catholic New World*, April 8, 2001.

37. Francis E. George, "Dwell In My Love: A Pastoral Letter on Racism," April 4, 2001.

38. Francis E. George, "Dwell in My Love," *Catholic New World*, April 8, 2001.

39. This and the following five quotations are from Francis E. George, "Dwell In My Love: A Pastoral Letter on Racism," April 8, 2001.

40. Francis E. George, "Dwell in My Love," *Catholic New World*, April 8, 2001.

41. This and the following five quotations are from Francis E. George, "The Spirit of Unity with God and the Signs of Unity in the Church," The Cardinal's Column, *Catholic New World*, June 6, 2001.

42. Francis E. George, "When the Medium is the Message: Tales of the Southside Catholic Conference," The Cardinal's Column, *Catholic New World*, August 5, 2001.

43. This and the following quotation are from Francis E. George, "Conversations in Spirituality: Religious Dialogue," The Cardinal's Column, *Catholic New World*, February 4, 2007.

TWELVE: A Missionary to the Culture

1. Francis E. George, "Evangelizing Our Culture," in *The New Evangelization*, ed. Steven Boguslawski and Ralph Martin (New York: Paulist Press, 2008), 44.

2. Francis E. George, "The Bishop's Sacramentality," Origins, Catholic News Service, November 8, 2001.

3. This, the following two quotations, and the subsequent extended quotation are from Francis E. George, "External and Internal Threats to the Church's Mission: Address to Pope John Paul II at 'Ad Limina' Visits with Bishops from Illinois, Wisconsin and Indiana," Origins, Catholic News Service, June 10, 2004.

4. Francis E. George, Address at Priests' Day on October 7, 2014, Private Collection.

5. Francis E. George, "The Cathedral as the Seat of Episcopal Ministry," Cathedral of St. James, Brooklyn, (unpublished manuscript, June 4, 1999), Private Collection.

6. This and the following quotation are from "Cardinal George Talks About His Ministry, Life and Facing Death," *Catholic New World*, November 16-29, 2014.

7. Francis E. George, "From the Bishop," *Central Washington Catholic*, May-June, 1996.

8. Archbishop José H. Gomez, Statement on the Death of Cardinal Francis E. George, O.M.I., Archbishop Emeritus of Chicago, April 17, 2015.

9. Francis E. George, "Entering into the Mysteries of Christ Through Living the Liturgy," The Cardinal's Column, *Catholic New World*, November 25, 2001.

10. Francis E. George, "The Ecclesiology of Communion: From Jurisdiction to Relationship," in *The New Evangelization: Faith, People, Context and Practice*, ed. Paul Grogan and Kirsteen Kim (London: Bloomsbury T&T Clark, 2015), 97.

11. Francis E. George, "A Conversation Begins: Cardinal George's 1st Column," The Cardinal's Column, *Catholic New World*, September 23, 1998.

12. This and the next three quotations are from Francis E. George, "Celebrating the Millennium: A Moment of Conversion," The Cardinal's Column, *Catholic New World*, September 20, 1998.

13. "Cardinal Calls for New Ways of Evangelizing in Global Society," Catholic News Service, October 12, 1999.

14. Francis E. George, "Homily at Red Mass Celebrated at St. Matthew Cathedral in Washington, D.C.," October 4, 1998, *Congressional Record* vol. 144, no. 151, (Washington: Government Publishing Office, October 21, 1998).

15. This and the following three quotations are from John L. Allen, Jr., "Chicago's Exiting Cardinal: 'The Church is About True/False, Not Left/Right,'" *Crux*, November 17, 2014.

16. "Cardinal George Goes Door-to-Door with Chicago Parishioners," Catholic News Service, April 11, 2000.

17. Francis E. George, "Pentecost: Why the Church is Alive and Young," The Cardinal's Column, *Catholic New World*, May 22, 2005.

18. "Chicago Cardinal Says He is Grateful to Meet with Young People," Catholic News Service, July 25, 2002.

19. This and the following quotation are from "In Catechesis Session, Cardinal George Urges Youths to Stay Faithful," Catholic News Service, August 17, 2005.

20. This and the following three quotations are from Francis E. George, "Pastoral Letter: Becoming an Evangelizing People," *Catholic New World*, November 21, 1997.

21. Francis E. George, "The Role of the Laity and the Contemporary Cultural Milieu, June 20, 2013.

22. This and the following four quotations are from Francis E. George, "Becoming an Evangelizing People," Cardinal's Column, *Catholic New World*, November 21, 1997.

23. This and the following quotation are from "Cardinal Says Americans Must Criticize as Well as Love Culture," Catholic News Service, June 13, 2001.

24. This and the following three quotations are from Francis E. George, "External and Internal Threats to the Church's Mission: Address to Pope John Paul II at 'Ad Limina' Visits with Bishops from Illinois, Wisconsin and Indiana," Origins, Catholic News Service, June 10, 2004.

25. This and the following quotation are from Robert E. Barron, "A Lion of The American Church: Thoughts on The Passing of Cardinal George," *Catholic New World*, April 23, 2015.

26. This and the following three quotations are from Francis E. George, "Evangelizing American Culture," in *The New Catholic Evangelization*, ed. Kenneth Boyack, (New York: Paulist Press, 1992), p. 43.

27. This and the following quotation are from Francis E. George, "Immigra-

tion and the Law," The Cardinal's Column, *Catholic New World*, July 18, 2010.

28. This and the following two quotations are from Francis E. George, "Homily at Red Mass Celebrated at St. Matthew Cathedral in Washington, D.C.," October 4, 1998, *Congressional Record* vol. 144, no. 151 (Washington: Government Publishing Office, October 21, 1998).

29. Francis E. George, "External and Internal Threats to the Church's Mission: Address to Pope John Paul II at 'Ad Limina' Visits with Bishops from Illinois, Wisconsin and Indiana," Origins, Catholic News Service, June 10, 2004.

30. Francis E. George, "Presidential Address at the Fall Plenary Assembly of the United States Conference of Catholic Bishops," November 15, 2010.

31. This and the following two quotations are from "Cardinal Francis E. George Answers Questions at Parish Leadership Day 2009 at Maria High School," February 7, 2009, https://www.youtube.com/watch?v=S8XJdXCw-0A.

32. Francis E. George, "Address: People of Life: Entering the New Millennium," In God's Image: Called to Build a Culture of Life Conference, Washington, D.C., March 5, 1999, https://www.youtube.com/watch?v=7lGiYu4B2tw&t=131s.

33. Francis E. George, "Law and Culture," *Ave Maria Law Review*, Spring 2003.

34. This and the following two quotations are from Francis E. George, "Address: People of Life: Entering the New Millennium," March 5, 1999.

35. This and the following quotation are from Francis E. George, "Law and Culture," 2003.

36. The following five quotations are from Francis E. George, "Welcoming and Praying, In Season and Out of Season," The Cardinal's Column, *Catholic New World*, July 11, 1999.

37. Francis E. George, "January 22: Happy Anniversary?," The Cardinal's Column, *Catholic New World*, January 19, 2003.

38. "Cardinal Francis George Answers Questions at Parish Leadership Day 2009 at Maria High School," February 7, 2009, https://www.youtube.com/watch?v=S8XJdXCw-0A.

39. This and the following two quotations are from Francis E. George, "January 22: Happy Anniversary?," January 19, 2003

40. This and the following quotation are from "Cardinal Francis George An-

swers Questions at Parish Leadership Day 2009 at Maria High School," February 7, 2009.

41. Francis E. George, "When Law Encourages Violence," The Cardinal's Column, *Catholic New World*, May 25, 2008.

42. This and the following quotation are from Francis E. George, "American Freedom and the Catholic Church," The Cardinal's Column, *Catholic New World*, June 29–July 12, 2014.

43. This and the following two quotations are from Francis E. George, "Welcoming and Praying, In Season and Out of Season," July 11, 1999.

44. This and the following six quotations are from a prepared statement of Francis E. George, February 14, 2004, retained by the Joseph Cardinal Bernardin Archives and Records Center of the Archdiocese of Chicago.

45. This and the following two quotations are from Francis E. George to Archdiocese of Chicago parishioners, "'Same-sex Marriage:' What Do Nature and Nature's God Say?," January 1, 2013.

46. Francis E. George, "Legislation Creating 'Same-Sex' Marriage: What's at Stake?," The Cardinal's Column, *Catholic New World*, January 6–19, 2013.

47. This and the following two quotations are from Francis E. George, "'Same-sex Marriage:' What Do Nature and Nature's God Say?," January 1, 2013.

48. This and the following three quotations are from Francis E. George, "Legislation Creating 'Same-Sex' Marriage: What's at Stake?," January 6–19, 2013.

49. This and the following two quotations are from Francis E. George, "Easter 2011: God Sets us Free, Even When Laws Enslave," The Cardinal's Column, *Catholic New World*, April 24, 2011.

50. This and the following three quotations are from Francis E. George, "Legislation Creating 'Same-Sex' Marriage: What's at Stake?," January 6–19, 2013.

51. The document, *Considerations Regarding Proposals to Give Legal Recognition to Unions Between Homosexual Persons*, was published by the Congregation for the Doctrine of the Faith under the signature of its prefect Cardinal Joseph Ratzinger, and with approval of Pope John Paul II, on June 3, 2003, the memorial of St. Charles Lwanga and his companion martyrs.

52. This and the remaining quotations from the August 3, 2003, sermon are from Francis E. George, "Same-Sex Unions: Newspaper Headline Deplored,"

Origins, Catholic News Service, August 14, 2003.

53. This and the following two quotations are from Francis E. George, "Statement to the Press," December 27, 2011.

54. This and the following two quotations are from Francis E. George, "Statement to the Press," January 6, 2012.

55. Francis E. George, "Easter: The Font of Prayer and Service," Undergraduate Theological Symposium, University of Notre Dame (unpublished manuscript, March 31, 2008), Private Collection.

56. "Cardinal George Seen as an Intellectual Leader in Church," *Catholic New World*, December 8–21, 2013.

57. This and the following two quotations are from Francis E. George, "Evangelizing American Culture," 53.

58. Ibid., 52.

59. Ibid., 53.

60. Francis E. George, "What kind of Democracy Leads to Secularism?" Address at the Library of Congress, February 13, 2007.

61. Francis E. George, "Address at the Basilica of the National Shrine of the Immaculate Conception" (unpublished manuscript, December 4, 2004), Private Collection.

62. Francis E. George, "A Tale of Two Churches," The Cardinal's Column, *Catholic New World*, September 7–20, 2014.

63. Francis E. George, "Grace and Moral Theology: The Culture of Faith and the Formation of Disciples," Address at the Lateran University, Rome (unpublished manuscript, November 20, 2003), Private Collection.

64. Francis E. George, "Notre Dame Law School Olin Lecture: Law and Culture" (unpublished manuscript, January 30, 2003), Private Collection.

65. This and the following extended quotation are from Francis E. George, "The Wrong Side of History," The Cardinal's Column, *Catholic New World*, Oct 21–Nov 3, 2012.

66. This and the following four quotations are from Francis E. George, "Address at the Basilica of the National Shrine of the Immaculate Conception" December 4, 2004, Private Collection.

67. This and the following three quotations are from Manya Brachear Pash-

man, "Cardinal George Marks 50 Years as Priest, Reflects on Changing Secular, Spiritual Worlds," *Chicago Tribune*, December 18, 2013.

68. This and the following quotation are from Francis E. George, "The Role of the Laity and the Contemporary Cultural Milieu, June 20, 2003."

THIRTEEN: An Instrument of the Lord

1. This and the following quotation are from Francis E. George, "What God has Joined Together ...," The Cardinal's Column, *Catholic New World*, January 16, 2011.

2. Francis E. George, "Catholics and Latter-day Saints: Partners in the Defense of Religious Freedom," Brigham Young University (unpublished manuscript, February 23, 2010), Private Collection.

3. This and the following quotation are from Francis E. George, "How the Latin Liturgy Gets Put into English," The Cardinal's Column, *Catholic New World*, May 20, 2001.

4. This and the following four quotations are from Francis E. George, "Entering into the Mysteries of Christ Through Living the Liturgy," The Cardinal's Column, *Catholic New World*, November 25, 2001.

5. Margaret Ramirez, "Bishops May Alter the Words of Mass," *Chicago Tribune*, June 15, 2006.

6. This and the following six quotations are from Francis E. George, "L.A. in L.A.: Liturgiam Authenticam in Los Angeles," The Cardinal's Column, *Catholic New World*, June 25, 2006.

7. Liturgical Institute, "About the Liturgical Institute," Video, December 3, 2010, https://www.youtube.com/watch?v=vfUF1JEzxLg&t=45s.

8. This and the following quotation are from "Glorious Lives: Cardinal Francis George," *Shalom World Television*, 2018.

9. Francis E. George, "The Bishop's Sacramentality," November 8, 2001.

10. This and the following quotation are from Francis E. George, "Address to Priests of the Diocese of Corner Brook: Called to the Cross" (unpublished manuscript, June 29, 2006), Private Collection. It's noteworthy that he spoke these words in the immediate wake of the McCormack scandal and just weeks before his first cancer diagnosis.

11. "Cardinal Says He'll Seek Sanctions for Negligent Bishops," Catholic News Service, June 11, 2002.

12. Francis E. George, "External and Internal Threats to the Church's Mission: Address to Pope John Paul II at 'Ad Limina' Visits with Bishops from Illinois, Wisconsin and Indiana," Origins, Catholic News Service, June 10, 2004.

13. The following quotations are from the official minutes from various meetings between officials from the USCCB and Holy See dicasteries.

14. This and the following quotation are from Manya Brachear Pashman, "Chicago's Cardinal: Francis George Rose to Lead Hometown's Catholics," *Chicago Tribune*, April 18, 2015.

15. This and the following five quotations are from "The World Over with Raymond Arroyo," *Eternal Word Television Network*, November 20, 2014. Remaining citations from this interview are in-text.

16. This and the following quotation are from Francis E. George, "Address at Conference of Diocesan Attorneys" (unpublished manuscript, April 21, 2013), Private Collection.

17. This and the following quotation are from "Cardinal George Warns Obama Against Moving U.S. Towards Despotism," Catholic News Agency, March 17, 2009.

18. "Cardinal Praises Expanded Health Care But Fears Remain on Abortion," Catholic News Service, March 23, 2010.

19. This and the following three quotations are from "Cardinal George: Sr. Keehan Chose Obama Over Catholic Bishops," Catholic News Agency, June 16, 2010.

20. This and the following six quotations are from Francis E. George, "Presidential Address at the Fall Plenary Assembly of the United States Conference of Catholic Bishops," November 15, 2010.

21. This and the following five quotations are from "On Life Issue, Cardinal George Says Obama on 'Wrong Side of History,'" Catholic News Service, April 24, 2009.

22. Cardinal Francis E. George to President Barack Obama, April 28, 2009, located by the author among Cardinal George's personal items retained by the Joseph Cardinal Bernardin Archives and Records Center of the Archdiocese of

Chicago in October 2018. This is noteworthy since, in recent years, McCarrick's activity in such endeavors took place at a time when he was allegedly sidelined by Pope Benedict XVI under a cloud of suspicion on account of sexual misconduct.

23. "Cardinal George says Notre Dame Made a Unilateral Decision," Catholic News Agency, April 6, 2009.

24. This and the following three quotations are from Kathleen Gilbert, "President of US Bishops' Conference: Notre Dame Obama Invite an 'Extreme Embarrassment,'" *LifeSiteNews*, March 31, 2009.

25. Francis E. George to Reverend John I. Jekins, C.S.C., May 12, 2009, located by the author among Cardinal George's personal items retained by the Joseph Cardinal Bernardin Archives and Records Center of the Archdiocese of Chicago in October 2018.

26. This and the following quotation are from "Cardinal Praises Expanded Health Care But Fears Remain on Abortion," Catholic News Service, March 23, 2010.

27. This and the following two quotations are from Francis E. George, "Catholics and Latter-day Saints: Partners in the Defense of Religious Freedom," February 23, 2010.

28. Francis E. George, "Catholic Participation in Political Life, Revisited," The Cardinal's Column, *Catholic New World*, October 10, 2004.

29. This and the following two quotations are from Francis E. George, "Why a New Apologetics Is Needed," Origins, Catholic News Service, December 4, 1997.

30. This and the following quotation are from "Pope Begins Lenten Retreat Led by Cardinal George of Chicago," Catholic News Service, March 5, 2001.

31. "Cardinal Denies He's Leaving Chicago," *Chicago Tribune*, November 2, 2001.

32. This and the following two quotations are from Francis E. George, "Contexts for Living the Scriptural Text (unpublished manuscript, October 2008), Private Collection.

33. George Pell, *Prison Journal*, vol. 3 (San Francisco: Ignatius Press, 2021), 101.

34. "CNN Presents: The Last Days of Pope John Paul II: The Untold Sto-

ries," *Cable News Network* transcript, April 1, 2006, http://transcripts.cnn.com/TRANSCRIPTS/0604/01/cp.02.html.

35. Francis E. George, "Apostolic Governance: The Power of the Keys," The Cardinal's Column, *Catholic New World*, May 8, 2005.

36. Francis E. George, "Address at National Conference of Community and Justice: Pope Benedict XVI and Interfaith Relations," June 24, 2005.

37. This and the following quotation are from "CNN Presents: The Last Days of Pope John Paul II: The Untold Stories."

38. John L. Allen, Jr., "NCR Interview with Cardinal Francis George," *National Catholic Reporter*, March 2, 2013.

39. This and the following two quotations are from Francis E. George, "Pope Benedict XVI," The Cardinal's Column, *Catholic New World*, February 17, 2013.

40. This and the following quotation are from Allen, "NCR Interview with Cardinal Francis George, March 2, 2013."

41. This and the following quotation are from Austen Ivereigh, *The Great Reformer* (New York: Henry Holt and Company, 2014), 359.

42. Ibid., 356.

43. This and the following two quotations are from "Cardinal Francis George on Pope Francis," *Chicago Tribune*, December 19, 2013.

44. Brachear Pashman, "Cardinal George Marks 50 Years as Priest, Decemeber 18, 2013."

45. Allen, "NCR Interview with Cardinal Francis George, March 2, 2013"

46. This and the following sixteen quotations are from John L. Allen, Jr., "What 'America's Ratzinger' Would Like to Ask Pope Francis," *Crux*, November 16, 2014.

FOURTEEN: Simply Catholic

1. Francis E. George, "Pilgrimage of Love: Ministry of the Bishop and his Life with God," The Cardinal's Column, *Catholic New World*, February 14, 1999.

2. Francis E. George, "Knowing the Place for the First Time," The Cardinal's Column, *Catholic New World*, April 28, 2002.

3. This and the following three quotations are from Francis E. George, "Will the Real Vatican II Please Stand Up?," The Cardinal's Column, *Catholic New*

World, June 11, 2006.

4. This and the following quotation are from Francis E. George, "Address on Ecclesial Identity of Religious Life to National Board of Vicars for Religious" (unpublished manuscript, March 18, 2012), Private Collection.

5. Francis E. George, address at Mundelein Seminary, 2014, Private Collection.

6. Francis E. George, "Address on Ecclesial Identity of Religious Life to National Board of Vicars for Religious, March 18, 2012."

7. This is from Francis E. George, "How Liberalism Fails the Church," *Commonweal*, June 17, 2004.

8. Francis E. George, "Kenrick Lecture at Kenrick-Glennon Seminary in St. Louis" (unpublished manuscript, March 22, 2000), Private Collection.

9. This and the following three quotations are from Francis E. George, "How Liberalism Fails the Church," *Commonweal*, June 17, 2004.

10. Barron, "A Lion of The American Church, April 23, 2015."

11. This and the following four quotations are from Francis E. George, "Christmas Homily at Midnight Mass" (unpublished manuscript, 2013), Private Collection.

12. This and the following quotation are from the written description accompanying George's coat of arms.

13. This and the following quotation are from Francis E. George, "Address at the Basilica of the National Shrine of the Immaculate Conception" (unpublished manuscript, December 4, 2004), Private Collection.

14. "Constitutions and Rules of the Congregation of the Missionary Oblates of Mary Immaculate" (1982), no. 2.

15. Francis E. George, "The Role of the Laity and the Contemporary Cultural Milieu, June 20, 2013."

16. Francis E. George, "The Cultural Context of Catholicism in the United States: Address at the Spring Assembly of the United States Conference of Catholic Bishops," (unpublished manuscript, June 2004), Private Collection.

17. Francis E. George, talk on The Difference God Makes, retrieved from https://www.youtube.com/watch?v=WaXLP0zm0Qo.

18. This and the following three quotations are from "Cardinal George Shares Thoughts on Future," *Catholic New World*, January 6, 2013.

19. This and the following quotation are from the written description accompanying George's coat of arms.

20. George Weigel, "Cardinal Francis George," *First Things*, December 2014.

21. "Cardinal's Impact Will Be Felt for Years to Come, Says Portland Priest," Catholic News Service, April 21, 2015.

22. Patrick T. Reardon, "A Rare Look Inside Cardinal's World," *Chicago Tribune*, March 5, 2008.

23. Weigel, "Cardinal Francis George, December 2014."

24. "Chicago's New Archbishop Impresses Reporters At First Press Conference," *The Wanderer*, April 17, 1997.

25. This and the following nine quotations are from Cathleen Falsani, "The Man in the Red Dress: My Unlikely Friendship with Cardinal Francis George," Religion Dispatches blog, April 23, 2015.

26. Francis E. George, "Pilgrimage of Love: Ministry of the Bishop and his Life with God," The Cardinal's Column, *Catholic New World*, February 14, 1999.

27. Francis E. George, "Entering into the Mysteries of Christ Through Living the Liturgy," The Cardinal's Column, *Catholic New World*, November 25, 2001.

28. This and the following quotation are from "Glorious Lives: Cardinal Francis George," *Shalom World Television*, 2018.

29. Francis E. George, "October: Praying the Rosary and Respecting Life," The Cardinal's Column, *Catholic New World*, October 11, 2009.

30. *Oblate Prayer* (Rome: General Administration of the Missionary Oblates of Mary Immaculate, 2016), 21.

31. This and the following quotation are from "Glorious Lives: Cardinal Francis George," *Shalom World Television*, 2018.

32. Daniel Lipinski, "Recognizing Archbishop Blase Joseph Cupich and Cardinal Francis George of Chicago, Illinois," Congressional Record vol. 160, no. 141 (Washington: Government Publishing Office, November 18, 2014).

33. Alfredo Fricano, quoted by Joyce Duriga, "Longtime Chicago barber made Cardinal George laugh and look good," Catholic News Service, April 22, 2015.

34. This and the following three quotations are from Duriga, "Cardinal George Talks About 50 Years as a Priest," Decemeber 22, 2013.

35. Handwritten Notes.

36. Francis E. George, "On Death and Other Limitations," The Cardinal's Column, *Catholic New World*, August 26, 2012.

37. "Archdiocese Releases Thousands of Pages of Priest Sex Abuse Files" WBBM 780 Radio Chicago, November 6, 2014, https://chicago.cbslocal.com/2014/11/06/archdiocese-to-release-thousands-of-pages-of-priest-sex-abuse-files/.

38. Duriga, "Cardinal George Talks About 50 Years as a Priest," Decemeber 22, 2013.

39. Francis E. George, "The Cardinal I Never Knew: George Mundelein," The Cardinal's Column, *Catholic New World*, March 5, 2000.

40. This and the following three quotations are from Francis E. George, "Story Lines, Ours and God's," The Cardinal's Column, *Catholic New World*, November 16, 2014.

41. Francis E. George, Final Public Homily as Archbishop of Chicago, November 16, 2014, Private Collection.

42. Pashman, "Chicago's Cardinal: Francis George Rose to Lead Hometown's Catholics," April 18, 2015.

43. This and the following two quotations are from "Cardinal George Awarded Chicago's Highest Honor," ABC 7 Chicago Television, December 10, 2014, https://abc7chicago.com/news/cardinal-george-to-be-honored-with-medal-of-merit/430892/.

44. This and the following quotation are from Fran Spielman, "Archbishop Emeritus Awarded Medal of Merit," *Chicago Sun-Times*, December 11, 2014.

45. This and the following two quotations are from *The Wanderer*.

46. Laurie Goodstein, "Cardinal Francis E. George, Who Urged 'Zero Tolerance' in Abuse Scandal, Dies at 78," *New York Times*, April 18, 2015.

47. Monifa Thomas, "Cardinal George Says Doctors Have 'Run Out of Tricks' for Him," *Associated Press*, January 30, 2015.

48. *Chicago Tribune* video interview with Bishop Raymond E. Goedert, April 21, 2014, https://www.youtube.com/watch?v=LHZvqtxS3DM.

49. "Glorious Lives: Cardinal Francis George," *Shalom World Television*, 2018.

50. Francis E. George, "Why Doesn't God Love Everyone Equally?," The

Cardinal's Column, *Catholic New World*, February 27, 2011.

51. Cardinal George Mundelein rests beneath the high altar in the Chapel of the Immaculate Conception at Mundelein Seminary, and Cardinal Albert Meyer is buried in the cemetery on the seminary grounds.

52. Francis E. George, "Easter Sunday Homily" (unpublished manuscript, April 22, 2012), Private Collection.

About the Author

Michael R. Heinlein is editor of OSV's SimplyCatholic.com and a regular contributor to OSV's periodicals. He earned a degree in theology from The Catholic University of America in Washington, D.C. He is author of *The Handy Little Guide to Spiritual Communion* (OSV), *Black Catholics on the Road to Sainthood* (OSV), and the Teeny Tiny Theology children's series (OSV). He finds great inspiration in the lives of the saints and the spirituality of the Pauline Family, and often is found using whatever spare time he has for genealogical research. His greatest treasures are his Catholic Faith and his family. He is married to Gretchen, with whom he has three children.